My Dear Son

LETTERS FROM JOHN MCDOUGALL (WEAVER),
ISLE OF LISMORE, SCOTLAND,
TO HIS SON, JOHN, IN AMERICA

MARGARET A. MILLER

abbott press

Front cover: Achuaran, Isle of Lismore, October 2013
by Margaret A. Miller

Abbott Press books may be ordered through booksellers or by contacting:

Abbott Press
1663 Liberty Drive
Bloomington, IN 47403
www.abbottpress.com
Phone: 1 (866) 697-5310

ISBN: 978-1-4582-1806-3 (sc)
ISBN: 978-1-4582-1807-0 (e)

Library of Congress Control Number: 2014919150

Print information available on the last page.

Abbott Press rev. date: 8/13/2015

Contents

Acknowledgements

John McDougall, last weaver on the Isle of Lismore, Scotland, wrote to his son, John (b. 1837) from 1870 to 1888 after his son had left the family home for other parts of Scotland and the United States. Ruth MacDougall McCartin, a granddaughter of the younger John McDougall, organized and transcribed the letters with her cousin, Gertrude Smith Inglis, and her sister, Margaret Carasik. This book would not be possible without their work. Ruth McCartin titled the letters *We are Still in the Land of the Living*, and gave them to the Lismore Historical Society (Comann Eachdraidh Lios Mòr) in 2011. Special thanks to the Society for making copies of the original letters and annotated transcripts available to me.

Permissions

Comann Eachdraidh Lios Mòr (The Lismore Historical Society) gave permission to use images of the letters in this book. The Society's website is located at http://www.lismoregaelicheritagecentre.org/.

The following gave permission to use other documents as well as photographs and maps:

- Anne McIlraith Aburn
- Barbara Wilcox Bitetto
- Krista Louise Bitetto
- Mark Francis Bitetto
- Margaret MacDougall Carasik
- Jim Cassatt
- Bruce Lindsay Guthrie
- Martha Catherine Alter Hines
- Carolyn Wilcox Knowles
- Alec John (Jock) MacDougall
- Eric James MacDougall
- Mark John McCartin
- Lynn David Miller
- National Library of Scotland
- *Redwood Gazette*
- Registrar General for Scotland
- Jean Aufderheide Stark
- Lee Ann Tiffany Stearns
- Sue Robson Tiffany
- *The Oban Times*
- *The Scotsman*
- David H. White
- Chiaki Wilcox
- Robert Tiffany Wilcox

Introduction

John McDougall (labeled weaver throughout this book) was born on the Isle of Lismore in the West Highlands of Scotland in 1803. He was the oldest of John McDugald and Mary Carmichael's three children, all born in the hamlet of Ballimackillichan. (See Notes about Names, Language and Spelling in this book, below.) His father had served in the 91st Regiment and settled on Lismore as a young man. John McDougall (weaver) married Catherine McCallum, born in 1809 to John McCallum and Anne Carmichael in the Lismore hamlet of Balure. John (weaver) and Catherine raised their eight children at Ballimackillichan, and lived there until Catherine's death in 1886.

John McDougall (weaver) lived the life of a cottar as a landless resident of Ballimackillichan where he provided weaving services to the island. He was the last weaver on the Isle of Lismore and superintendent of the island's Sabbath School from 1844 to 1874.

Although he was not wealthy, his life was far from simple. He had not only lived to see the birth of his own children, but their departure from Lismore, as well. Letters he wrote to his son, John (born 1837), who migrated to the United States in 1872, reveal a devout man, living a principled life, who was active in his community and in frequent contact with friends and family throughout Scotland and North America. By 1879, his son had settled in Redwood County, Minnesota. By then, John (weaver) was extending compliments and local news through his son to a person he called McCorquodale, a former member of the Lismore community who had also migrated to Redwood County. He was also in contact through letters to his son, with members of Catherine McCallum's family, including her sister-in-law, Ann McCallum and Ann's children, who had migrated to Minnesota from Lismore. John (weaver) shared family news through his letters and inquired about the health and well-being of family and friends in the United States. Although Lismore was his home for all but the last two of his 85 years, he influenced the development of families and communities in Scotland and the United States through simple, direct and consistent guidance to his children, recorded in the following letters.

Ruth McCartin, born in the United States, was a grandchild of the younger John McDougall (born 1837) who had migrated to the United States. She saved the letters and gave them to the Lismore Historical Society in 2011. (Ruth, herself, passed away November 4, 2012.) The letters allow John McDougall, the weaver's, own words to express his perspective on life, religion and family relationships. The collection, reproduced here, includes his letters as well as transcripts, photographs, maps, family trees and a chronology of events for enrichment.

The book provides a view of Scotland at a time of emigration through the eyes of a local cottar and community member. It is relevant to descendants of John McDougall (weaver), his wife's extended family (McCallums, Carmichaels, and McColls), other members of the Lismore community, historians of Highland churches, and scholars of Scottish land reform, migration patterns, and the Highland's impact on communities in the New World.

Additional Information

The letters begin in December 1870 when John McDougall (weaver), and Catherine McCallum write their oldest son, John McDougall (b. 1837 Lismore), working in Dunoon, Scotland. Their letters end in 1888 after the older John McDougall (weaver) and Catherine McCallum have passed away and the younger John has settled in the United States. The collection, which continues to 1913, includes a few from the younger John McDougall in Minnesota to a friend, Donald McConochie, in Oban, Scotland, as well as letters to the younger John McDougall from family members and friends.

John McDougall (weaver) served for more than 30 years as Superintendent of the island's Sabbath School, a voluntary role. Although he, himself, appears to have been an active member of the Independent Chapel at Achuaran on Lismore, the Sabbath School appears to have served a range of Protestant groups, including Presbyterian, Baptist and Congregational.

The younger John (identified as John McDougall, b. 1837 throughout this book), and his siblings had left Lismore by December 1870 when the first letter in the collection appears, leaving their parents to care for themselves. By 1874, their parents report being lonely on Lismore without any children nearby. (See, for example, the letter of April 17, 1874.) Robert Hay's recent book (Hay 2013, *How an Island Lost its People*), explores the social, political and other dynamics that influenced the migration of young people from the island, including that of John McDougall, the weaver's, children.

The letters from other family members include some from my great grandmother, Margaret McDougall Milne, youngest child of John McDougall (weaver) and Catherine McCallum. Her letters are especially important due to her death in 1888, sixteen months after migrating to Minnesota with her husband and six children when her youngest son, my grandfather, was three years old. Her early death had a significant impact on the family.

The letters are a poignant reminder of ways in which medicine, communications and transportation have changed. However, they are also a reminder of enduring human goodness and strength. Preparing the book has helped me understand my own identity as a descendant of the authors. I hope others will find the letters informative, engaging and inspiring as well.

Additional Acknowledgements

This book is possible in its current form because many people provided moral and logistical support. Robert Hay, Curator, and Lorraine King, Assistant Curator of the Lismore Historical Society (Comann Eachdraidh Lios Mòr), made digital copies of the scanned letters available for use in this book. Margaret Black, former curator, Laura Gloag, genealogist, and other members of the Lismore community shared their knowledge and insight about details in the letters. For example, Laura provided information about the children of John McDougall (weaver) and members of the McCallum families that helped me understand the names of people mentioned in the letters. Margaret Black alerted me to connections between details mentioned in the letters and the Napier Commission's report of 1883, gave me a copy of *The Oban Times* article mentioned in the letter of April 17, 1874, took me to visit places mentioned in the letters, and shared information about the history and social structure of the island. I am grateful for their support.

Archie MacColl, owner of the Ballimackillichan estate on Lismore, took the time to review maps and census data to determine the specific building on the estate in which the John McDougall (weaver) family would have lived. David White found and shared detailed maps of Lismore which pinpoint the location of the McDougall home on Ballimackillichan. Together, Margaret Black, David White and Archie MacColl found the building and showed it to me on a windy day in October 2013.

Mrs. Maureen Crossan of the Old Schoolhouse Bed & Breakfast, and her daughters, Helen and Katy, shared their insights with me about the Gaelic language, the cultural history of Lismore, and phrases used in the letters. Mrs. Crossan and Elizabeth Kilmurray of Newfield Terrace hosted me on visits to Lismore. They not only provided excellent food and shelter, but took an interest in the research and opened doors to members of the community who shed light on the details.

Mary MacDougall invited me home for tea on a chilly day in October 2012, as I wandered in the rain near her home shortly after I arrived, looking for the hamlet of Balure, home of McCallum family members. Barbara MacDougall shared knowledge of her husband's family on the island, descended from Peter McDougall, a schoolteacher. We wondered if we were related.

The MacDougall McCallum Heritage Foundation provided a scholarship for travel to Oban and Lismore in 2013 for research related to this book. The Foundation's interest in the book encouraged me and helped focus my research.

My aunt, Sue Robson Tiffany, provided details about a portrait of the Alexander Milne family, in which Dougald Milne Tiffany, the youngest, sat on his exhausted mother's lap before the family left Scotland for the United States in 1887. My grandfather, Dougald, had shared the details with Sue Tiffany, pointing to the contrast between his exhausted mother in the family photograph and an earlier picture. (See the images of Margaret McDougall Milne in plates 1.8 and 35.4, following letters #1 and #35.) Aunt Sue's husband is my Uncle John Milne Tiffany, son of Dougald Milne Tiffany. He is also a grandson of Margaret McDougall Milne and great grandson of John McDougall (weaver).

Anne Aburn of New Zealand provided information about her ancestors, the Duncan McCallums of Lismore, including stories about the migration of her ancestors to New Zealand, Australia, and North America. The details helped me understand references to McCallum family members throughout the letters and provided rich detail for family trees that appear in Appendixes 8 and 9.

Mary MacDougall Brown copied and sent me copies of genealogical worksheets that had been prepared by Gertrude Smith Inglis, which proved invaluable.

Margaret MacDougall Carasik of the MacDougall McCallum Heritage Foundation, a granddaughter of John McDougall (b. 1837), helped in numerous ways throughout the project. She provided photographs and documents for the book. She also introduced me to Anne Aburn and many others who shared photographs, news articles and memories of people mentioned in the letters, enriching my understanding of them. Margaret's enthusiasm for the project was infectious.

At this point, I take you to the letters. They are a provocative picture of life in Scotland and the United States in the late 19th century at a time of significant social change. The purpose is to share what I have learned.

Margaret A. Miller
April 2015

Family Tree #1

John McDougall (weaver) (b. 1803 Lismore), Catherine McCallum (b. 1809 Lismore) and their Children

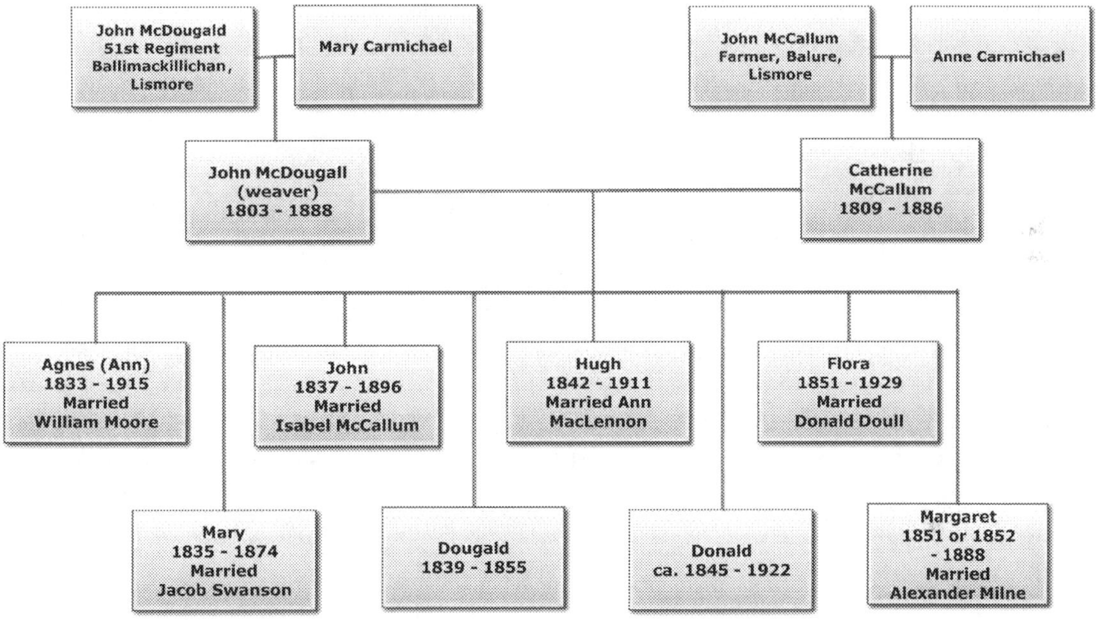

Sources: Gloag (2014b); Guthrie (2013); Inglis (undated); National Records of Scotland (Pre-1855a, Pre-1855b, 1855 – 2013a, 1855 – 2013b); Wilcox (1977)

Notes about Names, Languages and Spelling Used in the Letters and this Book

Names and Places: The names of many people in the letters include names of the communities in which they lived. For example, the letter of April 4, 1871, refers to "ann black baligarve". Baligarve is a hamlet to the north of Ballimackillichan on Lismore and would have been the home of Ann Black. The letter of August 29, 1872, refers to the death of Alexander Carmichael Balure. Mr. Carmichael would have lived in the Lismore community of Balure. Where possible, I have included recent photographs of the communities immediately after the letters in which they are mentioned.

Languages: The letters have been written in English. However, members of the Lismore community who are Gaelic speakers have told me the letters express thoughts as they would have been spoken in Gaelic, translated verbatim into English. The letters, themselves, reflect a variety of languages, including Scottish Gaelic and Scots. In addition, they include English expressions in use in Scotland, but less common in American English. The letters frequently include phonetic spellings and benefit from being read aloud. Context is helpful, too. Here are a few examples.

Term Used in Letter [Term used for translation]	Language	Translation & Source	How Used
bern [bairn]	Scots	offspring of any age (*Concise Scots Dictionary*, p. 27)	"your Cusen ann McNicol Mrs McPerson was buried last Thursday left two nice berns father and motherless" (See letter #26, January 24, 1882.)
dauch [deoch]	Gaelic	drink, dram (*Am Faclair Beag)*	"he said to his mother he wished he had a drink out from dauch" (See letter #26, January 24, 1882.) The letter may have been alluding to the Gaelic expression, "deoch an dorais", which means "stirrup cup" or "parting drink". (Lismore residents, personal conversation, 2013. See also the Gaelic dictionary, *Am Faclair Beag*.)
foge [fog]	Scots	grass left in the field during winter; moss (*Concise Scots Dictionary*, p. 204)	"and rember death and Judghment dear John if you will take our advice dont be like the rowing stone will not getter foge ..." (See letter #26, January 24, 1882.)
oxter	Scots, Northern English	the armpit; the under part of the (upper) arm (*Concise Scots Dictionary*, p. 466)	"Gilbart was a good man and so hugh should be he was in my oxter when the Lord reveld my blessed Saviour to my soul and throw my sins in the osion of love". (See letter #26, January 24, 1882.)
plaiden [plaid]	Gaelic	blankets, course flannel (*Am Faclair Beag*)	"we wonder that none of you did not writ to let us know whither you got th plaiden ... the were four yards of plaiden". (See letter #3, April 4, 1871.)
throng [trang]	Gaelic	very busy (*Am Faclair Beag*)	"I hear Uncle John is well and throng working away..." (See letter #14, August 18, 1877.)
translate	English	move from one place or condition to another: *she had been translated from familiar surroundings to a foreign court* (*Oxford Dictionaries*)	"Your mother was scercely able to tranceleted till now She is a great deal better now". (See letter #2, January 16, 1871.)

Spelling of Names:
I have transcribed names as they appear in the letters and in the records available to me, realizing that the spellings may be inconsistent. For example, Gilbert Hugh (Gib) MacDougall and Anna MacDougall Aufderheide, grandchildren of John McDougall (weaver) and Catherine McCallum, who were born in Minnesota, spelled their names MacDougall. Nonetheless, their father's gravestone in Redwood Falls, Minnesota is marked McDougall. (See Plate 37.2.)

Dougald Milne Tiffany's middle name was recorded on his birth certificate in 1885 in Thurso, Scotland as McDougall, but was recorded later in the United States as MacDougall. He was the son of Margaret McDougall and Alexander Milne and, was, like Gilbert Hugh (Gib) MacDougall, a grandson of John McDougall (weaver) and Catherine McCallum.

The Transcripts:
I prepared the transcripts that follow each letter by reviewing images of the original handwritten letters and the typewritten transcripts prepared by Ruth MacDougall McCartin, Gertrude Smith Inglis and Margaret MacDougall Carasik. I inserted explanatory notes and clarifications in brackets, including those provided by Mrs. McCartin, Mrs. Inglis, Mrs. Margaret Black and others. I have included notes immediately after some letters to provide additional information and summarized each in Appendix 1 ("The Letters - A List.")

The transcripts are intended to be verbatim copies with the same spelling, punctuation and capitalization that appear in the original letters. Any errors of transcription are strictly my own. Margaret A. Miller

Places Mentioned in the Book - Scotland

Lynn D. Miller

Plate A7.2

The Letters

Letter #1

December 13th 1870

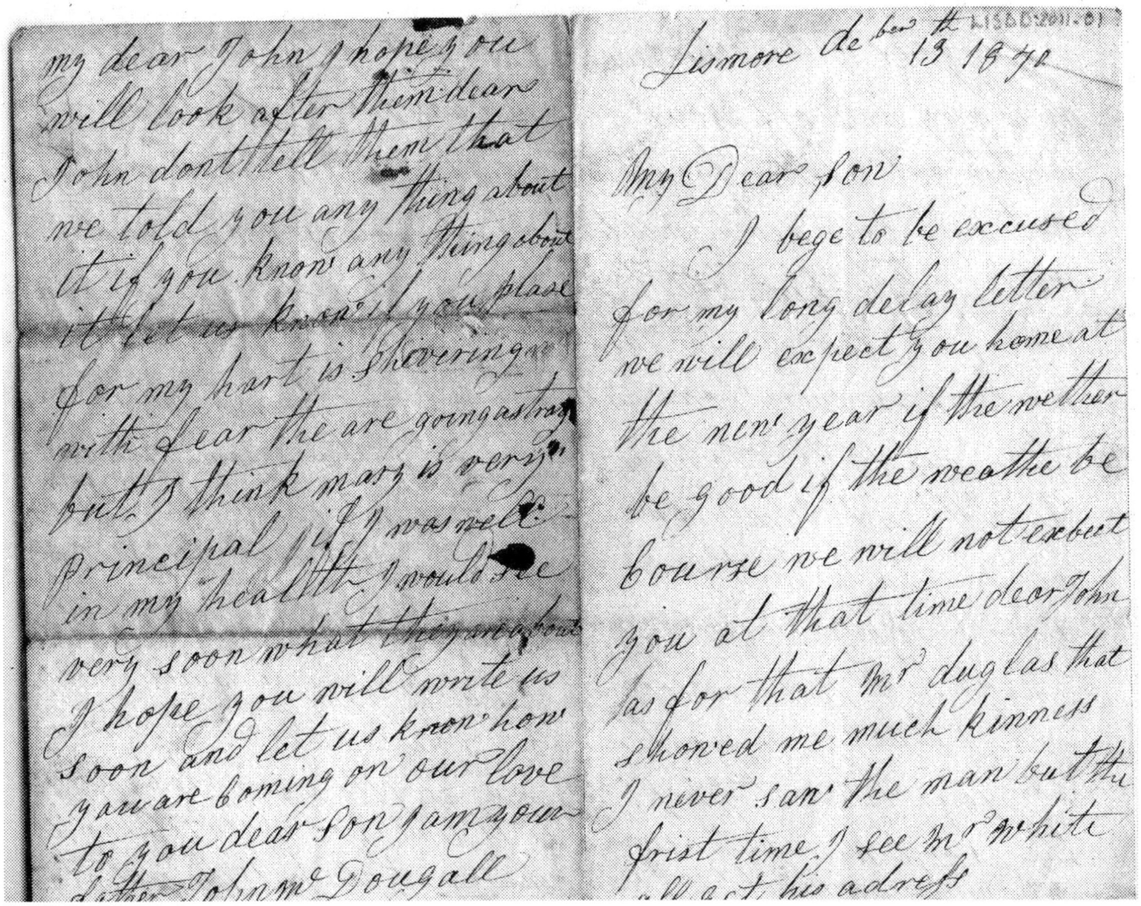

Lismore Debr 13th 1870

My Dear Son
I bege to be excused
for my long delay letter
we will expect you home at
the nen year if the wether
be good if the weathe be
bourse we will not exbect
you at that time dear John
as for that Mr duglas that
showed me much kinness
I never saw the man but the
frist time I see Mr White
[illegible] his adress

my dear John I hope you
will look after them dear
John dont tell them that
we told you any thing about
it if you know any thing about
it let us know if you plase
for my hart is shivering
with fear the are going astray
but I think mary is very
principal if I was well
in my health I would see
very soon what they [illegible]
I hope you will write us
soon and let us know how
you are coming on our love
to you dear son I am your
father John McDougall

Image db063

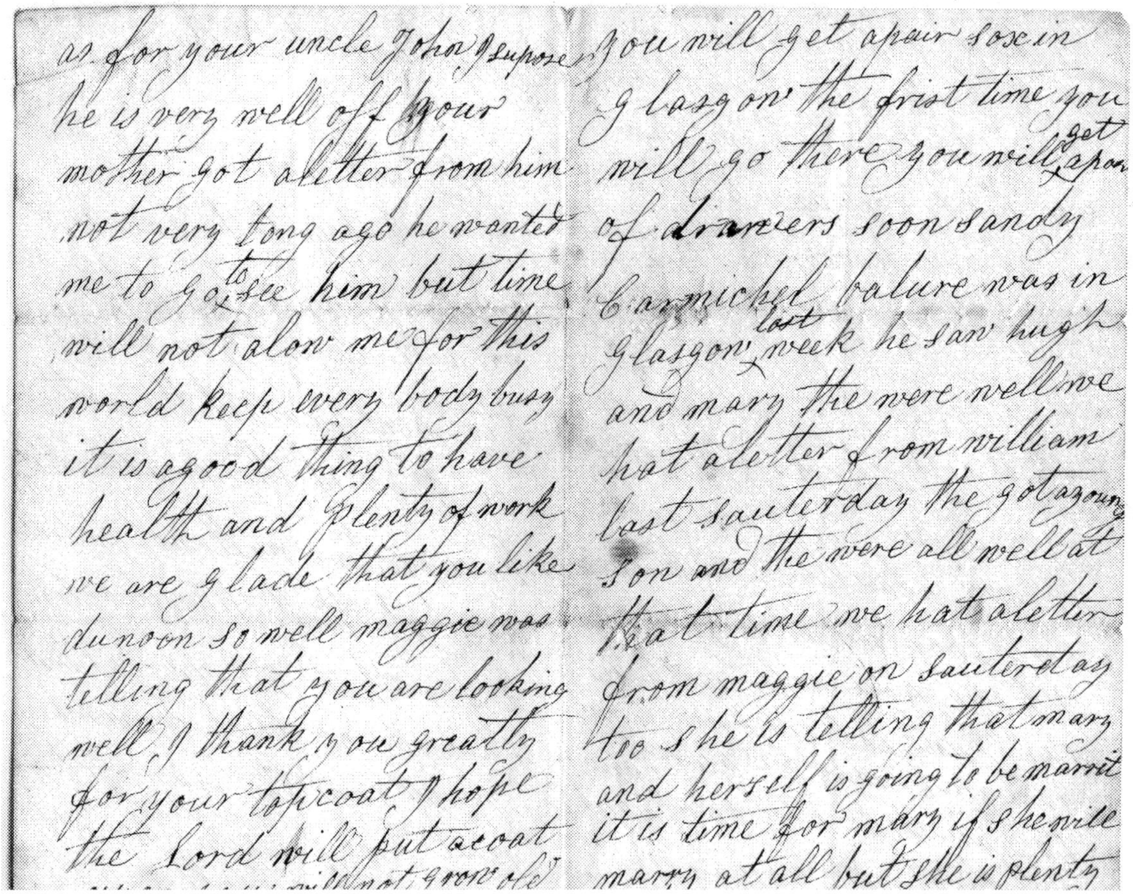

as for your uncle John I supose
he is very well off your
mother got aletter from him
not very long ago he wanted
me to go to see him but time
will not alow me for this
world keep every body busy
it is agood thing to have
health and plenty of work
we are glade that you like
dunoon so well maggie was
telling that you are looking
well I thank you greatly
for your topcoat I hope
the Lord will put acoat
... will not grow old

you will get apair sox in
Glasgow the frist time you
will go there you will get apair
of drawers soon sandy
Carmichel balure was in
Glasgow last week he saw hugh
and mary the were well we
hat aletter from william
last sauterday the got ayoung
son and the were all well at
that time we hat aletter
from maggie on sauterday
too she is telling that mary
and herself is going to be marrit
it is time for mary if she will
marry at all but she is plenty

Image db064

LETTER FROM JOHN MCDOUGALL (b. 1803 Lismore) WHO LIVED AT BALLIMACKILLICHAN, ISLE OF LISMORE TO JOHN MCDOUGALL (b. 1837 Lismore) IN DUNOON, SCOTLAND

Lismore de^{ber} 13th 1870

My Dear Son

I bege to be excused for my long delay letter we will expect you home at the new year if the wether be good if the weathe be Course we will not exbect you at that time dear John as for that Mr duglas that showed me much kinness I never saw the man but the frist time I see Mr White all get his adress

As for your uncle John [McCallum] I supose he is very well off your mother got a letter from him not very long ago he wanted me to go to see him but time will not alow me for this world keep every body busy it is a good thing to have health and plenty of work we are glade that you like dunoon so well maggie [son John's sister] was telling that you are looking well I thank you greatly for your topcoat I hope the Lord will put a coat upon you will not grow old

You will get a pair sox in Glasgow the frist time you will go there you will get a pair of drawers soon Sandy Carmichel balure was in Glasgow last week he saw hugh and mary [son John's brother and sister] the were well we hat a letter from William last Sauterday the got a young Son and the were all well at that time we hat a letter from maggie on Sauterday too She is telling that mary and herself is going to be marrit it is time for mary if she will marry at all but she is plenty a time

my dear John I hope you will look after them dear John dont tell them that we told you any thing about it if you know any thing about it let us know if you plase for my hart is shivering with fear the are going astray but I think mary is very principal if I was well in my health I would see very soon what they are about I hope you will write us soon and let us know how you are coming on our love to you dear son I am your

father John McDougall

People and Places Mentioned in the Letter of December 13th, 1870

Plate 1.1. John McDougall (weaver) and Catherine McCallum McDougall

Photo taken by Robert W. Wilcox, 1965, on visit to home of Catherine (Kate) Guthrie, cousin of Dougald Milne Tiffany. The photos were on display in her home in Montrose, Scotland.

Plate 1.2. Catherine McCallum McDougall (b. 1809 Balure, Lismore)

Plate 1.3. **John McDougall (b. 1837), son of John McDougall (weaver) and Catherine McCallum**

Plate 1.4. Photo Back

This photograph was taken in New York, date unknown.

Ballimackillichan

Plate 1.5.

Plate 1.6
Home of John McDougall (weaver) and Catherine McCallum McDougall, Remaining Section
Ballimackillichan, Lismore
2012

Ballimackillichan is a farm owned by Archie MacColl, who was born there. Archie, in black jacket, stands with Lismore resident Margaret Black where outer walls of the McDougall home would have stood. (See Plate 1.5.) In Plate 1.6, he confers with Margaret Black and David White of Lismore about the home's location.

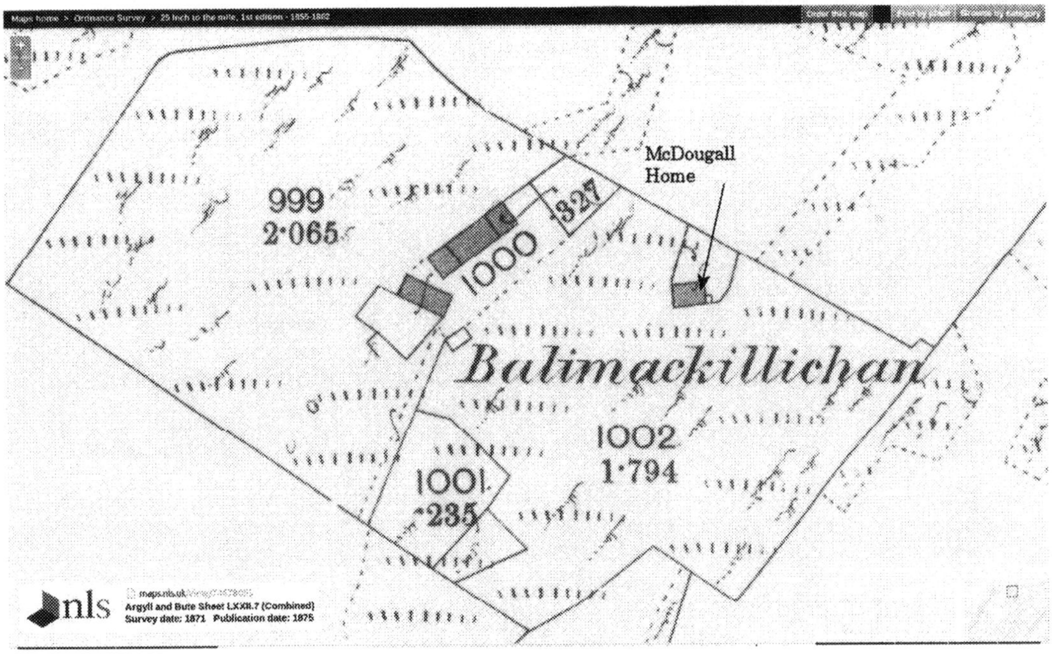

Reproduced by Permission of the National Library of Scotland

Plate 1.7. Ordnance Survey Map Showing Location of John McDougall (weaver) Home on Balimackillichan, Lismore

Plate 1.8. Margaret McDougall Milne ("Maggie") as a Young Woman

BALURE AREA, ISLE OF LISMORE

Plate 1.9. Sign to the Balure Area from the Main Road, Isle of Lismore

Plate 1.10. Along the Road to Balure

Plate 1.11. Pasture in the Balure Area of Lismore

Plate 1.12. Road from Balure to the Main Road, Isle of Lismore

GLASGOW

Plate 1.13. Open Air Market, Dumbarton Road, Partick

Plate 1.14. Partick Library, Dumbarton Road, Glasgow

The Library is a half-block from the Partick Church in which Margaret McDougall and Alexander Milne were married, November 17, 1876.

Plate 1.15. Kelvingrove Art Gallery and the Kelvin River, Glasgow

The Kelvingrove Art Gallery is located near the University of Glasgow. The Gallery and the Kelvin River are within walking distance of the Partick area. The Art Gallery would not have been available to Margaret McDougall and Alexander Milne; it opened to the public in May 1901.

Letter #2

January 16th 1871

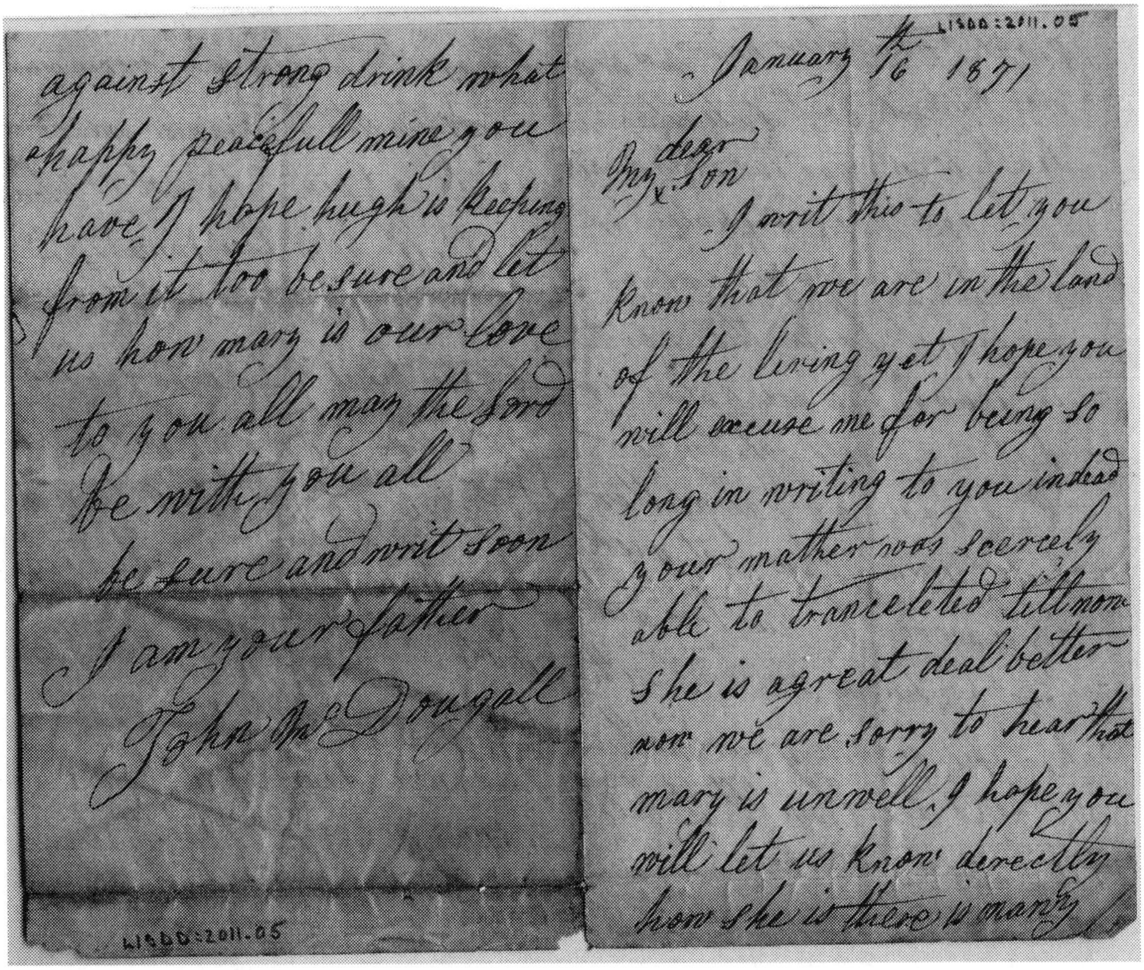

LISDD:2011.05

January 16th 1871

My dear Son

I writ this to let you
know that we are in the land
of the living yet I hope you
will excuse me for being so
long in writing to you indead
your mather was scercely
able to tranceleted till now
She is a great deal better
now we are sorry to hear that
mary is unwell I hope you
will let us know derectly
how she is there is many

against strong drink what
a happy peacefull mine you
have I hope hugh is keeping
from it too be sure and let
us how mary is our love
to you all may the Lord
be with you all
be sure and writ soon
I am your father
John McDougall

LISDD:2011.05

Image db077

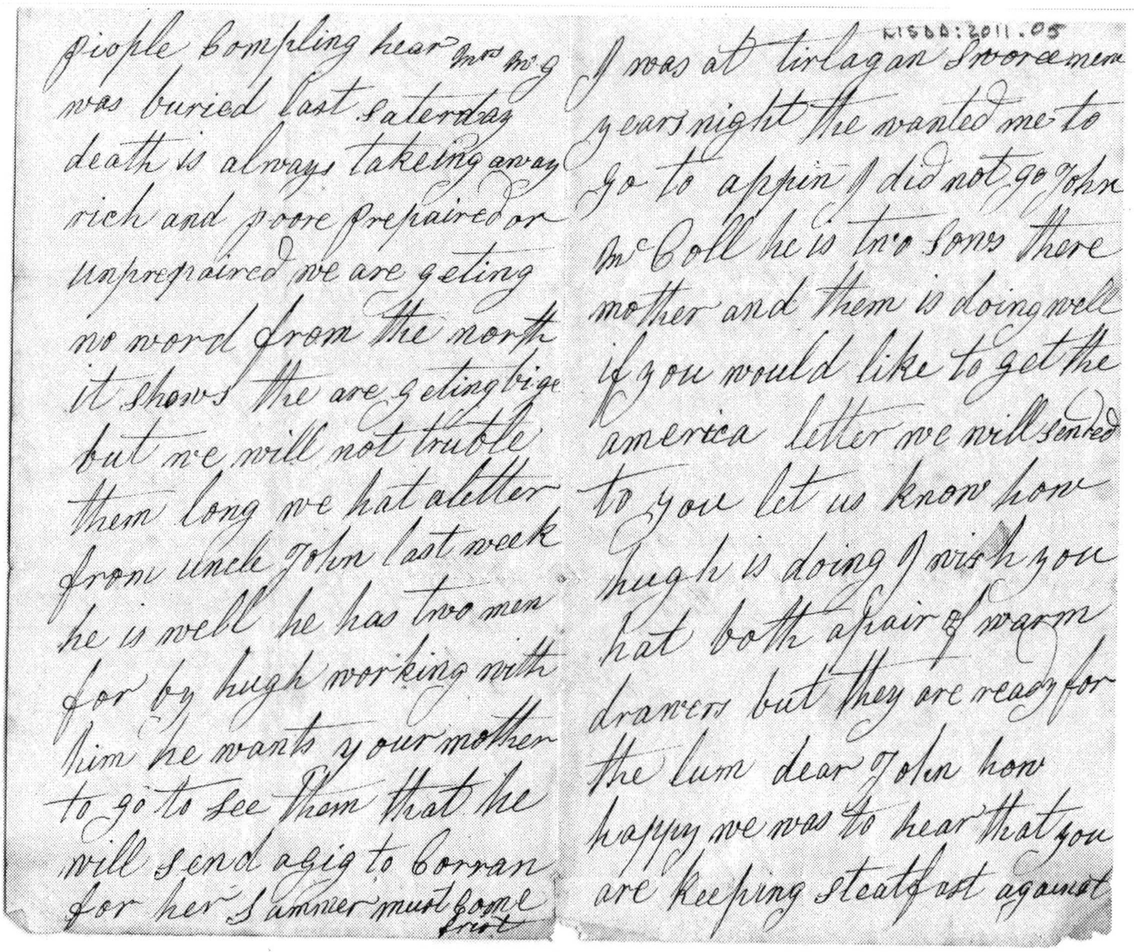
pieople Bompling hear Mrs McG
was buried last saterday
death is always takeing away
rich and poore prepaired or
unprepaired we are geting
no word from the north
it shows the are getingbige
but we will not truble
them long we hat aletter
from uncle John last week
he is well he has two men
for by hugh working with
him he wants your mother
to go to see them that he
will send agig to Corran
for her Summer must come
frist

I was at tirlagan Swora new
years night the wanted me to
go to appin I did not go John
McColl he is two sons there
mother and them is doingwell
if you would like to get the
america letter we will sendit
to you let us know how
hugh is doing I wish you
hat both apair of warm
drawers but they are ready for
the lum dear John how
happy we was to hear that you
are keeping steatfast against

Image db078

LETTER FROM JOHN MCDOUGALL (b. 1803 Lismore) WHO LIVED AT BALLIMACKILLICHAN, ISLE OF LISMORE TO JOHN MCDOUGALL (b. 1837 Lismore) IN GLASGOW

January 16th 1871

My dear Son

I writ this to let you know that we are in the land of the living yet I hope you will excuse me for being so long in writing to you indead your mother was scercely able to tranceleted* till now She is a great deal better now we are sorry to hear that mary is unwell. I hope you will let us know derectly how she is there is many piople Compling hear Mrs McG [Mrs. McGregor, wife of Revd Gregor MacGregor, died 6th Jan 1871] was buried last saterday death is always takeing away rich and poore prepaired or unprepaired we are geting no word from the north it shows the are geting bige but we will not truble them long we hat a letter from uncle John last week he is well he has two men for by hugh working with him he wants your mother to go to see them that he will send a gig to Corran for her Summer must come frist I was at tirlagan sworee [soiree] new years night [Old New Year January] the wanted me to go to appin I did not go John McColl he is two sons there mother and them is doing well if you would like to get the america letter we will sended to you let us know how hugh is doing I wish you hat both a pair of warm drawers but they are ready for the lum dear John how happy we was to hear that you are keeping steatfast against against strong drink what a happy peacefull mine you have I hope hugh is keeping from it too be sure and let us how mary is our love to you all may the Lord be with you all

be sure and writ soon

I am your father

John McDougall

* translate – "move from one place or condition to another: *she had been translated from familiar surroundings to a foreign court...*" (*Oxford Dictionaries)*

Note: In this letter, John McDougall (weaver) indicated that Catherine McCallum had been invited to visit by "uncle John," probably her brother, John McCallum (b. 1818). By 1873, John McCallum was living in Strontian, Sunart, a village northwest of Lismore on the Ardnamurchan Peninsula. (See Letter #7.) Strontian is twelve miles inland from the village of Ardgour, where a ferry takes travelers from the peninsula to the mainland across the Corran Narrows. The "gig" mentioned by John McDougall (weaver) probably would have met Catherine McCallum at Ardgour after she would have crossed the Corran Narrows from the mainland to visit her brother.

Plate 2.1. The Inn at Ardgour, as Seen from the Ferry, *The Corran*

In this photograph, the ferry is departing Ardgour and the Ardnamurchan Peninsula to cross the Corran Narrows and return to the mainland, September 2014.

Plate 2.2. Approaching Nether Lochaber from Ardhour on *The Corran*

The ferry is approaching Nether Lochaber on the mainland after leaving Ardgour.

Plate 2.3. Tirlagan, Lismore

Plate 2.4. Mr. Duncan MacGregor, Isle of Lismore
Viewing Grave Marker of Rev. Mr. Gregor MacGregor
Parish Minister, 1836 - 1885
Lismore Parish Church, Old Graveyard

Plate 2.5. Grave Markers of Rev. Gregor MacGregor and His Wife
Lismore Parish Church, Old Graveyard

Letter #3

April 4th 1871

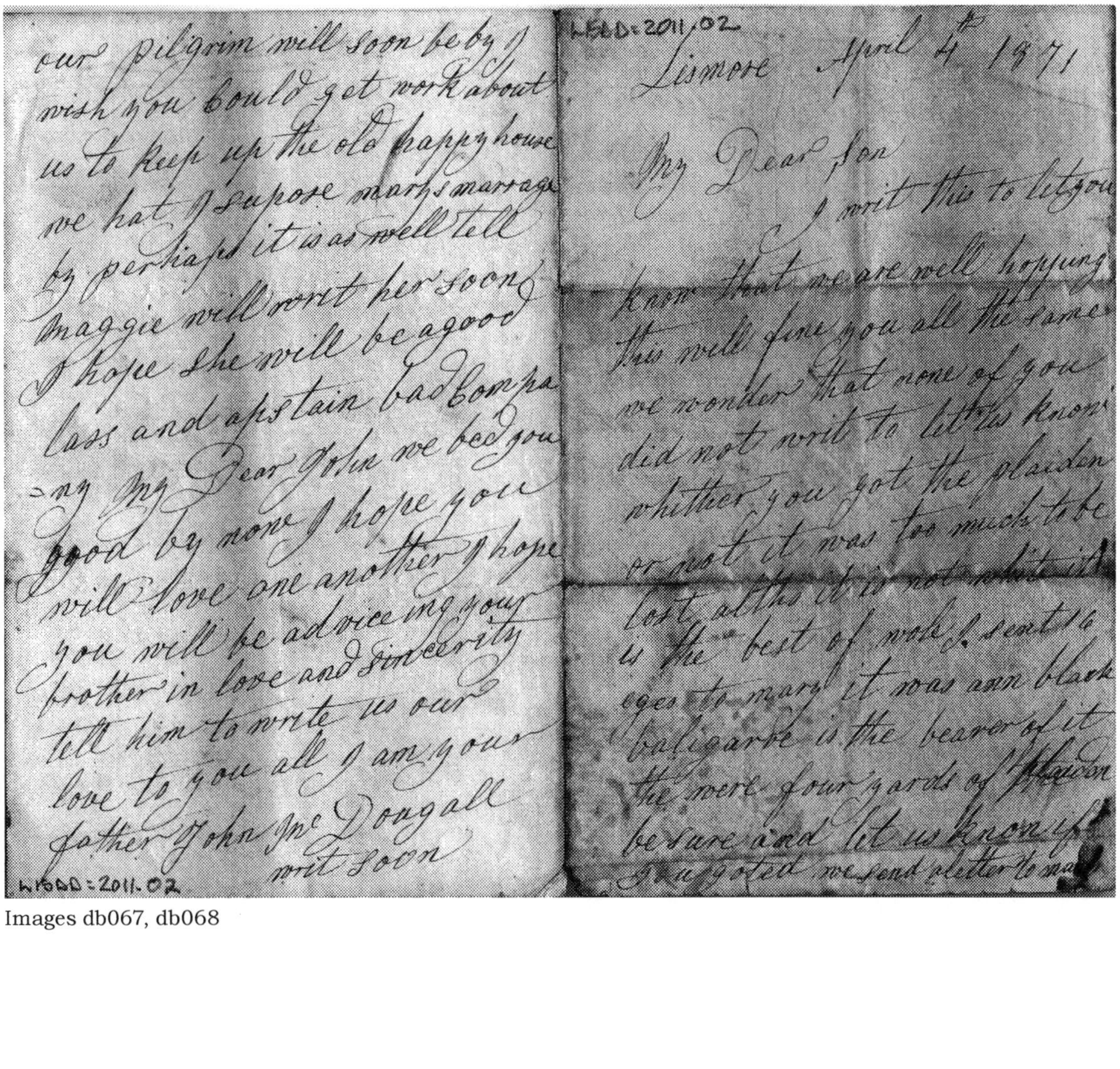

Lismore April 4th 1871

My Dear Son

I writ this to let you
know that we are well hopping
this will fine you all the same
we wonder that none of you
did not writ to let us know
whither you got the plaiden
or not it was too much to be
lost altho it is not white it
is the best of wole I sent 16
eges to mary it was ann black
baligarve is the bearer of it
the were four yards of plaiden
be sure and let us know if
I suggoted we send a letter to ma

our piligrim will soon be by I
wish you could get work about
us to keep up the old happy house
we hat I supose marys marrage
by perhaps it is as well tell
Maggie will writ her soon
I hope she will be a good
lass and apstain bad compa
=ny My Dear John we bed you
good by now I hope you
will love one another I hope
you will be adviceing your
brother in love and sincerity
tell him to write us our
love to you all I am your
father John McDougall
writ soon

Images db067, db068

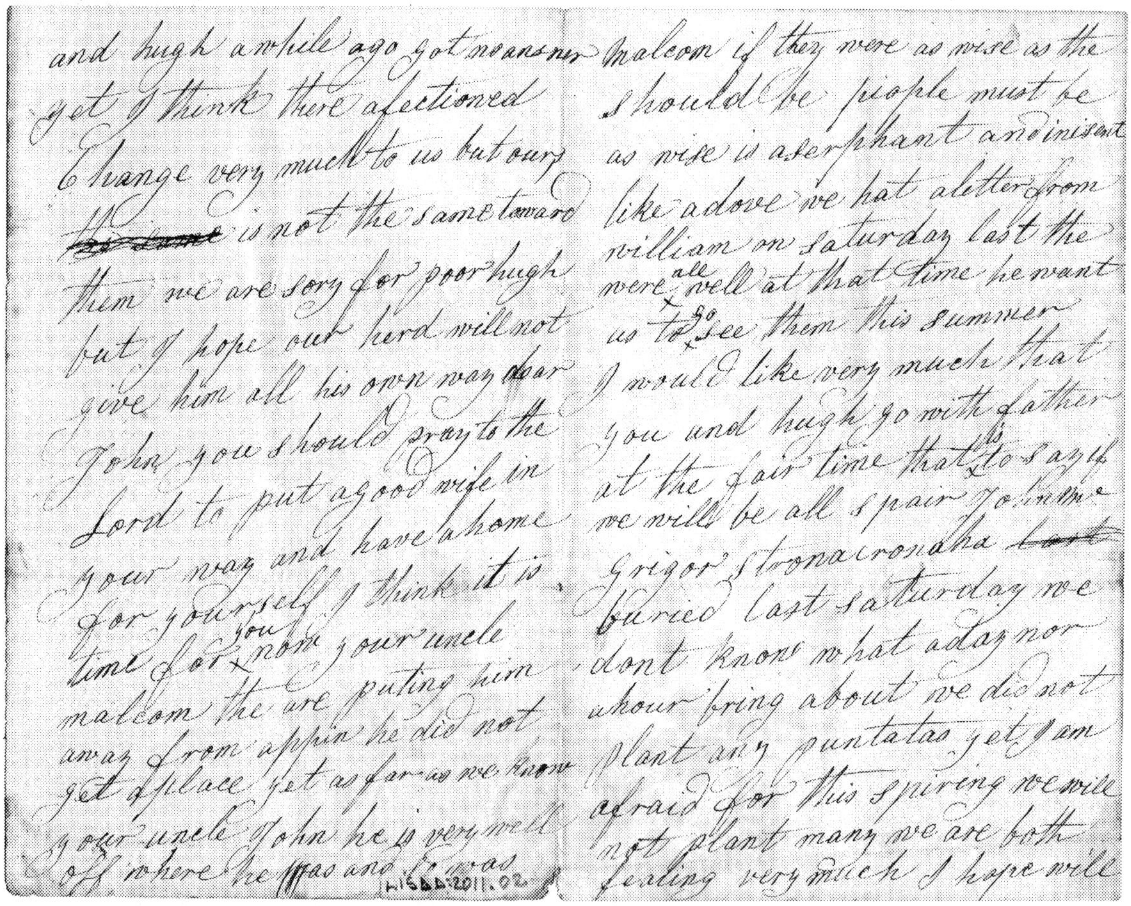

and hugh a while ago got no answer
yet I think there afectioned
Change very much to us but ours
[illegible] is not the same toward
them we are sory for poor hugh
but I hope our lord will not
give him all his own way dear
John you should pray to the
Lord to put a good wife in
your way and have a home
for yourself I think it is
time for you now your uncle
malcom the are puting him
away from appin he did not
get a place yet as far as we know
your uncle John he is very well
off where he was and [illegible] was

malcom if they were as wise as the
should be piople must be
as wise is a serphant and inisent
like a dove we hat a letter from
william on saturday last the
were all well at that time he want
us to go see them this summer
I would like very much that
you and hugh go with father
at the fair time that is to say if
we will be all spair Johnnie
Grigor Stronaironaha ~~last~~
buried last saturday we
dont know what a day nor
a hour bring about we did not
plant any puntatas yet I am
afraid for this spiring we will
not plant many we are both
fealing very much I hope will

Image db069

LETTER FROM JOHN MCDOUGALL (b. 1803 Lismore) AND CATHERINE MCCALLUM MCDOUGALL (b. 1809 Lismore) WHO LIVED AT BALLIMACKILLICHAN, ISLE OF LISMORE TO JOHN MCDOUGALL (b. 1837 Lismore) IN GLASGOW

Lismore April 4th 1871

My Dear Son

I writ this to let you know that we are well hopping this will fine you all the same we wonder that none of you did not writ to let us know whither you got the plaiden or not it was too much to be lost altho it is not white it is the best of wole I sent 16 eges to mary it was ann black baligarve is the bearer of it the were four yards of plaiden be sure and let us know if you goted we send a letter to mary and hugh awhile ago got no answer yet I think there afectioned Change very much to us but ours is not the same toward them we are sory for poor hugh but I hope our herd will not give him all his own way dear John you should pray to the Lord to put a good wife in your way and have a home for yourself I think it is time for you now your uncle malcom the are puting him away from appin he did not get a place yet as far as we know your uncle John he is very well off where he was and so was malcom if they were as wise as the should be piople must be as wise is a serphant and inisent like a dove we hat a letter from william on Saturday last the were all well at that time he want us to go see them this summer I would like very much that you and hugh go with father at the fair time that is to say if we will be all spair John McGrigor Stronacronaha buried last saturday we dont know what a day nor a hour bring about we did not plant any puntatas yet I am afraid for this spiring we will not plant many we are both fealing very much I hope will our pilgrim will soon be by I wish you Could get work about us to keep up the old happy house we hat I supose marys marrage by perhaps it is as well tell Maggie will writ her soon I hope she will be a good lass and apstain bad Company My Dear John we bed you good by now I hope you will love one another I hope you will be adviceing your brother in love and sincerity tell him to write us our love to you all I am your father

John McDougall

writ soon

Plate 3.1. Baligarve

Plate 3.2. Ewe and Lamb
Killean, Isle of Lismore, April 2011

Port Appin

Note: The letter refers to Appin, which, like Port Appin, is on the mainland immediately across the Lynn of Lorn from the Isle of Lismore.

Plate 3.3. Looking toward Port Appin from the Isle of Lismore, 2012

Letter #4

1871

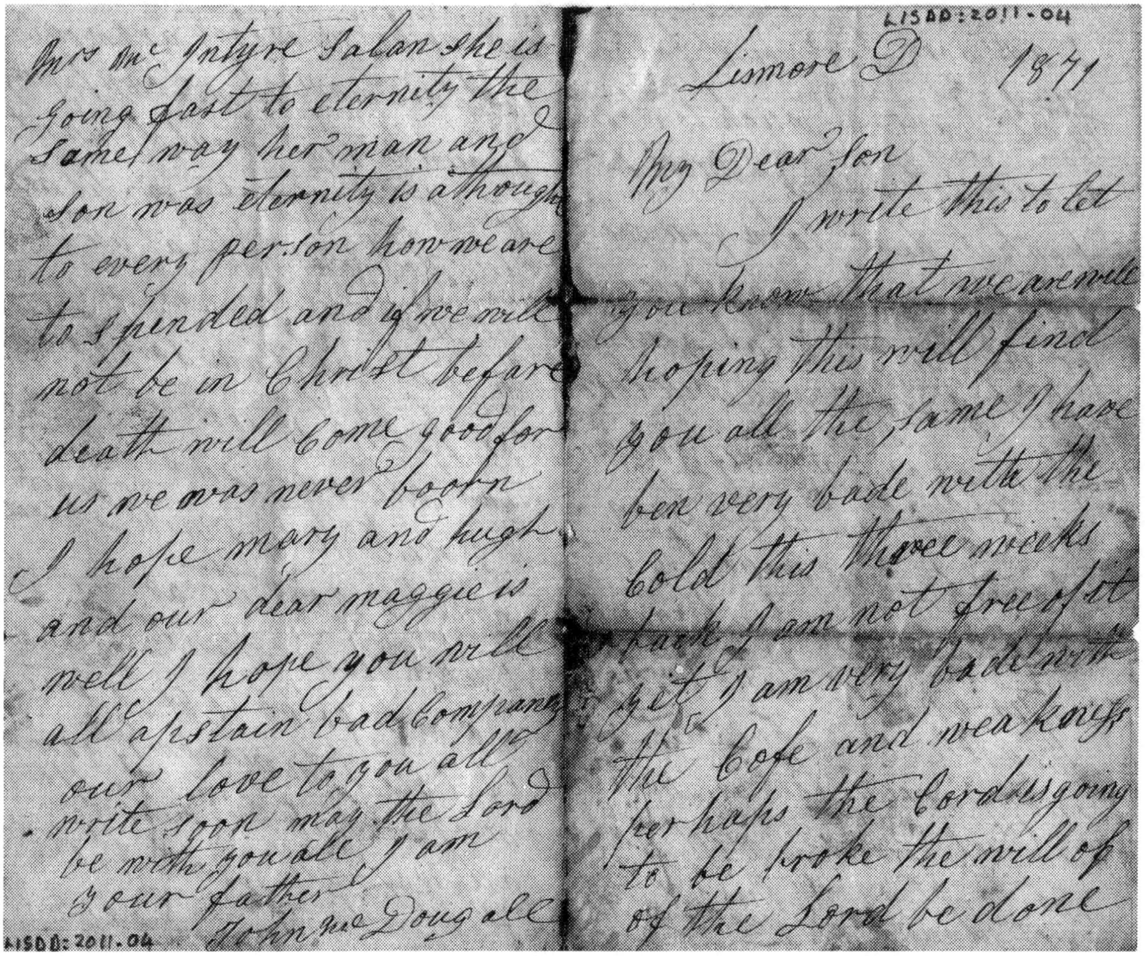

LISAD:2011-04

Lismore D 1871

My Dear Son

I write this to let you know that we are well hoping this will find you all the same I have ben very bade with the cold this three weeks back I am not free of it yet I am very bade with the cofe and weakness perhaps the Cord is going to be broke the will of of the Lord be done

Mrs Mc Intyre Salan she is going fast to eternity the same way her man and son was eternity is a thought to every person how we are to spended and if we will not be in Christ before death will come good for us we was never boorn I hope mary and hugh and our dear maggie is well I hope you will all apstain bad Company our love to you all write soon may the Lord be with you all I am your father

John Mc Dougall

LISAD:2011-04

Image db074

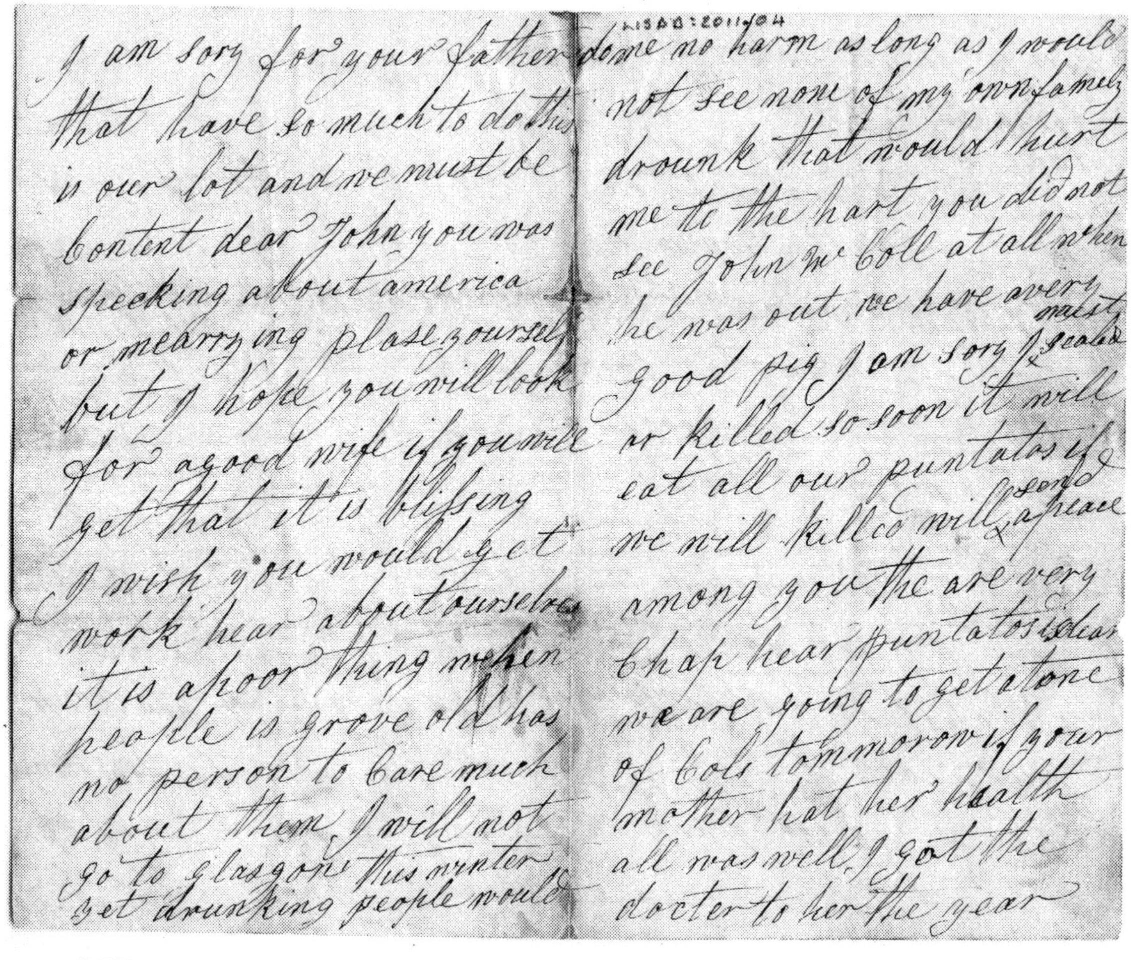

I am sory for your father
that have so much to do this
is our lot and we must be
content dear John you was
speecking about america
or mearrying plase yourself
but I hope you will look
for a good wife if you will
get that it is blissing
I wish you would get
work hear about ourselves
it is a poor thing when
people is grove old has
no person to care much
about them I will not
go to glasgow this winter
get drunking people would
done no harm as long as I would
not see none of my own famely
drounk that would hurt
me to the hart you did not
see John Mc Coll at all when
he was out we have a very
good pig I am sory I must sealed
or killed so soon it will
eat all our puntatos if
we will kill we will send a peace
among you the are very
chap hear puntatos dear
we are going to get a tone
of cols tommorow if your
mother hat her health
all was well I got the
docter to her the year

Image db075

**LETTER FROM JOHN MCDOUGALL (b. 1803 Lismore)
WHO LIVED AT BALLIMACKILLICHAN, ISLE OF LISMORE
TO JOHN MCDOUGALL (b. 1837 Lismore) IN GLASGOW**

Lismore D 1871

My dear Son

I write this to let you know that we are well hoping this will find you all the same I have been very bade with the Cold this three weeks back I am not free of it yet I am very bade with the Cofe and weakness perhaps the Cord is going to be broke the will of of the Lord be done

I am sory for your father that have so much to do this is our lot and we must be Content dear John you was speeking about america or mearrying plase yourself but I hope you will look for a good wife if you will get that it is blissing I wish you would get work hear about ourselves it is a poor thing when people is grove old has no person to Care much about them I will not go to glasgow this winter yet drunking people would do me no harm as long as I would not see none of my own famely drounk that would hurt me to the hart you did not see John McColl at all when he was out we have a very good pig I am sory I must sealed [sell it?] or killed so soon it will eat all our puntatos if we will killed will send a peace among you the are very Chap hear puntatos is dear we are going to get a tone of Cols tommorow if your mother hat her health all was well I got the doctor to her the year Mrs McIntyre Salan she is going fast to eternity the same way her man and Son was eternity is a thought to every person how we are to spended and if we will not be in Christ before death will come good for us we was never boorn I hope mary and hugh and our dear maggie is well I hope you will all apstain bad company

our love to you all

write soon may the Lord be with you all I am

your father

John McDougall

Plate 4.1. Sailean (Salan), Lismore

Plate 4.2. Sailean (Salan)

Plate 4.3. Sailean (Salan)

Plate 4.4. Sailean (Salan)

***The Oban Times,* March 4, 1871**

LISMORE

SOIREE – The annual soiree of the Achachuran Sabbath School was held in the Independent Chapel there on the evening of Thursday the 23rd ult. The chair was occupied by the Rev. John McGregor; and about 100 children were present, besides a considerable number of parents and others interested in the school. After tea, the chairman addressed the meeting, and addresses were also given by Messrs J. McDougall and J. McDonald. The children sang a number of hymns very nicely. The soiree, which proved to be very successful, broke up about 10 o'clock.

PLOUGHING MATCH – The annual competition in ploughing came off last, the 24th ult, on Mr. McGregor's farm at Achachuaran. The day was favourable, and the ground was suitable for the purpose. In all, ten ploughs were on the ground, and completed their work satisfactorily. The judges were Messrs Duncan McDonald, Ardintenny Benderloch; Archibald McCorquodale, Kilandrist; and Donald Buchanan, Baleveolan; and they were awarded the prizes as follows:

1st, Alexander McColl, Point; 2nd, Alexander Buchanan, Achachuaran; 3rd, Alex. Carmichael, Balure; 4th, Dugald McGregor, Achachuaran; 5th, Alexander McColl, Ballimackillichan.

After the completion of the day's work, the committee, judges, ploughmen, and onlookers were entertained to dinner by Mr. McGregor.

(*The Oban Times,* March 4, 1871, p. 2)

Letter **#5**

March 1, 1872

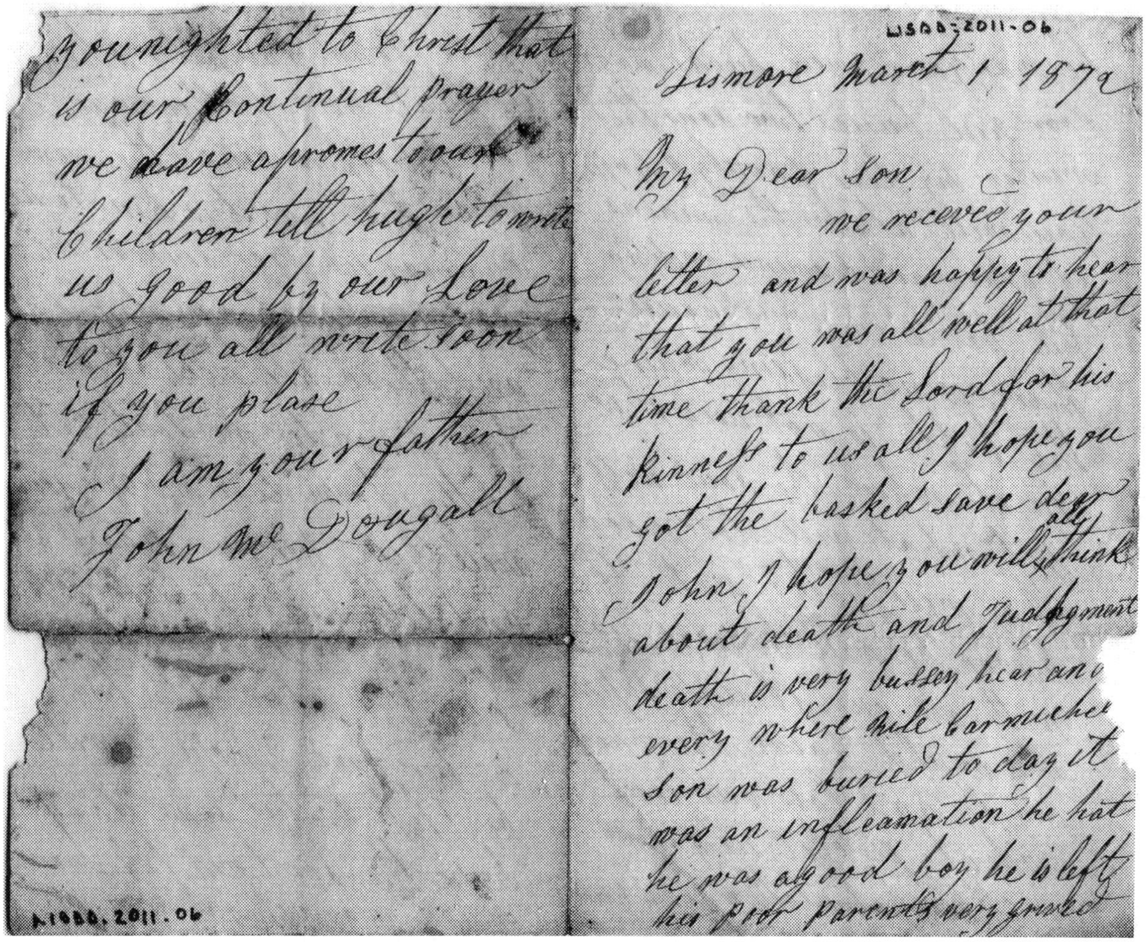
younighted to Christ that
is our Continual prayer
we have a promes to our
Children tell hugh to write
us Good by our Love
to you all write soon
if you plase
I am your father
John McDougall

Lismore March 1, 1872
My Dear Son
we receved your
letter and was happy to hear
that you was all well at that
time thank the Lord for his
kinness to us all I hope you
got the basked save dear
John I hope you will ally think
about death and Judgment
death is very bussey hear and
every where mile Carmichee
Son was buried to day it
was an infleamation he hat
he was a good boy he is left
his poor Parents very grived

Image db080

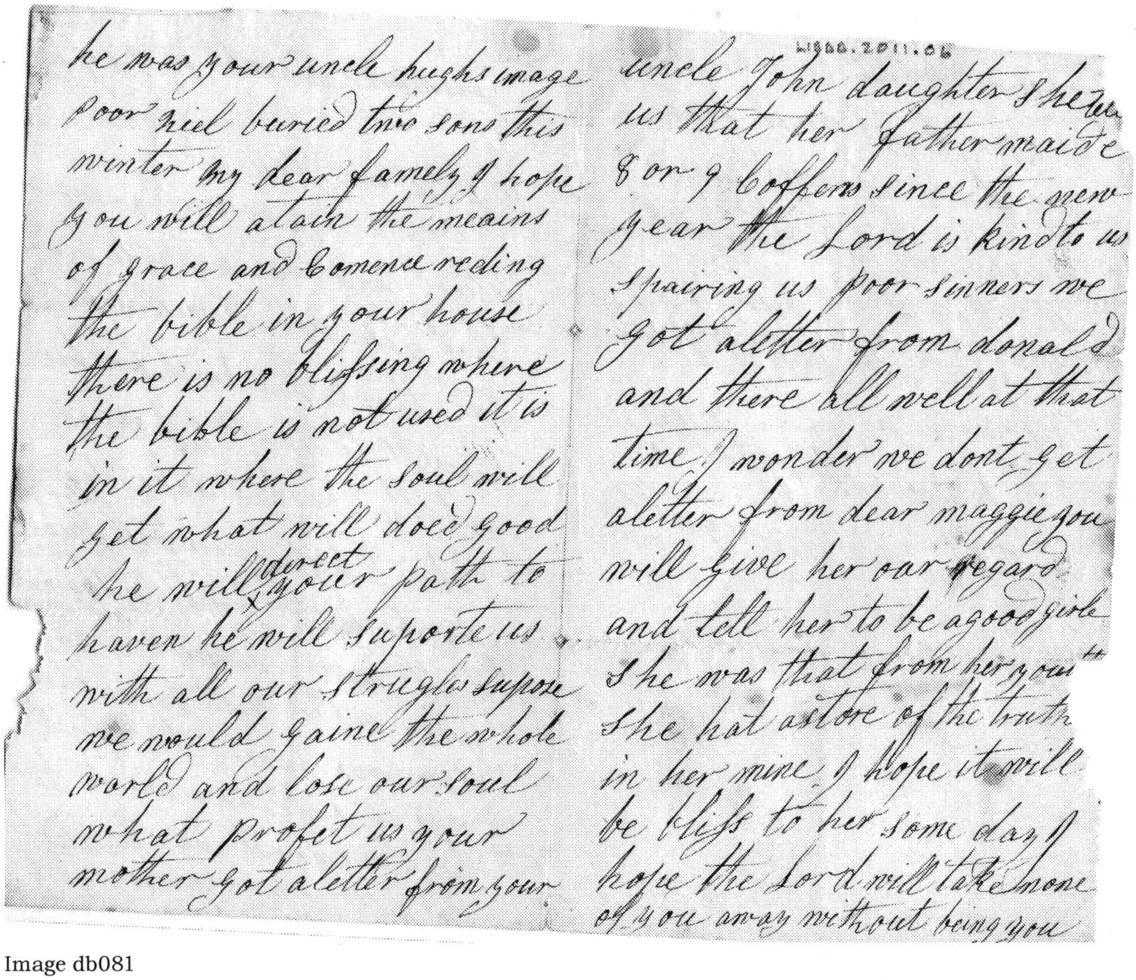
LI500.2011.06
he was your uncle hughs image
poor niel buried two sons this
winter my dear famely I hope
you will atain the meains
of grace and Comence reding
the bible in your house
there is no blissing where
the bible is not used it is
in it where the soul will
get what will doee good
he will direct your path to
haven he will suporte us
with all our struglss supose
we would gaine the whole
world and lose our soul
what profet us your
mother got aletter from your
uncle John daughter she tel
us that her father maide
8 or 9 Coffens since the new
year the Lord is kind to us
spairing us poor sinners we
got aletter from donald
and there all well at that
time I wonder we dont get
aletter from dear maggie you
will give her our regard
and tell her to be agood girle
she was that from her youth
she hat astore of the truth
in her mine I hope it will
be bliss to her some day I
hope the Lord will take none
of you away without being you

Image db081

LETTER FROM JOHN MCDOUGALL (b. 1803 Lismore) WHO LIVED AT BALLIMACKILLICHAN, ISLE OF LISMORE TO JOHN MCDOUGALL (b. 1837 Lismore) IN GLASGOW

Lismore March 1 1872

My Dear Son

we receved your letter and was happy to hear that you was all well at that time thank the Lord for his kinness to us all I hope you got the basked save dear John I hope you will all think about death and Judgment death is very bussey hear and every where Nile Carmichel Son was buried to day it was an infleamation he hat he was a good boy he is left his poor parents very grived he was your uncle hughs image poor niel buried two sons this winter My dear famely I hope you will atain the meains of grace and Comence reding the bible in your house there is no blissing where the bible is not used it is in it where the soul will get what will doed good he will direct your path to haven he will suporte us with all our strugles supose we would gaine the whole world and lose our Soul what profet us your mother got a letter from your uncle John daughter she tell us that her father maide 8 or 9 Coffens since the new year the Lord is kind to us spairing us poor sinners we got a letter from donald and there all well at that time I wonder we dont get a letter from dear maggie you will give her our regard and tell her to be a good girle She was that from her youth She hat a store of the truth in her mine I hope it will be bliss to her some day I hope the Lord will take none of you away without being you younighted to Christ that is our Continual prayer we have a promes to our Children tell hugh to write us Good by our Love to you all write soon if you plase

I am your father

John McDougall

Notes:

"[H]e was your uncle hughs image" might be a reference to John McDougall's (weaver) brother, Hugh, born 12 September 1808. (NRS, 1855 – 2013a)

"[Y]our uncle John daughter" might be a reference to Ann (born 1863), a niece of Catherine McCallum and the daughter of John McCallum (born 1818 Balure) and Flora Carmichael. (Gloag, 2014a)

Plate 5.1. Achuaran Farm, Lismore

John McDougall (weaver) was head of the Lismore Sabbath School for 30 years that met in this Independent Chapel. It is now being used for storage on Achuaran Farm, a sheep farm located in the north-central area of the island.

Inside the Building

Plate 5.2.

Plate 5.3.

Letter **#6**

August 29th 1872

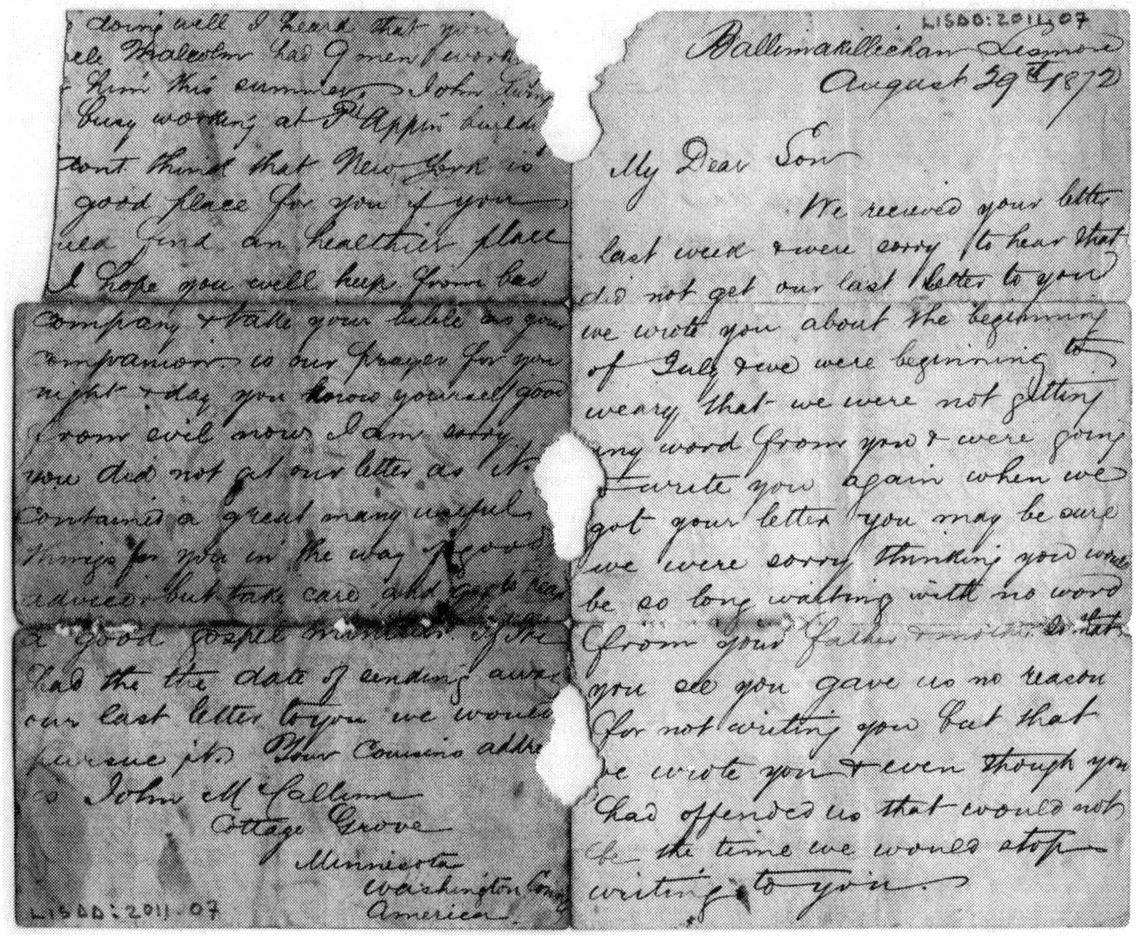

LISDO:2011.07

Ballimakillechan Lismore
August 29th 1872

My Dear Son

We received your letter last week & were sorry to hear that did not get our last letter to you we wrote you about the beginning of July & we were beginning to weary that we were not getting any word from you & were going to write you again when we got your letter you may be sure we were sorry thinking you would be so long waiting with no word from your father & mother & that you see you gave us no reason for not writing you but that we wrote you & even though you had offended us that would not be the time we would stop writing to you.

doing well I heard that your uncle Malcolm had 9 men working with him this summer, John being busy working at Pt Appin building. I dont think that New York is good place for you if you could find an healthier place I hope you will keep from bad company & take your bible as your companion. is our prayer for you night & day you know yourself good from evil now I am sorry you did not get our letter as it contained a great many useful things for you in the way of good advice but take care and try to hear a good gospel minister. If he had the the date of sending away our last letter to you we would pursue it. Your Cousins address is John McCallum Cottage Grove Minnesota Washington County America

LISDO:2011.07

Image db084

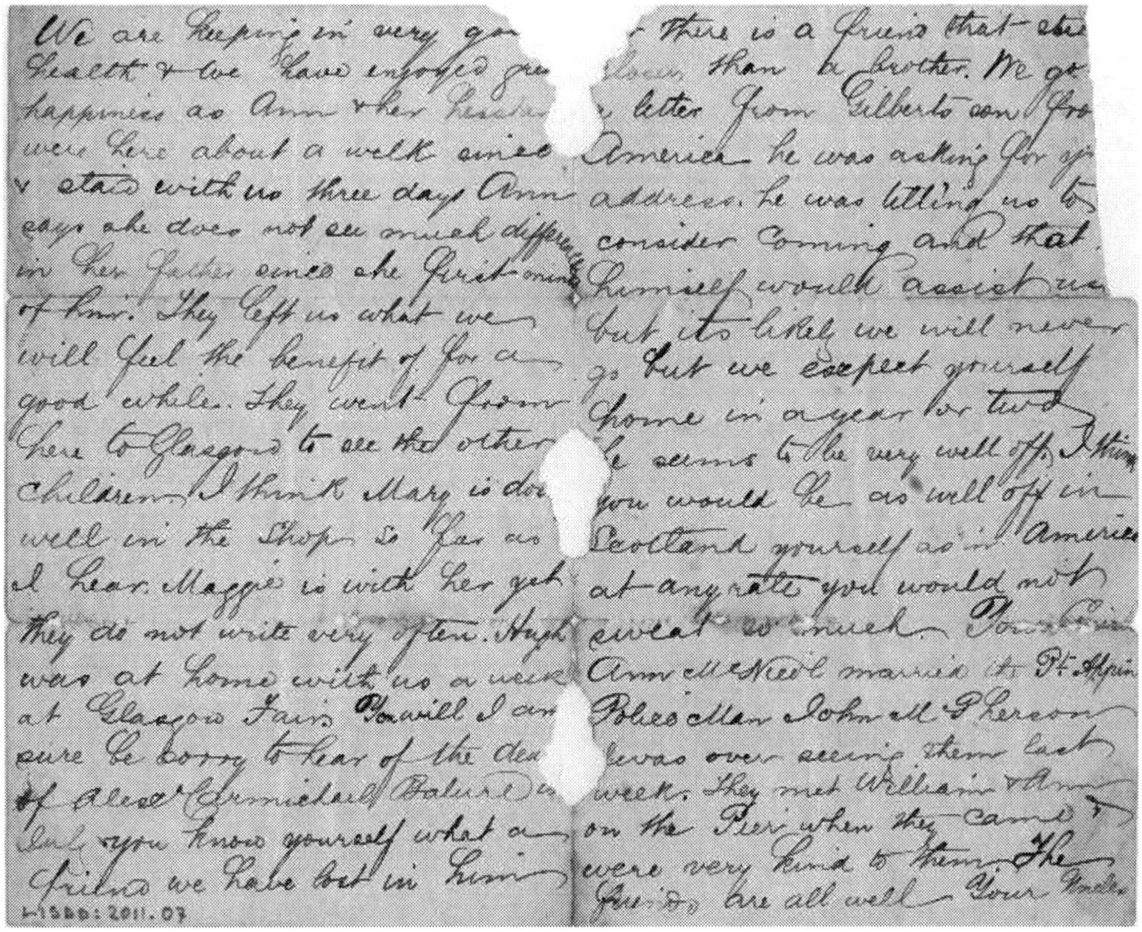

We are keeping in very go
health & we have enjoyed gre
happiness as Ann & her husban
were here about a week since
& staid with us three days Ann
says she does not see much diffe
in her father since she first mind
of him. They left us what we
will feel the benefit of for a
good while. They went from
here to Glasgow to see the other
children. I think Mary is doi
well in the Shop so far as
I hear. Maggie is with her yet
they do not write very often. Hugh
was at home with us a week
at Glasgow Fair. You will I am
sure be sorry to hear of the dea
of Alexr Carmichael Baliure
Ind you know yourself what a
friend we have lost in him

there is a friend that sti
closer than a brother. We go
letter from Gilberts son fro
America he was asking for yo
address. he was telling us to
consider coming and that
himself would assist us
but its likely we will never
go but we expect yourself
home in a year or two
he seems to be very well off. I think
you would be as well off in
Scotland yourself as in America
at anyrate you would not
sweat so much. Your Cousin
Ann McNeil married its Pt Appin
Police Man John McPherson
I was over seeing them last
week. They met William & Ann
on the Pier when they came &
were very kind to them. The
friends are all well Your Uncle

H-1580: 2011.07

Image db084a page 2

LETTER FROM JOHN MCDOUGALL (b. 1803 Lismore) AND CATHERINE MCCALLUM MCDOUGALL (b. 1809 Lismore) WHO LIVED AT BALLIMACKILLICHAN, ISLE OF LISMORE TO JOHN MCDOUGALL (b. 1837 Lismore) IN GLASGOW

Ballimackillichan Lismore
August 29th 1872

My Dear Son

We recieved your letter last week & were sorry to hear that did not get our last letter to you we wrote you about the beginning of July & we were beginning to weary that we were not getting any word from you & were going to write you again when we got your letter you may be sure we were sorry thinking you would be so long waiting with no word from your father & mother. Is[?] that you see you gave us no reason for not writing you but that we wrote you & even though you had offended us that would not be the time we would stop writing to you.

We are keeping in very good health & we have enjoyed great happiness as Ann & her husband were here about a week since & staid with us three days Ann says she does not see much difference in her father since she first mind of him. They left us what we will feel the benefit of for a good while. They went from here to Glasgow to see the other children. I think Mary is doing well in the shop so far as I hear. Maggie is with her yet they do not write very often. Hugh was at home with us a week at Glasgow Fair. You will I am sure be sorry to hear of the death of Aleser [Alexander] Carmichael Balure in July you know yourself what a friend we have lost in him [___] there is a friend that stais[?] closer than a brother. We got a letter from Gilberts son from America he was asking for your address. he was telling us to consider coming and that himself would assist us but its likely we will never go but we expect yourself home in a year or two he seems to be very well off. I think you would be as well off in Scotland yourself as in America at any rate you would not sweat so much. Your cousin Ann McNicol married the Pt Appin Police Man John McPherson I[?] was over seeing them last week. They met William & Ann on the Pier when they came & were very kind to them. The friends are all well Your Uncles [___] doing well I heard that you [un]cle Malcolm had 9 men working [___] him this summer. John Living[stone] busy working at Pt Appin building dont think that New York is good place for you if you [co]uld find an healthier place I hope you well keep from bad company & take your bible as your companion is our prayer for you night & day you know yourself good from evil now I am sorry you did not get our letter as it contained a great many useful things for you in the way of good advice but take care and go to hear a good gospel minister If we had the the date of sending away our last letter to you we would pursue it. Your cousins address is

John McCallum
Cottage Grove
Minnesota
Washington County
America.

(rest of letter missing)

Note: "Gilberts son from America" might refer to John McCallum (b. 1847), whose address appears at the end of the letter. He was the son of Catherine McCallum's brother, Gilbert (b. 1813 Balure), and Ann McCallum (b. 1814). He was also the brother of Isabel McCallum (b. 1850).

Agnes (Ann) McDougall (b. 1833), her husband, William Moore, and their son James

Plate 6.1. Ann (Agnes) McDougall Daughter of John McDougall (weaver) and Catherine McCallum

Plate 6.2. William Moore, Husband of Ann (Agnes)

Plate 6.3. James Moore (b. 1868) Son of Ann (Agnes) McDougall and William Moore Grandson of John McDougall (weaver) and Catherine McCallum

Plate 6.4. Drummond, Home of William Moore Family, Evanton, 1965
Balure Area, Lismore

Plate 6.5. Looking toward Eileen Dubh (Black Island) near Balure

Plate 6.6. The Broch, near Balure

Plate 6.7. Port Appin

Plate 6.8. Port Appin Pier

Plate 6.9. Port Appin Beach and Pier, June 2010 with Lismore in the Distance

Letter **#7**

June 6th 1873

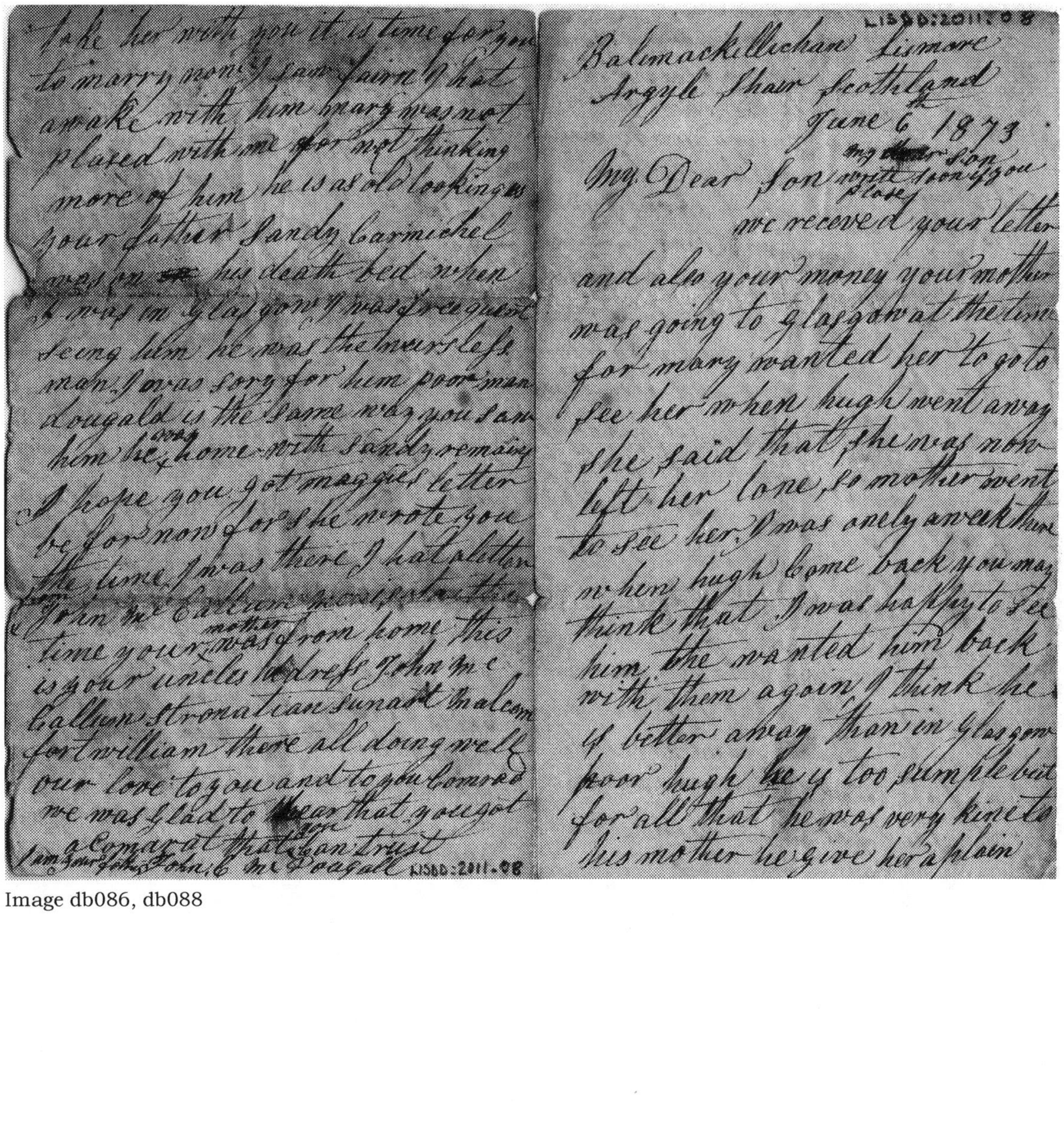

take her with you it is time for you
to marry now I saw fairn [illegible] that
awake with him mary was not
plased with me for not thinking
more of him he is as old looking as
your father Sandy Carmichel
was on his death bed when
I was in glasgow I was frequent
seing him he was the mearsless
man I was sory for him poor man
dougald is the same way you saw
him he was home with Sandy remains
I hope you got maggies letter
before now for she wrote you
the time I was there I hat a letter
from John Mc Callum [illegible]
time your mother was from home this
is your uncles address John Mc
Callum Strontian Sunart Malcom
fortwilliam there all doing well
our love to you and to you comrad
we was glad to hear that you got
a comrad that you can trust
I am your father John C McDougall LISDD:2011.08

LISDD:2011.08
Balmackillichan Lismore
Argyle Shair Scothland
June 6th 1873
My Dear Son write soon if you please my dear son
we receved your letter
and also your money your mother
was going to glasgow at the time
for mary wanted her to go to
see her when hugh went away
she said that she was now
left her lone so mother went
to see her I was onely a week there
when hugh come back you may
think that I was happy to see
him she wanted him back
with them again I think he
is better away than in glasgow
poor hugh he is too sumple but
for all that he was very kine to
his mother he give her a plain

Image db086, db088

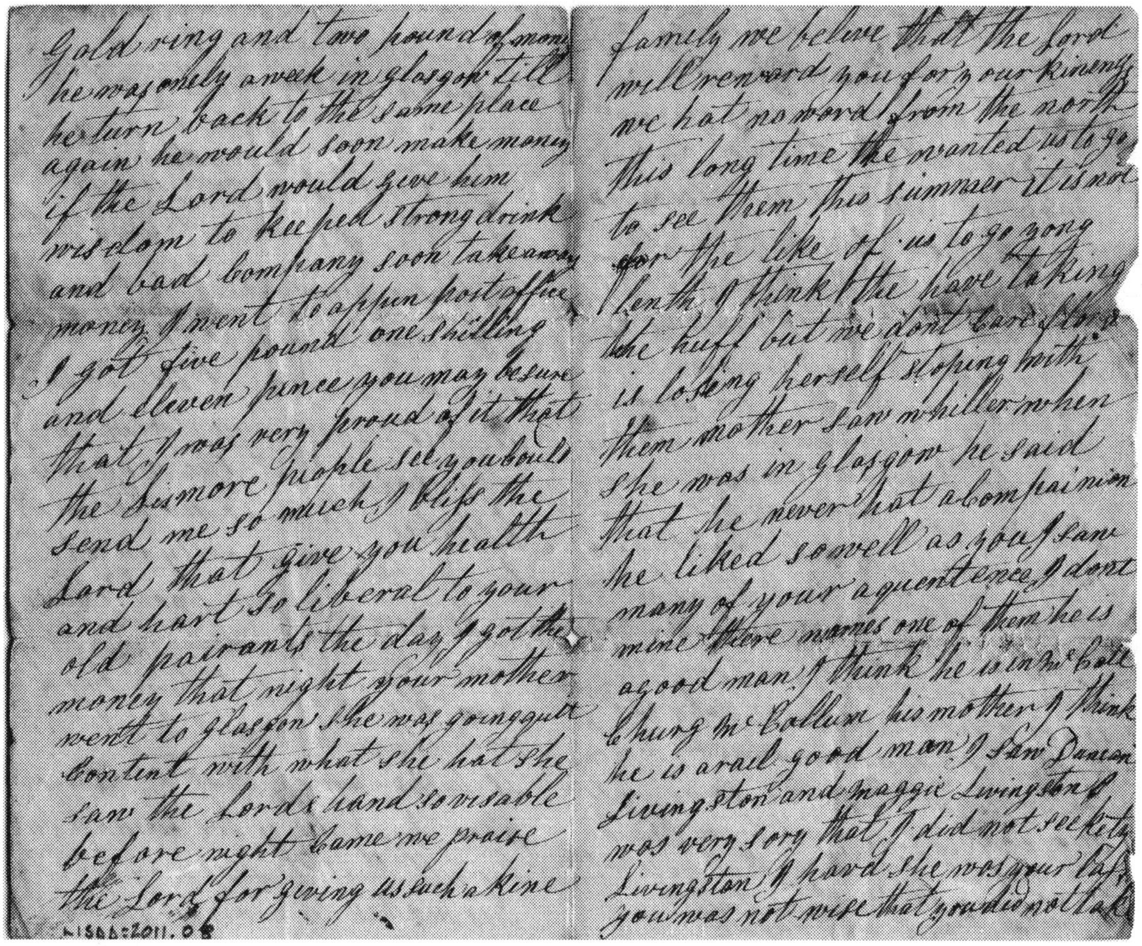

Gold ring and two pound of mony
he was onely a week in glasgow till
he turn back to the same place
again he would soon make mony
if the Lord would give him
wisdom to keeped strong drink
and bad company soon take away
money I went to appin postoffice
I got five pound one shilling
and eleven pince you may be sure
that I was very proud of it that
the seemore people see you boult
send me so much I bliss the
Lord that give you health
and hart so liberal to your
old pairants the day I got the
money that night your mother
went to glasgow she was going quit
content with what she hat she
saw the Lords hand so visable
before night came we praise
the Lord for giving us such a kine

family we belive that the Lord
will reward you for your kinens
we hat no word from the north
this long time the wanted us to go
to see them this summer it is not
for the like of us to go gong
lenth I think the have taking
the huff but we dont care Flora
is losing herself stoping with
them mother saw m'hiller when
she was in glasgow he said
that he never hat a compainion
that he liked so well as you I saw
many of your aquentence I dont
mine there names one of them he is
a good man I think he is in MColle
Church MCollum his mother I think
he is a rail good man I saw Duncan
Livingston and maggie Livingston I
was very sory that I did not see kity
Livingston I hard she was your lass
you was not wise that you did not tak

HISDA:2011.08

Image db087, db089

LETTER FROM JOHN MCDOUGALL (b. 1803 Lismore) WHO LIVED AT BALLIMACKILLICHAN, ISLE OF LISMORE TO JOHN MCDOUGALL (b. 1837) DELHI, REDWOOD COUNTY, MINNESOTA USA

Balimackillichan Lismore

Argyle Shair Scothland

June 6th 1873

My Dear Son My Son write soon if you plase

We receved your letter and also your money your mother was going to glasgow at the time for mary wanted her to go to see her when hugh went away she said that she was now left her lone so mother went to see her. I was onely a week there when hugh Came back you may think that I was happy to see him the wanted him back with them again I think he is better away than in Glasgow poor hugh he is too sumple but for all that he was very kine to his mother he give her a plain Gold ring and two pound of money he was onely a week in glasgow till he turn back to the same place again he would soon make money if the Lord would give him wisdom to keeped strong drink and bad Company soon take away money I went to appin post office I got five pound one shilling and eleven pence you may be sure that I was very proud of it that the Lismore people see you Could send me so much I bliss the Lord that give you health and hart so liberal to your old pairants the day I got the money that night your mother went to glasgow she was going quit Content with what she hat she saw the Lords hand so visable before night Came we praise the Lord for giving us such a kine family we belive that the Lord will reward you for your kineness we hat no word from the north this long time the wanted us to go to see them this summer it is not for the like of us to go yong lenth I think the have taking the huff but we dont care flora is losing herself stoping with them mother saw whiller when she was in glasgow he said that he never hat a Compainion he liked so well as you I saw many of your aquentence I dont mine there names one of them he is a good man I think he is in McColl Churg McCallum his mother I think he is a rail good man I saw Duncan Livingston and Maggie Livingston I was very sory that I did not see kety Livingston I hard she was your lass you was not wise that you did not tak take her with you it is time for you to marry now I saw[?] fairn [Fairn?] I hat[?] awake with him mary was not plased with me for not thinking more of him he is as old looking as your father Sandy Carmichel was on his death bed when I was in Glasgow I was freequent seing him he was the nursless[?] man I was sory for him poor man dougald is the same way you saw him he was home with Sandy remains I hope you got maggies letter befor now for she wrote you the time I was there I hat a letter from John McCallum Minisota the time your mother was from home this is your uncles adress

John McCallum Stronatian Sunart

Malcom fortwilliam

there all doing well our love to you and to you Comrad

we was Glad to hear that you got a Comarat that you Can trust

I am your father John, C McDougall

Plate 7.1. Sign on the Village Shop
Strontian, Sunart
September 2014

In this letter, John McDougall (weaver) mentioned that he had heard from Catherine McCallum's nephew, John McCallum (b. 1847), who was living in Minnesota. ("John McCallum Minisota" was the son of Catherine's brother, Gilbert.)

John McDougall (weaver) also included addresses for Catherine's brothers, Malcolm and John. Malcolm McCallum (b. 1811), was living in Fort William, a garrison town northeast of Lismore. John McCallum (b. 1818), who bore the same name as his nephew, was living in Strontian, Sunart, a village on the Ardnamurchan Peninsula, northwest of Lismore and southwest of Fort William. (See Letter 2, above.)

For more information about the McCallum families, see notes after Letter 14, Letter 26, Letter 30 and Appendix 9.

Letter #8

Undated Fragments

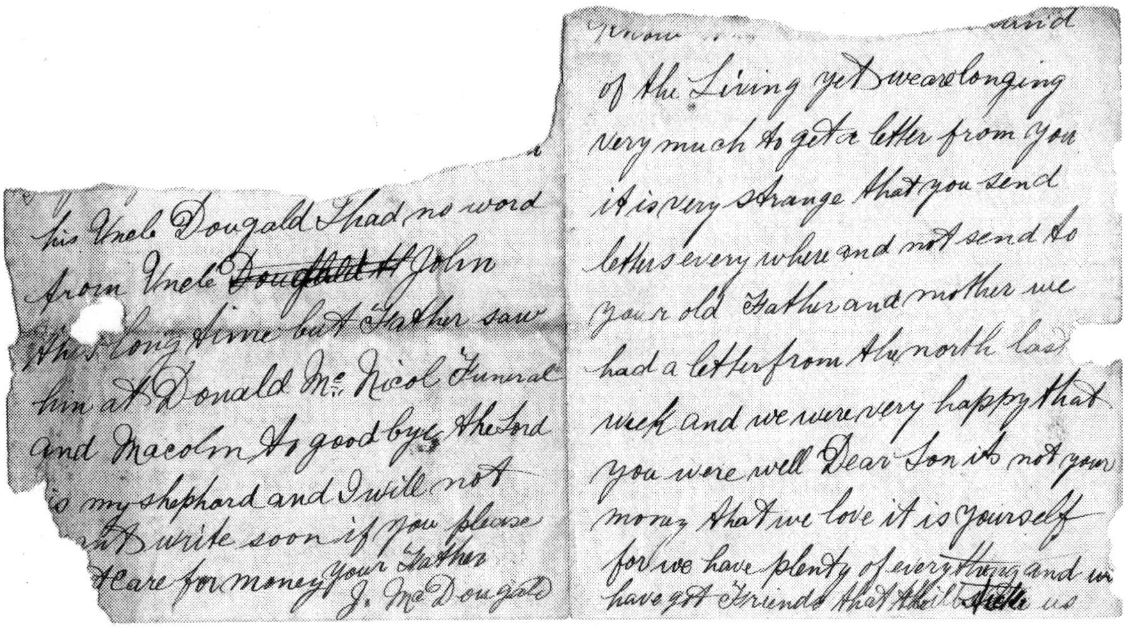

his Uncle Dougald & had no word
from Uncle ~~Dougald~~ John
this long time but Father saw
him at Donald McNicol Funeral
and Macolm to good bye the Lord
is my shephard and I will not
...t write soon if you please
care for money your Father
J. McDougald

know ... and
of the Living yet we are longing
very much to get a letter from you
it is very strange that you send
letters every where and not send to
your old Father and mother we
had a letter from the north last
week and we were very happy that
you were well Dear Son it's not your
money that we love it is yourself
for we have plenty of everything and we
have got friends that will ~~tickle~~ us

Image db221

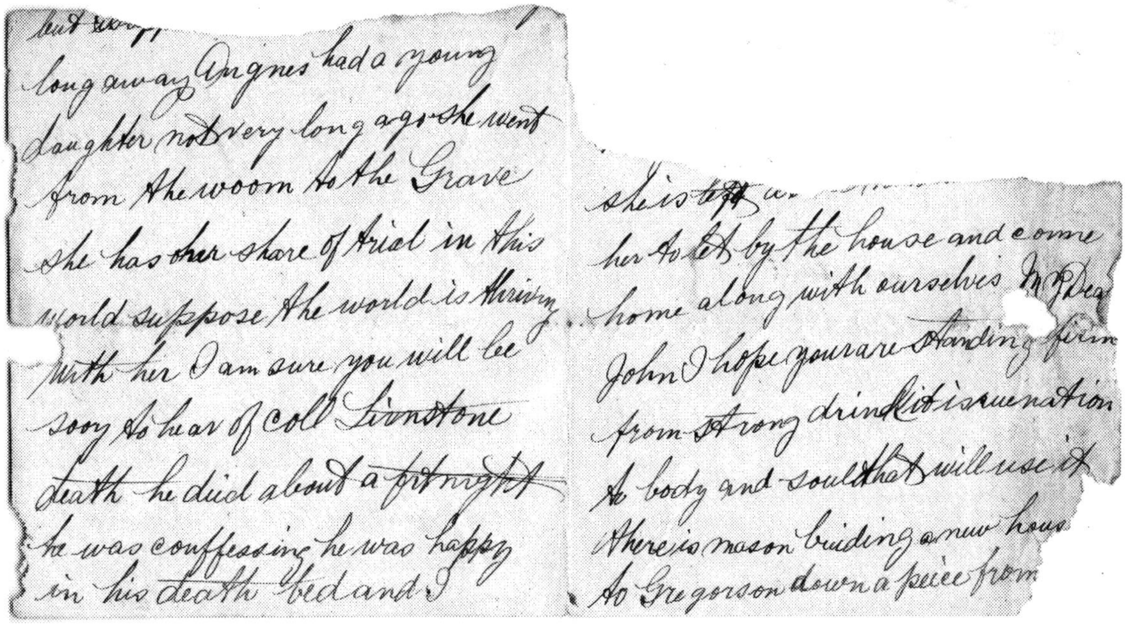

but ...
long away Angnes had a young
daughter not very long ago she went
from the woom to the Grave
she has her share of trial in this
world suppose the world is thriving
with her I am sure you will bee
sorry to hear of coll Livingstone
death he died about ~~a fortnight~~
he was confessing he was happy
in his death bed and I

she is ~~off~~ ...
her to let by the house and come
home along with ourselves My Dear
John I hope you are standing firm
from strong drink it is ruenation
to body and soul that will use it
there is mason biding a new hous
to Gregorson down a peice from

Image db222

LETTER FROM JOHN MCDOUGALL (b. 1803 Lismore) WHO LIVED AT BALLIMACKILLICHAN, ISLE OF LISMORE TO HIS SON JOHN MCDOUGALL (b. 1837) DELHI, REDWOOD COUNTY MINNESOTA, USA

(date unknown)

(fragments of a letter)

[___]and of the Living yet we are longing very much to get a letter from you it is very strange that you send letters every where and not send to your old Father and mother we had a letter from the north last week and we were very happy that you were well Dear Son its not your money that we love it is yourself for we have plenty of everything and we have got Friends that [___] us

[___] but[___] long away Angnes [Ann McDougall Moore] had a young daughter not very long ago she went from the woom to the Grave she has her share of trial in this world suppose the world is thriving with her I am sure you will be soory to hear of Coll Livinstone death he died about a fortnight he was conffessing he was happy in his death bed and I [___] she is left [___] her to let by the house and come home along with ourselves My Dear John I hope you are standing firm from strong drink it is ruenation to body and soul that will use it there is mason buiding a new house [___] to Gregorson down a peice from [___]

[___]his Uncle Dougald I had no word from Uncle John this long time but Father saw him at donald McNicol Funeral and Malcolm to good bye the Lord is my shephard and I will not want write soon if you please ... t care for money Your Father

J. McDougald

Letter #9

April 17th 1874

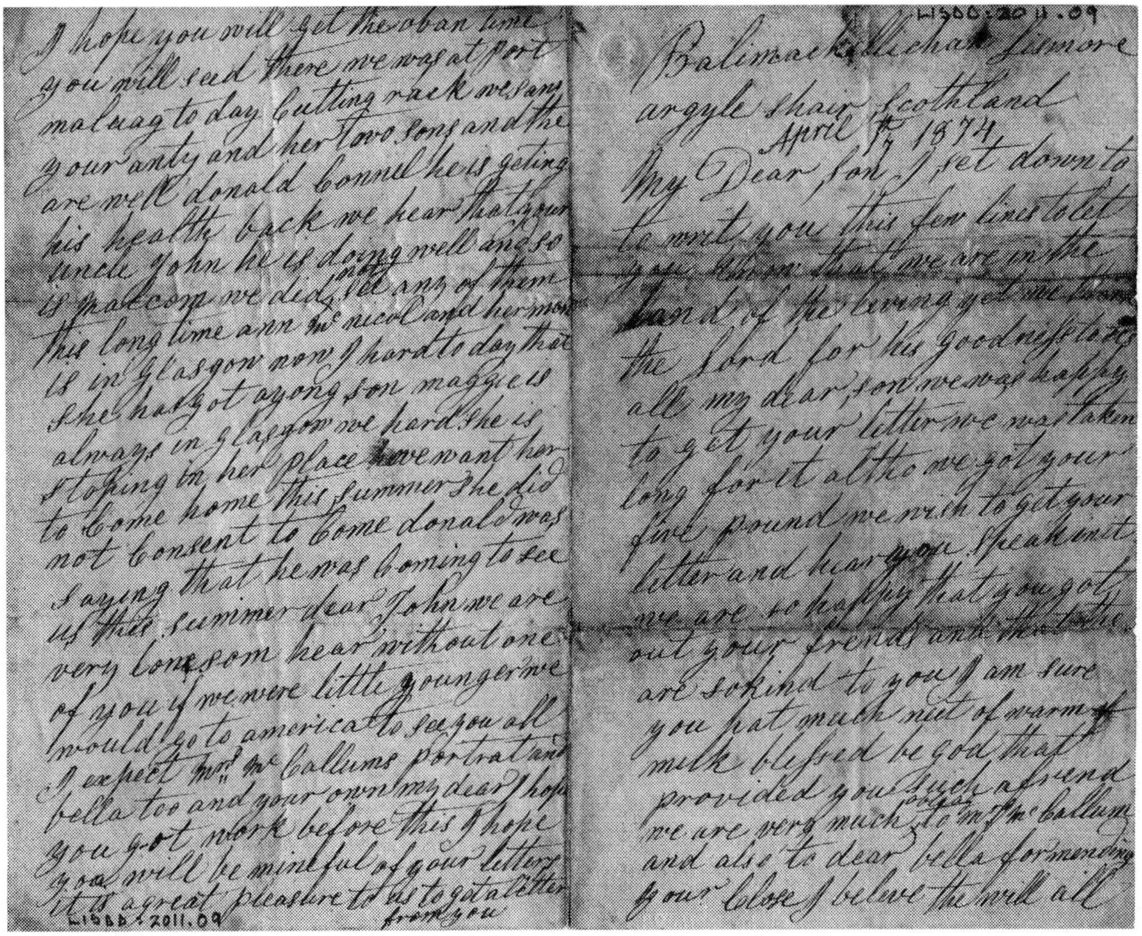

I hope you will get the oban time
you will sead there we was at port
malaag to day Cutting rack we saw
your anty and her two sons and the
are well donald Connel he is geting
his health back we hear that your
uncle John he is doing well and so
is malcom we did not see any of them
this long time ann Mc nicol and her mon
is in Glasgow now I hard to day that
she hat got a yong son maggie is
always in glasgow we hard she is
stoping in her place we want her
to Come home this summer she did
not Consent to Come donald was
saying that he was Coming to see
us this summer dear John we are
very lonesom hear without one
of you if we were little younger we
would go to america to see you all
I expect Mrs Mc Callums portrat and
bella too and your own my dear I hope
you got work before this I hope
you will be mindful of your letters
it is a great pleasure to us to get a letter
from you

LISDD : 2011.09

Balimackillichan Lismore
argyle shair Scotland
April 17th 1874
My Dear son I set down to
to writ you this few lines to let
you know that we are in the
land of the living yet we [illegible]
the Lord for his Goodness to us
all my dear son we was happy
to get your letter we was taken
long for it altho we got your
five pound we wish to get your
letter and hear you speak in it
we are so happy that you got
out your frends and the [illegible]
are so kind to you I am sure
you hat much need of warm
milk blessed be God that
provided you such a frend
we are very much obligd to Mrs Mc Callum
and also to dear bella for mending
your Close I beleve the will all

LISDD : 2011.09

Image db091

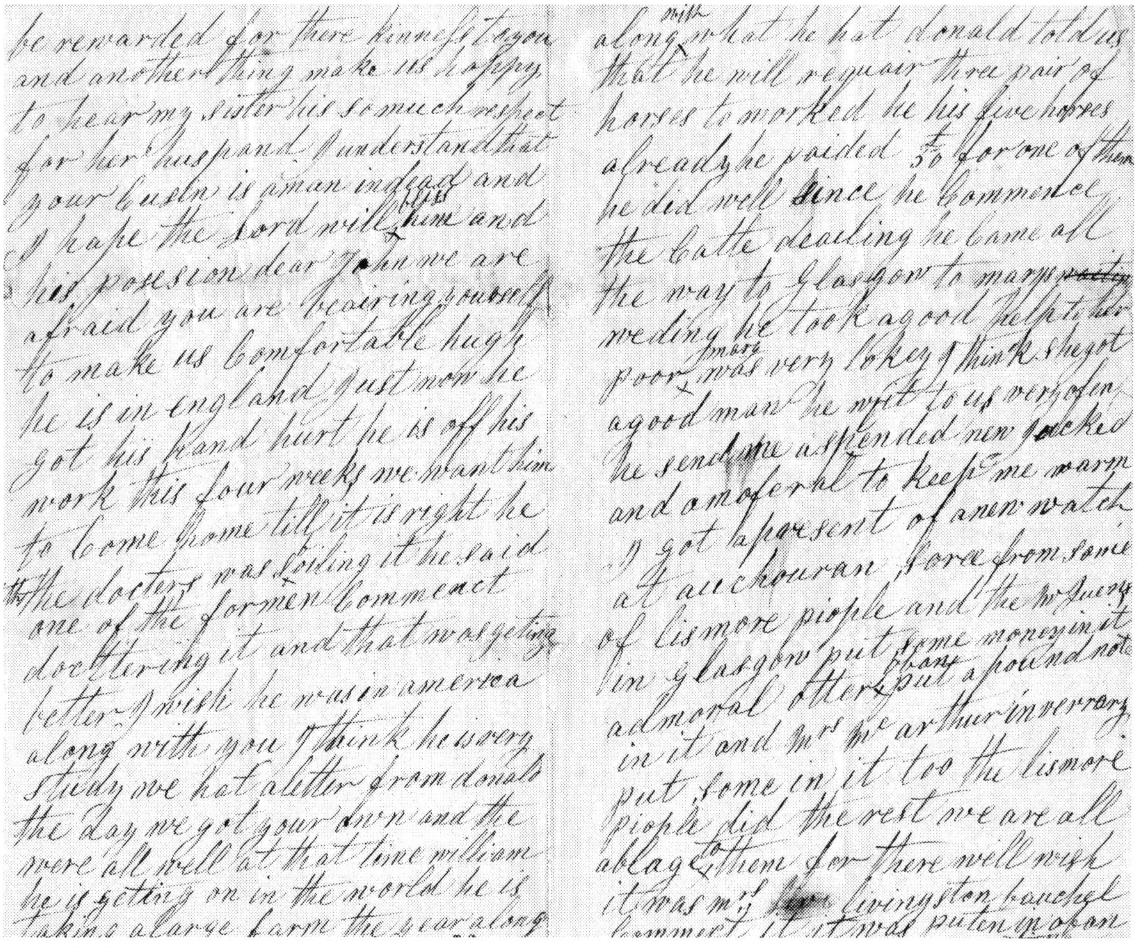

be rewarded for there kinnes to you
and another thing make us happy
to hear my sister his so much respect
for her husband I understand that
your husbn is a man indead and
I hope the Lord will bless him and
his posesion dear John we are
afraid you are beairing yourself
to make us comfortable hugh
he is in england just now he
got his hand hurt he is off his
work this four weeks we want him
to come home till it is right he
the doctors was spoiling it he said
one of the formen commenct
docttering it and that was geting
better I wish he was in america
along with you I think he is very
study we hat a letter from donald
the day we got your own and the
were all well at that time william
he is getting on in the world he is
taking a large farm the year along
with what he hat donald told us
that he will requair three pair of
horses to worked he his five horses
already he paided £50 for one of them
he did well since he commence
the cattle dealing he came all
the way to Glasgow to marry [illegible]
weding he took a good help to her
poor mary was very lokey I think she got
a good man he writ to us very ofen
he send me a splended new jacked
and a moferal to keep me warm
I got a present of a new watch
at auchouran store from some
of lismore piople and the McQueen
in Glasgow put some money in it
admoral otter brane put a pound note
in it and Mrs McArthur inverrary
put some in it too the lismore
piople did the rest we are all
ablage to them for there well wish
it was Mrs [illegible] livingston bachel
commenct it it was puten in opan

Image db092

LETTER FROM JOHN MCDOUGALL (b. 1803 Lismore) AND CATHERINE MCCALLUM MCDOUGALL (b. 1809 Lismore) WHO LIVED AT BALLIMACKILLICHAN, ISLE OF LISMORE TO JOHN MCDOUGALL (b. 1837) DELHI, REDWOOD COUNTY, MINNESOTA USA

Balimackillichan Lismore
Argyle Shair Scothland
April 17th 1874

My Dear Son

I set down to writ you this few lines to let you know that we are in the land of the living yet we thank the Lord for his goodness to us all my dear son we was happy to get your letter we was taken long for it altho we got your five pound we wish to get your letter and hear you speak in it we are so happy that you got out your frends and that the are so kind to you I am sure you hat much neet of warm milk blissed be god that provided you such a friend we are very much obliag to Mrs McCallum and also to dear bella for mending your Close I beleve the will all be rewarded for the kinness to you and another thing make us happy to hear my sister his so much respect for her huspand I understand that your Cusin is a man indead and I hope the Lord will bliss him and his posesion dear John we are afraid you are beairing yourself to make us Comfortable hugh he is in england Just now he got his hand hurt he is off his work this four weeks we want him to Come home till it is right he [...]th the docters was sboiling it he said one of the formen Commenct doctering it and that was geting better I wish he was in america along with you I think he is very study we hat a letter from donald the day we got your own and the were all well at that time william he is geting on in the world he is taking a large farm the year along with what he hat donald told us that he will requair three pair of horses to worked he his five horses already he paided £50 for one of them he did well since he commence the Cattle deailing he Came all the way to Glasgow to marys weding he took a good help to her poor mary was very lokey I think she got a good man he writ to us very ofen he send me a splended new jacked and a moferal [muffler] to keep me warm

I got a present of a new watch at auchouran soree [soiree] from some of lismore piople and the McQuenz [McQueens] in Glasgow put some money in it admoral otter oban put a pound note in it and Mrs McArthur inverrary put some in it too the lismore piople did the rest we are all oblage to them for there well wish it was Mrs livingston bauchel Commect it it was puten in oban time I hope you will get the oban time you will seed there we was at port maluag to day Cutting rack [wrack] we saw your anty and her two sons and the are well donald Connel he is geting his health back we hear that your uncle John he is doing well and so is Malcom we did not see any of them this long time ann mcnicol and her man is in Glasgow now I hard today that she has got a yong son maggie is always in Glasgow we hard she is Stoping in her place we want her to Come home this summer she did not Consent to Come donald was saying that he was coming to see us this summer dear John we are very lonesom hear without one of you if we were little younger we would go to america to see you all I expect Mrs McCallums portrat and bella too and your own my dear I hope you got work before this I hope you will be mineful of your letters it is a great pleasure to us to get a letter from you

(rest of letter missing)

Plate 9.1. Isabel McCallum

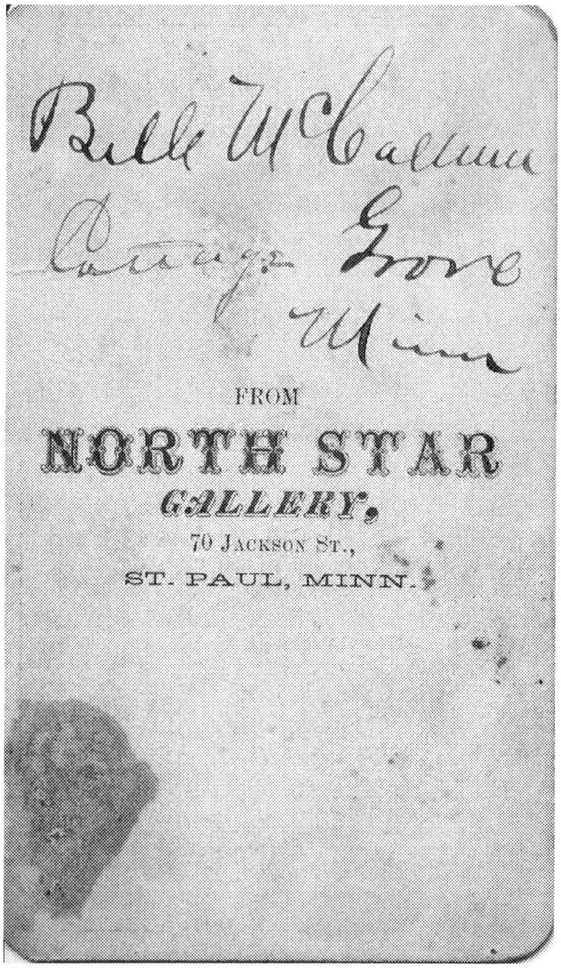

Plate 9.2. Photo Back

Plate 9.3. John McDougall (b. 1837) and Isabel McCallum McDougall (b. 1850)

Plate 9.4. *The Oban Times*, February 21, 1874
Article about the Achuaran Soiree

LISMORE - Soiree

The annual soiree in connection with the Auchuaran Sabbath School was held in the Independent Chapel here on Friday last. There was a good attendance both of the general public and of children. The Rev Mr Livingston, in the absence of Mr Macgregor, our usual genial chairman, occupied the chair. After tea and its "accompaniments" had been disposed of, the chairman treated his audience to a very humorous address. Throughout the evening several hymns etc suitable to the occasion were sung by the children, finishing with "St George's Edinburgh," in which the audience joined. In the intervals between the singing, addresses were delivered by Mr Ross, UP Manse, and others. Oranges having been distributed among the children, a very happy and enjoyable evening was brought to a close.

PRESENTATION. – Advantage was taken of the occasion to present Mr John Macdougall, superintendent of the Sabbath School, with a silver watch and a sum of money, contributed by friends in Lismore and at a distance. Mr Macdougall has, for the last thirty years, laboured untiringly as a Sabbath School teacher, without fee or reward, and with no motive but "love to his neighbor." In presenting the testimonial, Mr Livingston mentioned that it was not merely given in appreciation of his (Mr Macdougall's) services, but also on account of his sterling worth and exemplary Christian character. Mr Macdougall feelingly returned suitable thanks.
(*The Oban Times*, 21 February 1874)
By permission, *The Oban Times*

Plate 9.5. Bachuil (Bauchel)

In his letter, John McDougall (weaver) reports, “Mrs. Livingston bauchel commest it ... [an article about the soiree] was puten in oban time.” (See the letter and article, above.) Ballimackillichan is located directly behind Bachuil, within walking distance.

Plate 9.6. Achuaran, Isle of Lismore

Plate 9.7. The Independent Chapel Building, Achuaran

The building, now used for storage, is located on Achuaran Farm; Archie MacGillivray is the tenant.

***The Oban Times*, January 9, 1875**

LISMORE – CHRISTMAS – We are sorry to say that Christmas was almost neglected in these quarters. There were hardly any preparations made for it.

SCHOLASTIC – Mr. Maceachern, schoolmaster, Balegrundle, has resigned his appointment for another at Salen, Mull.
(*The Oban Times,* January 9, 1875, p. 2)
By permission, *The Oban Times*

Letter **#10**

March 12, 1875

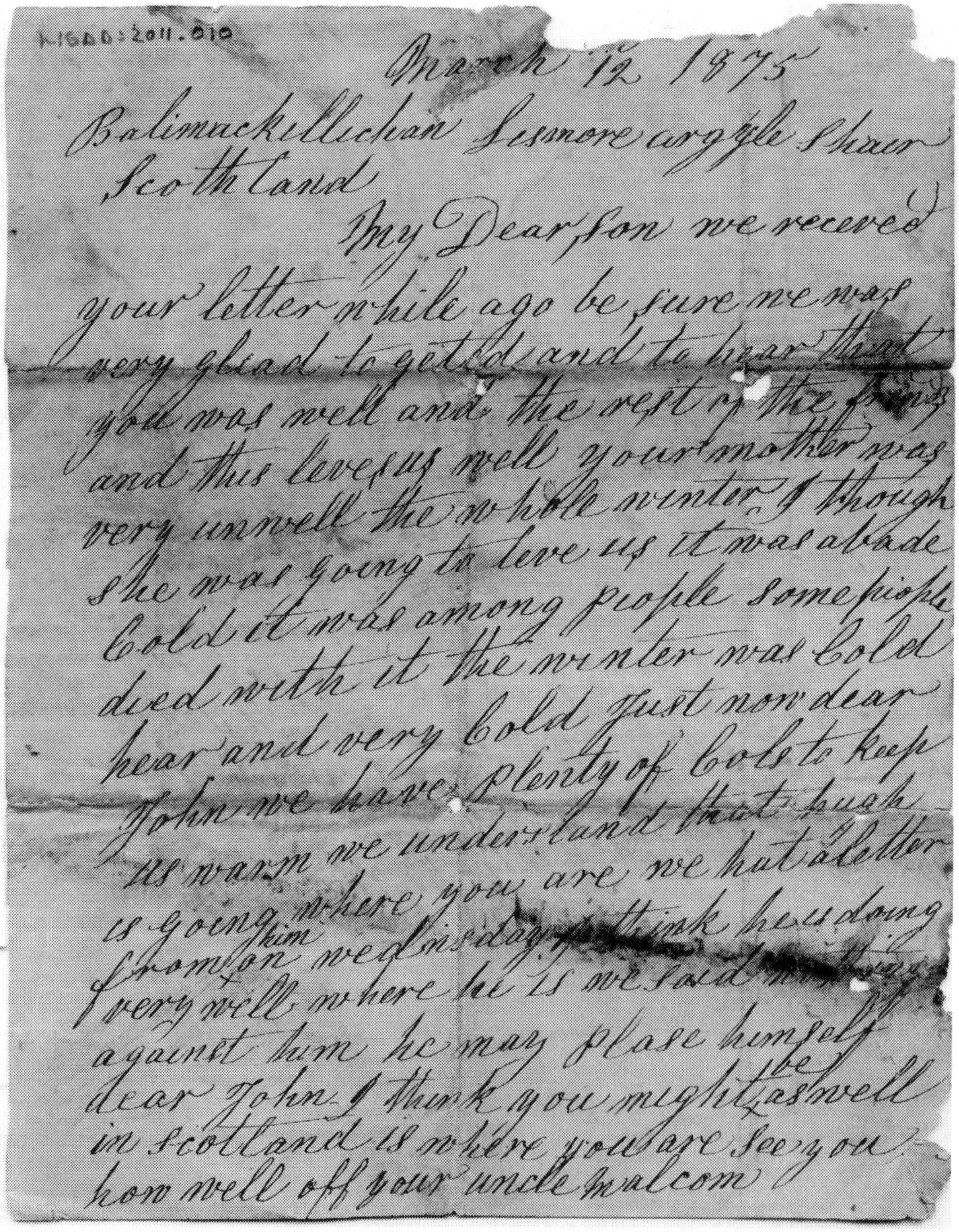
K1GAD:2011.010

March 12 1875

Balimackillichan Lismore argyle Shear
Scothland

My Dear Son we receved
your letter while ago be sure we was
very glead to getdd and to hear that
you was well and the rest of the frinds
and this leves us well your mother was
very unwell the whole winter I though
she was going to leve us it was a bade
Cold it was among people some piople
died with it the winter was Cold
hear and very Cold just now dear
John we have plenty of Cole to keep
us warm we understand that hugh
is going where you are we hat aletter
from him on wednsday I think he is doing
very well where he is we said nothing
against him he may plase himself
dear John I think you might be aswell
in scotland is where you are see you
how well off your uncle malcom

Image db096

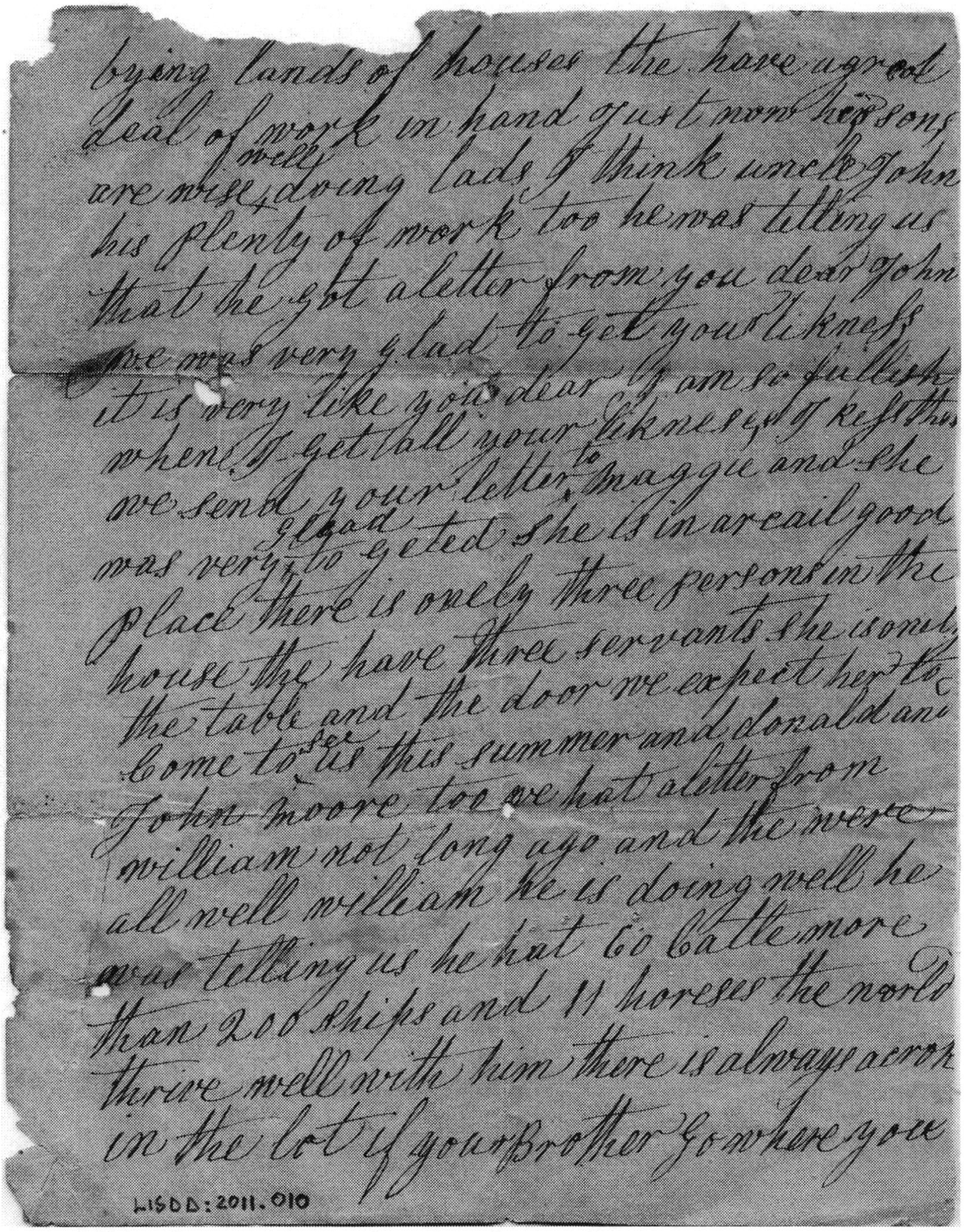
bying lands of houses the have a great
deal of work in hand just now her sons
are wise well doing lads I think uncle John
his plenty of work too he was telling us
that he got a letter from you dear John
we was very glad to get your likness
it is very like you dear I am so fullish
when I get all your liknesses I keps them
we send your letter to maggie and she
was very glad to geted she is in areail good
place there is onely three persons in the
house the have three servants she is onely
the table and the door we expect her to
come to see us this summer and donald and
John moore too we hat a letter from
william not long ago and the were
all well william he is doing well he
was telling us he hat 60 Catle more
than 200 ships and 11 horeses the world
thrive well with him there is always a crop
in the lot of your Brother Jo where you

LISDD:2011.010

Image db097

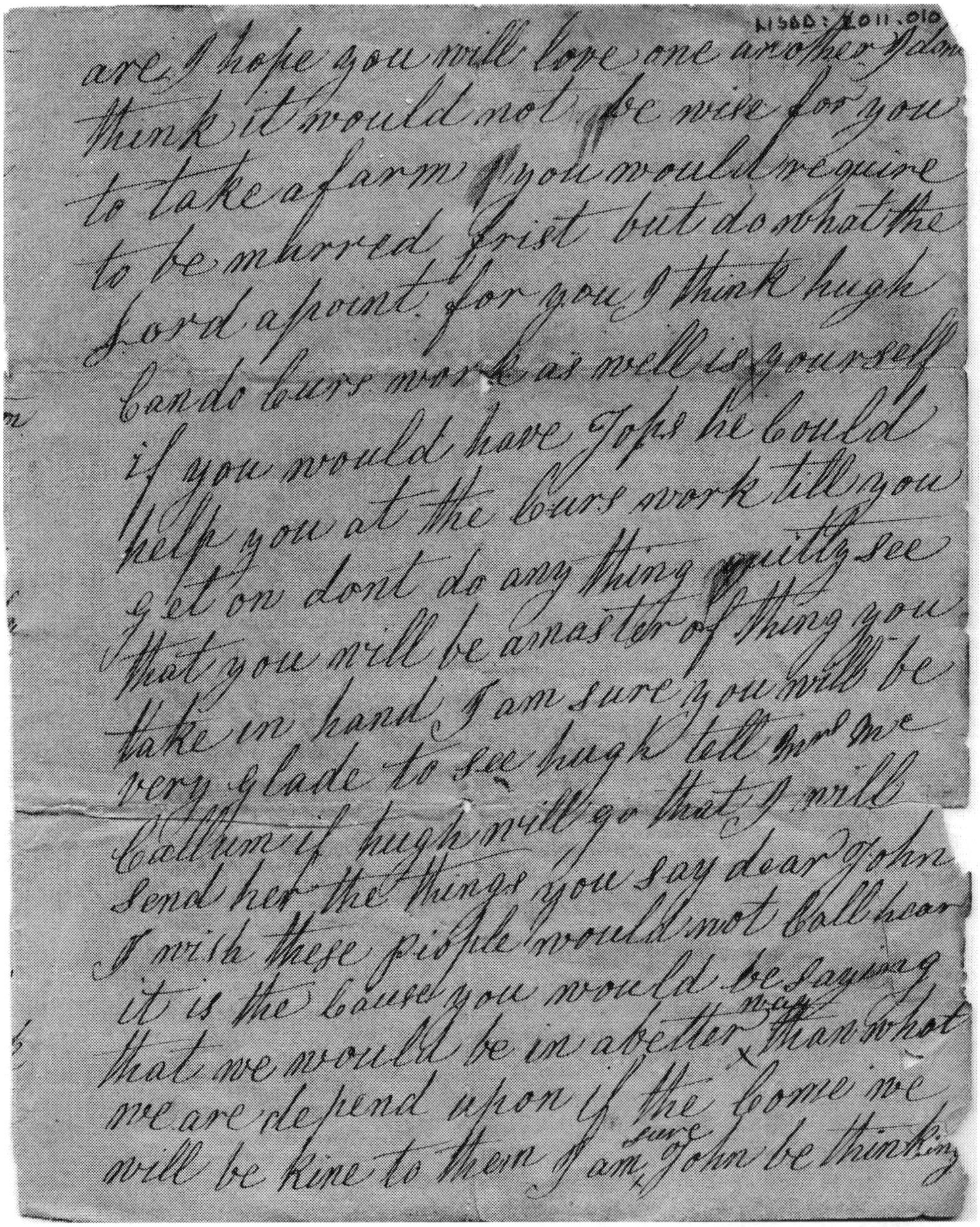

are I hope you will love one another I don[t]
think it would not be wise for you
to take a farm you would require
to be marred frist but do what the
Lord apoint for you I think hugh
can do curs work as well is yourself
if you would have Jops he could
help you at the curs work till you
get on dont do any thing quitly see
that you will be a master of thing you
take in hand I am sure you will be
very glade to see hugh tell Mrs Mc
Callum if hugh will go that I will
send her the things you say dear John
I wish these piople would not call hear
it is the cause you would be saying
that we would be in a better way than what
we are depend upon if the come we
will be kine to them I am sure John be thinking

Image db098

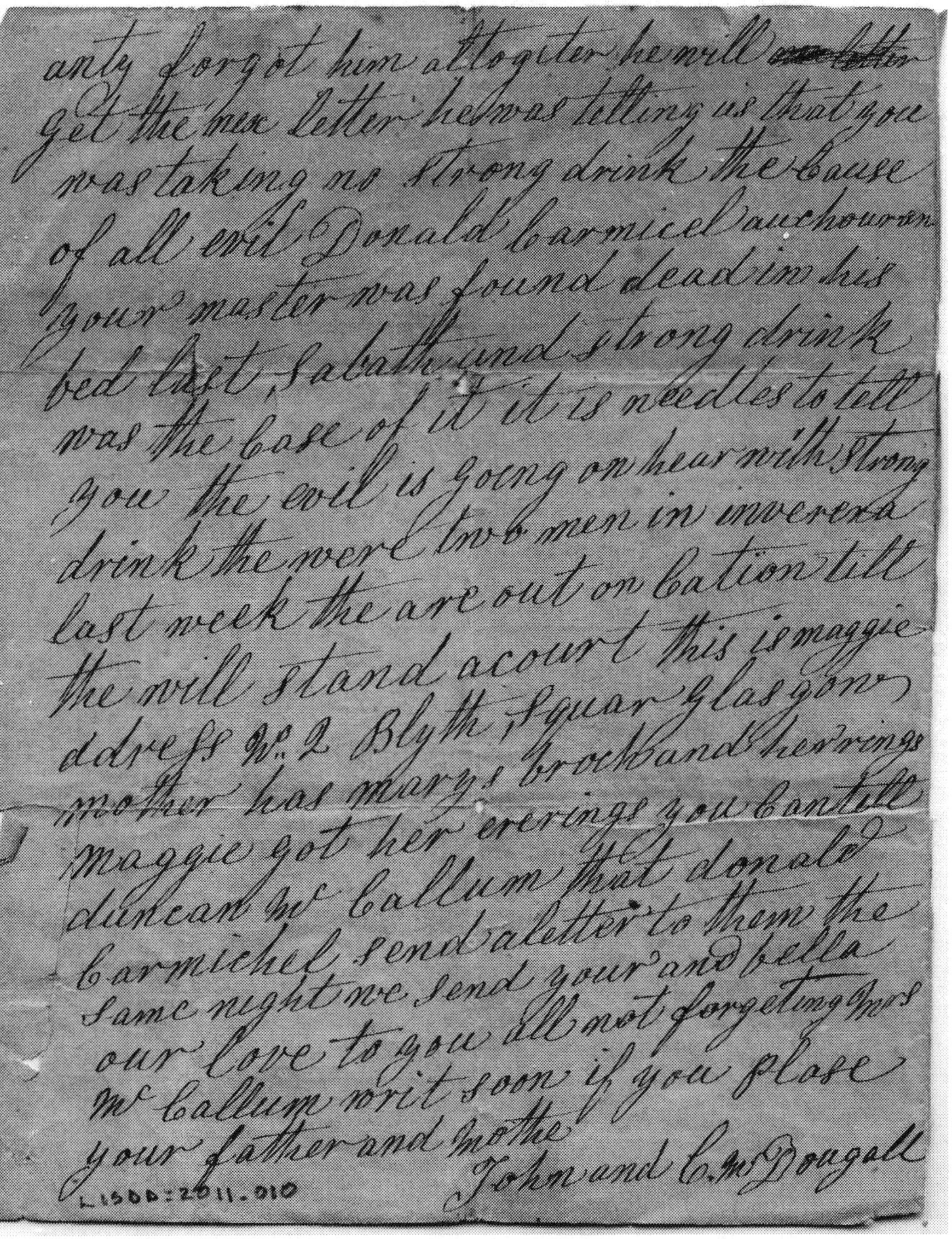

anty forgot him altogiter he will
get the nex letter he was telling us that you
was taking no strong drink the cause
of all evil Donald carmicel auchouran
your master was found dead in his
bed last Sabath and strong drink
was the case of it it is needles to tell
you the evil is going on hear with strong
drink the were two men in inverera
last week the are out on cation till
the will stand a court this is maggie
ddress No 2 Blyth Squar Glasgow
mother has marys brock and herrings
maggie got her erings you can tell
duncan Mc callum that donald
carmichel send a letter to them the
same night we send your and bella
our love to you all not forgeting Mrs
Mc callum writ soon if you plase
your father and mothe
John and C. McDougall

L1500:2011.010

Image db099

LETTER FROM JOHN MCDOUGALL (b. 1803 Lismore) AND CATHERINE MCCALLUM MCDOUGALL (b. 1809 Lismore) WHO LIVED AT BALLIMACKILLICHAN, ISLE OF LISMORE TO JOHN MCDOUGALL (b. 1837) DELHI, REDWOOD COUNTY, MINNESOTA USA

March 12 1875

Balimackillichan Lismore Argyle Shair

Scothland

My Dear Son we receved your letter while ago be sure we was very glead to geted and to hear that you was well and the rest of the frends and this leves us well Your mother was very unwell the whole winter I though she was going to leve us it was a bade cold it was among people some piople died with it the winter was Cold hear and very Cold Just now dear John we have plenty of Cols to keep us warm we understand that hugh is going where you are we hat a letter from him on wednsday I think he is doing very well where he is we said nothing against him he may plase himself dear John I think you might be as well in Scotland is where you are See you how well off your uncle Malcom bying lands of houses the have a great deal of work in hand Just now his sons are wise well doing lads I think uncle John [McCallum] his plenty of work too he was tilling us that he got a letter from you dear John we was very glad to get your likness it is very like you dear I am so fullish when to get all your liknesses I kess them we send your letter to Maggie and she was very glead to geted She is in a reail good place there is onely three persons in the house the have three servants she is onely the table and the door we expect her to come to see us this summer and donald and John Moore too we hat a letter from William [Moore] not long ago and the were all well william he is doing well he was telling us he hat 60 Cattle more than 200 ships [sheep?] and 11 horeses the world thrive well with him there is always a crop in the lot if your Brother [Hugh] Go where you are I hope you will love one another I dont think it would not be wise for you to take a farm you would require to be marred frist but do what the Lord apoint for you I think hugh Can do Curs work as well is yourself if you would have Jops he Could help you at the Curs [course?] work till you get on dont do anything quitly see that you will be a master of thing you take in hand I am sure you will be very glade to see hugh tell Mrs McCallum if hugh will go that I will send her things you say dear John I wish these piople would not Call hear it is the Cause you would be saying that we would be in a better way than what we are depend upon if the Come we will be kine to them I am sure John be thinking anty forgot him altogeter he will get the nex letter he was telling us that you was taking no strong drink the Cause of all evil Donald Carmicel auchouran your master was found dead in his bed last Sabath and strong drink was the case of it it is needles to tell you the evil is going on hear with strong drink the were two men in inverera last week the are out on Cation till the will stand a court this is maggie adress W.2 Blyth Squar Glasgow mother has marys broch and her rings maggie got her ererings you can tell duncan McCallum that donald Carmichel send a letter to them the same night we send your and bella [son John's wife, Isabel McCallum] our love to you all not forgeting Mrs McCallum [Bella's mother, Ann] writ soon if you plase your father and mothe

John and C. McDougall

Notes:

William Moore was the husband of Agnes (Ann) McDougall, oldest daughter of John McDougall (weaver) and Catherine McCallum.

Mary, their second daughter, had passed away, June 18, 1874..

Letter **#11**

December 11th 1875

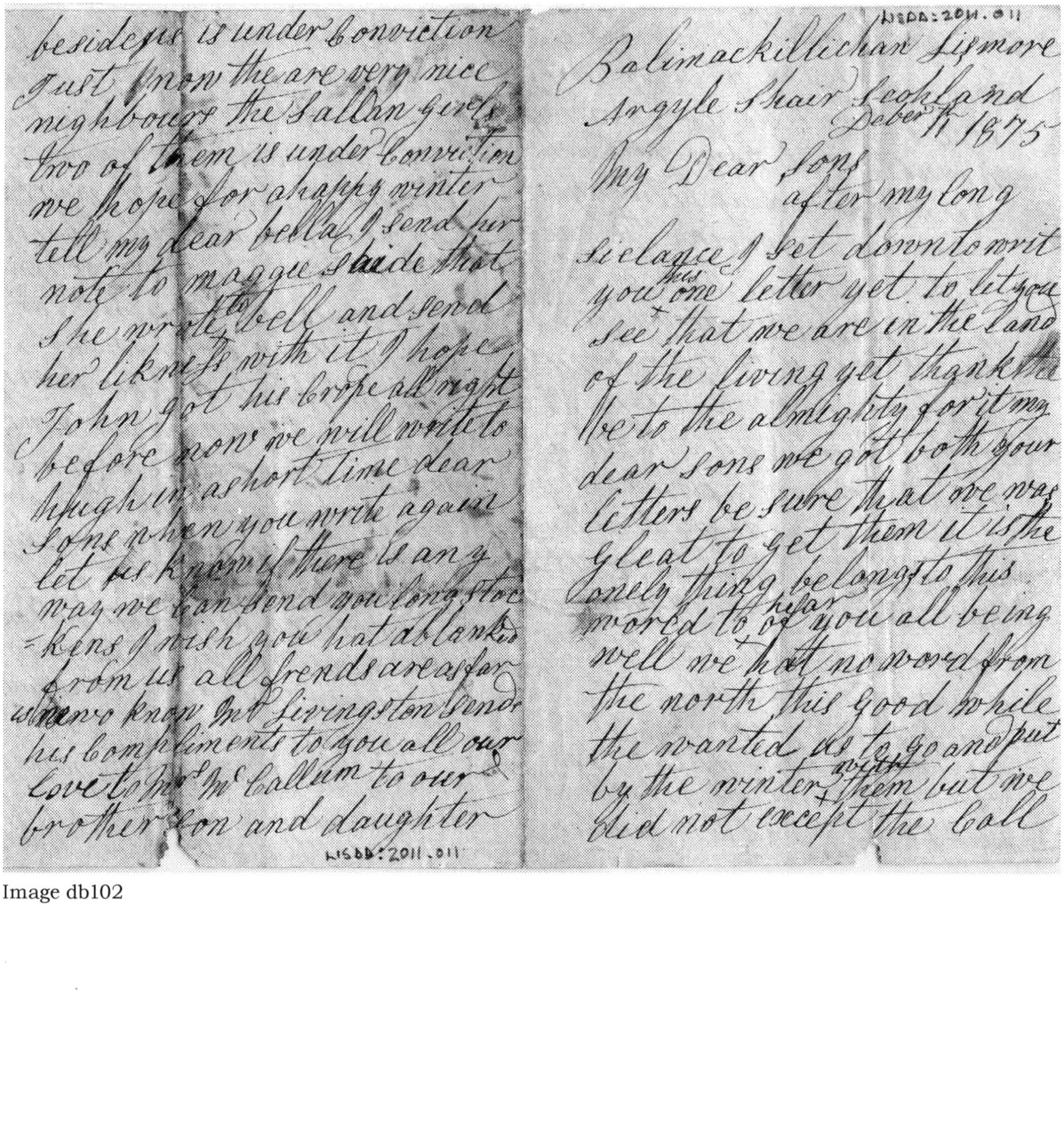

besides us is under Conviction
just now the are very nice
neighbours the Sallan girls
two of them is under Conviction
we hope for a happy winter
tell my dear bella I send her
note to maggie saide that
She wrote to bell and send
her likness with it I hope
John got his crope all right
before now we will write to
hugh in a short time dear
Sons when you write again
let us know if there is any
way we can send you long stoc
=kens I wish you hat a blanket
from us all frends are as far
as we know Mr Livingston sends
his compliments to you all our
love to Mr McCallum to our
brother son and daughter

NSDA:2011.011

NSDA:2011.011

Balimackillichan Lismore
Argyle Shair Scohland
Decber 11 1875
My Dear Sons
after my long
sielance I set down to writ
you this one letter yet to let you
see that we are in the land
of the living yet thanks
be to the almighty for it my
dear sons we got both your
letters be sure that we was
gleat to get them it is the
onely thing belongs to this
world to hear of you all being
well we hat no word from
the north this good while
the wanted us to go and put
by the winter with them but we
did not except the call

Image db102

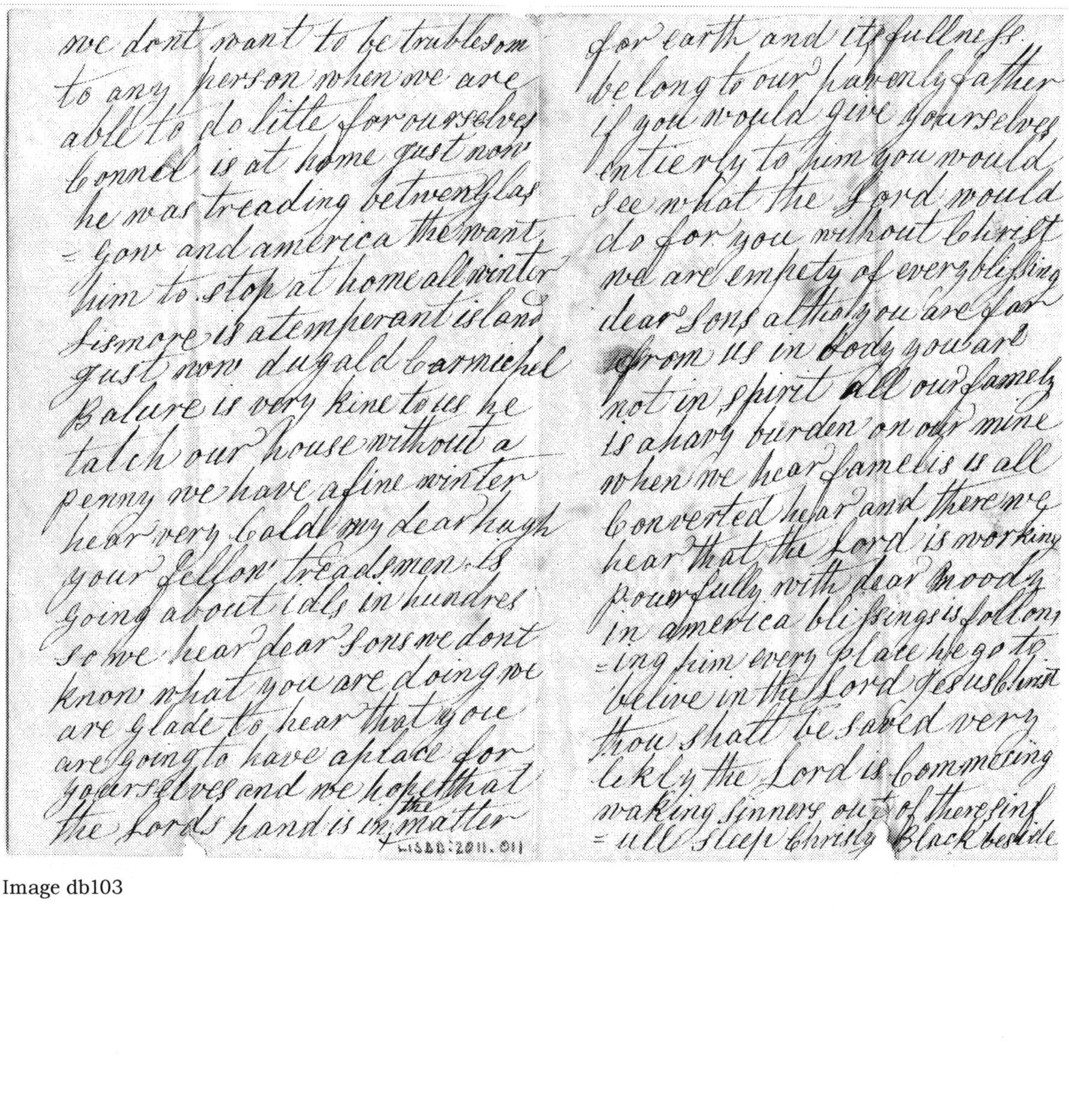
we dont want to be trublesom
to any person when we are
able to do litle for ourselves
Connel is at home just now
he was treading betwen Glas
= gow and america the want
him to stop at home all winter
Lismore is a temperant island
just now dugald Carmichel
Balure is very kine to us he
tatch our house without a
penny we have a fine winter
hear very Cold my dear hugh
your fellow treadsmen is
Going about idls in hundres
so we hear dear Sons we dont
know what you are doing we
are glade to hear that you
are going to have a place for
yourselves and we hope that
the Lords hand is in the matter

for earth and its fullness
belong to our havenly father
if you would give yourselves
entierly to him you would
see what the Lord would
do for you without Christ
we are empety of every blissing
dear Sons altho you are far
from us in body you are
not in spirit all our famely
is a havy burden on our mine
when we hear famelis is all
Converted hear and there we
hear that the Lord is working
powerfully with dear moody
in america blissings is follow
= ing him every place he go to
belive in the Lord Jesus Christ
thou shalt be saved very
likly the Lord is Commencing
waking sinners out of there sinf
= ull sleep Christy Black beside

Image db103

LETTER FROM JOHN MCDOUGALL (b. 1803 Lismore) AND CATHERINE MCCALLUM MCDOUGALL (b. 1809 Lismore) WHO LIVED AT BALLIMACKILLICHAN, ISLE OF LISMORE TO THEIR SONS JOHN MCDOUGALL (b. 1837) AND HUGH MCDOUGALL (b. 1842) MINNESOTA

Balimackillichan Lismore Argyle Shair

Scohland

Deber 11th 1875

My Dear Sons

after my long sielance I set down to writ you this one letter yet to let you see that we are in the land of the living yet thank the be to the almighty for it my dear sons we got both your letters be sure that we was gleat to get them it is the onely thing belongs to this world to hear of you all being well we hat no word from the north this good while the wanted us to go and put by the winter with them but we did not except the Call we dont want to be trublesom to any person when we are able to do litle for ourselves Connel is a home just now he was treading between Glasgow and america the want him to stop at home all winter Lismore is a temperant island Just now dugald Carmichel Balure is very kine to us he tatch our house without a penny we have a fine winter hear very Cold my dear hugh your fellow treadsmen is Going about idle in hundres so we hear dear sons we dont know what you are doing we are Glade to hear that you are going to have a place for yourselves and we hope that the Lords hand is in the matter for earth and its fullness belong to our havenly father if you would give yourselves entierly to him you would see what the Lord would do for you without Christ we are empety of every blissing dear sons altho you are far from us in body you are not in spirit all our famely is a havy burden on our mine when we hear famelis is all Converted hear and there we hear that the Lord is working powerfully with dear Moody in america blissings is following him every place he go to belive in the Lord Jesus Christ thou shalt be saved very likly the Lord is Commecing waking sinners out of there sinfull sleep Christy Black beside beside us is under Conviction Just know the are very nice nighbours the Sallan girls two of them is under Conviction we hope for a happy winter tell my dear bella I send her note to Maggie saide that she wrote to bell and send her likness with it I hope John got his Crope all right before now we will write to hugh in a short time dear Sons when you write again let us know if there is any way we can send you long stockens I wish you hat a blanked from us all frends are as far is newo (?) know Mr Livingston sends his Compliments to you all our love to Mrs McCallum to our brother son and daughter

Note: The last phrase, "to our brother son and daughter", might mean "to our brother's son and daughter." If so, the phrase might refer to Isabel McCallum and her brother, John McCallum (b. 1847). Although Isabel was the wife of John McDougall (b. 1837), she and her brother, John, were also his cousins; their father, Gilbert McCallum (b. 1813), was a younger brother of Catherine McCallum, the mother of John McDougall (b. 1837).

Plate 11.1. Remains of John McDougall's (weaver) House, Ballimackillichan

As noted in the letter of December 11, 1875, the house was thatched. Lismore residents, Archie MacColl (back to camera), Margaret Black and David White, stand where the missing walls of the original home stood.

Plate 11.2. Thatched Crofter's Cottage
Lismore Historical Society, Isle of Lismore

Letter #12

January 1876

This letter is from Hugh McDougall in Glasgow to his brother, John, in Minnesota.

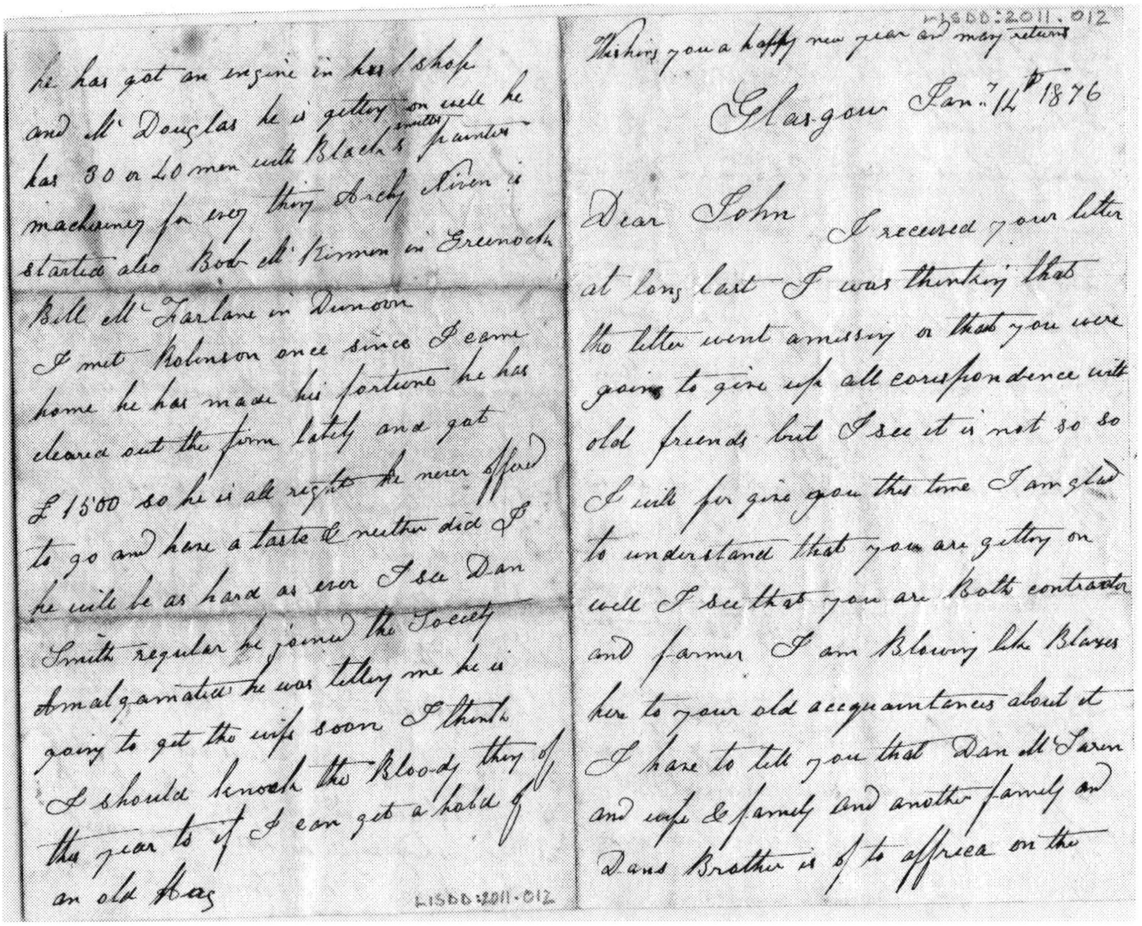

he has got an engine in his shop
and Mc Douglas he is getting on well he
has 30 or 40 men with Black's writer painter
machinery for every thing Archy Niven is
started also Bob McKinnon in Greenock
Bill McFarlane in Dunoon
I met Robinson once since I came
home he has made his fortune he has
cleared out the firm lately and got
£1500 so he is all right he never offered
to go and have a taste & neither did I
he will be as hard as ever I see Dan
Smith regular he joined the Society
Amalgamation he was telling me he is
going to get the wife soon I think
I should knock the bloody thing of
the year to if I can get a hold of
an old Hag

LISDD:2011-012

LISDD:2011.012

Wishing you a happy new year and many returns

Glasgow Jan.y 14th 1876

Dear John I received your letter
at long last I was thinking that
the letter went amissing or that you were
going to give up all correspondence with
old friends but I see it is not so so
I will forgive you this time I am glad
to understand that you are getting on
well I see that you are both contractor
and farmer I am blowing like blazes
here to your old acquaintances about it
I have to tell you that Dan McLaren
and wife & family and another family and
Dans Brother is of to affrica on the

Image db142

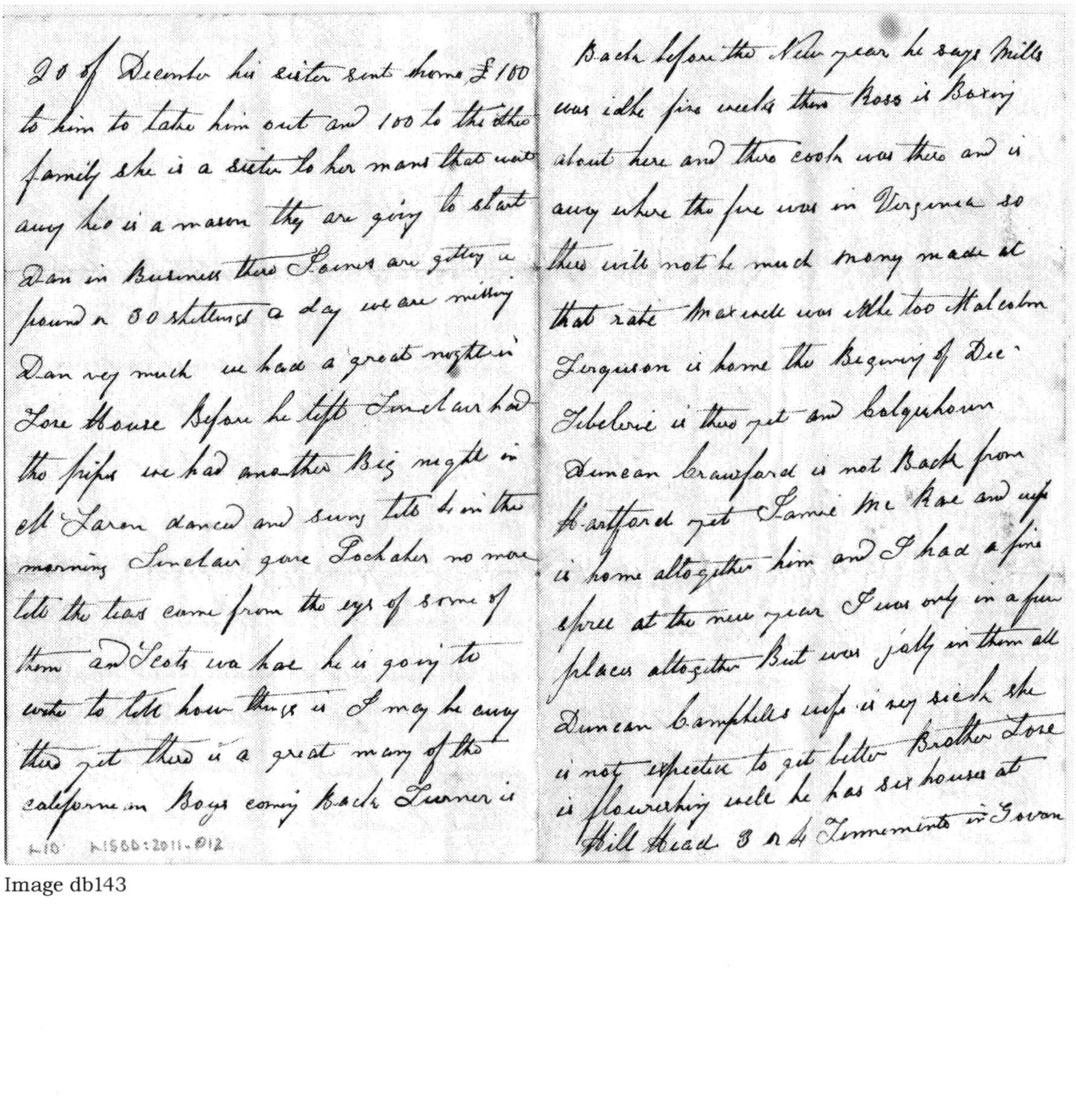
20 of December his sister sent home £100
to him to take him out and 100 to the other
family she is a sister to her mans that went
away he is a mason they are going to start
Dan in Business there Lairds are getting a
pound or 30 shillings a day we are missing
Dan very much we had a great night in
Lore House Before he left Sinclair had
the pipes we had another Big night in
McLaren danced and sung till 4 in the
morning Sinclair gave Pochaker no more
till the tears came from the eys of some of
them and Scots wa hae he is going to
write to tell how things is I may be away
there yet there is a great many of the
californian Boys coming Back Turner is

Back before the New year he says Mills
was idle five weeks there Ross is Boxing
about here and there cook was there and is
away where the fire was in Virginia so
there will not be much money made at
that rate Maxwell was idle too Malcolm
Ferguson is home the Beginning of Dec
Tibelerie is there yet and Colquhoun
Duncan Crawford is not Back from
Hartford yet Lamie McRae and wife
is home altogether him and I had a fine
spree at the new year I was only in a few
places altogether But was jolly in them all
Duncan Campbells wife is very sick she
is not expected to get better Brother Lore
is flourishing well he has six houses at
Hill Head 3 or 4 Tennements in Govan

L10 A1560:2011.012

Image db143

LETTER FROM HUGH MCDOUGALL (b. 1842 Lismore) IN GLASGOW TO HIS BROTHER JOHN MCDOUGALL (b. 1837 Lismore) IN MINNESOTA

Wishing you a happy new year and many returns

Glasgow Jan^{y} /4th 1876

Dear John

I received your letter at long last – I was thinking that the letter went amissing or that you were going to give up all corespondence with old friends but I see it is not so so I will for give you this time I am glad to understand that you are getting on well I see that you are Both contractor and farmer I am Blowing like Blazes here to your old accquaintences about it I have to tell you that Dan McLaren and wife & famely and another famely and Dans Brother is of to Affrica on the 20 of December his sister sent home £100 to him to take him out and 100 to the other family she is a sister to her mans that went away he is a mason they are going to start Dan in Business there farmers are getting a pound n 30 shillings a day we are missing Dan very much we had a great night in Lore House Before he left Sinclair had the pipes we had another Big night in McLaren danced and sung till 4 in the morning Sinclair gave Lochaber no more [on the pipes] till the tears came from the eyes of some of them and Scots wa hae he is going to write to tell how things is I may be away there yet there is a great many of the Californian Boys coming Back Turner is Back before the New year he says Mills was idle five weeks there Ross is Boxing about here and there cook[?] was there and is away where the fire was in Virginia so there will not be much money made at that rate Maxwell was idle too Malcolm Ferguson is home the Beginning of Dec Fibelvie is there yet and Colquhoun Duncan Crawford is not Back from Hartford yet Jamie McRae and wife is home altogether him and I had a fine spree at the new year I was only in a few places altogether But was jolly in them all Duncan Campbells wife is very sick she is not expected to git better Brother Lose is flourishing well he has six houses at Hill Head 3 or 4 Tennements in Govan he has got an engine in his shop and McDouglas he is getting on well he has 30 or 40 men with Blacksmiths painters machinery for everything Archy Niven is started also Bob McKinnon in Greenoch Bill McFarlane in Dunoon

I met Robinson once since I came home he has made his fortune he has cleared out the firm lately and got £1500 so he is all right he never offered to go and have a taste & neither did I he will be as hard as ever I see Dan Smith regular he joined the Society Amalgamation he was telling me he is going to get the wife soon I think I should knock the Bloody thing of this year to if I can get a hold of an old Hag

(rest of letter missing)

Plate 12.1. Gravestone of Hugh MacDougall and his Wife, Ann MacDougall
Redwood Falls Cemetery
Redwood Falls, Minnesota

Redwood Falls

The following are views of the Dougald Milne Tiffany Farm in Redwood Falls, Minnesota.

Note: Dougald Milne Tiffany (b. 1885, Thurso, Scotland, d. 1977, Redwood Falls, Minnesota), was the son of Margaret McDougall Milne (Maggie) and the nephew of John and Hugh McDougall.

Plate 12.2. Jared Jerome Tiffany with his Granddaughter, Margaret Elizabeth Tiffany, Redwood Falls, 1917

Plate 12.3. Dougald Milne Tiffany Farm
Redwood Falls, Minnesota, 1917

Plate 12.4. Dougald Milne Tiffany Farm
Redwood Falls, Minnesota
1940s

Plate 12.5. Moving Cattle
Dougald Milne Tiffany Farm
Redwood Falls
1948

Plate 12.6. Robert Tiffany Wilcox, Grandson of Dougald Milne Tiffany
on his Grandfather's Allis Chalmers Tractor
Redwood Falls
1949

Plate 12.7. Cattle on the Dougald Milne Tiffany Farm
Redwood Falls
January 1950

***The Oban Times*, March 18, 1876**

LISMORE – *SOIREE – The annual soiree in connection with the Achuaran Sabbath School, Lismore, was held here on the evening of the 10th inst. In the unavoidable absence of our usual genial chairman, the Rev. Mr. Macgregor, the chair was taken by Mr John Macdougall, superintendent of the Sabbath School. There was a large attendance. Mr Macdougall's opening address was characterised by common sense and feeling. An address was given by Mr Campbell, Appin School. The latter gentlemen also gave a Gaelic reading ("Calum Posta.") Throughout the evening, a number of hymns were sung, and the singing, which was heartily joined in, was led by Messrs Connell and Maccoll. Creature comforts were not neglected, there being an abundance of "good things." Addresses were also given by several present interested in the Sabbath School, and all spent a very enjoyable evening. (The Oban Times, March 18, 1876, p. 2)*

By permission, *The Oban Times*

Note: Calum Posta (Calum the Postman) was the central character in a 19th century Gaelic dialogue developed by Dr. Norman MacLeod to question changes in the price of postage and criticize the Queen and her advisors. (Kidd 2000, p. 9)

***The Oban Times*, March 25, 1876**

LISMORE – *REVIVAL – This movement, which commenced in December last, is still going on under favourable conditions, though the meetings are not of so exciting a character as they were at first nor so well attended.*

WEATHER –Since this month set in the weather has been very severe. In some places the snow drift is several feet deep. No accident has occurred. Ploughing is far behind, owing to the unfavourable weather. Long line fishing is prosecuted with fair success. Cod sell at from 1s to 1s 6d each. (*The Oban Times*, March 25, 1876, p. 2)

By permission, *The Oban Times*

***The Oban Times*, June 17, 1876**

LISMORE – *SACRAMENT – The Lord's Supper was dispensed in the Parish Church of this island on Sunday, when the venerable minister, Rev. G. McGregor, was assisted by the Rev. Mr Dewar, Appin, and Rev. Mr McGregor, Skipness.*

WEATHER – The weather continues to be very cold. Showers of snow fell last week, and since it is observed that the corn crop has turned pale and appears drooping. Potato shaws are not so regular on the drills as might be expected. The grazing meadows are luxuriantly clothed with verdant green, and look well; still, vegetation is behind that of last year, owing to the dryness of April and May.

The money order office, which was to have been opened early this year, is postponed in the meantime.

SCHOOL-HOUSE – We understand that the Baligrundle school buildings are contracted by Messrs McCallum, Fort-William. (*The Oban Times*, June 17, 1876, p. 2)

By permission, *The Oban Times*

Letter **#13**

January 30th 1877

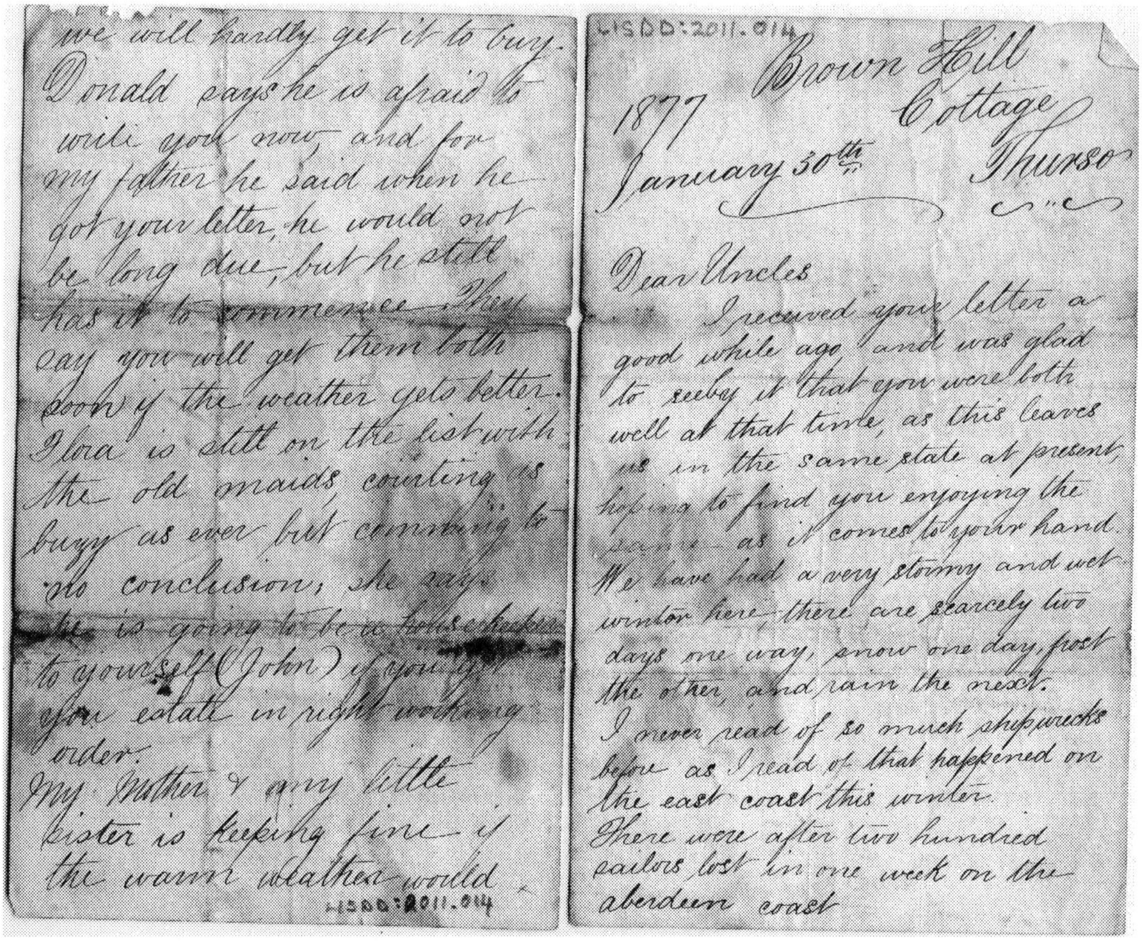

we will hardly get it to buy.
Donald says he is afraid to
write you now, and for
my father he said when he
got your letter he would not
be long due, but he still
has it to commence. They
say you will get them both
soon if the weather gets better.
Flora is still on the list with
the old maids counting as
busy as ever but coming to
no conclusion; she says
she is going to be a housekeeper
to yourself (John) if you get
your estate in right working
order.
My Mother & my little
sister is keeping fine if
the warm weather would

4SDD:2011.014

4SDD:2011.014

Brown Hill
Cottage
Thurso
1877
January 30th

Dear Uncles
I received your letter a
good while ago and was glad
to see by it that you were both
well at that time, as this leaves
us in the same state at present,
hoping to find you enjoying the
same as it comes to your hand.
We have had a very stormy and wet
winter here there are scarcely two
days one way, snow one day, frost
the other, and rain the next.
I never read of so much shipwrecks
before as I read of that happened on
the east coast this winter.
There were after two hundred
sailors lost in one week on the
aberdeen coast

Image db151

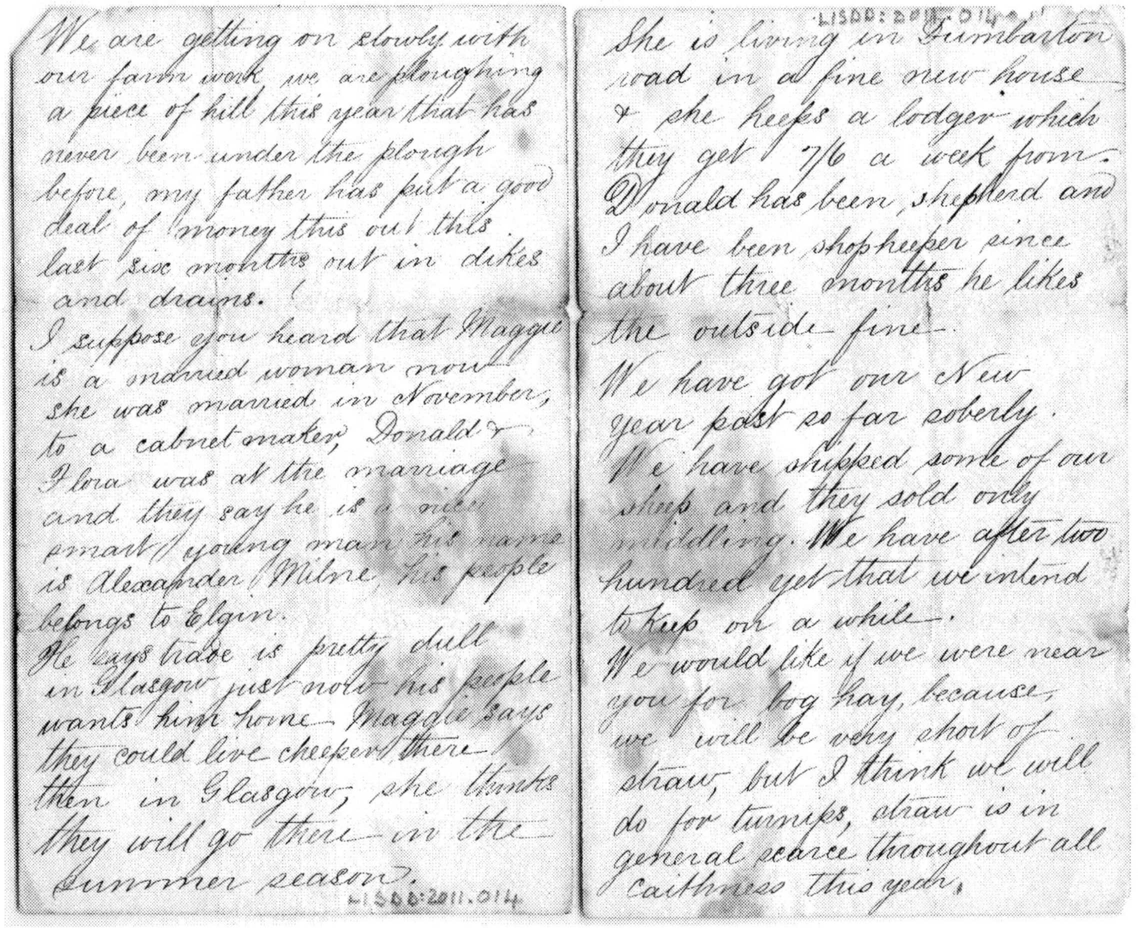
We are getting on slowly with
our farm work we are ploughing
a piece of hill this year that has
never been under the plough
before, my father has put a good
deal of money this out this
last six months out in dikes
and drains.
I suppose you heard that Maggie
is a married woman now
she was married in November,
to a cabnet maker, Donald &
Flora was at the marriage
and they say he is a nice
smart young man his name
is Alexander Milne, his people
belongs to Elgin.
He says trade is pretty dull
in Glasgow just now his people
wants him home Maggie says
they could live cheeper there
then in Glasgow, she thinks
they will go there in the
Summer season.

She is living in Dumbarton
road in a fine new house
& she keeps a lodger which
they get 7/6 a week from.
Donald has been, shepherd and
I have been shopkeeper since
about three months he likes
the outside fine.
We have got our New
year past so far soberly.
We have shipped some of our
sheep and they sold only
middling. We have after two
hundred yet that we intend
to keep on a while.
We would like if we were near
you for bog hay, because
we will be very short of
straw, but I think we will
do for turnips, straw is in
general scarce throughout all
Caithness this year.

Image db152

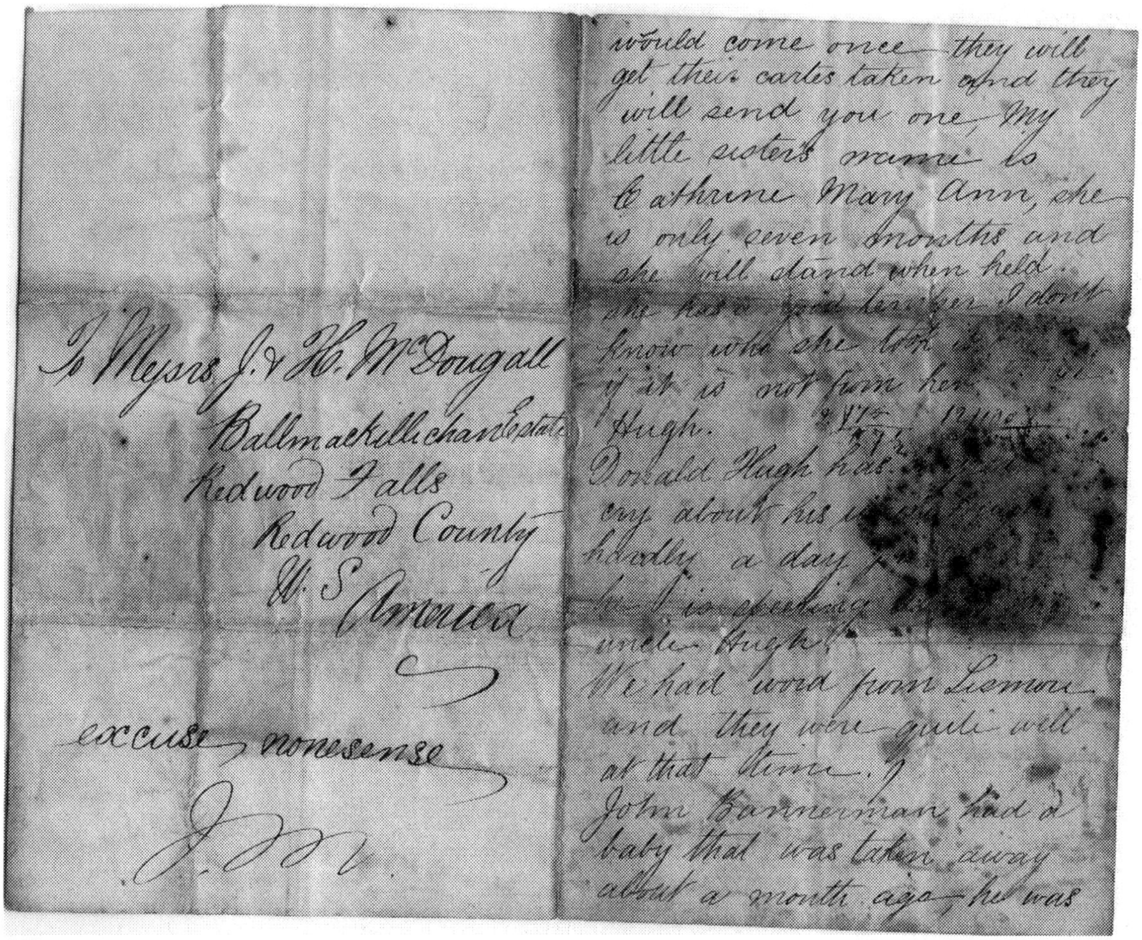
To Messrs J. & H. McDougall
Ballmackellichan Estate
Redwood Falls
Redwood County
U. S. America

excuse nonesense

would come once they will
get their cartes taken and they
will send you one. My
little sister's name is
Cathrine Mary Ann, she
is only seven months and
she will stand when held.
She has a [illegible] I don't
know who she took [illegible]
if it is not from her [illegible]
Hugh.
Donald Hugh has [illegible]
cry about his [illegible]
hardly a day [illegible]
[illegible] is speaking [illegible]
uncle Hugh.
We had word from Lismore
and they were quite well
at that time.
John Bannerman had a
baby that was taken away
about a month ago he was

Image db148

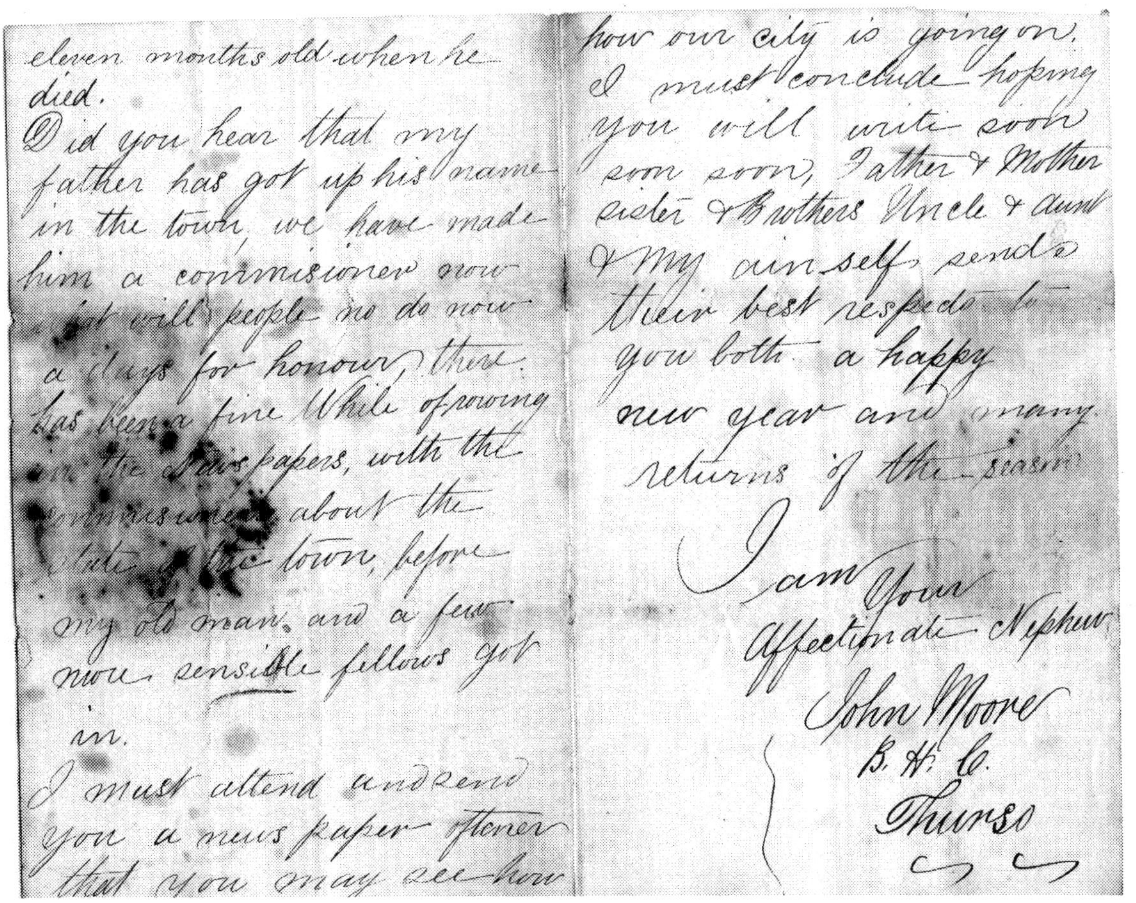

eleven months old when he
died.
Did you hear that my
father has got up his name
in the town, we have made
him a commissioner now
what will people no do now
a days for honour, there
has been a fine While of rowing
in the News papers, with the
commissioners about the
state of the town, before
my old man, and a few
more sensible fellows got
in.
I must attend and send
you a news paper oftener
that you may see how

how our city is going on.
I must conclude hoping
you will write soon
soon soon, Father & Mother
sister & Brothers Uncle & Aunt
& my ain self, sends
their best respects to
you both a happy
new year and many
returns of the season

I am Your
Affectionate Nephew
John Moore
B. H. C.
Thurso

Image db149

TO JOHN AND HUGH MCDOUGALL - BALLIMACKILLICHAN ESTATES REDWOOD FALLS, REDWOOD COUNTY, US AMERICA FROM JOHN MOORE (b. 1858, son of Agnes (Ann) McDougall Moore) THURSO - BROWN HILL COTTAGE

Note: The letter below is from John Moore, son of Agnes (Ann) McDougall Moore, to his uncles, John and Hugh McDougall in the US. John Moore was born in 1858 and died on December 31, 1881, at age 23. This letter would have been written when he was 18 or 19 years old, after Hugh McDougall migrated to the US.

To Mysrs J. & H. McDougall

Ballimackillichan Estates

Redwood Falls

Redwood County

US America

excuse nonsense

JM

Brown Hill Cottage

Thurso

1877 January 30th

Dear Uncles

I received your letter a good while ago, and was glad to see by it that you were both well at that time, as this leaves us in the same state at present, hoping to find you enjoying the same as it comes to your hand. We have had a stormy and wet winter here, there are scarcely two days one way, snow one day, frost the other, and rain the next.

I never read of so much shipwrecks before as I read of that happened on the east coast this winter.

There were after two hundred sailors lost in one week on the Aberdeen coast

We are getting on slowly with our farm work, we are ploughing a piece of hill this year that has never been under plough before, my father has put a good deal of money this out this last six months out in dikes and drains.

I suppose you heard that Maggie [Margaret McDougall, his aunt] is a married woman now. She was married in November, to a cabnet maker, Donald & Flora [his aunt Flora McDougall] was at the marriage and they say he is a nice smart young man his name is Alexander Milne, his people belongs to Elgin.

He says trade is pretty dull in Glasgow just now his people wants him home Maggie says they could live cheeper there then in Glasgow, she thinks they will go there in the summer season.

She is living in Dumbarton road in a fine new house & she keeps a lodger which they get 7/6 a week from. Donald has been shepherd and I have been shop keeper since about three months he likes the outside fine.

We have got our New Year past so far soberly. We have shipped some of our sheep and they sold only middling. We have after two hundred yet that we intend to keep on a while.

We would like if we were near you for bog hay, because, we will be very short of straw, but I think we will do for turnips, straw is in general scarce throughout all Caithness this year. We will hardly get it to buy.

Donald says he is afraid to write you now, and for my father [William Moore] he said when he got your letter he would not be long due, but he still has it to commence – They say you will get them both soon if the weather gets better.

Flora is still on the list with the old maids, courting as buzy as ever but comming to no conclusion, she says she is going to be a housekeeper to yourself (John) if you get you estate in right working order.

My Mother & my little sister is keeping fine if the warm weather would come once they will get their cartes [photographs] taken and they will send you one, My little sister's name is Cathrine Mary Ann she is only seven months and she will stand when held. she has a good temper I don't know who she took it from if it is not from her Uncle Hugh.

Donald Hugh [his brother] has a great cry about his Uncle Hugh hardly a day passes ... he is speaking about his uncle Hugh.

We had word from Lismore and they were quite well at that time.

John Bannerman had a baby that was taken away about a month ago, he was eleven months old when he died.

Did you hear that my father has got up his name in the town, we have made him a commisioner now. What will people no do now a days for honour, there has been a fine While of rowing in the Newspapers, with the commisioners about the state of the town, before my old man and a few more sensible fellows got in.

I must attend and send you a newspaper oftener that you may see how our city is going on. I must conclude hoping you will write soon soon soon, Father & Mother sister & Brothers Uncle & Aunt & my ain self send their best respects to you both a happy new year and many returns of the season

I am Your

Affectionate Nephew

John Moore

B.H.C. [Brown Hill Cottage]

Thurso

Plate 13.1. Alexander Milne (top center) with his Parents and Siblings, 1875
A note on the photo back lists the individuals as
"William, Alex, James,
Joseph, James, Jessie Gunn Milne, John and Jane."

**Plate 13.2. Partick South Parish Church (Scale Model)
Glasgow, 2012**

Margaret McDougall and Alexander Milne were married at 371 Dumbarton Road, Glasgow, November 17, 1876, according to the record of marriage, District of Anderston, Burgh of Glasgow. The record lists Flora McDougall and William Milne as witnesses. However, the Partick South Parish Church, which was located at 259 Dumbarton Road, Glasgow and shown in the scale model above maintained by the church, has been identified as the one in which they were married. The church was demolished and replaced in 1988.

Plate 13.3. **Plate 13.4.**

The Partick South Parish Church, 259 Dumbarton Road, Glasgow, 1983. Before It Was Replaced

Plate 13.5. Catherine (Kate) Doull Guthrie with Dougald Milne Tiffany at her Home in Montrose, Scotland, 1966

Flora McDougall did marry. Her husband was Donald Doull, a master plumber. Their daughter, Catherine ("Cousin Kate") Guthrie (September 18, 1884 - January 11, 1972) is shown in the photograph above with her cousin, Dougald Milne Tiffany (January 22, 1885 - May 1977), son of Alexander Milne and Margaret McDougall. The photograph was taken in 1966 at Catherine Guthrie's home in Montrose when Dougald M. Tiffany, his wife, Jennie June, their daughter, Margaret Tiffany Wilcox, and granddaughter, Barbara Wilcox Bitetto, visited from the US.

Letter #14

August 18, 1877

Note: The following letter was transcribed by John Moore, grandson of John McDougall (weaver) and Catherine McCallum McDougall. It includes a note from him.

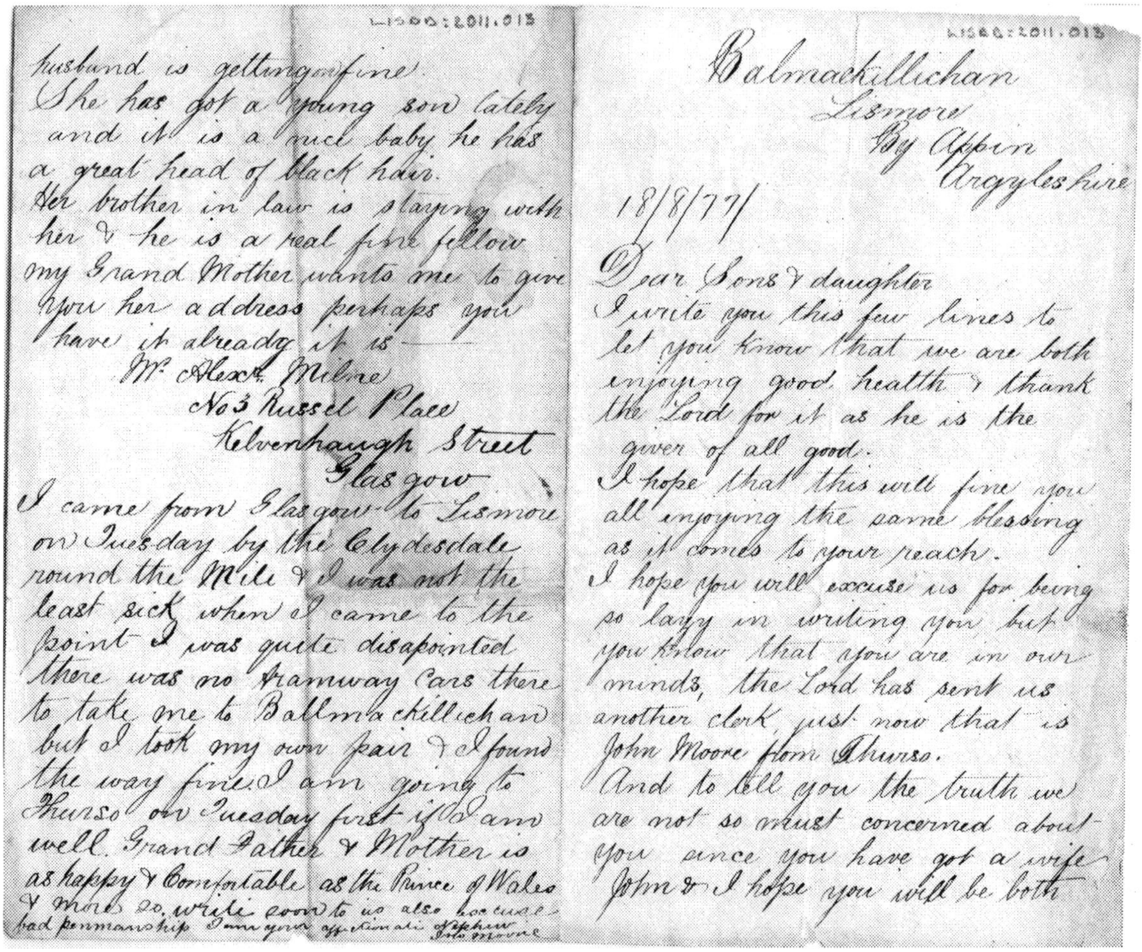

Balmackillichan
Lismore
By Appin
Argyleshire

18/8/77

Dear Sons & daughter
I write you this few lines to let you know that we are both enjoying good health & thank the Lord for it as he is the giver of all good.
I hope that this will fine you all enjoying the same blessing as it comes to your reach.
I hope you will excuse us for being so lazy in writing you but you know that you are in our minds, the Lord has sent us another clerk just now that is John Moore from Thurso.
And to tell you the truth we are not so must concerned about you since you have got a wife John & I hope you will be both

husband is getting on fine
She has got a young son lately and it is a nice baby he has a great head of black hair.
Her brother in law is staying with her & he is a real fine fellow
my Grand Mother wants me to give you her address perhaps you have it already it is
Mr Alexr Milne
No 3 Russel Place
Kelvinhaugh Street
Glasgow
I came from Glasgow to Lismore on Tuesday by the Clydesdale round the Mile & I was not the least sick when I came to the point I was quite disapointed there was no tramway Cars there to take me to Ballmachillichan but I took my own fair & I found the way fine. I am going to Thurso on Tuesday first if I am well. Grand Father & Mother is as happy & Comfortable as the Prince of Wales & more so, write soon to us also excuse bad penmanship I am your affectionate nephew John Moore

Image db145

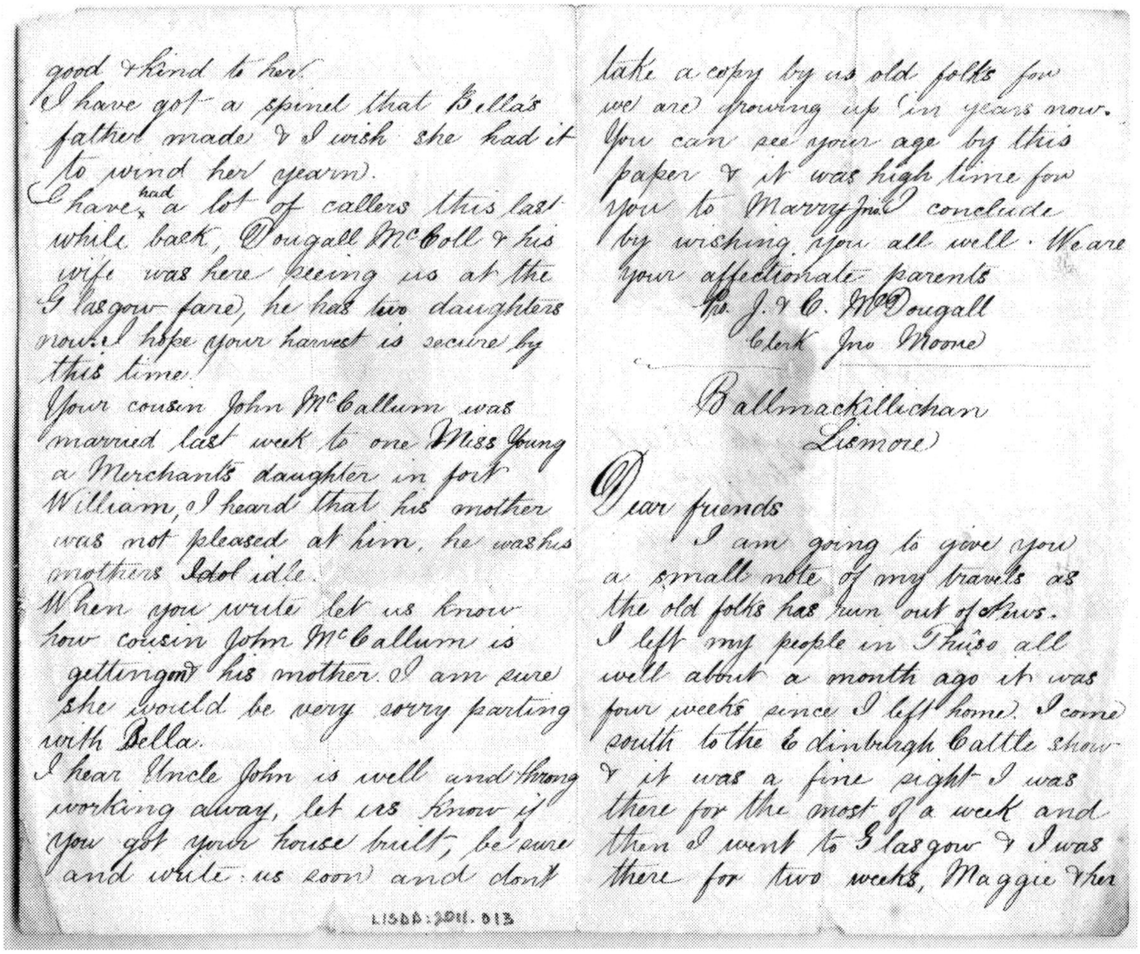

good & kind to her.
I have got a spinel that Bella's father made & I wish she had it to wind her yearn.
I have had a lot of callers this last while back, Dougall McColl & his wife was here seeing us at the Glasgow fare, he has two daughters now. I hope your harvest is secure by this time.
Your cousin John McCallum was married last week to one Miss Young a Merchant's daughter in fort William, I heard that his mother was not pleased at him, he was his mothers Idol idle.
When you write let us know how cousin John McCallum is getting on his mother. I am sure she would be very sorry parting with Bella.
I hear Uncle John is well and strong working away, let us know if you got your house built, be sure and write us soon and dont

take a copy by us old folks for we are growing up in years now. You can see your age by this paper & it was high time for you to Marry. I conclude by wishing you all well. We are your affectionate parents
pr. J. & C. McDougall
Clerk Jno Moore

Ballmackillichan
Lismore

Dear friends
I am going to give you a small note of my travels as the old folks has run out of News. I left my people in Thurso all well about a month ago it was four weeks since I left home. I come south to the Edinburgh Cattle show & it was a fine sight I was there for the most of a week and then I went to Glasgow & I was there for two weeks, Maggie & her

Image db146

LETTER FROM JOHN MCDOUGALL (b. 1803 Lismore) AND CATHERINE MCCALLUM MCDOUGALL (b. 1809 Lismore) WHO LIVED AT BALLIMACKILLICHAN, ISLE OF LISMORE TO JOHN MCDOUGALL (b. 1837 Lismore) AND HUGH MCDOUGALL (b. 1842 Lismore) MINNESOTA

Balmackillichan
Lismore
By Appin
Argyleshire

18/8/77

Dear Sons & daughter

I write you this few lines to let you know that we are both enjoying good health & thank the Lord for it as he is the giver of all good.

I hope that this will fine you all enjoying the same blessing as it comes to your reach.

I hope you will excuse us for being so lazy in writing you but you know that you are in our minds, the Lord has sent us another clerk, just now that is John Moore from Thurso.

And to tell you the truth we are not so must concerned about you since you have got a wife John & I hope you will be both good & kind to her.

I have got a spinel that Bella's father made & I wish she had it to wind her yearn.

I have had a lot of callers this last while back, Dougall McColl & his wife was here seeing us at the Glasgow fare, he has two daughters now. I hope your harvest is secure by this time.

Your cousin John McCallum was married last week to one Miss Young a Merchant's daughter in fort William, I heard that his mother was not pleased at him, he was his mothers idle.

When you write let us know how cousin John McCallum is getting on & his mother. I am sure she would be very sorry parting with Bella.

I hear Uncle John is well and throng [busy] working away, let us know if you got your house built, be sure and write us soon and don't take a copy by us old folks for we are growing up in years now.

You can see your age by this paper & it was high time for you to Marry Jno. I conclude by wishing you all well. We are your affectionate parents.

Mr. J. & C. MacDougall

Clerk Jno Moore

Ballmackillichan

Lismore

Dear friends

I am going to give you a small note of my travels as the old folks [John & Catherine McDougall] has run out of News. I left my people in Thurso all well about a month ago it was four weeks since I left home. I come south to the Edinburgh Cattle show & it was a fine sight I was there for the most of a week and then I went to Glasgow & I was there for two weeks, Maggie & her husband is getting on fine.

She has got a young son lately and it is a nice baby he has a great head of black hair.

Her brother in law is staying with her & he is a real fine fellow my Grand Mother wants me to give you her address perhaps you have it already it is -

Mr. Alex[d] Milne

No 3 Russel Place

Kelvenhaugh Street

Glasgow

I came from Glasgow to Lismore on Tuesday by the Clydesdale round the Mile [Mull of Kinty] & I was not the least bit sick when I came to the point I was quite disapointed there was no tramway cars there to take me to Ballmackillichan but I took my own pair & I found the way fine. I am going to Thurso on Tuesday first if I am well. Grand Father & Mother is as happy & Comfortable as the Prince of Wales & more so. write soon to us also excuse bad penmanship I am your affectionate Nephew

Jno Moore

Notes:

This letter refers to three different John McCallums.

1.) The following phrase probably refers to John McCallum (Fort William) (b. 1847), the son of Malcolm McCallum (b. 1811 Balure), the second brother of Catherine McCallum. "Your cousin John McCallum was married last week to one Miss Young a Merchant's daughter in fort William..."

2.) The following probably refers to John McCallum (also born 1847), of Ortonville, Minnesota, the son of Gilbert McCallum (b. 1813 Balure) who was a brother of Catherine McCallum. "When you write let us know how cousin John McCallum is getting on & his mother..." This particular John McCallum was also the brother of Isabel McCallum McDougall.

3.) The following probably refers to Catherine McCallum's fourth and youngest brother, John, (b. 1818 Balure): "I hear Uncle John is well and throng [busy] working away..."

See Appendix 9 for additional information.

This letter also refers to the marriage of John McDougall (b. 1837) and is consistent with the following report: "Mr. John McDougall returned last evening with a better half." (*Redwood Falls Gazette,* Thursday, Feb 1, 1877, Local News, last page) The newspaper provides no additional information.

"Maggie & her husband is getting on fine.
She has got a young son lately and it is a nice
baby he has a great head of black hair"

James Alexander Milne, the first child of Margaret McDougall Milne and Alexander Milne, was born July 10, 1877, near Elgin. (Wilcox, 1977) He is the young son mentioned in John Moore's note in the letter of August 18, 1877, above.

Plate 14.1. James Alexander Milne
with Grand Nephew, Robert Tiffany (Bob) Wilcox and
Grand Niece, Carolyn Ruth Wilcox
1948 or 1949, Boise, Idaho

Plate 14.2. James Alexander Milne with Niece Margaret Tiffany Wilcox and her Children at her Home, Boise, Idaho

The children are Margaret Frances (Dondee), Carolyn Ruth and Robert Tiffany (Bob) Wilcox.

Plate 14.3. James Alexander Milne (second from left)
with Carolyn Ruth Wilcox (front left), Robert Tiffany Wilcox (on horse), Robert Wilson Wilcox, Margaret Frances (Dondee) Wilcox (in front), and George A. Wilcox (on right), July 1950

Plate 14.4. Margaret Milne Marquardt and her Cousin, John Milne Tiffany
Tiffany Family Reunion, Redwood Falls, Minnesota, June 2012
They are grandchildren of Margaret McDougall and Alexander Milne. Margaret (1911 - 2015) was the daughter of James Alexander Milne. John (b. 1928) is the son of Dougald Milne Tiffany.

Plate 14.6. Point, Isle of Lismore, Looking toward Sheep Island

Letter **#15**

January 29th 1879

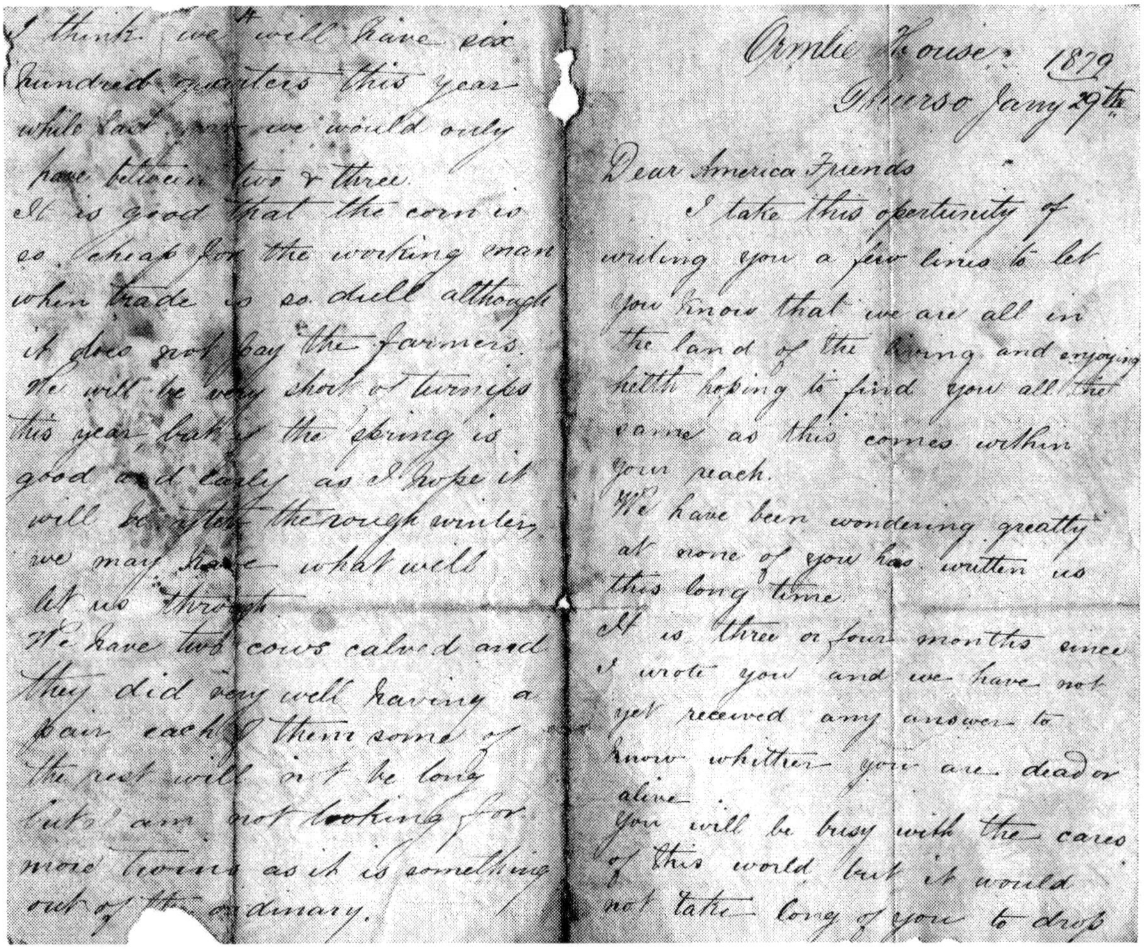

Armlie House 1879
Thurso Jany 29th

Dear America Friends

I take this opertunity of writing you a few lines to let you know that we are all in the land of the living and enjoying helth hoping to find you all the same as this comes within your reach.

We have been wondering greatly at none of you has written us this long time

It is three or four months since I wrote you and we have not yet received any answer to know whither you are dead or alive

You will be busy with the cares of this world but it would not take long of you to drop

I think we will have six hundred quarters this year while last year we would only have between two & three.

It is good that the corn is so cheap for the working man when trade is so dull although it does not pay the farmers.

We will be very short of turnips this year but if the spring is good and early as I hope it will be after the rough winter we may have what will let us through

We have two cows calved and they did very well having a pair each & there some of the rest will not be long but I am not looking for more twins as it is something out of the ordinary.

Image db168

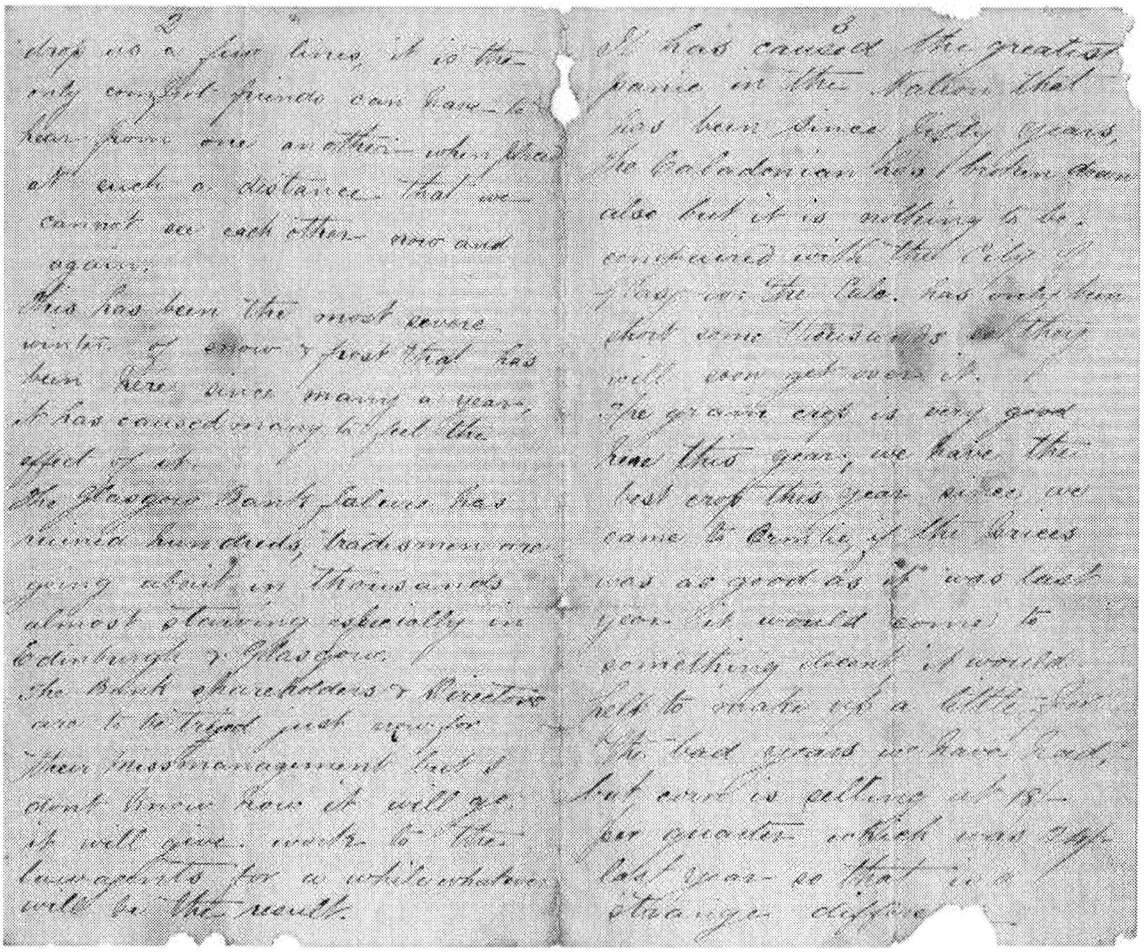

2

drop us a few lines, it is the
only comfort friends can have to
hear from one another when placed
at such a distance that we
cannot see each other now and
again.
This has been the most severe
winter of snow & frost that has
been here since many a year,
it has caused many to feel the
effect of it.
The Glasgow Bank failure has
ruined hundreds, tradesmen are
going about in thousands
almost starving especially in
Edinburgh & Glasgow.
The Bank shareholders & Directors
are to be tried just now for
their missmanagement but I
dont know how it will go
it will give work to the
lawagents for a while whatever
will be the result.

3

It has caused the greatest
panic in the Nation that
has been since fifty years,
the Caledonian has broken down
also but it is nothing to be
compared with the City of
Glasgow. The Cale. has only been
short some thousands but they
will soon get over it.
The grain crop is very good
here this year, we have the
best crop this year since we
came to Brnihe, if the prices
was as good as it was last
year it would come to
something decent it would
help to make up a little for
the bad years we have had,
but corn is selling at 18/-
per quarter which was 24/-
last year so that is a
strange differ

Image MM Scan 6 db168a page 2

TO JOHN MCDOUGALL (b. 1837 Lismore)
DELHI, REDWOOD COUNTY, MINNESOTA USA
FROM ORMLIE HOUSE, THURSO
MOORE (Agnes (Ann) McDougall's family (b. 1833))

Ormlie House
Thurso
1879 Jany 29th

Dear America Friends

I take this opertunity of writing you a few lines to let you know that we are all in the land of the living and enjoying helth hoping to find you all the same as this comes within your reach.

We have been wondering greatly at none of you has written us this long time.

It is three or four months since I wrote you and we have not yet received any answer to know whither you are dead or alive

You will be busy with the cares of this world but it would not take long of you to drop drop us a few lines, it is the only comfort friends can have to hear from one another when placed at such a distance that we cannot see each other now and again.

This has been the most severe winter of snow & frost that has been here since many a year, it has caused many to feel the effect of it.

The Glasgow Bank falure has ruined hundreds, tradesmen are going about in thousands almost starving especially in Edinburgh & Glasgow.

The Bank shareholders & Directors are to be tried just now for their Missmanagement but I don't know how it will go, it will give work to the law agents for a while whatever will be the result.

It has caused the greatest panic in the Nation that has been since fifty years, The Caladonian has broken down also but it is nothing to be compaired with the City of Glasgow: The Cala. has only been short some thousands so they will soon get over it.

The grain crop is very good here this year, we have the best crop this year since we came to Ormlie, if the prices was as good as it was last year it would come to something decent, it would help to make up a little for the bad years we have had, but, corn is selling at 18/- per quarter which was 14/- last year so that is a strange difference.

I think we will have six hundred quarters this year while last year we would only have between two & three.

It is good that the corn is so cheap for the working man when trade is so dull although it does not pay the farmers. We will be very short of turnips this year, but if the spring is good and early as I hope it will be after the rough winter, we may have what will let us through.

We have two cows calved and they did very well having a pair each of them some of the rest will not be long but I am not looking for more twins as it is something out of the ordinary.

(rest missing)

Letter **#16**

February 17, 1879

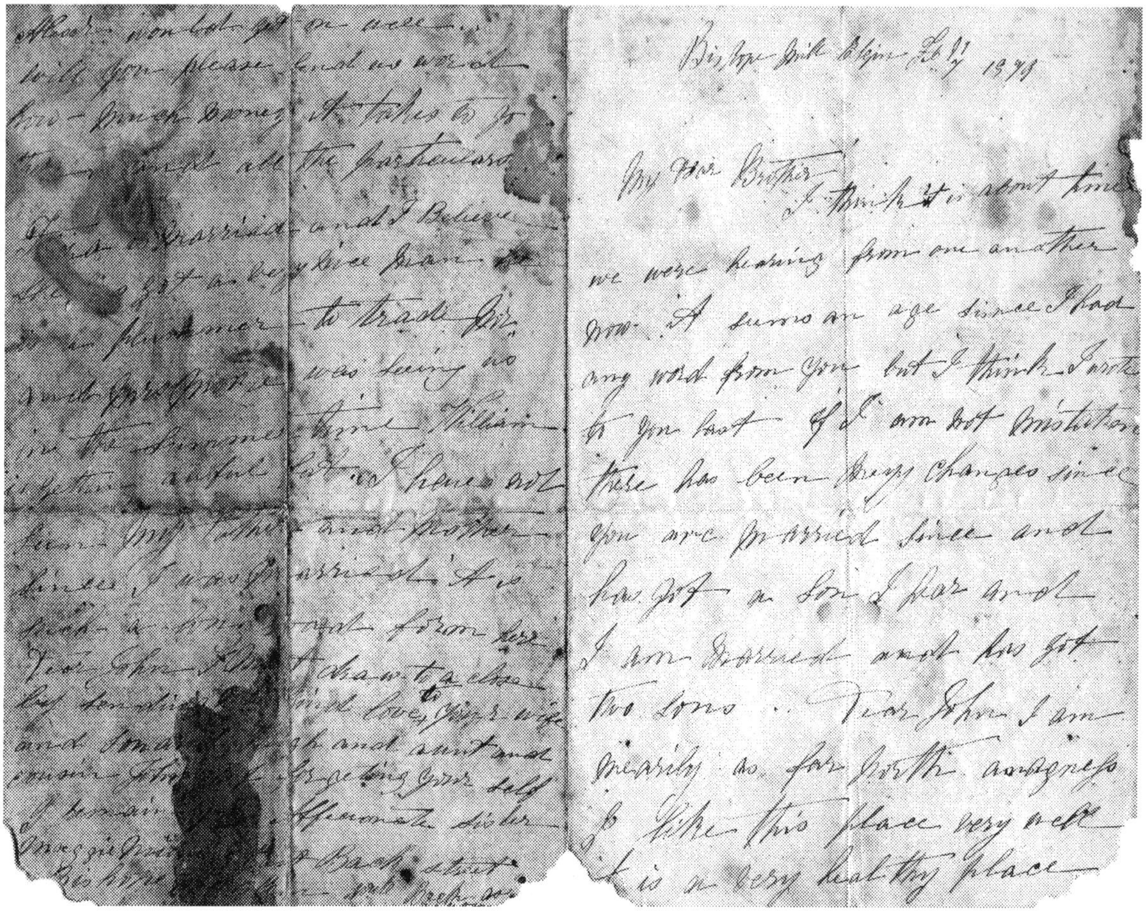

Bishops Mill Elgin Feby 17 1879

My Dear Brother
I think it is about time
we were hearing from one another
now. It seems an age since I had
any word from you but I think I wrote
to you last if I am not mistaken
there has been many changes since
you are married since and
has got a son I hear and
I am married and has got
two sons. Dear John I am
nearly as far North as [illegible]
I like this place very well
it is a very healthy place

Image db165

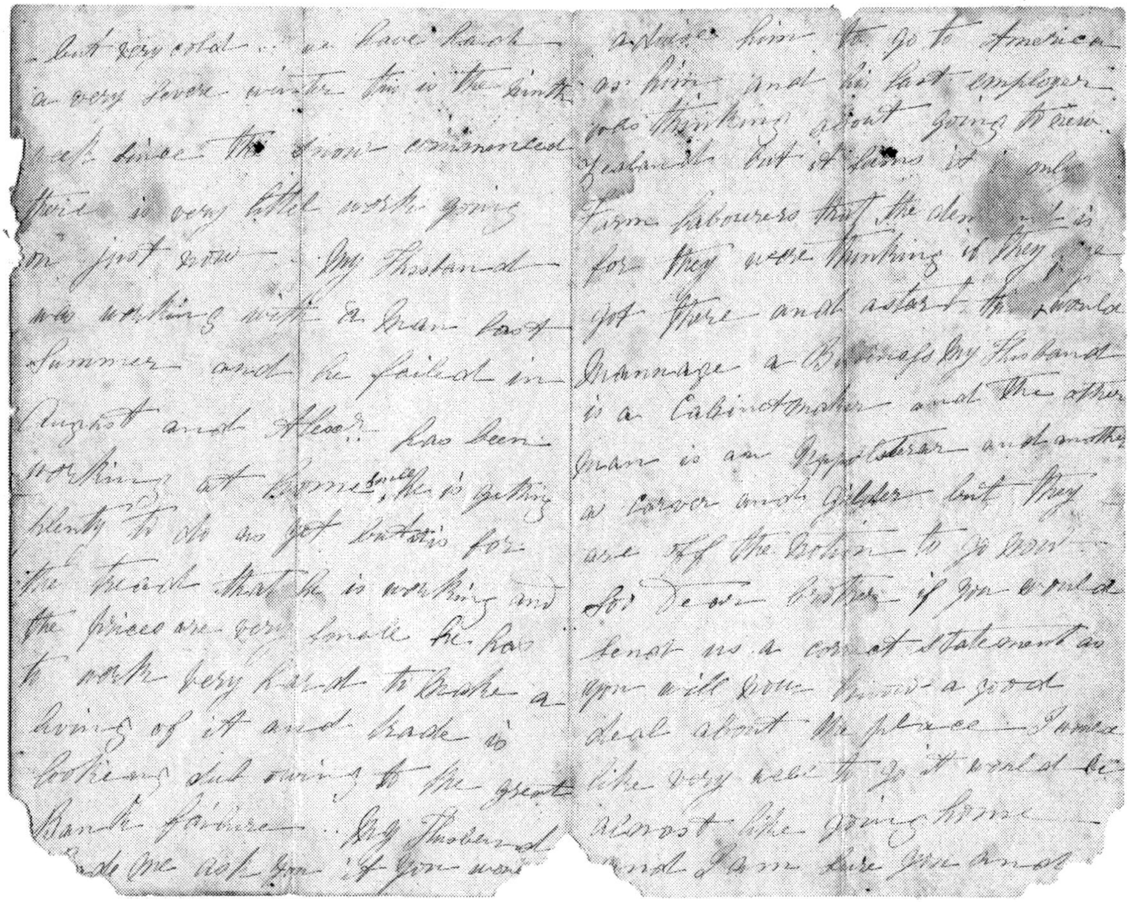

but very cold .. we have had
a very severe winter this is the sixth
week since the snow commenced
there is very little work going
on just now. My Husband
was working with a man last
Summer and he failed in
August and Alex.. has been
working at home since he is getting
plenty to do as yet but [illegible] for
the trade that he is working and
the prices are very small he has
to work very hard to make a
living of it and trade is
looking dull owing to the great
Bank failure. My Husband
bade me ask you if you would
advise him to go to America
as him and his last employer
was thinking about going to New
Zealand but it seems it is only
Farm labourers that the demand is
for they were thinking if they
got there and start they would
manage a Business My Husband
is a Cabinetmaker and the other
man is an Upholsterer and another
a Carver and Gilder but they
are off the notion to go now
so Dear Brother if you would
send us a correct statement as
you will now know a good
deal about the place I would
like very well to go it would be
almost like going home
and I am sure you must

Image db166

LETTER TO JOHN MCDOUGALL (1837 - 1896) IN MINNESOTA FROM HIS SISTER, MARGARET MCDOUGALL MILNE (1851 or 1852 - 1888)

Bishope Mill Elgin

Feb. 17 1879

My Dear Brother

I think it is about time we were hearing from one another now. It seems an age since I had any word from you but I think I wrote you last if I am not mistaken there has been many changes since you are married since and has got a son I hear and I am married and has got two sons [James Alexander b. 1877, John b. 1878] Dear John I am nearily as far North as Agness [sister Agnes (Ann) McDougall Moore, b. 1833 Lismore] I like this place very well It is a very healthy place - but very cold ... we have had a very severe winter this is the ninth week since the snow commenced there is very littel work going on just now -- My Husband was working with a Man last Summer and he failed in August and Alesar [Alexander] has been working at home since he is getting plenty to do as yet but it is for the tread [trade] that he is working and the prices are very Smale he has to work very hard to Make a living of it and trade is looking dul owing to the great Bank failure .. My Husbend [...]ade me ask you if you would advise him to go to America as him and his last employer was thinking about going to New Zealand but it Seems it is only Farm labourers that the demand is for they were thinking if they ... got there and astart that would Mannage a Business My Husband is a Cabinetmaker and the other man is an Uppolsterar and another a carver and gilder but they are off the Notion to go now – Soo Dear brother if you would send us a correct statement as you will now know a good deal about Me place – I would like very well to go it would be almost like going home and I am sure you and Alesar [Alexander] would get on well ... Will you please send me word how - Much money it takes to go there and all the particulars. Flory is married and I Believe She is got a very nice Man he is a plummer to trade Mr. and Mrs Moore [Ann McDougall] was seeing us in the Summer time William is getting awful fat. I have not Seen my Father and Mother since I was married it is such a long road form here Dear John I must draw to a close by sending... kind love to your wife and Son and Hugh and aunt and cousin John not forgeting your self.

I remain your afffecionate sister

Maggie Milne [___] East Back street

Bishope Mill Elgin write back as...

Notes:

John Milne, son of Margaret and Alexander Milne, was born December 5, 1878, at 7, East Back Street, Bishopmill, Elgin. (NRS, 1855 – 2013a; General Register for Scotland, GROS, number 135/00 0255)

"[C]ousin John" might refer to John McCallum, b. 1847, son of Gilbert McCallum and Ann McCallum McCallum. He was the cousin of John McDougall (b. 1837) and brother of Isabel McCallum. (See Appendix 9.)

Plate 16.1. Margaret McDougall Milne ("Maggie") Holding Baby John Milne, Alexander Milne (on right) Holding James Alexander Milne 1878

"My Husband is a Cabinetmaker"

Plate 16.2. Cabinet Made by Margaret McDougall's Husband, Alexander Milne
At Clinic of Dr. S. Francis Ceplecha, 1971
Redwood Falls, Minnesota

"I would like very well to go
it would be almost like going home"

Plate 16.3. Dougald Milne Tiffany (1885 – 1977),
Son of Margaret McDougall and Alexander Milne
Feeding Cattle on his Farm, Redwood Falls, Minnesota
January 1950
Temperature: - 25° F (- 31.67° C)

Plate 16.4. Margaret Tiffany Wilcox (1913 – 1976), Granddaughter of Margaret McDougall and Alexander Milne, Viewing a Backdoor Garden Elgin, August 1966

Letter #17

July 29, 1879

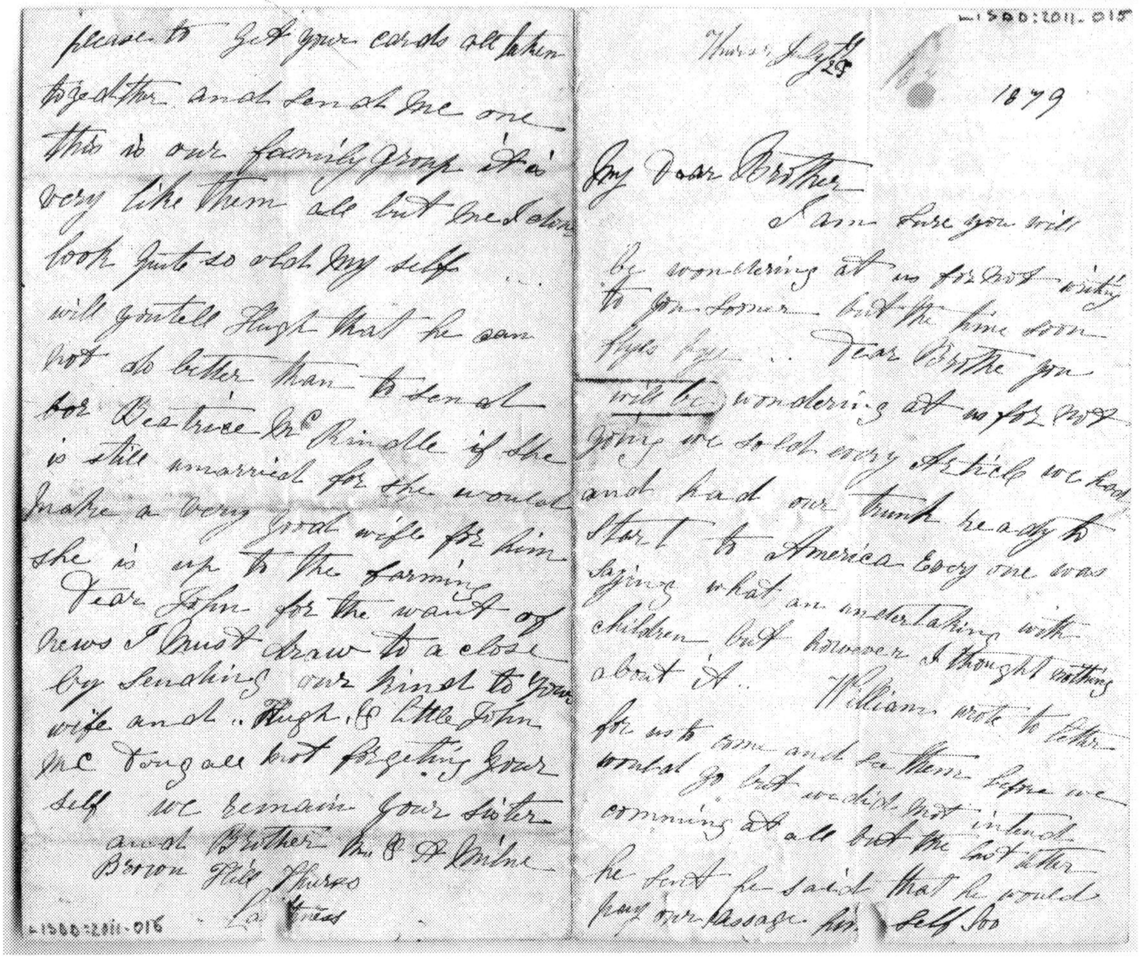

Thurs July 29

1879

My Dear Brother

I am sure you will
be wondering at us for not writing
to you sooner but the time soon
flys bye. Dear Brothe you
will be wondering at us for not
going we sold every Article we had
and had our trunk ready to
start to America every one was
saying what an undertaking with
children but however I thought nothing
about it. William wrote to letter
for us to come and be there before we
would go but we did not intend
comming at all but the last letter
he sent he said that he would
pay our passage him self too

L1500:2011-015

please to get your cards all taken
togather and send me one
this is our family group it is
very like them all but me I dont
look Just so old my self
will you tell Hugh that he can
not do better than to send
for Beatrice McKindle if she
is still unmarried for she would
make a very good wife for him
she is up to the farming
Dear John for the want of
news I must draw to a close
by sending our kind to your
wife and Hugh & little John
McDougall but forgeting your
self we remain your sister
and Brother M & A Milne
Barron Hill Thurso
Caithness

L1500:2011-016

Image db155

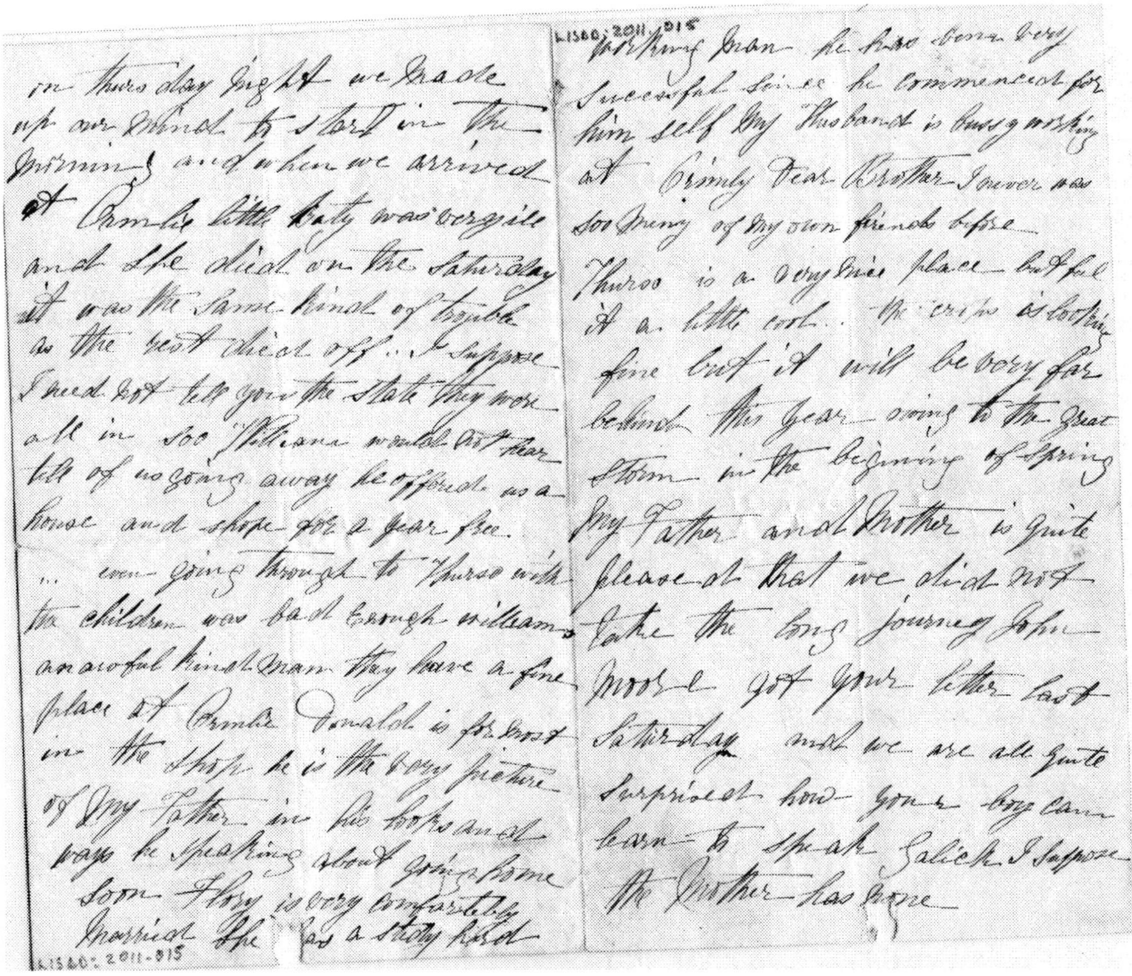

on thursday night we made
up our mind to start in the
morning and when we arrived
at Crimly little Katy was verry ill
and she died on the Saturday
it was the same kind of trouble
as the rest died off ... I suppose
I need not tell you the state they were
all in so William would not hear
tell of us going away he offered us a
house and shop for a year free.
... our going through to Thurso with
the children was bad enough william
an awful kind man they have a fine
place at Crimly Donald is foreman
in the shop he is the very picture
of my Father in his looks and
ways he speaking about going home
soon Flory is very comfortably
married she has a steady kind
LISAD: 2011-015

LISAD: 2011-015
working man he has done very
successful since he commenced for
him self my Husband is busy working
at Crimly Dear Brother I never was
so many of my own friends before
Thurso is a very nice place but feel
it a little cool. the crop is looking
fine but it will be very far
behind this year owing to the great
storm in the beginning of spring
my Father and Mother is quite
pleased that we did not
take the long journey John
Mood got your letter last
Saturday and we are all quite
surprised how your boy can
learn to speak Galick I suppose
the Mother has gone

Image db156

LETTER TO JOHN MCDOUGALL (1837 - 1896) IN MINNESOTA FROM HIS SISTER, MARGARET MCDOUGALL MILNE (1851 or 1852 - 1888)

Thurso July 29th 1879

My Dear Brother

I am sure you will be wondering at us for not writing to you sooner but the time soon flyes bye .. Dear Brother you will be wondering at us for not going we sold every Article we had and had our trunk ready to start to America Every one was saying what an undertaking with children but however I thought nothing about it .. William wrote to [two?] letter for us to come and see them before we would go but we did not intend comming at all but the last letter he sent he said that he would pay our passage himself Soo on thursday night we made up our minds to start in the morning and when we arrived at Ormlie little Katy was very ill and she died on the Saturday it was the same kind of trouble as the rest died off .. I suppose I need not tell you the state they were all in soo William would not hear tell of us going away he offered us a house and shope for a year free ... even going through to Thurso with the children was bad Enough Williams an awful kind man they have a fine place at Ormlie Donald is for most in the shop he is the very picture of My Father in his looks and ways he speaking about going home [Lismore] soon Flory [her sister Flora, born 1851 on Lismore] is very comfortebly married She has a stedy hard working man he has ben very Sucessful since he commenced for him self My Husband [Alexander Milne born 1850 near Elgin] is bussy working at Ormily Dear Brother I never was soo miny of my own friends before Thurso is a very nice place but feel it a little cool .. the crops is looking fine but it will be very far behind this year owing to the Great Storm in the beginning of Spring My Father and Mother is quite pleased that we did not take the long journey John Moore got your letter last Saturday and we are all quite Surprised how your boy [John McDougall, born 1877 in Minnesota] can learn to speak Galick I suppose the Mother has none

Please to get your cards [pictures?] all taken togedhther and send me one this is our family group it is very like them all but me I dont[?] look quite so old myself ... will you tell Hugh [her brother born 1842 Lismore] that he can not do better than to send for Beatrice McRindle if she is still umarried for she would make a very good wife for him she is up to the farming

Dear John for the want of news I must draw to a close by sending our kind to your wife and .. Hugh & little John McDougall not forgeting your self we remain your sister and Brother

M.. & A Milne

Brown Hill
Thurso

Caithness

Letter **#18**

August 22nd 1879

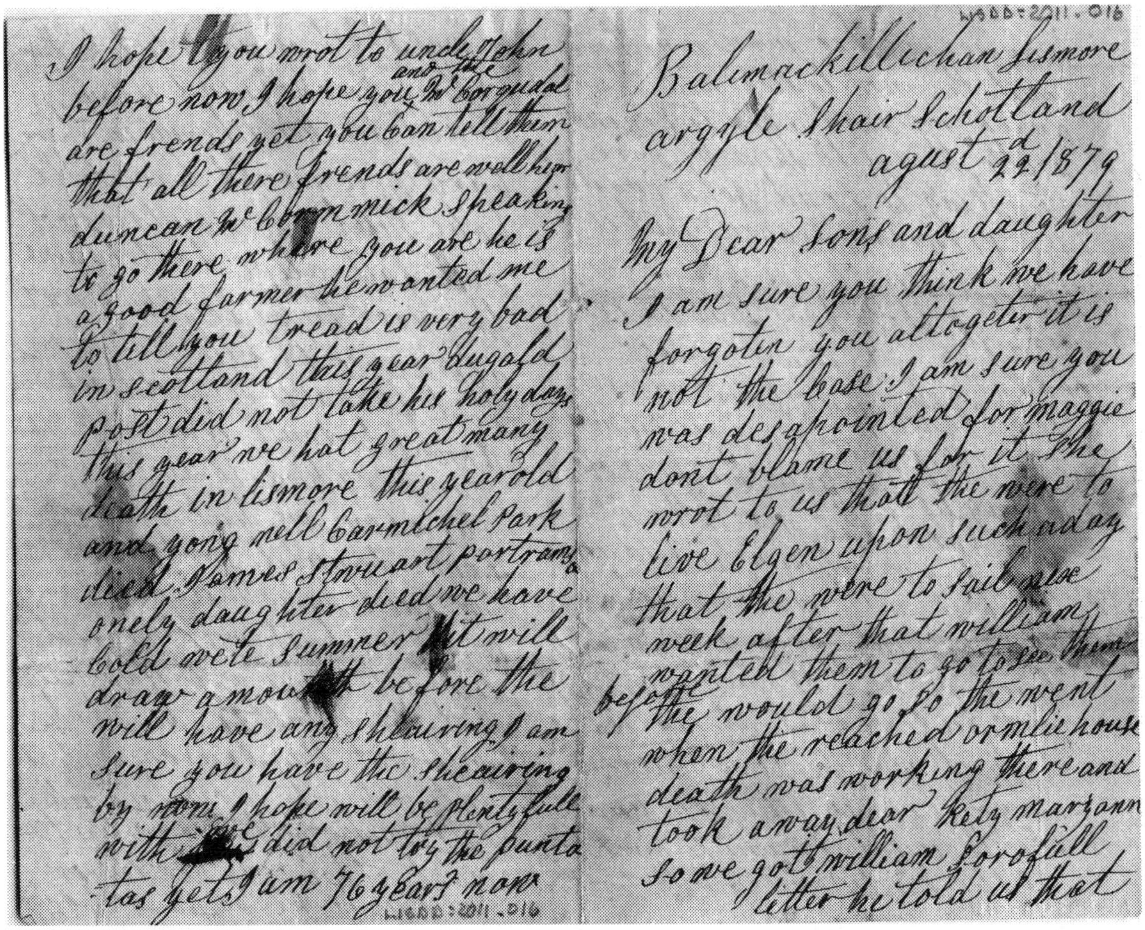

Balmackillechan Lismore
argyle Shair Schotland
agust 22d/1879

My Dear Sons and daughter
I am sure you think we have
forgoten you altogeter it is
not the case I am sure you
was desapointed for maggie
dont blame us for it the
wrot to us that the were to
live Elgen upon such a day
that the were to sail nex
week after that william
wanted them to go to see them
before the would go so the went
when the reached ormlie house
death was working there and
took away dear Katy marjann
so we got william sorofull
letter he told us that

I hope you wrot to uncle John
before now I hope you and the Mc Corquedal
are frends yet you can tell them
that all there frends are well hear
duncan Mc Cormmick speaking
to go there where you are he is
a good farmer he wanted me
to tell you tread is very bad
in scotland this year dugald
post did not take his holydays
this year we hat great many
death in lismore this year old
and yong nell Carmichel Park
died James Stewart portramo
onely daughter died we have
cold wete summer it will
draw a mounth before the
will have any shearing I am
sure you have the shearing
by now I hope will be plentyfull
with you we did not try the punta
-tas yet I am 76 years now

Image db158

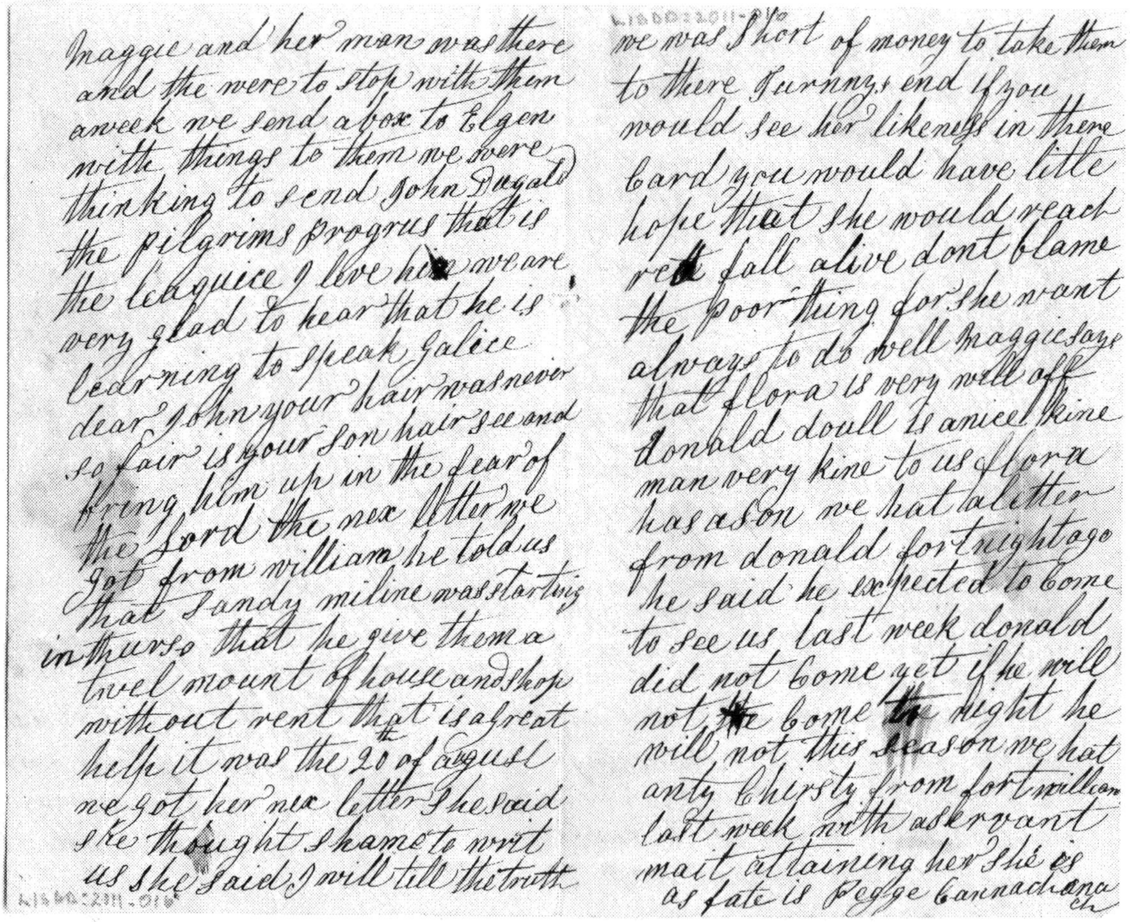

maggie and her man was there
and the were to stop with them
aweek we send a box to Elgen
with things to them we were
thinking to send John Dugald
the pilgrims progres that is
the lenguice I love him we are
very glad to hear that he is
learning to speak Galice
dear John your hair was never
so fair is your son hair see and
bring him up in the fear of
the Lord the nex letter we
got from william he told us
that Sandy miline was starting
in thurso that he give them a
twel mount of house and shop
without rent that is a great
help it was the 20th of august
we got her nex letter she said
she thought shame to writ
us she said I will tell the truth

we was short of money to take them
to there Jurnny's end if you
would see her likeness in there
card you would have little
hope that she would reach
rest fall alive dont blame
the poor thing for she want
always to do well maggie says
that flora is very well off
donald doull is a nice kine
man very kine to us flora
has a son we hat a letter
from donald fortnight ago
he said he expected to come
to see us last week donald
did not come yet if he will
not come the night he
will not this season we hat
anty Chirsty from fort william
last week with a servant
mait attaining her she is
as fate is Pegge Cannachanach

Image db160

LETTER FROM JOHN MCDOUGALL (b. 1803 Lismore) AND CATHERINE MCCALLUM MCDOUGALL (b. 1809 Lismore) WHO LIVED AT BALLIMACKILLICHAN, ISLE OF LISMORE TO JOHN MCDOUGALL (b. 1837 Lismore) AND HUGH MCDOUGALL (b. 1842 Lismore) MINNESOTA

Balimackillichan
Lismore

Argyle Shair Schotland

Agust 22d 1879

Dear Sons & daughter

I am sure you think we have forgoten you altogeter it is not the Case I am sure you was desapointed for maggie dont blame us for it She wrot to us that the were to live Elgen upon such a day that the were to sail nex week after that William wanted them to go to see them before the would go so the went when the reached ormlie house death was working there and took away dear kety mary ann so we got william sorofull letter he told us that Maggie and her man was there and the were to stop with them a week we send a box to Elgen with things to them we were thinking to send John Dugald the pilgrims progrus that is the leaquice [bequeath?] I live [leave?] him we are very glad to hear that he is learning to speak Galice dear John your hair was never so fair is your son hair see and bring him up in the fear of the Lord the nex letter we got from william he told us that Sandy miline was starting in thurso that he give them a twel mount [twelve months] of house and shop without rent that is a great help it was the 20th of august we got her nex letter she said she thought shame to writ us she said I will tell the truth we was Short of money to take them to there Jurrnys end if you would see her likeness in there Card you would have litle hope that she would reach red[?] fall alive dont blame the poor thing for she want always to do well Maggie says that flora is very well off donald doull is a nice kine man very kine to us flora has a son we hat a letter from donald fortnight ago he said he expected to Come to see us last week donald did not Come yet if he will not Come the night he will not this season we hat anty Chirsty [Black] from fort willliam last week with a servant mait attaining her she is as fate is Pegge Cannachanach [Buchanan]

I hope you wrote to uncle John before now I hope you and the McCorqudal are frends yet you can tell them that all there frends are well hear Duncan McCormmick speaking to go there where you are he is a good farmer he wanted me to tell you tread [trade] is very bad in scotland this year dugald post [post runner] did not take his holy days this year we hat great many death in lismore this year old and yong Nell Carmichel Park died James Stwuart [Stuart] port Ramsa[Ramsay] onely daughter died we have Cold wete Summer it will draw a mouth before the will have any sheairing by now I am sure you have the sheairing by now I hope will be plenty full with we did not try the puntatas yet I am 76 years now

(rest of letter missing)

Plate 18.1. Fort William Railway Station, Train to Mallaig 2012

Plate 18.2. Catherine (Kate) Doull Guthrie with Margaret Tiffany Wilcox In garden of Kate Guthrie, Montrose, 1965

Catherine Guthrie was the daughter of Flora McDougall (b. 1851) and Donald Doull. Margaret Wilcox was the daughter of Dougald Milne Tiffany and granddaughter of Margaret McDougall (b. 1851 or 1852) and Alexander Milne.

Plate 18.3. Port Ramsay, Lismore
2013

Letter #19

August 23rd 1879

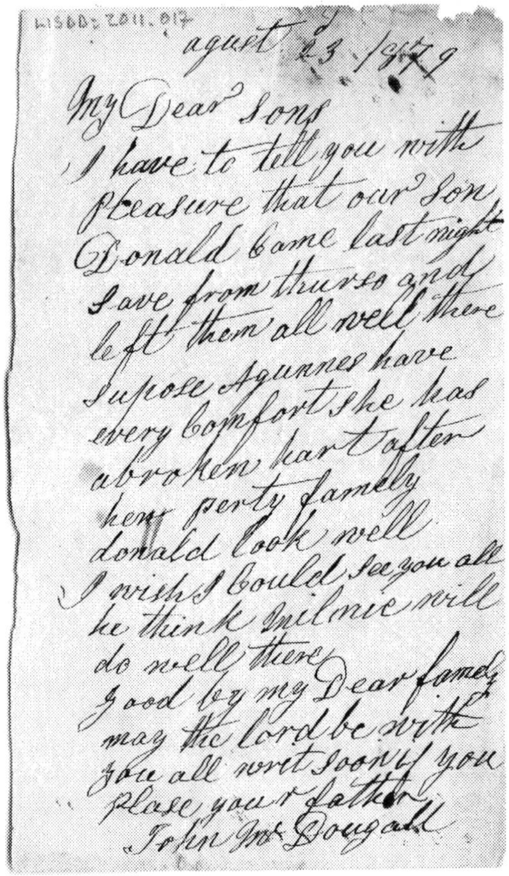
LISDD: 2011.017

aguest 23 1879

My Dear Sons
I have to tell you with
pleasure that our Son
Donald Came last night
Save from thurso and
left them all well there
Supose Agunnes have
every Comfort She has
abroken hart after
her perty famelly
donald look well
I wish I Could see you all
he think Quilmie will
do well there
good by my Dear famely
may the lord be with
you all writ soon if you
plase your father
John McDougall

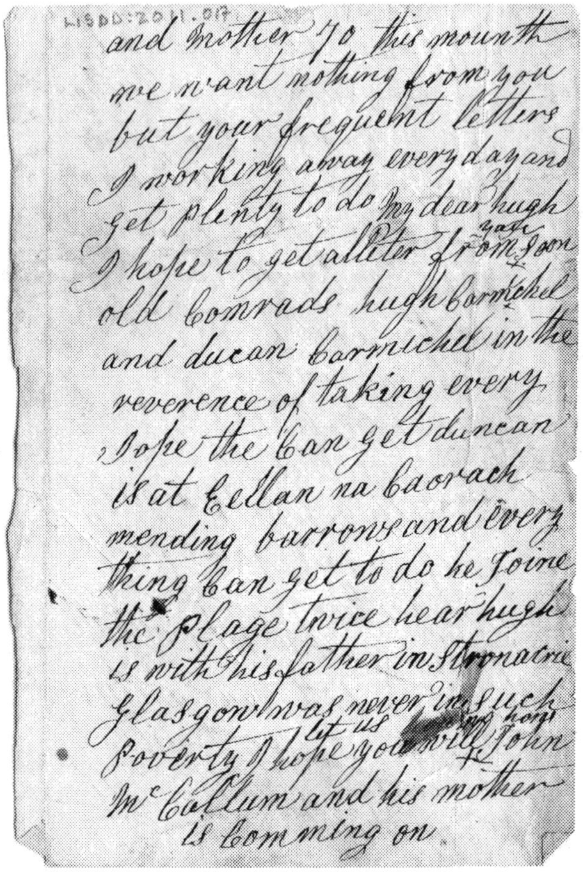
LISDD: 2011.017

and mother 70 this mounth
we want nothing from you
but your frequent letters
I working away every day and
get plenty to do my dear hugh
I hope to get alleter from you soon
old Comrads hugh Carmichel
and ducan Carmichel in the
reverence of taking every
hope the Can get duncan
is at Eellan na Caorach
mending barrows and every
thing Can get to do he Joine
the plage twice hear hugh
is with his father in Stronacrie
Glasgow was never in such
poverty I hope you will let us no how John
Mc Collum and his mother
is comming on.

Image db162

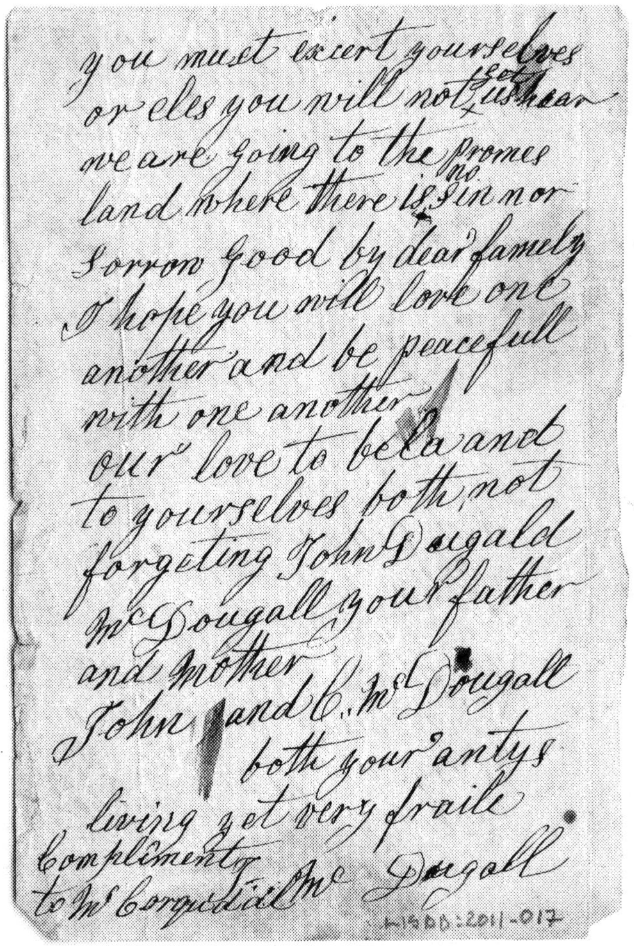

you must excert yourselves
or eles you will not see us hear
we are going to the promes
land where there is no sin nor
Sorrow Good by dear famely
I hope you will love one
another and be peacefull
with one another
our love to bela and
to yourselves both; not
forgeting John Dougald
McDougall your father
and Mother
John and C. McDougall
both your antys
living yet very fraile
Compliments
to Mr Corquodail McDougall

NSDD:2011-017

NSDD:2011.017

Image db163

LETTER FROM JOHN MCDOUGALL (b. 1803 Lismore) AND CATHERINE MCCALLUM MCDOUGALL (b. 1809 Lismore) WHO LIVED AT BALLIMACKILLICHAN, ISLE OF LISMORE TO JOHN MCDOUGALL (b. 1837 Lismore) AND HUGH MCDOUGALL (b. 1842 Lismore) MINNESOTA

Agust 23d 1879

My Dear Sons

I have to tell you with pleasure that our Son Donald Came last night save[safe?] from thurso and left them all well there supose Agunnes [Agnes] have every Comfort she has a broken hart after her perty family

donald look well

I wish I Could see you all he think Milnie will do well there

Good by my Dear famely may the lord be with you all writ soon if you plase your father

John McDougall

.... and mother 70 this mounth we want nothing from you but your frequent letters I working away every day and get plenty to do My dear hugh I hope to get alleter [a letter] from you soon old Comrads hugh Carmichel and ducan Carmichel in the reverence of taking every Iope [job?] the Can get duncan is at Eellan na Caorach [Eilean na Caorach – Sheep Island] mending barrows and everything can get to do he Joine the plage twice dear hugh is with his father in Stronacrie

Glasgow was never in such poverty I hope you will let us no how John McCallum and his mother is comming on

you must excert yourselves or eles you will not get us hear we are going to the promes land where there is no sin nor sorrow good by dear famely I hope you will love one another and be peacefull with one another

our love to bela and to yourselves both, not forgeting John Dugald McDougall your father and Mother

John and C. McDougall

Both your antys living yet very fraile

Compliments to McCorqudal McDugall

"[D]uncan is at Eellan na Caorach mending barrows"

© David H. White

Plate 19.1. Eilean na Caorach (Sheep Island)

© David H. White

Plate 19.2. Eilean na Caorach
with Lime Kiln and Cottage Faintly Visible near the Shore

The following article appeared in *The Scotsman* December 13, 1879, 3 ½ months after the letter above was written. It describes a boat accident between Port Appin and Lismore Point near Sheep Island.

Fatal Boat Accident At Appin- 13th December 1879

Scotsman Archives

An accident resulting in the loss of three lives took place between Appin and Lismore on Wednesday evening.

It was pay-day at the limestone quarry on Sheep Island, off Port Appin, and some of the men were more or less under the influence of liquor. Five of them proposed to cross over to Lismore in a boat of 10 ½ feet keel. Mr Maclachlan, manager of the works, interfered, and succeeded in locking up one of the men, while the other four, named Donald Black, Alexander Macgregor, Alexander Buchanan and Dugald Carmichael, launched the small boat, but they had scarcely put off when they commenced quarrelling and one of them jumped overboard.

The noise of the quarrelling in the boat attracted the attention of a young man named Hugh McIntyre, who hurrying down to the water's edge, saw the occupants of the boat were hardly in a fit state to manage the boat and jumped in to pilot it across to Lismore.

Shortly after another dispute arose, which ended in a fight and the boat was capsized. Carmichael was saved by a shepherd putting off a boat from Lismore and Buchanan by Dr Buchanan of Appin but Macgregor was found dead in the boat while McIntyre and Black had sunk. Black and Macgregor were married and leave families. McIntyre was unmarried.

Additional information:
It's believed that the men had been drinking that day at the Inn at Point on Lismore, before going to Sheep Island. When one of the bodies was eventually retrieved from the water, a heel mark impression was found on the side of his face. The Inn at Point was closed and no other has ever opened since.
(*The Scotsman*, December 13, 1879)
Permission of *The Scotsman*

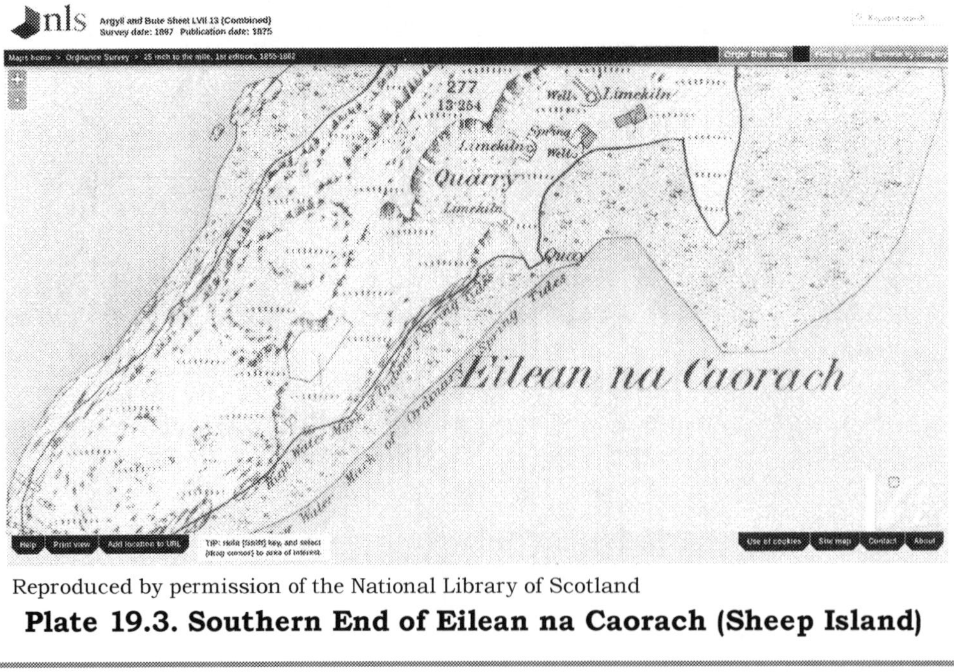

Reproduced by permission of the National Library of Scotland

Plate 19.3. Southern End of Eilean na Caorach (Sheep Island)

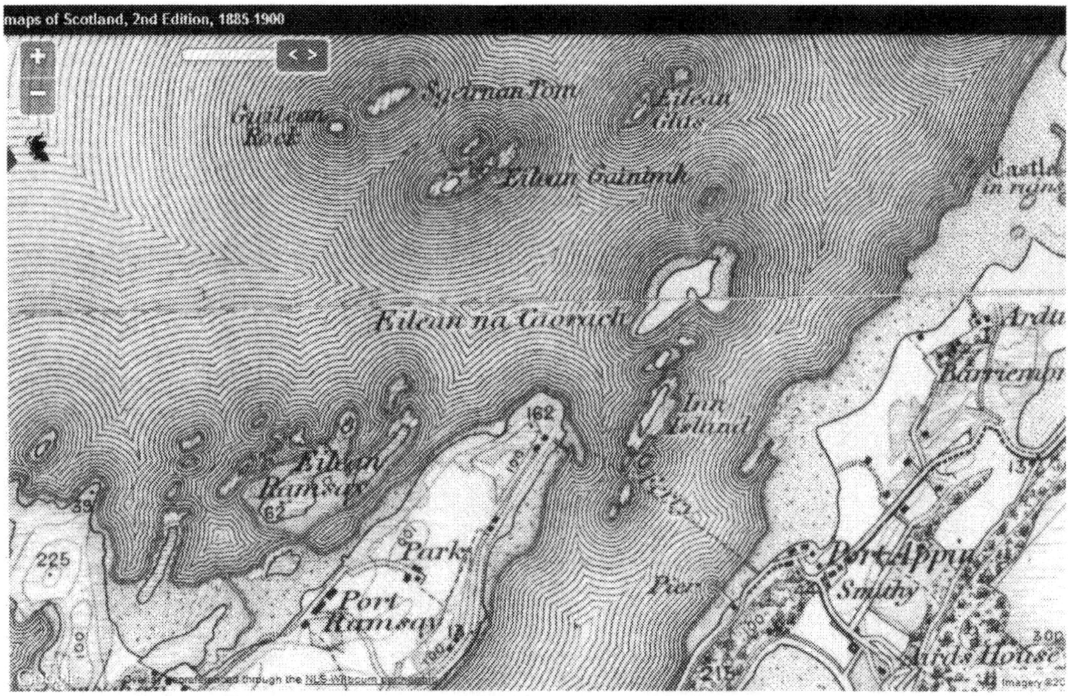

Reproduced by permission of the National Library of Scotland

Plate 19.4. Eilean na Caorach, Inn Island, Port Appin and Lismore Communities of Park and Port Ramsay

Letter #20

Date Unknown, about 1879

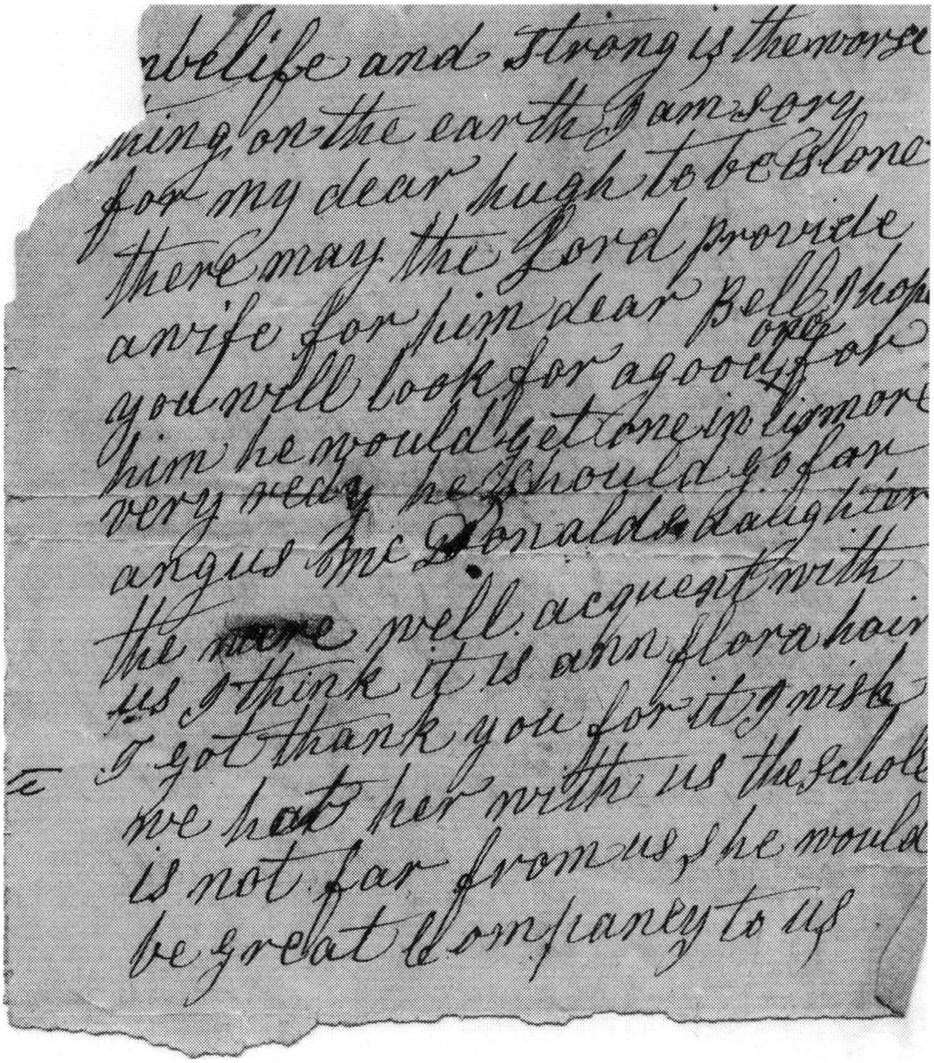
...welife and strong is the worse
ming on the earth I am sory
for my dear hugh to be alone
there may the Lord provide
a wife for him dear Bell I hope
you will look for a good one for
him he would get one in lismore
very ready he should go for
angus McDonald's daughter
the [illegible] well acquent with
us I think it is ann flora hair
I got thank you for it I wish
we had her with us the schole
is not far from us she would
be great companey to us

Image db175

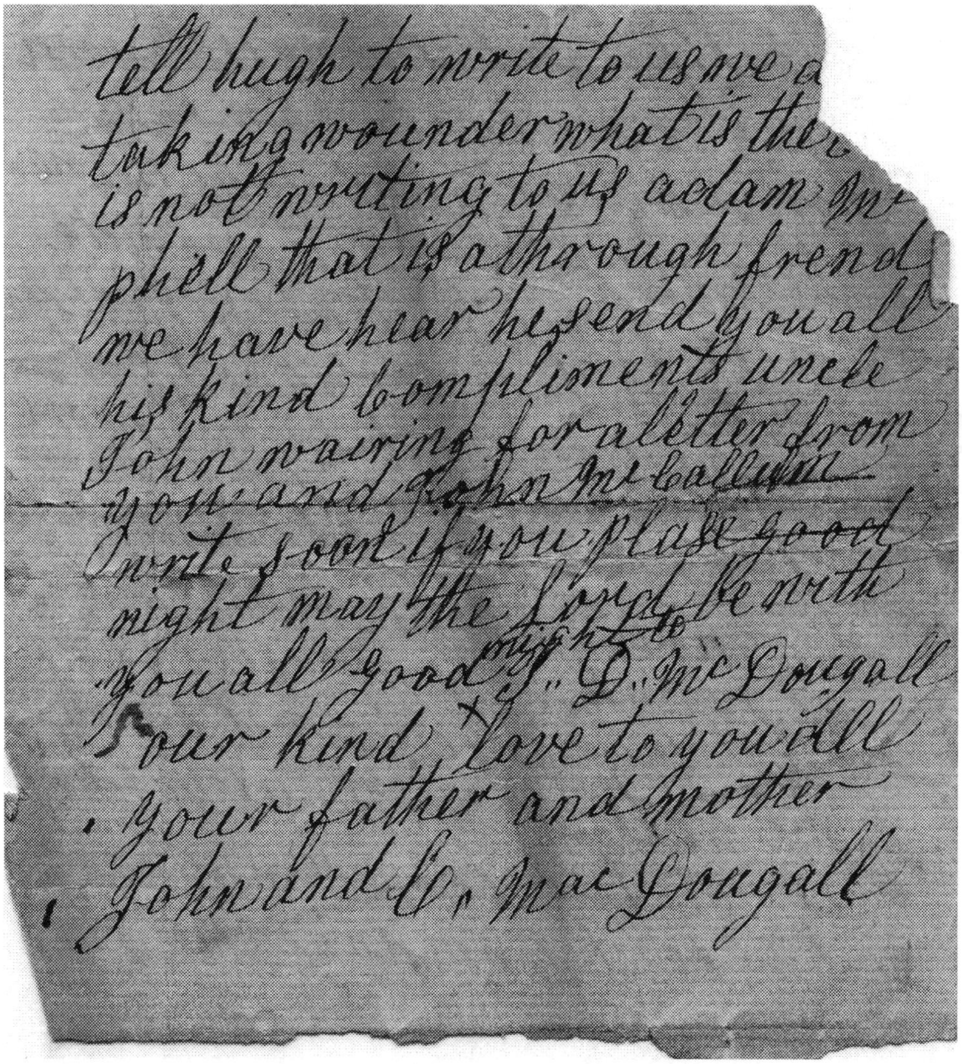
tell hugh to write to us we a
taking wounder what is the
is not writing to us adam M
phell that is a through frend
we have hear he send you all
his kind compliments uncle
John wairing for a letter from
you and John Mc Callum
write soon if you plase good
night may the Lord be with
you all good night to J. D. Mc Dougall
your kind love to you all
your father and mother
John and C. MacDougall

Image db176

LETTER FROM JOHN MCDOUGALL (b. 1803 Lismore) AND CATHERINE MCCALLUM MCDOUGALL (b. 1809 Lismore) WHO LIVED AT BALLIMACKILLICHAN, ISLE OF LISMORE TO THEIR SON JOHN MCDOUGALL (b. 1837 Lismore) DELHI, REDWOOD COUNTY, MINNESOTA USA

(date unknown, about 1879)

(fragments of a letter)... nbelife and strong is the worse thing on the earth I am sory for my dear hugh [their son, b. 1842 Lismore] to be is lone there may the Lord provide a wife for him dear Bell [John's wife, Isabel McCallum McDougall] I hope you will look for a good one for him he would get one in lismore very redy he should go for Angus McDonalds daughter the were well acquent with us I think it is ann flora hair I got thank you for it I wish we hat her with us the schole is not far from us she would be great Companey to us.

tell hugh to write us we a... taking wounder what is the ... is not writing to us adam Mcphell [McPhail] that is a through frend we have hear he send you all his kind Compliments uncle John wairing for a letter from you and John McCallum

write soon if you plase good night may be the Lord be with you all good night to J.. D.. McDougall

our kind love to you all

Your father and mother

John and C. MacDougall

Plate 20.1. John Dougald MacDougal (b. 1877, Delhi, Minnesota), First Child of John McDougall (b. 1837) and Isabel McCallum, with his Wife, Lela Cardwell MacDougal
Possibly at his retirement from the
Spokane, Portland & Seattle (SP&S) Railroad, 1949

Letter **#21**

December 27, Year Unknown

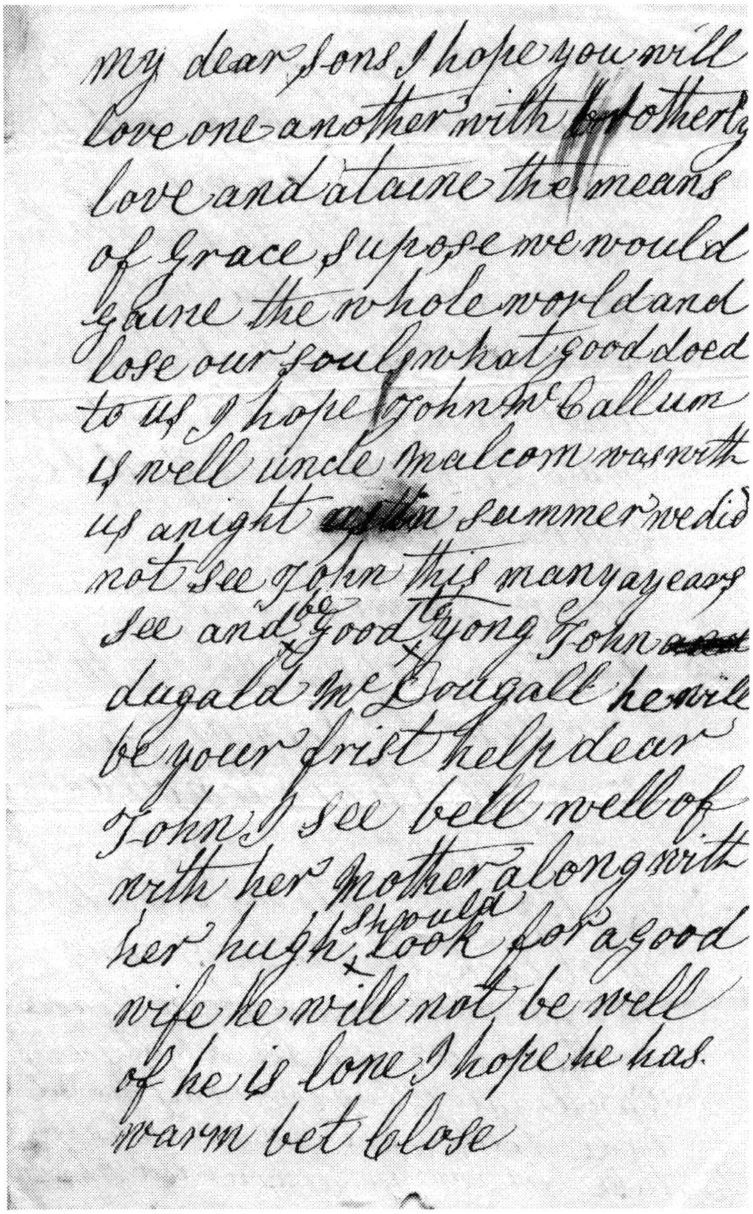

my dear sons I hope you will
love one another with brotherly
love and ataine the means
of Grace suppose we would
gaine the whole world and
lose our soul what good doed
to us I hope John McCallum
is well uncle malcom was with
us a night summer we did
not see John this many a years
see and be Good to yong John
dugald McDougall he will
be your frist help dear
John I see bell well of
with her mother along with
her hugh should look for a good
wife he will not be well
of he is lone I hope he has
warm bet close

Image db218

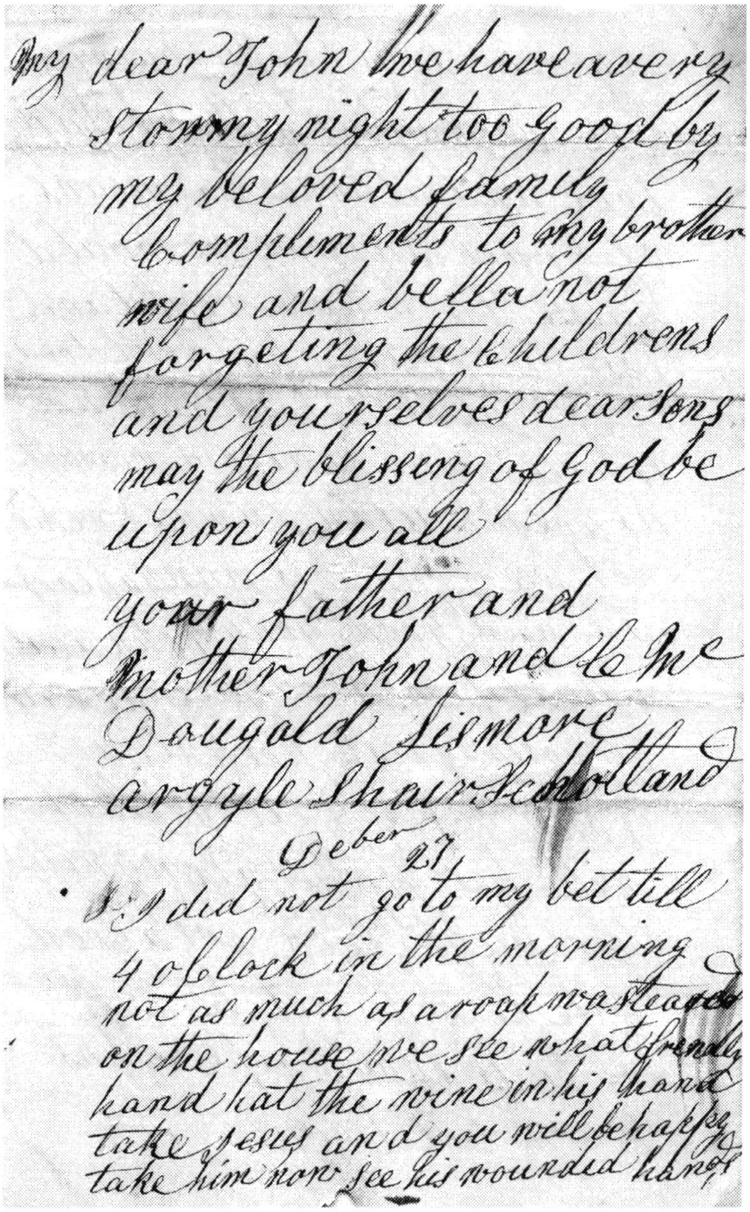
My dear John we have a very
stormy night too good by
my beloved family
compliments to my brother
wife and bella not
forgeting the childrens
and yourselves dear sons
may the blissing of God be
upon you all
your father and
mother John and C Mc
Dougald Lismore
argyle Shair Scotland
Deber 27
I did not go to my bet till
4 oclock in the morning
not as much as a roap was lead
on the house we see what frendly
hand hat the wine in his hand
take Jesus and you will be happy
take him now see his wounded hands

Image db219

LETTER FROM JOHN MCDOUGALL (b. 1803 Lismore) AND CATHERINE MCCALLUM MCDOUGALL (b. 1809 Lismore) WHO LIVED AT BALLIMACKILLICHAN, ISLE OF LISMORE TO JOHN AND HUGH MCDOUGALL DELHI, REDWOOD COUNTY, MINNESOTA USA

(date unknown)

(fragments of a letter)... my dear Sons I hope you will love one another with brotherly love and ataine the means of Grace Supose we would gaine the whole world and lose our souls what good doed to us I hope John McCallum is well uncle Malcom [Catherine McCallum's brother] was with us a night ... in Summer we did not see John this many a years See and be good to yong John dugald McDougall he will be your frist help dear John see bell [son John's wife Isabel McCallum MacDougall] well of with her Mother [Ann McCallum McCallum] along with her hugh should look for a good wife he will not be well of he is lone I hope he has warm bet Close [clothes] ...

My dear John we have a very Stormy night too Goodby my beloved family

Compliments to my brother wife and bella not forgetting the Childrens and yourselves dear Sons may the blissing of God be upon you all

Your father and Mother John and C McDougald Lismore Argyle Shair Scotland

Deber 27

I did not go to my bet till 4 oClock in the morning not as much of a roap was teared on the house [which had a thatched roof] we see what frendly hand hat the wine[vine?] in his hand take Jesus and you will be happy take him now see his wounded hands ...

Letter #22

March 22nd 1881

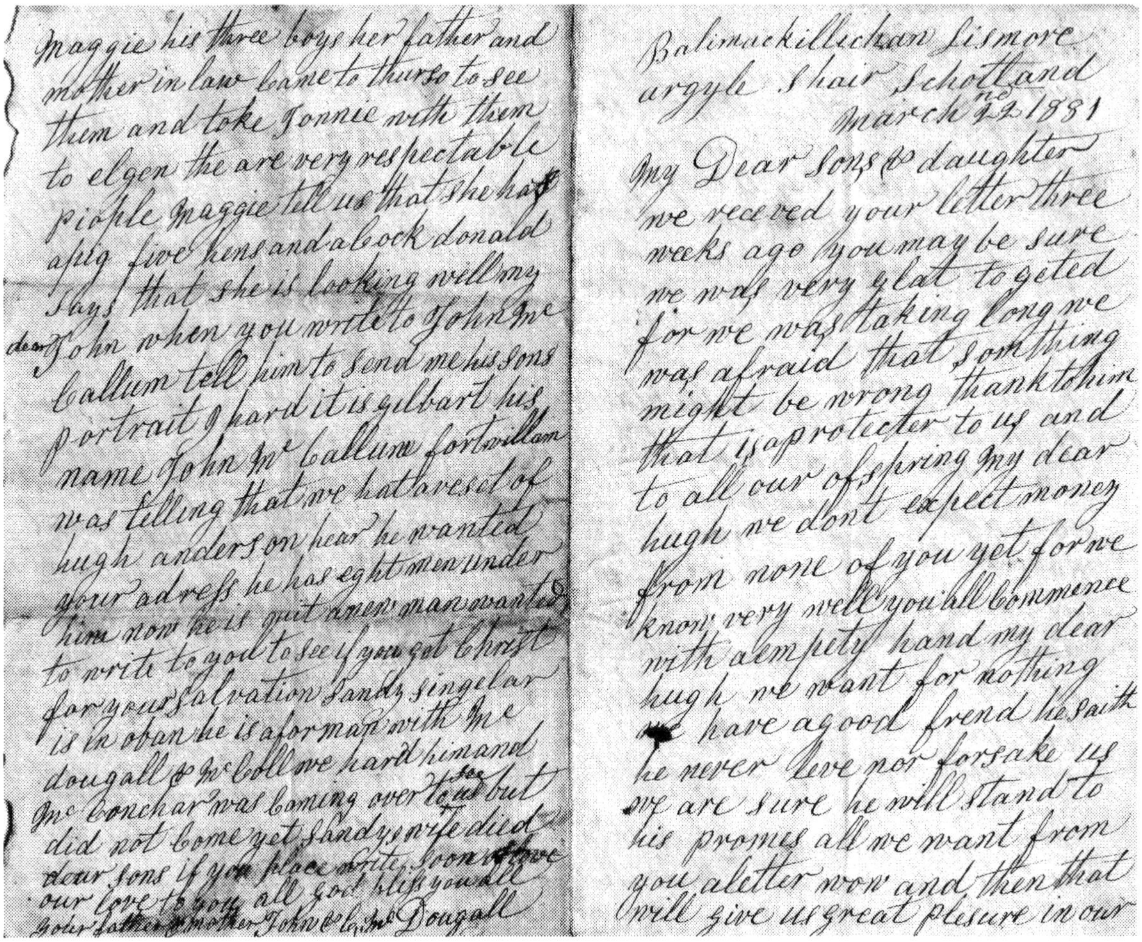

Balimackillichan Lismore
argyle Shair Schotland
March 22nd 1881
My Dear Sons & daughter
we receved your letter three
weeks ago you may be sure
we was very glat to geted
for we was taking long we
was afraid that somthing
might be wrong thank to him
that is a protecter to us and
to all our ofspring my dear
hugh we dont expect money
from none of you yet for we
know very well you'll commence
with a empety hand my dear
hugh we want for nothing
we have a good frend he saith
he never leve nor forsake us
we are sure he will stand to
his promes all we want from
you a letter now and then that
will give us great plesure in our

Maggie his three boys her father and
mother in law came to thurso to see
them and take Jonnie with them
to elgen the are very respectable
piople Maggie tell us that she has
a pig five hens and a cock donald
says that she is looking well my
dear John when you write to John Mc
Callum tell him to send me his sons
portrait I hard it is gilbart his
name John Mc Callum fortwilliam
was telling that we hat a resel of
hugh anderson hear he wanted
your adress he has eght men under
him now he is quit a new man wanted
to write to you to see if you got Christ
for your salvation Sandy singelar
is in oban he is a forman with Mc
dougall & Mc Coll we hard him and
Mc Conchar was coming over to see but
did not come yet Sandys wife died
dear sons if you please write soon we have
our love to you all God bliss you all
your father & mother John & [illegible] Mc Dougall

Image db181

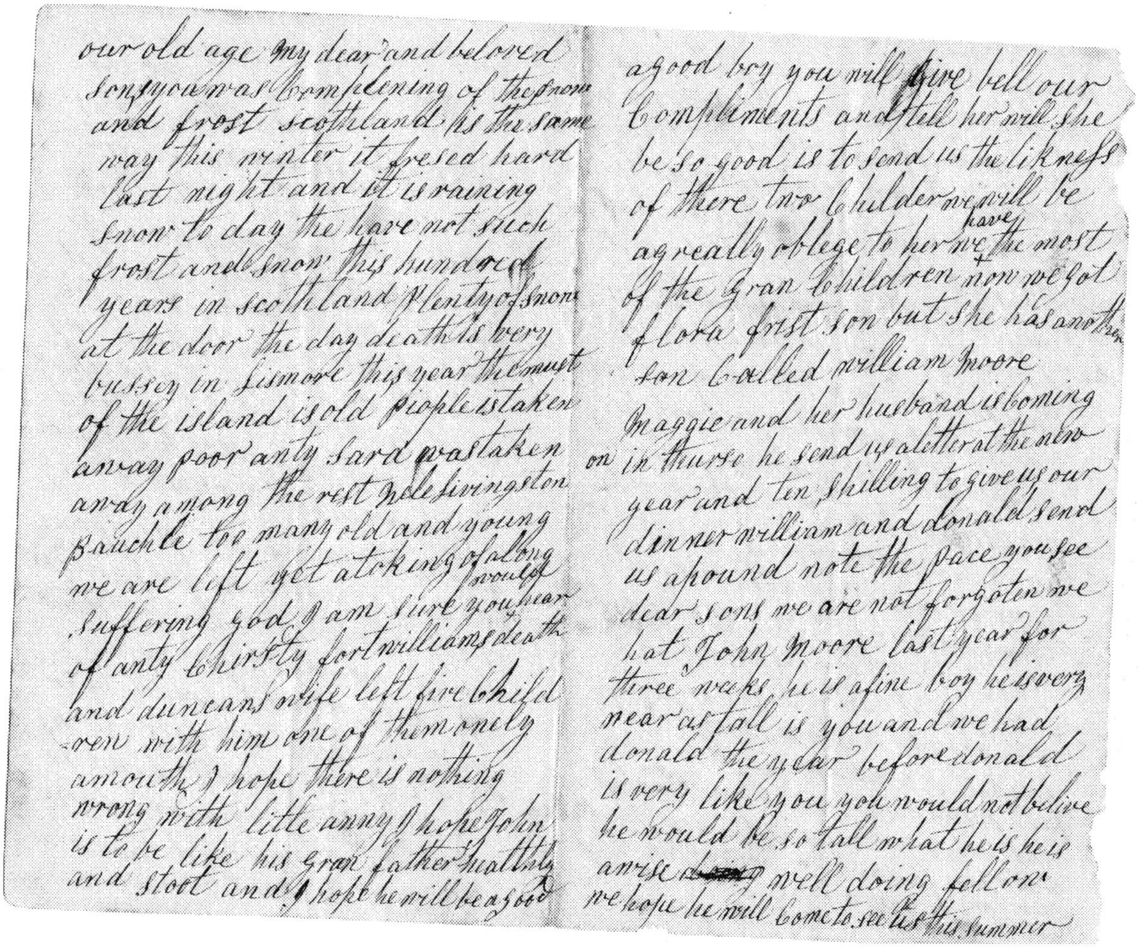
our old age my dear and beloved
sons you was complening of the snow
and frost scothland is the same
way this winter it fresed hard
last night and it is raining
snow to day the have not such
frost and snow this hundred
years in scothland plenty of snow
at the door the day death is very
bussey in lismore this year the must
of the island is old people is taken
away poor anty sara was taken
away among the rest nele livingston
bauchle too many old and young
we are left yet a toking of along
suffering god I am sure you would hear
of anty chirsty fort williams death
and duncans wife left five child
-ren with him one of them onely
a mouth I hope there is nothing
wrong with little anny I hope John
is to be like his gran father healthy
and stool and I hope he will be a good

a good boy you will give bell our
compliments and tell her will she
be so good is to send us the likness
of there two childer we will be
ag really oblege to her we have the most
of the gran children now we got
flora frist son but she has another
son called william moore
maggie and her husband is coming
on in thurso he send us a letter at the new
year and ten shilling to give us our
dinner william and donald send
us a pound note the pace you see
dear sons we are not forgoten we
hat John moore last year for
three weeks he is a fine boy he is very
near as tall is you and we had
donald the year before donald
is very like you you would not belive
he would be so tall what he is he is
a wise [illegible] well doing fellow
we hope he will come to see us this summer

Image db182

LETTER FROM JOHN MCDOUGALL (b. 1803 Lismore) AND CATHERINE MCCALLUM MCDOUGALL (b. 1809 Lismore) WHO LIVED AT BALLIMACKILLICHAN, ISLE OF LISMORE TO THEIR SONS JOHN MCDOUGALL (b. 1837) AND HUGH MCDOUGALL (b. 1842) LIVING IN THE USA

Balimackillichan Lismore
Argyle Shair Schotland
March 22nd 1881

My Dear Sons & daughter

we receved your letter three weeks ago you may be sure we was very glat to geted for we was taking long we was afraid that somthing might be wrong thank to him that is a protecter to us and to all our ofspring My dear hugh we dont expect money from none of you yet for we know very well you all Commence with a empety hand my dear hugh we want for nothing we have a good frend he saith he never leve nor forsake us we are sure he will stand to his promes all we want from you a letter now and then that will give us great plesure in our our old age My dear and beloved sons you was Complening of the snow and frost Scothland is the same way this winter it fresed hard last night and it is raining snow to day the have not such frost and snow this hundred years in Scothland Plenty of snow at the door the day death is very bussey in Lismore this year the must of the island is old piople is taken away poor anty Sara [Black?] was taken away among the rest Nele Livingston Bauchle too many old and young we are left yet a toking of a long suffering god I am sure you would hear of anty Chirsty [Black?] fort williams death and duncans wife left five Children with him one of them onely amouth[a month?] I hope there is nothing wrong with little anny I hope John is to be like his gran father healthly and stoot and I hope he will be a good boy a good boy you will give bell our Compliments and tell her will she be so good is to send us the likness of there two Childer we will be agreatly oblege to her we have the most of the gran Children now we got flora frist son but she has another son Called william Moore

Maggie and her husband is Coming on in Thurso he send us a letter at the new year and ten shilling to give us our dinner william and donald send us a pound note the pace you see dear sons we are not forgoten we hat John Moore last year for three weeks he is a fine boy he is very near as tall is you and we had donald the year before donald is very like you you would not belive he would be so tall what he is he is a wise well doing fellow we hope he will come to see us this summer

Maggie his three boys her father and mother in law Came to thurso to see them and take Jonnie with them to elgen the are very respectable piople Maggie tell us that she has a pig five hens and a Cock donald says that she is looking well my dear John when you write to John McCallum tell him to send me his sons portrait I hard it is gelbart his name John McCallum fort william was telling that we hat a veset of hugh anderson hear he wanted your adress he has eght men under him now he is quit anew man wanted to write to you to see if you got Christ for your salvation Sandy Singelar [Sinclair?] is in oban he is a forman not Come yet Sandys wife died dear Sons if you place write soon

our love to you all god bliss you all   Your father and mother John & C. McDougall

Plate 22.1. Anna MacDougall (b. 1879) (standing) and her Mother, Isabel (Bella) McCallum McDougall

Plate 22.2. Photo Back

This photograph was probably taken before Anna's marriage, which occurred in 1916. (Stark, 2014f)

Plate 22.3. Gustave (Gus) and Anna MacDougall Aufderheide
Their Wedding Photo, 1916

Plate 22.4. Gravestone of Anna MacDougall Aufderheide (b. 1879)
Redwood Falls Cemetery, Redwood Falls, Minnesota

Anna was the daughter of John McDougall and Isabel McCallum McDougall. She married Gustave (Gus) Aufderheide and had five children:

- Isabel Aufderheide
- Wilma Aufderheide
- Jean Aufderheide Stark
- Ernie Aufderheide
- John MacDougall Aufderheide

Plate 22.5. Members of the MacDougall, Aufderheide and McCallum Families Redwood Falls, Minnesota, July 1953

Front row (kneeling, from left to right):
Mary MacDougall Brown, Florence (Floss) McCallum Aufderheide (in white dress), Wilma (Billie) Aufderheide, Gilbert (Gil) McCallum (in white shirt)

Second row (standing, from left to right)
Morris L. McCallum; Isabel (Issy) Aufderheide (in white hat, glasses); possibly Ott McCallum, son of Les McCallum and grandson of John McCallum (Ortonville, b. 1847); Isabel McCallum (in dark dress); Marlese Briese Aufderheide or Isabel MacDougall Board (in white top), Ernest (Ernie) L. Aufderheide; Edith Bollum MacDougall (wife of Gilbert MacDougall); Gustave (Gus) Aufderheide; Gilbert (Gib) MacDougall (b. 1881, son of John McDougall & Isabel McCallum McDougall, brother of Anna MacDougall Aufderheide)

Notes:

1. According to Jean Aufderheide Stark, "Anna MacDougall Aufderheide [her mother] (wife of Gus) died when her youngest child, John MacDougall Aufderheide, was two years old. Anna's brother William (Bill) and his wife Maude Osborne MacDougall ('Auntie Bill') came to help at the Aufderheide home and were with the family for five years at which time Floss and Gus were married" (Stark, 2013).

2. In this letter, John McDougall (weaver) and Catherine McCallum ask their sons to have John McCallum "send me his sons portrait I hard it is gelbart his name". Jean Aufderheide Stark explains, "Gilbert McCallum of Ortonville born in 1878 was the oldest child of John [McCallum, Ortonville, Minnesota] and Mary [Secrest]. His nickname was Gil, and I'm sure he was named for his grandfather [Gilbert McCallum, b. 1813 Balure] who died before my grandmother [Isabel McCallum McDougall] was born" (Stark, 2014d). Gilbert (Gil) McCallum appears in the front row of Plate 22.5, above.

Letter **#23**

December 6th 1881

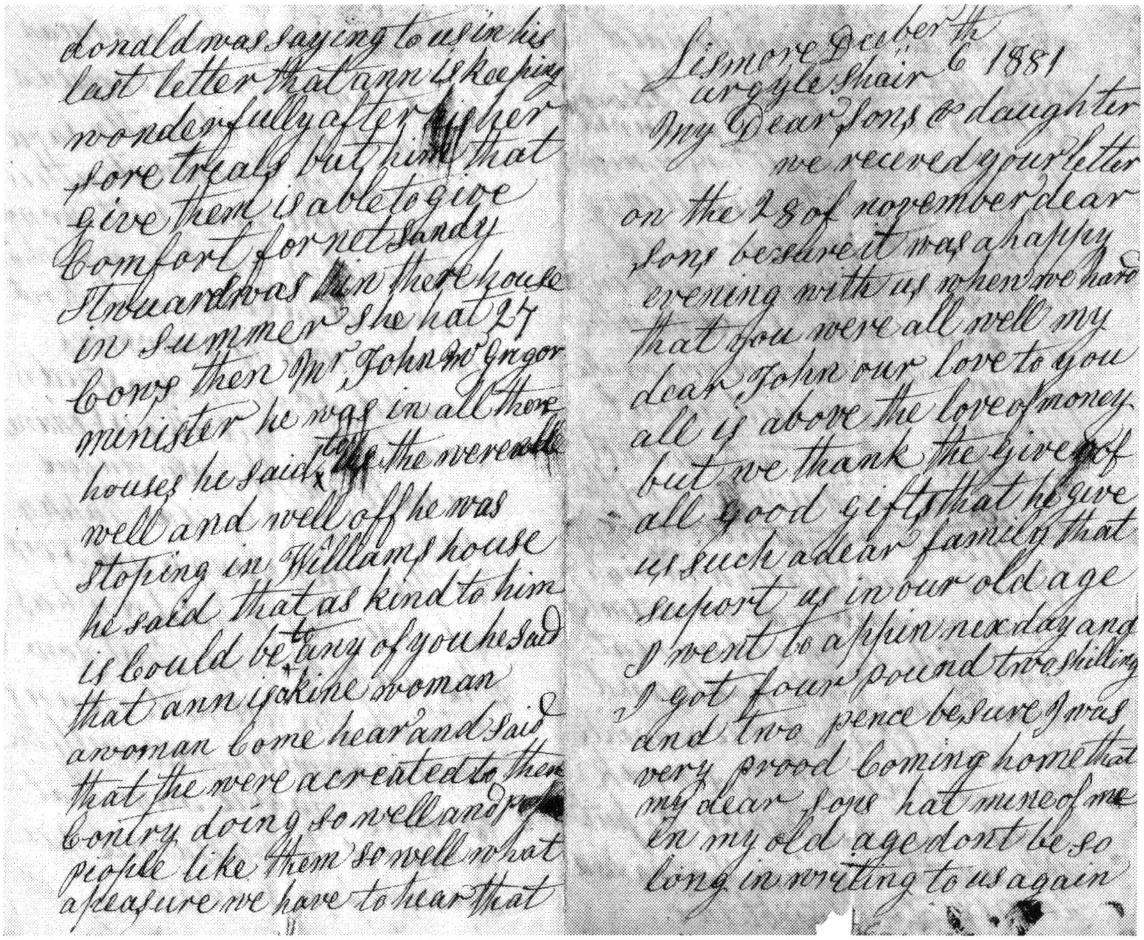

donald was saying to us in his
last letter that ann is keeping
wonderfully after her
sore treals but him that
give them is able to give
Comfort for net Sandy
Stewart was in there house
in Summer she hat 27
Cows then Mr John McGregor
minister he was in all there
houses he said the were all
well and well off he was
stoping in Williams house
he said that as kind to him
is could be to any of you he said
that ann is a kine woman
a woman Come hear and said
that the were acreated to them
contry doing so well and
people like them so well what
a pleasure we have to hear that

Lismore Decber 6th
argyle shair 6 1881
My Dear Sons & daughter
we receved your letter
on the 28 of november dear
sons be sure it was a happy
evening with us when we hard
that you were all well my
dear John our love to you
all is above the love of money
but we thank the giver of
all good gifts that he give
us such a dear famaly that
suport us in our old age
I went to appin nex day and
I got four pound two shilling
and two pence be sure I was
very prood Coming home that
my dear sons hat mind of me
in my old age dont be so
long in writing to us again

Image db184

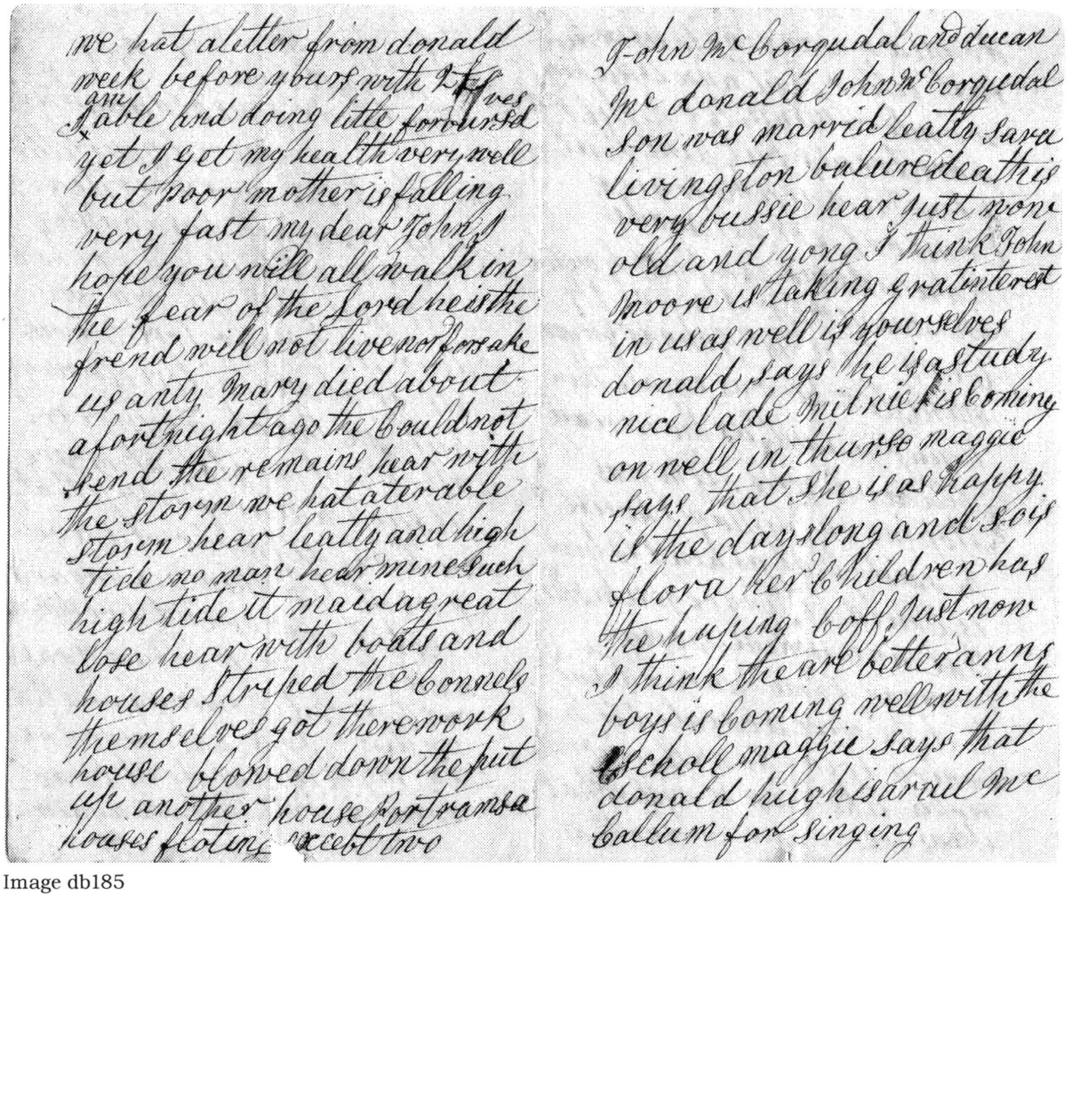
we hat aletter from donald
week before yours with 2 £
am
I able and doing litte for ourselves
yet I get my health very well
but poor mother is falling
very fast my dear John I
hope you will all walk in
the fear of the Lord he is the
frend will not live nor forsake
us anty Mary died about
a fortnight ago the could not
send the remains hear with
the storm we hat a terable
storm hear leatly and high
tide no man hear mine such
high tide it maid a great
lose hear with boats and
houses striped the connels
themselves got there work
house blowed down the put
up another house for transa
houses floting [illegible] xcebt two

John Mc Corqudal and ducan
Mc donald John Mc Corqudal
son was married leatly Sara
livingston balure death is
very bussie hear just now
old and yong I think John
moore is taking grat interest
in us as well is yourselves
donald says he is a study
nice lade milnie is coming
on well in thurso maggie
says that she is as happy
is the days long and soys
flora her children has
the huping coff just now
I think the are better anns
boys is coming well with the
scholl maggie says that
donald hugh is a raul Mc
callum for singing

Image db185

LETTER FROM JOHN MCDOUGALL (b. 1803 Lismore) AND CATHERINE MCCALLUM MCDOUGALL (b. 1809 Lismore) WHO LIVED AT BALLIMACKILLICHAN, ISLE OF LISMORE TO THEIR SONS JOHN MCDOUGALL (b. 1837) AND HUGH MCDOUGALL (b. 1842) LIVING IN THE USA

Lismore

Argyle Shair

Dceber 6th 1881

My Dear Sons & daughter

we receved your letter on the 28 of november dear Sons be sure it was a happy evening with us when we hard that you were all well my dear John our love to you all is above the love of money but we thank the giver of all good gifts that he give us such a dear family that suport us in our old age I went to appin nex day and I got four pound two shilling and two pence be sure I was very prood Coming home that my dear sons hat mine of me in my old age dont be so long in writing to us again

we hat a letter from Donald week before yours with 2£

I am able and doing little for ourselves yet I get my health very well but poor mother is falling very fast my dear John I hope you will all walk in the fear of the Lord he is the frend will not live nor forsake us anty Mary died about a fortnight ago the Could not send the remains hear with the storm we hat a terable storm hear leatly [lately] and high tide no man hear mine such high tide it maid a great lose hear with boats and houses Striped the Connels themselves got there work house blowed down the put up another house Portramsa [Port Ramsay] houses floting excebt two

John McCorqudal and ducan Mcdonald John McCorqudal son was marrid leatly sara livingstone balure death is very bussie hear just now old and yong I think John Moore is taking grat interest in us as well is yourselves

donald says he is a study nice lade Milnie is Coming on well in thurso maggie says that she is as happy is the days long and so is flora her children has the huping coff Just now I think the are better anns [Agnes'] boys is coming well with the scholl maggie says that donald hugh is a rail [real] McCallum for singing

donald was saying to us in his last letter that ann [Agnes] is keeping wonderfully after her sore trials but him that give them is able to give Comfort fornet Sandy Stwuard [Stewart?] was in there house in summer She hat 27 cows then Mr john McGrigor minister he was in all there houses he said to the were all well and well off he was stoping in Williams house he said that as kind to him is Could be to any of you he said that ann [Agnes] is a kine woman a woman Come hear and said that the were a created [credit?] to there Contry doing so well and piople like them so well what a peasure [pleasure?] we have to hear that

(rest of letter missing)

Note: "Mr john McGrigor minister" would have been John MacNab MacGregor. His father, Rev. Gregor MacGregor, was parish minister of Lismore from 1836 – 1885. Rev. John MacGregor served as his father's assistant and intended successor from December 27, 1876 – March 31, 1881, when he transferred to the Parish of Farr. (Scott, 1923, p. 100) Farr is located in the Highland region on the north coast of Scotland about 30 miles from Thurso. (NRS, undated) He would have been able to visit the McDougall children in Thurso from there.

***The Oban Times*, October 14, 1876**

LISMORE – CALL – The congregation of Lismore, at a meeting held in the Parish Church on the 4th inst., unanimously elected Mr John M. McGregor, present minister of the Parish of Skipness, to be assistant and successor to his father, the Rev. Gregor McGregor, Lismore. (The Oban Times, October 14, 1876, p. 4)

By permission, *The Oban Times*

Letter #24

December 31, 1881

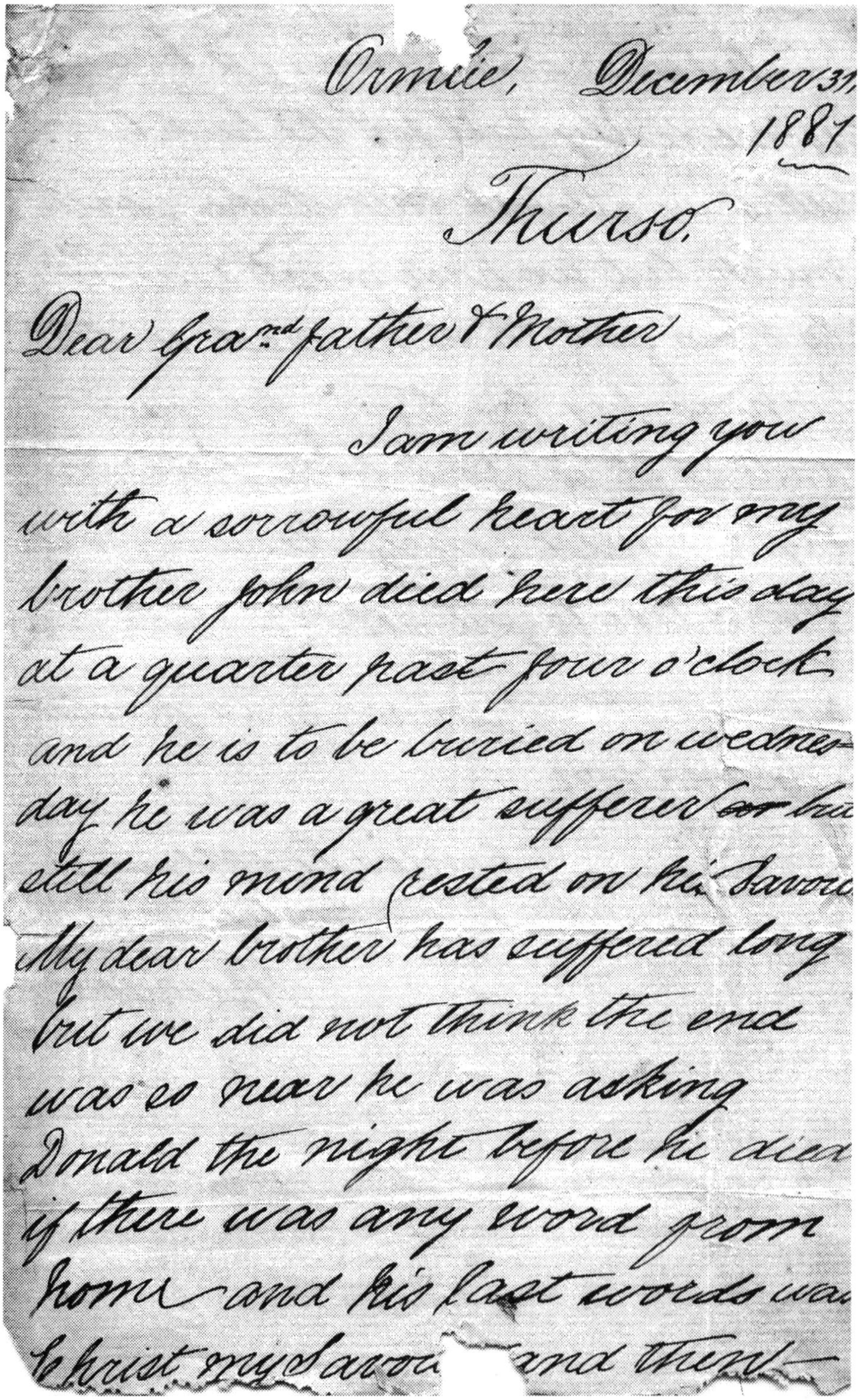

Ormlie, December 31
1881
Thurso.

Dear Grand father & Mother

I am writing you with a sorrowful heart for my brother john died here this day at a quarter past four o'clock and he is to be buried on wednesday he was a great sufferer ~~or~~ but still his mind rested on his Savour My dear brother has suffered long but we did not think the end was so near he was asking Donald the night before he died if there was any word from home and his last words was Christ my Savou and then

Image db178

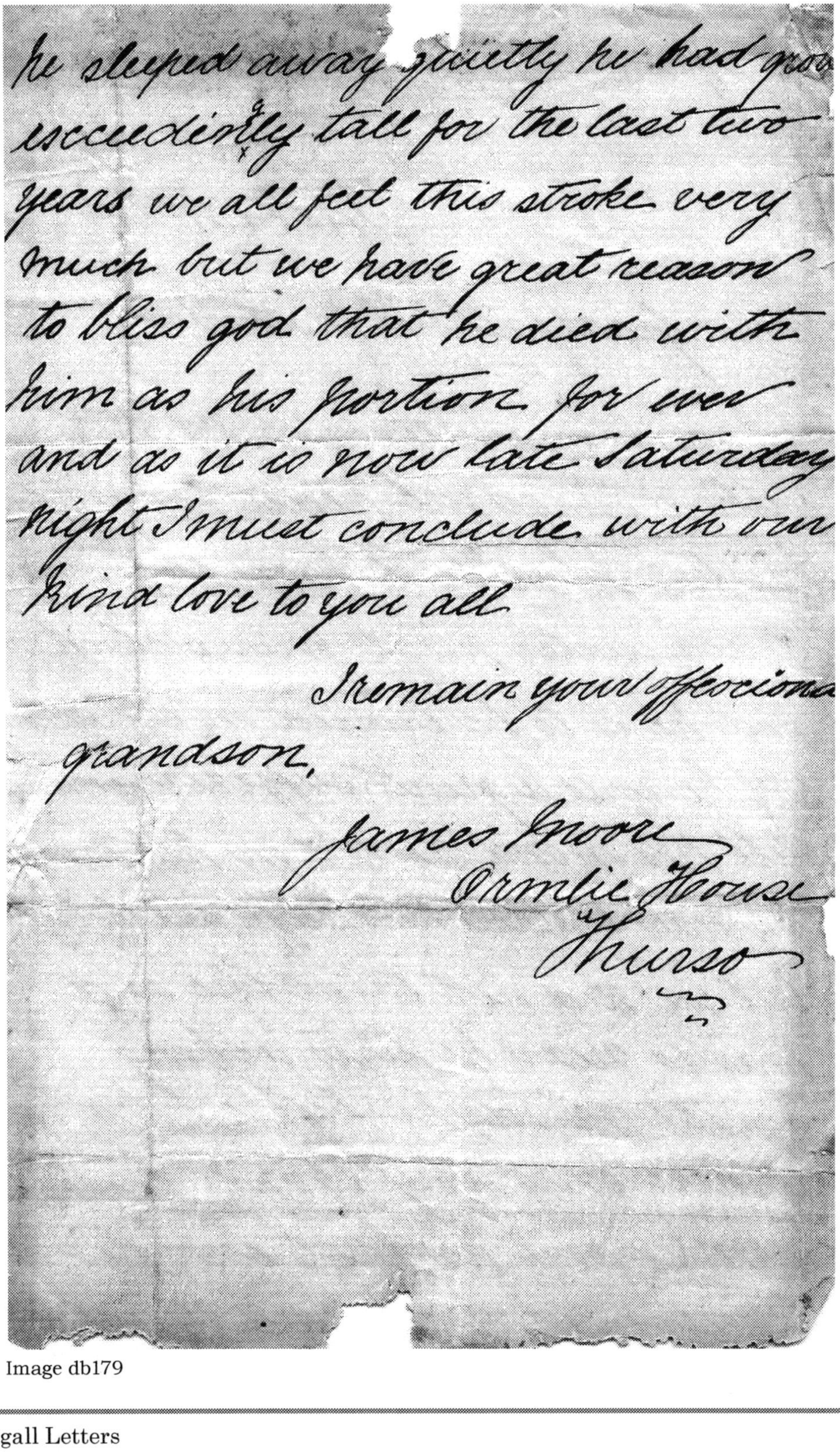

he sleeped away quietly he had grow
exceedingly tall for the last two
years we all feel this stroke very
much but we have great reason
to bliss god that he died with
him as his portion for ever
and as it is now late Saturday
night I must conclude with our
kind love to you all

I remain your affeccional
grandson,

James Moore
Ormlie House
Thurso

Image db179

LETTER TO JOHN MCDOUGALL (b. 1803 Lismore) AND CATHERINE MCCALLUM MCDOUGALL (b. 1809 Lismore) WHO LIVED AT BALLIMACKILLICHAN, ISLE OF LISMORE FROM THEIR GRANDSON JAMES MOORE (b. 1868 Thurso)

Ormlie, December 31, 1881
Thurso.

Dear Grandfather & Mother

I am writing you with a sorrowful heart for my brother John [Moore, b. 1858 died at age 23] died here this day at a quarter past four o'clock and he is to be buried on wednesday he was a great sufferer but still his mind rested on his Savior My dear brother has suffered long but we did not think the end was so near he was asking Donald the night before he died if there was any word from home and his last words was Christ my Savior and then he sleeped away quietly he had grown exceedingly tall for the last two years we all feel this stroke very much but we have great reason to bliss god that he died with him as his portion for ever and as it is now late Saturday night I must conclude with our kind love to you all

I remain your offeociona [affectionate] grandson,
James Moore
Ormlie House
Thurso

Letter **#25**

January 10th 1882

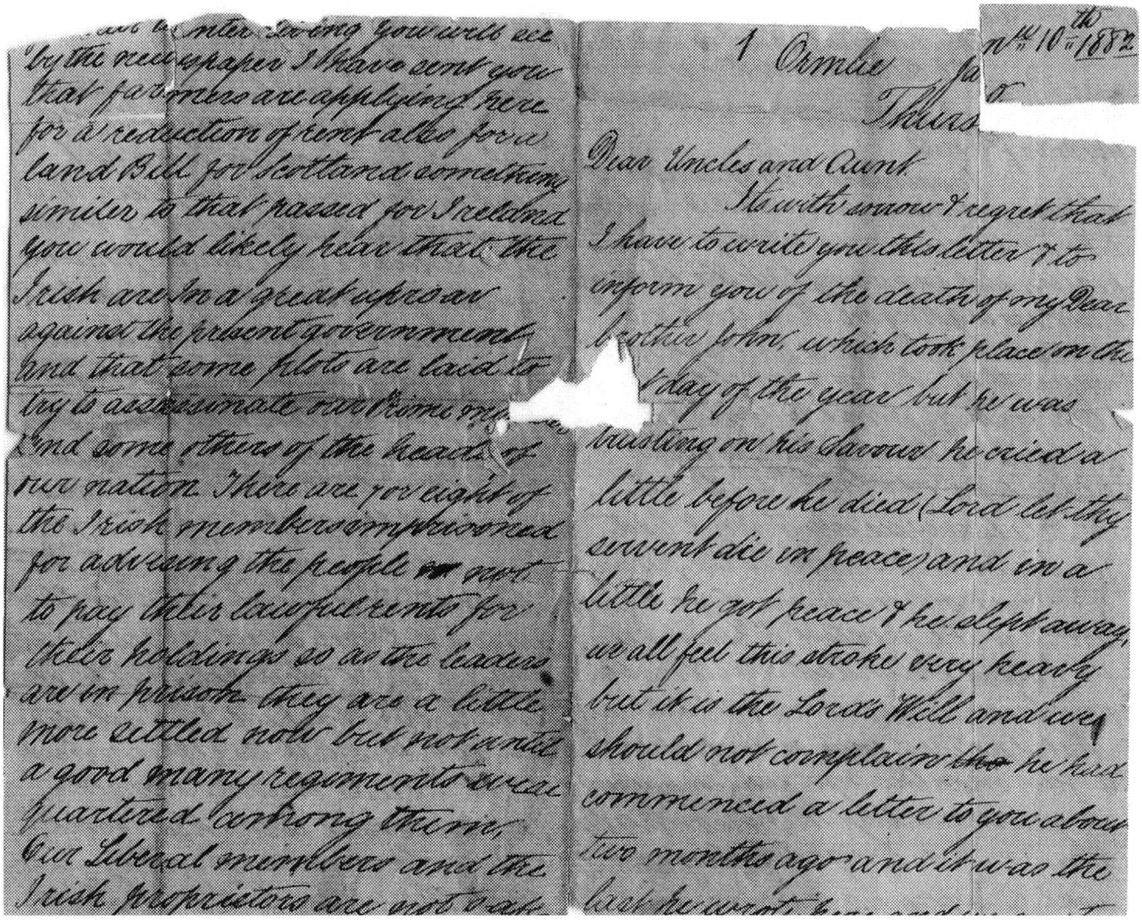

1 Ormlie Jan 10th 1882
Thurso

Dear Uncles and Aunt

Its with sorrow & regret that I have to write you this letter & to inform you of the death of my Dear brother John which took place on the [illegible] day of the year but he was trusting on his Saviour he cried a little before he died (Lord let thy servant die in peace) and in a little he got peace & he slept away we all feel this stroke very heavy but it is the Lords Will and we should not complain the he had commenced a letter to you about two months ago and it was the last he wrote [illegible]

[illegible] winter coming you will see by the newspaper I have sent you that farmers are applying here for a reduction of rent also for a land Bill for Scotland something similar to that passed for Ireland you would likely hear that the Irish are in a great uproar against the present government and that some plots are laid to try to assassinate our Prime min[illegible] and some others of the heads of our nation. There are [illegible] eight of the Irish members imprisoned for advising the people ~~or~~ not to pay their lawful rents for their holdings so as the leaders are in prison they are a little more settled now but not until a good many regiments were quartered among them, our Liberal members and the Irish proprietors are not [illegible]

Image db190

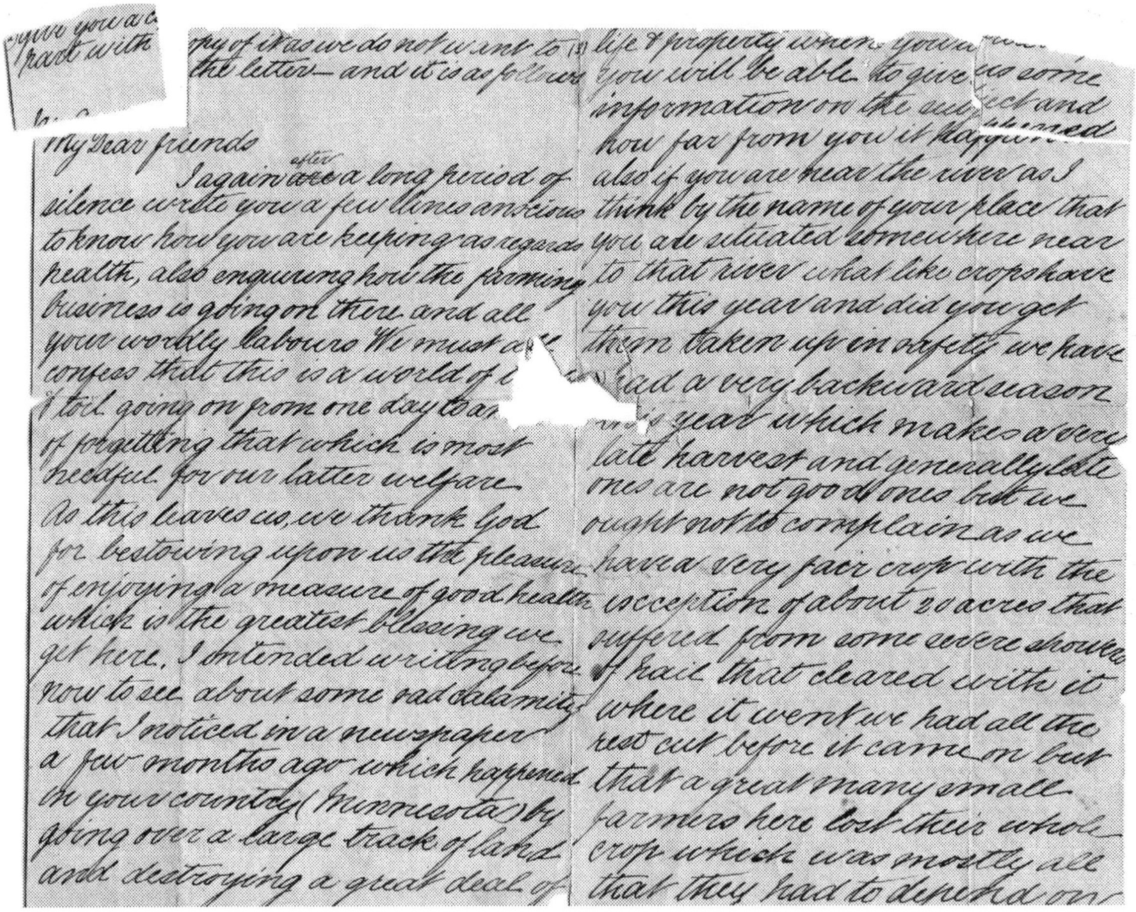

[illegible] your you a[illegible]
[illegible] with [illegible]py of it as we do not want to [illegible]
the letter— and it is as follows

My Dear friends

I again after a long period of silence write you a few lines anxious to know how you are keeping as regards health, also enquiring how the farming business is going on there and all your worldly labours We must all confess that this is a world of [illegible] & toil going on from one day to an[illegible] of forgetting that which is most needful for our latter welfare

As this leaves us, we thank God for bestowing upon us the pleasure of enjoying a measure of good health which is the greatest blessing we get here. I intended writing before now to see about some sad calamity that I noticed in a newspaper a few months ago which happened in your country (Minnesota) by going over a large track of land and destroying a great deal of life & property where you [illegible] you will be able to give us some information on the subject and how far from you it happened also if you are near the river as I think by the name of your place that you are situated somewhere near to that river what like crops have you this year and did you get them taken up in safety we have had a very backward season this year which makes a very late harvest and generally late ones are not good ones but we ought not to complain as we have a very fair crop with the exception of about 20 acres that suffered from some severe shower of hail that cleared with it where it went we had all the rest cut before it came on but that a great many small farmers here lost their whole crop which was mostly all that they had to depend on

Image db191

LETTER TO JOHN MCDOUGALL (b. 1803 Lismore) FROM NEPHEW JAMES MOORE (son of Agnes McDougall Moore, b. 1868 Thurso)

1 Ormlie

Janu 10th 1882

Thurso

Dear Uncles and Aunt.

Its with sorrow & regret that I have to write you this letter & to inform you of the death of my Dear brother John, which took place on the last day of the year but he was trusting on his Savour he cried a little before he died (Lord let thy servent die in peace) and in a little he got peace & he slept away, we all feel this stroke very heavy but it is the Lord's Will and we should not complain he had commenced a letter to you about two months ago and it was the last he wrote here and we are to give you a copy of it as we do not want to part with the letter – and it is as follows

My Dear friends [written by John Moore written before his death December 31, 1881]

I again after a long period of silence write you a few lines anxious to know how you are keeping as regards health, also enquiring how the farming business is going on there and all your wordly labours We must all confess that this is a world of ... & toil going on from one day to an... of forgetting that which is most needful for our latter welfare As this leaves us, we thank God for bestowing upon us the pleasure of enjoying a measure of good health which is the greatest blessing we get here. I intended writing before now to see about some sad calamity that I noticed in a newspaper a few months ago which happened in your country (Minnesota) by going over a large track of land and destroying a great deal of life & property when you write you will be able to give us some information on the subject and how far from you it happened also if you are near the river as I think by the name of your place that you are situated somewhere near to that river what like crops have you this year and did you get them taken up in safety we have had a very backward season this year which makes a very late harvest and generally late ones are not good ones but we ought not to complain as we have a very fair crop with the exception of about 20 acres that suffered from some severe showers of hail that cleared with it where it went we had all the rest cut before it came on but that a great many small farmers here lost their whole crop which was mostly all that they had to depend on

... you will see by the newspaper I have sent you that farmers are applying here for a reduction of rent also for a land Bill for Scotland something similer to that passed for Ireland you would likely hear that the Irish are in a great uproar against the present government and that some plots are laid to try to assassinate our Prime Minister and some others of the heads of our nation. There are 7 or eight of the Irish members imprisoned for advising the people not to pay their lawful rents for their holdings so as the leaders are in prison they are a little more settled now but not until a good many regiments were quartered among them, Our Liberal members and the Irish proprietors are not safe.

(rest of letter missing)

Letter **#26**

January 24th 1882

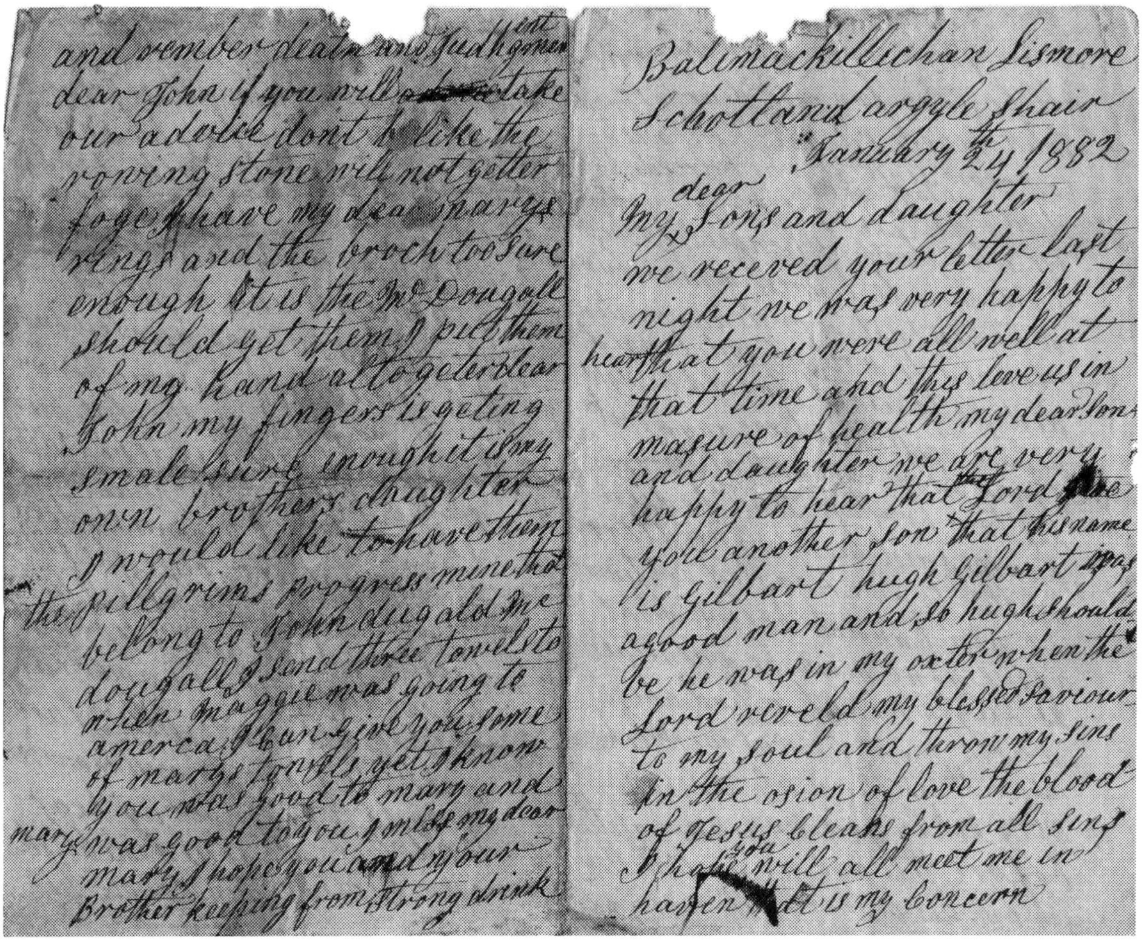

Balimackillichan Lismore
Schottand argyle Shair
January 24th 1882
My dear Sons and daughter
we receved your letter last
night we was very happy to
hear that you were all well at
that time and this leve us in
masure of health my dear Sons
and daughter we are very
happy to hear that Lord give
you another son that his name
is Gilbart hugh Gilbart was
a good man and so hugh should
be he was in my oxter when the
Lord reveld my blessed saviour
to my soul and throw my sins
in the osion of love the blood
of Jesus cleans from all sins
I hope you will all meet me in
haven that is my concern

and remember death and Judgment
dear John if you will take
our advice dont be like the
roving stone will not gether
foge I have my dear marys
rings and the broch too sure
enough it is the McDougall
should get them I put them
of my hand altogether dear
John my fingers is geting
smale sure enought it is my
own brothers daughter
I would like to have them
the pillgrims progress mine that
belong to John dugald Mc
dougall I send three towels to
when maggie was going to
america I can give you some
of marys towels yet I know
you was good to mary and
mary was good to you I miss my dear
mary I hope you and your
Brother keeping from strong drink

Image db187

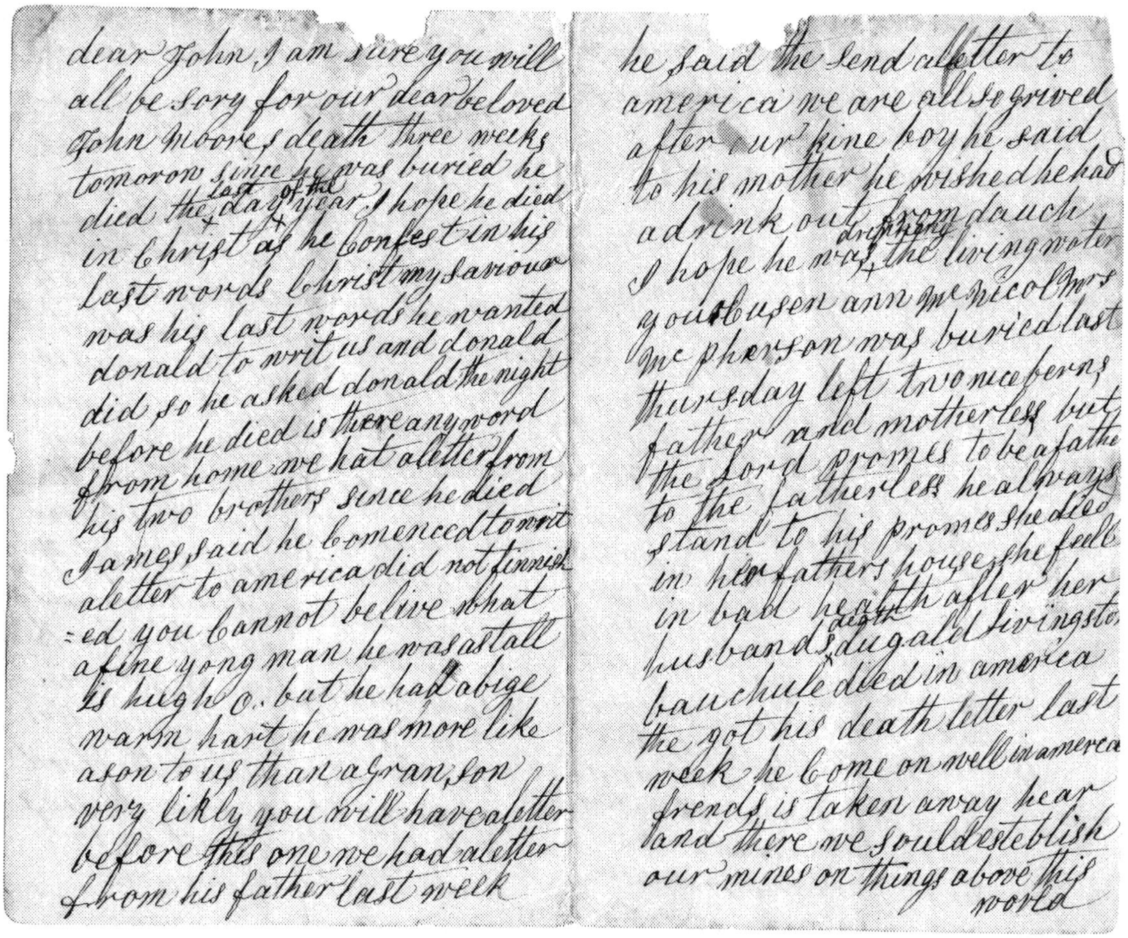

dear John, I am sure you will
all be sory for our dear beloved
John Moore's death three weeks
tomorow since he was buried he
died the last day of the year. I hope he died
in Christ as he confest in his
last words Christ my saviour
was his last words he wanted
donald to writ us and donald
did so he asked donald the night
before he died is there any word
from home we hat a letter from
his two brothers since he died
James said he comenced to writ
a letter to america did not finnish
=ed you cannot belive what
a fine yong man he was as tall
is hugh O.. but he had a bige
warm hart he was more like
a son to us than a gran son
very likly you will have a letter
before this one we had a letter
from his father last week

he said the send a letter to
america we are all so grived
after our fine boy he said
to his mother he wished he had
a drink out from dauch
I hope he was drinking the living water
your cusen ann mcnicol mrs
mc pherson was buried last
thursday left two nice berns
father and motherless but
the Lord promes to be a father
to the fatherless he always
stand to his promes she died
in her fathers house she fell
in bad health after her
husbands death dugald livingston
bauchule died in america
the got his death letter last
week he come on well in america
frends is taken away hear
and there we sould esteblish
our mines on things above this
world

Image db188

LETTER FROM JOHN MCDOUGALL (b. 1803 Lismore) AND CATHERINE MCCALLUM MCDOUGALL (b. 1809 Lismore) WHO LIVED AT BALLIMACKILLICHAN, ISLE OF LISMORE TO JOHN MCDOUGALL (b. 1837 Lismore) AND HUGH MCDOUGALL (b. 1842 Lismore) MINNESOTA

Balimackillichan
Lismore

Schotland argyle Shair

January 24th 1882

My dear Sons & daughter

we receved your letter last night we was very happy to hear that you were all well at that time and this leve us in masure of health my dear Son and daughter we are very happy to hear that the Lord give you another son that his name is Gilbart hugh Gilbart was a good man and so hugh should be he was in my oxter [armpit] when the Lord reveld my blessed Saviour to my soul and throw my sins in the osion [ocean] of love the blood of Jesus cleans from all sins I hope you will all meet me in haven that is my Concern

dear John I am sure you will all be sory for our dear beloved John Moores death three weeks tomorow since he was buried he died the last day of the year I hope he died in Christ as he Confest in his last words Christ my Saviour was his last words he wanted donald to writ us and donald did so he asked donald the night before he died is there any word from home we hat a letter from his two brothers since he died James said he Comenced to writ a letter to america did not finnished you Cannot belive what a fine yong man he was as tall is hugh o.. but he had a bige warm hart he was more like a son to us than a gran son very likly you will have a letter before this one we had a letter from his father last week he said the send a letter to america we are all so grived after our kine boy he said to his mother [Ann, Agnes] he wished he had a drink out from dauch I hope he was drinking the living water your Cusen ann McNicol Mrs McPerson was buried last thursday left two nice berns [bairns] father and motherless but the Lord promes to be a father to the fatherless he always stand to his promes she died in her fathers house she feell in bad health after her husbands death dugald livingston bauchule died in america the got his death letter last week he Come on well in amerca frends is taken away hear and there we sould esteblish our mines on things above this world

and rember death and Judghment dear John if you will take our advice dont be like the rowing stone will not getter foge [moss] I have my dear marys rings and the broch too sure enough it is the McDougall should get them I put them of my hand altogeter dear John my fingers is geting smale sure enough it is my own brothers daughter I would like to have them the pillgrims progress mine that belong to John dugald Mcdougall I send three towels to when Maggie was going to amerca I can give you some of marys towels yet I know you was good to mary and mary was good to you I miss my dear Mary I hope you and your Brother keeping from strong drink (rest of letter missing)

Note 1: The following summarizes the relationship between Catherine McCallum (b. 1809) and her niece, Isabel McCallum McDougall (b. 1850), wife of Catherine's son, John McDougall (b. 1837).

John McDougall (weaver) and Catherine McCallum (b. 1809 Balure) had eight children, including a son, John McDougall (b. 1837).

Catherine had several siblings, including a brother, Gilbert, who was born in 1813 (Balure). Gilbert married Ann McCallum (b. 1814 Lismore), daughter of Duncan McCallum and Isabella McColl.

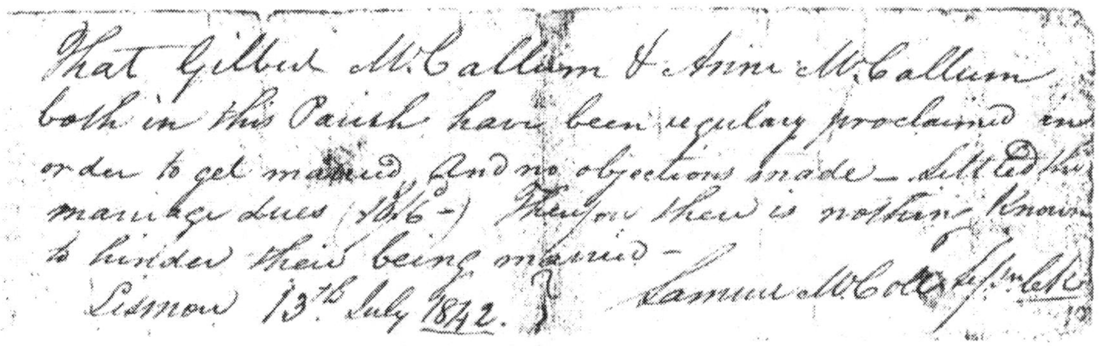
That Gilbert McCallum & Anne McCallum
both in this Parish have been regulary proclaimed in
order to get married, And no objections made — Settled the
marriage dues (1/6 -) Therefore there is nothing known
to hinder their being married —
Lismore 13th July 1842. Samuel McColl Sess. Clerk

Plate 26.1. Marriage Banns for Gilbert McCallum (b. 1813)
and Ann McCallum (b. 1814)
Lismore, 13th July 1842

Gilbert and Ann had two children, John McCallum (b. 1847) and Isabel McCallum (b. 1850.) Gilbert died in December 1849, a few weeks before Isabel's birth (March 1850). (Aburn, 2013a)

Ann migrated with her young children to the United States in 1855. She initially settled in New York, then migrated to Minnesota with her son, John McCallum and daughter, Isabel. Family research indicates the 1870 census shows them in Cottage Grove, Minnesota. (Aburn, 2013a)

The younger John McDougall (b. 1837) migrated to the United States in 1872, first to New York. (Aburn, 2000; Inglis, undated) Family notes indicate he moved to Cottage Grove, Minnesota between June 1873 and April 1874 where his aunt, Ann McCallum, and her two children, John and Isabel McCallum, had moved. (Inglis, undated) A brief item in *The Redwood Gazette* suggests the younger John McDougall married Ann's daughter, his cousin, Isabel McCallum, in January 1877. (The R*edwood Gazette,* Thursday, February 1, 1877, Local News) In their letter of August 18, 1877, his parents mention their relief at news of his marriage. See, also, editor's notes for Letter #30, a fragment of about 1884.

Note 2: Gilbert Hugh MacDougall, son of John McDougall and Isabel McCallum, was born in 1881 in Delhi, Minnesota.

Note 3: The word oxter means armpit (Scots, Northern English).

Note 4: "Gilbart was a good man," might refer to Gilbert McCallum (b. 1813 Balure), deceased husband of Ann McCallum, the father of Isabel McCallum McDougall, and the brother of Catherine McCallum.

Note 5: The following reference to "hugh" is unclear: "[A]nd so hugh should be he was in my oxter [armpit] when the Lord reveld my blessed Saviour to my soul." John McDougall (weaver) had a brother, Hugh McDougall (b. 1808). (NRS, pre-1855a)

Note 6: Foge means "Grass left in the field during winter; moss." (*Dictionary of the Scots Language* (2004), DSL foge, n.URL: http://www/dsl/ac.uk/dsl/.)

Note 7: The following reference to "Mary" is unclear: "I miss my dear Mary." The second child of John McDougall (weaver) and Catherine McCallum, Mary, died June 18, 1874. (See memorial stone and inscription from the Lismore Parish Church graveyard immediately following letter of July 27, 1888, below.) However, the letter of December 31, 1883, indicates that a Mary McCallum died "two years ago", about the time of this letter.

Note 8: The following might mean Catherine McCallum wants her niece and daughter-in-law, Isabel McCallum, to have the certain items. "I have my dear marys rings and the broch too sure enough it is the McDougall should get them ... it is my own brothers daughter I would like to have them."

Plate 26.2. Children of John McDougall and Isabel (Bell) McCallum McDougall About 1886

Front Row: Gilbert (Gib) (standing on left), William (Bill), Donald, Anna
John Dougald is standing in back.

Plate 26.3. Children of John McDougall (b. 1837) and Isabel (Bell) McCallum McDougall
(back, left to right) Gilbert (Gib), William (Bill);
(front, left to right) Donald, Anna, John

Plate 26.4. Gilbert Hugh (Gib) MacDougall (b. 1881) (in dark jacket on left) with his Cousin, Dougald Milne Tiffany (b. 1885)
Redwood Falls, Minnesota
1971

Plate 26.5. Children of Gilbert (Gib) MacDougall and Dougald Milne Tiffany
(left to right) John Milne Tiffany, Isabel MacDougall Board, D. William Tiffany,
Ruth MacDougall McCartin, John MacDougall
First Presbyterian Church
Redwood Falls, Minnesota
June 2008

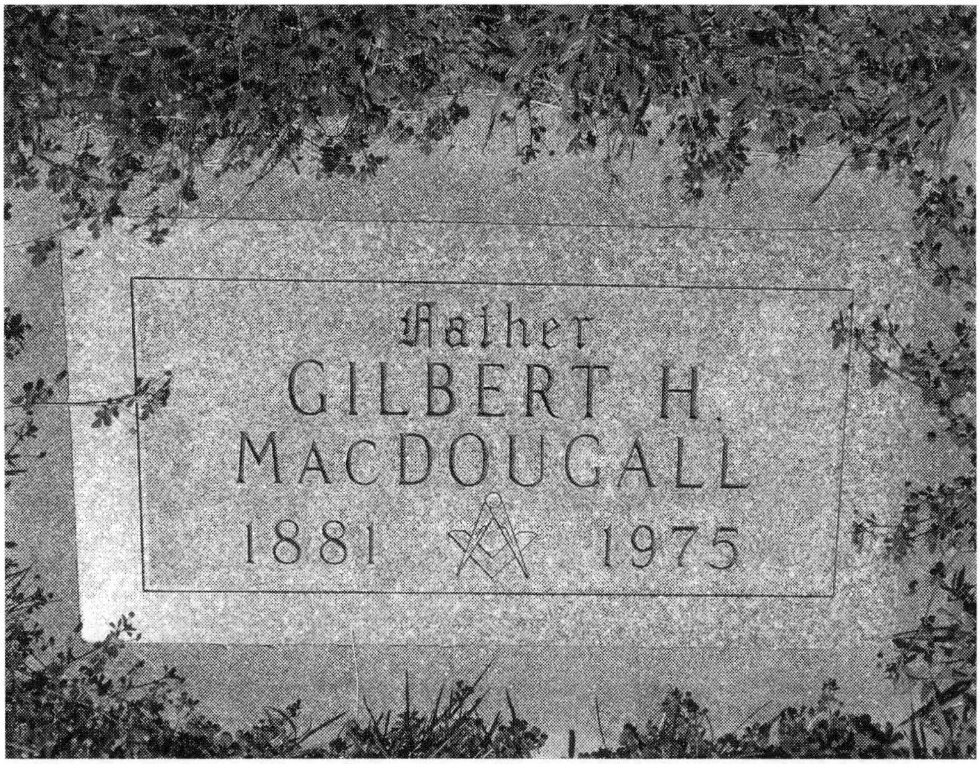

Plate 26.6. Gravestone of Gilbert Hugh (Gib) MacDougall
Redwood Falls Cemetery, Redwood Falls, Minnesota

Plate 26.7. Gravestone of Gilbert (Gib) MacDougall's Wife, Edith Bollum
Redwood Falls Cemetery, Redwood Falls, Minnesota

Letter #27

Undated

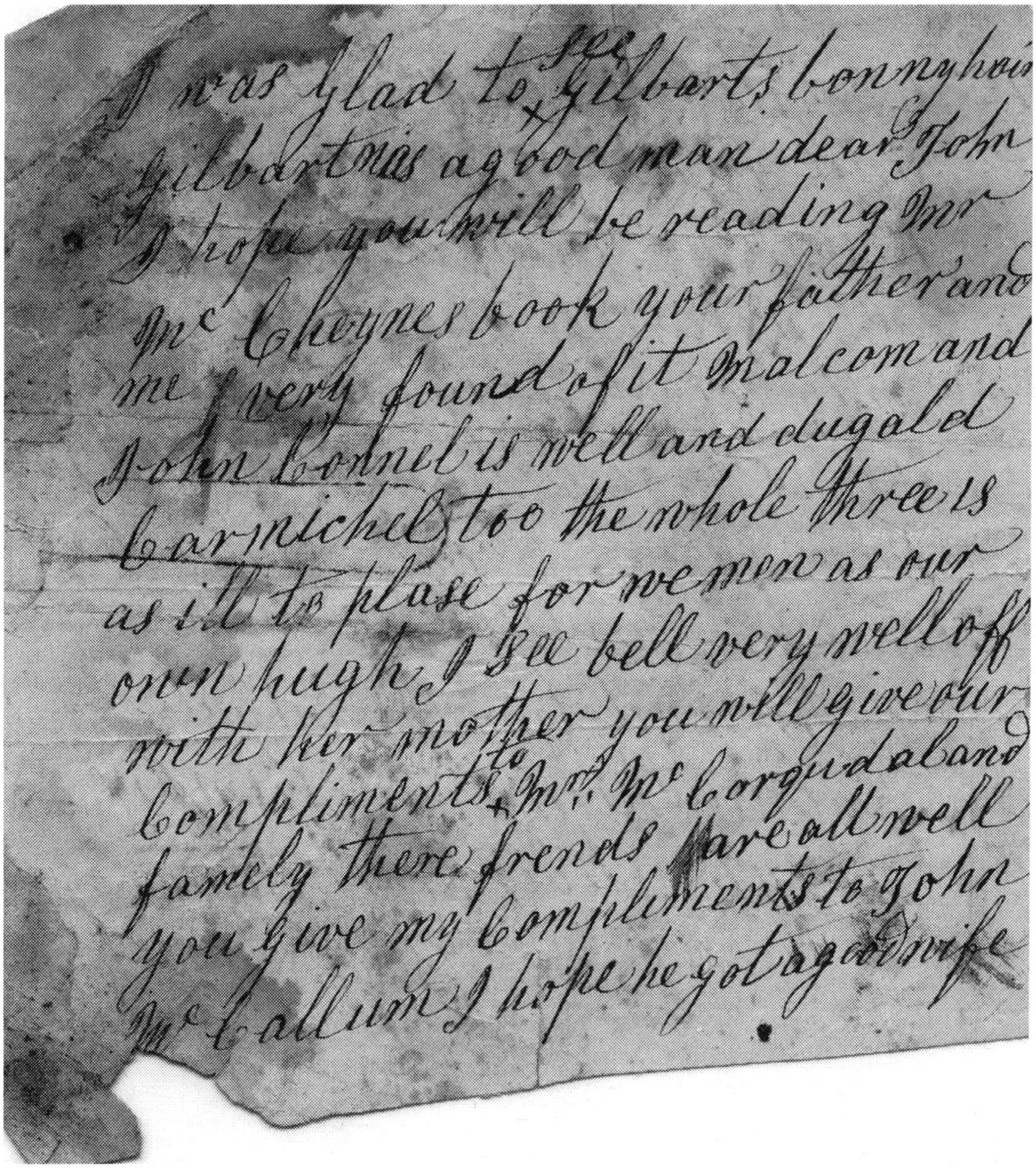

I was glad to see Gilbarts bonnyhoir
Gilbart was a good man dear John
I hope you will be reading Mr
Mc Cheynes book your father and
me very found of it Malcom and
John Connel is well and dugald
Carmichel too the whole three is
as ill to plase for wemen as our
own hugh I see bell very well off
with her mother you will give our
Compliments to Mrs Mc Corqudal and
famely there frends are all well
you give my Compliments to John
Mc Callum I hope he got a good wife

Image db214

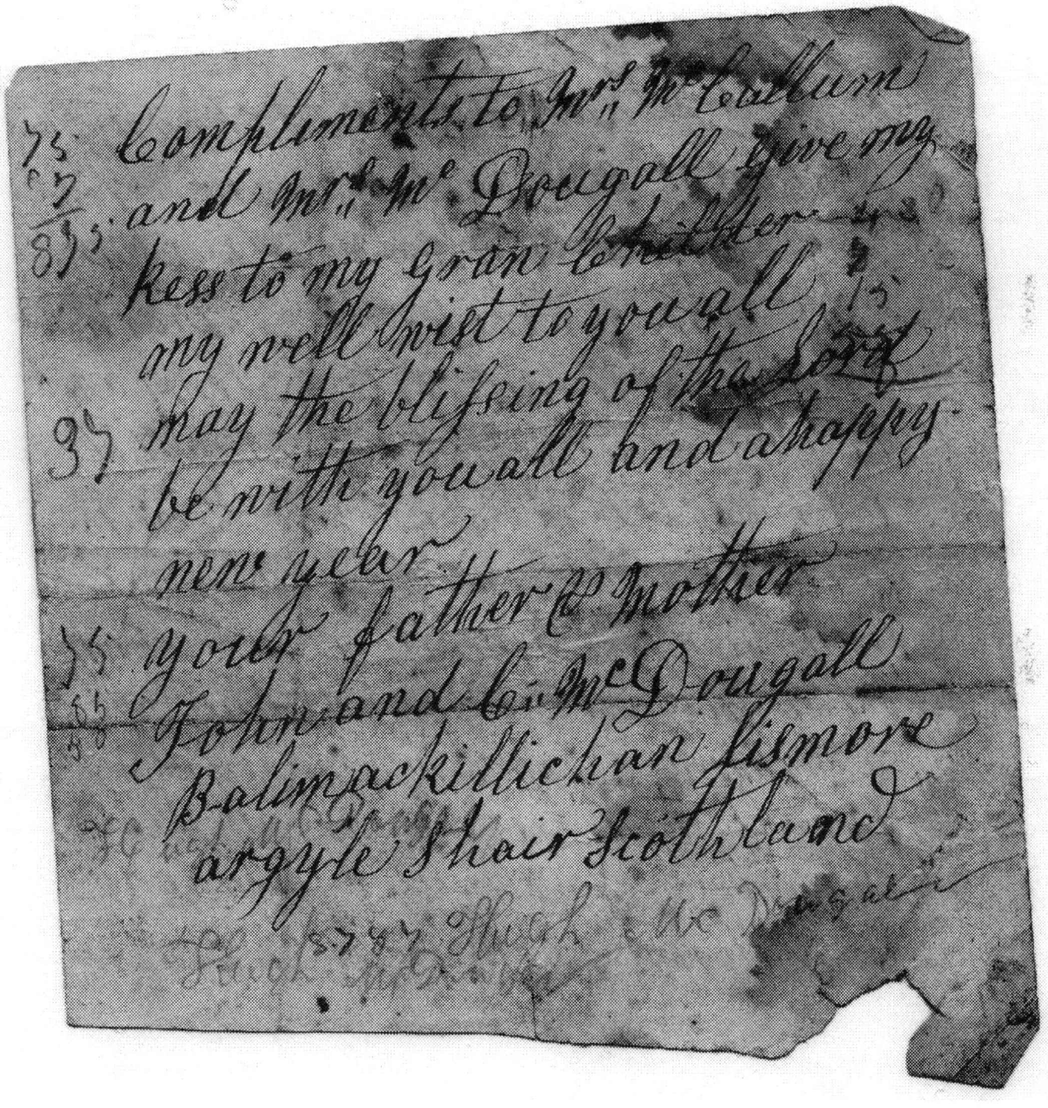

Compliments to Mrs McCallum
and Mrs McDougall give my
kess to my gran children
my well wist to you all
may the blissing of the Lord
be with you all and a happy
new year
your father & mother
John and C. McDougall
Balimackillichan Lismore
argyle Shair Scothland

Image db215

LETTER FROM JOHN MCDOUGALL (b. 1803 Lismore) AND CATHERINE MCCALLUM MCDOUGALL (b. 1809 Lismore) WHO LIVED AT BALLIMACKILLICHAN, ISLE OF LISMORE TO THEIR SON JOHN MCDOUGALL (b. 1837 Lismore) DELHI, REDWOOD COUNTY, MINNESOTA

(partial letter)

I was Glad to see Gilbarts [Gilbert Hugh, b. 1881 Delhi, Minnesota] bonny hair Gilbart was a good man dear John I hope you will be reading Mr McCheynes book your father and me very found of it Malcom and John Connel is well and dugald Carmichel too the whole three is as ill to plase for wemen as our own hugh I see bell [son John's wife, Isabel McCallum MacDougall, b. 1850 Lismore] very well off with her mother [Ann McCallum McCallum, b. 1814 Lismore, daughter of Duncan McCallum, b. 1790 Lismore and Isabella McColl, b. 1790 Lismore]

you will give our Compliments to Mr. McCorqudal and famely there friends are all well

you give my Compliments to John McCallum I hope he got a good wife

Compliments to Mrs. McCallum [Ann] and Mrs. McDougall [Isabel] give my kess to my gran childer

my well wist to you all

may the blissing of the Lord be with you all and a happy new year

Your father & Mother

John and C. McDougall

Ballimackillichan Lismore

Argyle Shair

Scothland

Note: This letter refers to a book by Scottish theologian, Robert Murray McCheyne (1813-1843). For more information, see Bonar (1843).

Plate 27.1. Along the Main Road, Lismore in Killean

Plate 27.2. Killean

Letter #28

Date Unknown

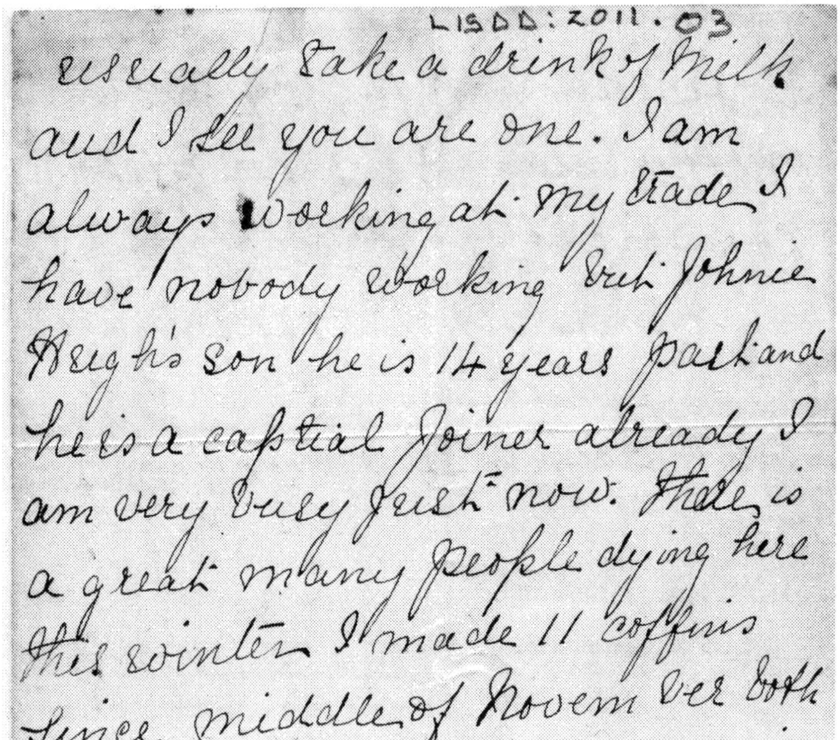
LISDD:2011.03

usually take a drink of milk
and I see you are one. I am
always working at my trade I
have nobody working with Johnie
Hugh's son he is 14 years past and
he is a capital joiner already I
am very busy just now. There is
a great many people dying here
this winter I made 11 coffins
since middle of November both
old and young. what a warning
to us all to prepare to meet to
our God. do not be so long in
writting this time John & Donald Mc
Callum Fortm. are well Donald is
no married yet. I must con-
-clude our best love to your wife

Image db071

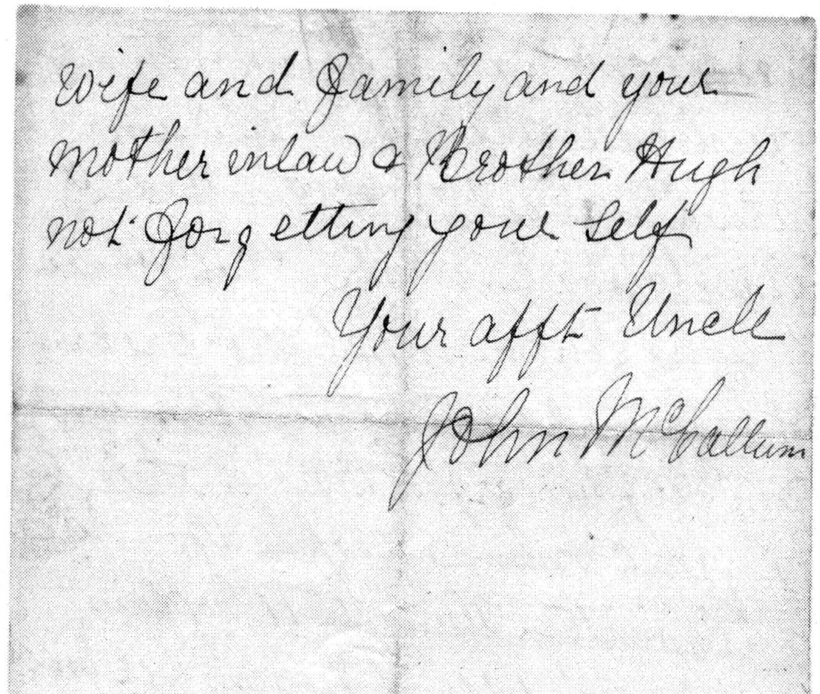

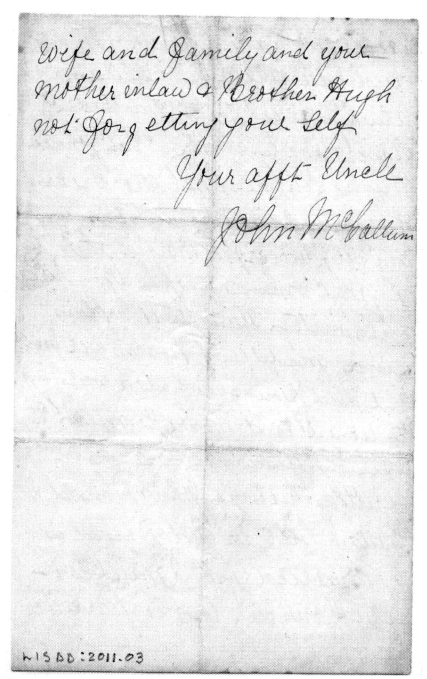

Wife and family and your
mother inlaw & Brother Hugh
not forgetting your self

Your affct Uncle

John McCallum

WISDD:2011.03

Image db072

TO JOHN MCDOUGALL (b. 1837 Lismore) DELHI, REDWOOD COUNTY, MINNESOTA, USA FROM JOHN MCCALLUM (John McDougall's Uncle)

(Fragment of letter)

.....usually take a drink of milk and I see you are one. I am always working at my trade I have nobody working but Johnie Hugh's son he is 14 years past and he is a captial Joiner already I am very busy just now. There is a great many people dying here this winter I made 11 coffins since middle of November both old and young. What a warning to us all to prepare to meet our God. do not be so long in writting this time John & Donald McCallum Fort^{m} [Fort William?] are well Donald is no married yet. I must conclude our best love to your wife wife and family and your mother inlaw & Brother Hugh and not forgetting your self

Your afft Uncle

John McCallum

Notes:

The author, John McCallum (b. 1818 Balure), refers to "John & Donald McCallum Fort William" who are likely to be his nephews, the sons of his brother, Malcolm McCallum, (b. 1811 Balure.) As noted in other parts of this book, John McCallum (b. 1818) and Malcolm were brothers of Catherine McCallum McDougall.

The interpretation, "Johnie Hugh's son", if correct, suggests that John McCallum (b. 1818) may have been reporting on John, the son of Hugh Carmichael. According to genealogical notes, John McCallum's wife, Flora Carmichael, whom he married in 1860, had a son named Hugh, born about 1849, whose father was a John Carmichael. Hugh Carmichael had a son, in turn, named John Carmichael, born about 1870, who might be the "Johnie" mentioned in this letter. (Gloag, 2014b)

The letter refers to "your wife ... and family" and would have been written sometime after the marriage of John McDougall and Isabel McCallum in January 1877. However, the letter could have been written much later. For example, the references to "Johnie Hugh's son" (if correctly understood) and "11 coffins since November" suggest John McCallum might have written this letter in late 1883 when Johnie would have been about 14.

Plate 28.1. Graveyard, Lismore Parish Church

The tall memorial standing in the photo center honors John McDougall (weaver), Catherine McCallum and their children.

(See photograph and inscription following letter of July 27, 1888.)

Letter **#29**

December 31st 1883

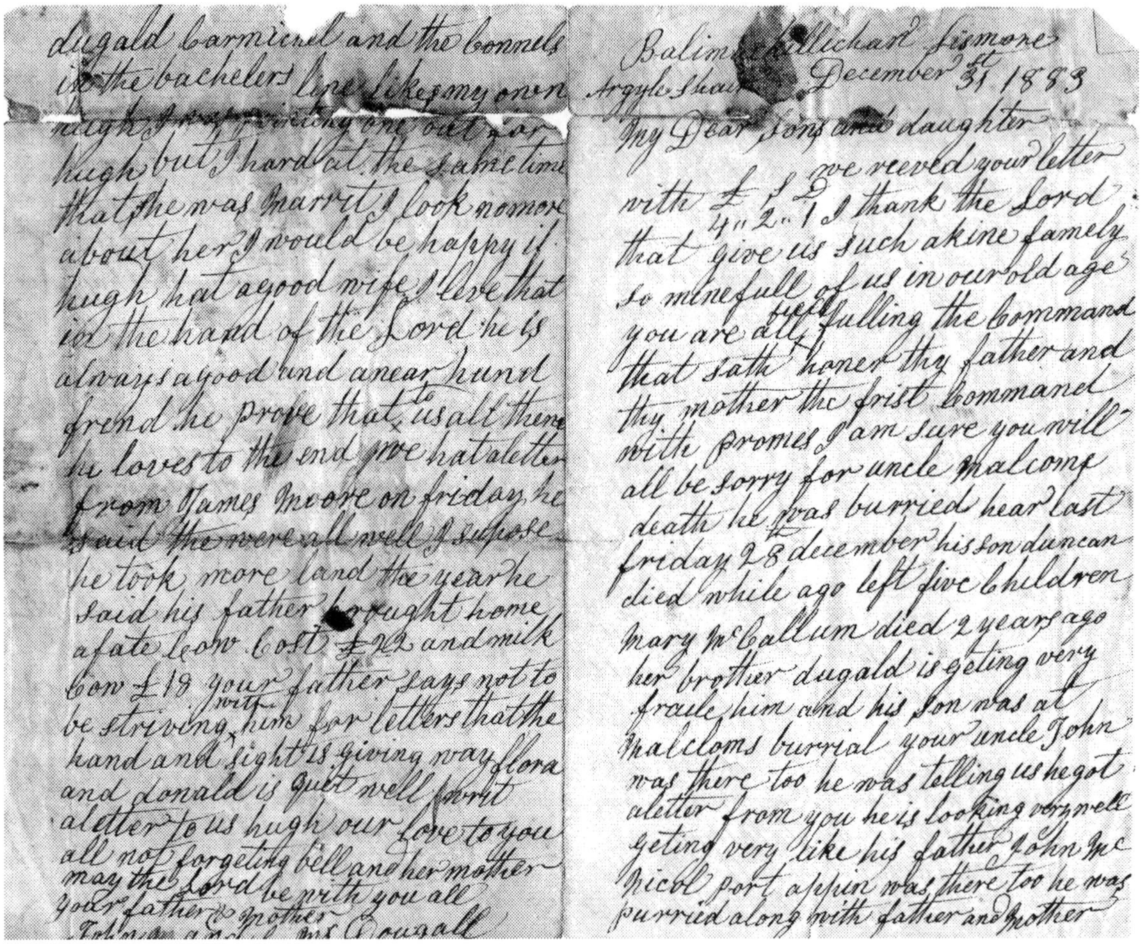

Balim[illegible] Kellichar Lismore
Argyle Shire December 31st 1883
My Dear Sons and daughter
we receved your letter
with £4" 2" 1 I thank the Lord
that give us such akine famely
so minefull of us in our old age
you are all fulfulling the Command
that sath honer thy father and
thy mother the frist Command
with promes I am sure you will
all be sorry for uncle Malcoms
death he was burried hear last
friday 28 december his son duncan
died while ago left five Children
Mary McCallum died 2 years ago
her brother dugald is geting very
fraile him and his son was at
Malcoms burrial your uncle John
was there too he was telling us he got
aletter from you he is looking very well
geting very like his father John Mc
Nicol port appin was there too he was
purried along with father and mother

dugald Carmicel and the Connels
in the bachelers line likes my own
[illegible] I was [illegible] one out for
hugh but I hard at the same time
that she was marred I look nomore
about her I would be happy if
hugh hat agood wife I leve that
in the hand of the Lord he is
always agood and anear hand
frend he prove that to us all there
he loves to the end we hat aletter
from James Moore on friday he
said the were all well I suppose
he took more land the year he
said his father brought home
afate Cow Cost £12 and milk
Cow £19 your father says not to
be striving with him for letters that the
hand and sight is giving way flora
and donald is quit well write
aletter to us hugh our Love to you
all not forgeting bell and her mother
may the Lord be with you all
your father & mother
John and [illegible] McDougall

Image db193

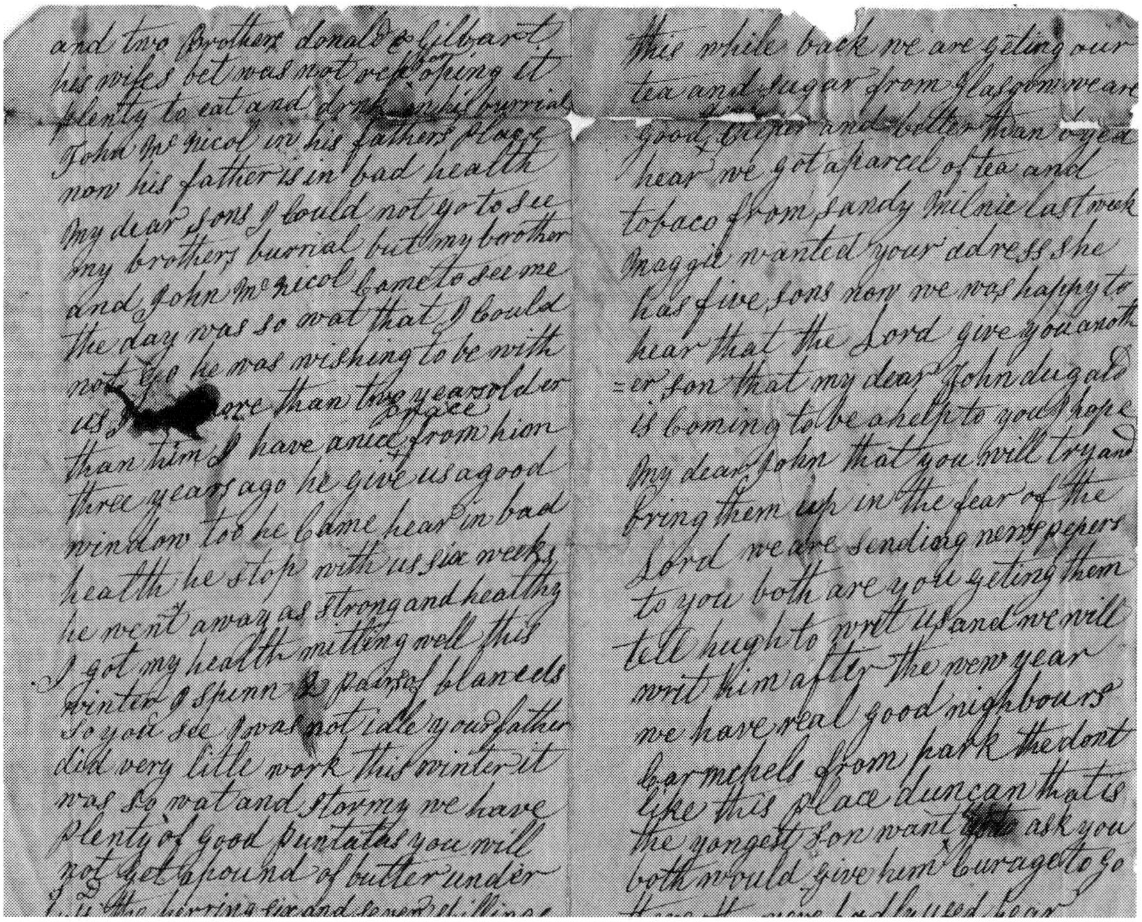

and two Brothers donald & Gilbart
his wifes bet was not vex hoping it
plenty to eat and drink in his burrial
John McNicol in his fathers place
now his father is in bad health
My dear sons I could not go to see
my brothers burrial but my brother
and John McNicol came to see me
the day was so wat that I could
not go he was wishing to be with
us I [illegible] more than two years older
than him I have a nice place from him
three years ago he give us a good
window too he came hear in bad
health he stop with us six weeks
he went away as strong and healthy
I got my health mitteng well this
winter I spinn 2 pairs of flanells
so you see I was not idle your father
did very little work this winter it
was so wat and stormy we have
plenty of good puntatas you will
not get a pound of butter under
[illegible] the hirring six and seven shillings

this while back we are geting our
tea and sugar from Glasgow we are
good cheaper and better than ever
hear we got a parcel of tea and
topaco from sandy Milnie last week
Maggie wanted your adress she
has five sons now we was happy to
hear that the Lord give you anoth
=er son that my dear John dugald
is coming to be a help to you I hope
My dear John that you will try and
bring them up in the fear of the
Lord we are sending news papers
to you both are you geting them
tell hugh to writt us and we will
writ him after the new year
we have real good nighbours
Carmichels from park the dont
like this place duncan that is
the yongest son want [illegible] ask you
both would give him curage to go
[illegible]

Image db194

LETTER FROM JOHN MCDOUGALL (b. 1803 Lismore) AND CATHERINE MCCALLUM MCDOUGALL (b. 1809 Lismore) WHO LIVED AT BALLIMACKILLICHAN, ISLE OF LISMORE TO THEIR SONS JOHN MCDOUGALL (b. 1837 Lismore) AND HUGH MCDOUGALL (b. 1842 Lismore) DELHI, REDWOOD COUNTY, MINNESOTA

Balimackillichan Lismore
Argyle Shair
December 31st 1883

My Sons and daughter

we rceved your letter with £4 2S 1D I thank the Lord that give us such a kine famely so minefull of us in our old age you are all full fulling the Command that sath honer thy father and thy mother the frist Command with promes I am sure you will all be sorry for uncle Malcoms death he was burried hear last friday 28th december his son duncan died while ago left five Children Mary McCallum died 2 years ago her brother dugald is geting very fraile him and his son was at Malcloms burrial your uncle John was there too he was telling us he got a letter from you he is looking very well geting very like his father John McNicol port appin was there too he [Uncle Malcolm?] was purried [buried] along with father and Mother and two Brothers donald & Gilbart his wifes bet was not rebeber[?] oping [open?] it plenty to eat and drnk on his burrial John McNicol in his fathers place now his father is in bad health

My dear Sons I Could not go to see my brothers burrial but my brother and John McNicol Came to see me the day was so wat that I Could not go he was wishing to be with us I [am] more than two years older than him I have a nice prace from him three years ago he give us a good window too he Came hear in bad health he stop with us six weeks he went away as strong and healthy I got mitling well this winter I spinn 2 pairs of blaneds so you see I was not idle your father did very litle work this winter it was so wat and stormy we have plenty of good puntatas you will not get a pound of butter under 1S 4D the herring six and seven shillings [the hundred]

this while back we are geting our tea and sugar from Glasgow we are good deal cheper and better than byed [bought] hear we got a parcel of tea and tobaco from Sandy Milnie last week Maggie wanted your adress she has five sons now we was happy to hear that the Lord give you another Son that my dear John dugald is Coming to be a big help to you I hope My dear John that you will try and bring them up in the fear of the Lord we are sending newspepers to you both are you geting them tell hugh to writ us and we will writ him after the new year we have real good nighbours Carmichels from park the dont like this place duncan that is the yongest son want us to ask you both would give him Curage to go there they were badly used hear [See Note 2, below.]

dugald Carmichel and the Connels in the bachelers line like my own hugh I was pointing one out for hugh but I hard at the same time that she was Marrit I look no more about her I would be happy if hugh hat a good wife I leve that in the hand of the

Lord he is always a good and a near hand frend he prove that to us all thene[?]he loves to the end we hat a letter from James Moore on friday he said the were all well I supose he took more land the year he said his father brought home a fate Cow Cost £22 and milk Cow £18 your father says not to be striving with him for letters that the hand and sight is giving way flora and donald is quit well writ a letter to us hugh our love to you all not forgeting bell and her mother may the Lord be with you all

Your father & Mother

John and C. McDougall

"we was happy to hear that the Lord give you another Son"

Plate 29.1. Gravestones of William Moore MacDougall and his Wife, Maude Ellen Scribner Redwood Falls Cemetery, Redwood Falls, Minnesota

William Moore MacDougall was born September 23, 1883 to John McDougall (b. 1837 Lismore) and Isabel McCallum.

Note 1: The following suggests that Malcolm McCallum (b. 1811 Balure) was buried with his parents, his oldest brother, Donald (b. 1803 Balure), and younger brother, Gilbert McCallum (b. 1813 Balure):

"[Uncle Malcolm?] was purried [buried] along with father and Mother and two Brothers donald & Gilbart".

Malcolm McCallum's parents were John McCallum (married about 1802) and Anne Carmichael (b. 1771/1772 Appin). His brother, Gilbert, was Isabel McCallum McDougall's father. His sister, Catherine McCallum McDougall, was Isabel's mother-in-law as well as her aunt. For more information about the family of John McCallum (married about 1802) and Anne Carmichael (b. 1771/1772), see Appendix 9.

Note 2: This letter refers to the Carmichaels from the Lismore township of Park. The family's difficulties are recorded in a report of The Napier Commission, appointed by Parliament to address challenges faced by crofters (tenants) and cottars (occupiers of dwelling houses) in crofting parishes of the Western Highlands. The Commission travelled to sites throughout the Highlands in 1883, including Lismore, and interviewed crofters selected by members of the community to represent them. The Commission's work influenced passage of the Crofters Holding (Scotland) Act, 1886, which addressed security of tenure, rights to holdings and other matters, and defined key terms, such as "permanent improvements" and "holdings". For more information, see The Napier Commission (1883) vol. 3, pages 2322 – 2358, including such sections as "Dugald Carmichael, Labourer, Balamaillachean (34)—examined", pages 2329-2333, and "Mrs Mary Carmichael, late of Park—examined", pages 2357-2358. See also Hay, 2013.

Letter **#30**

Fragment about 1884

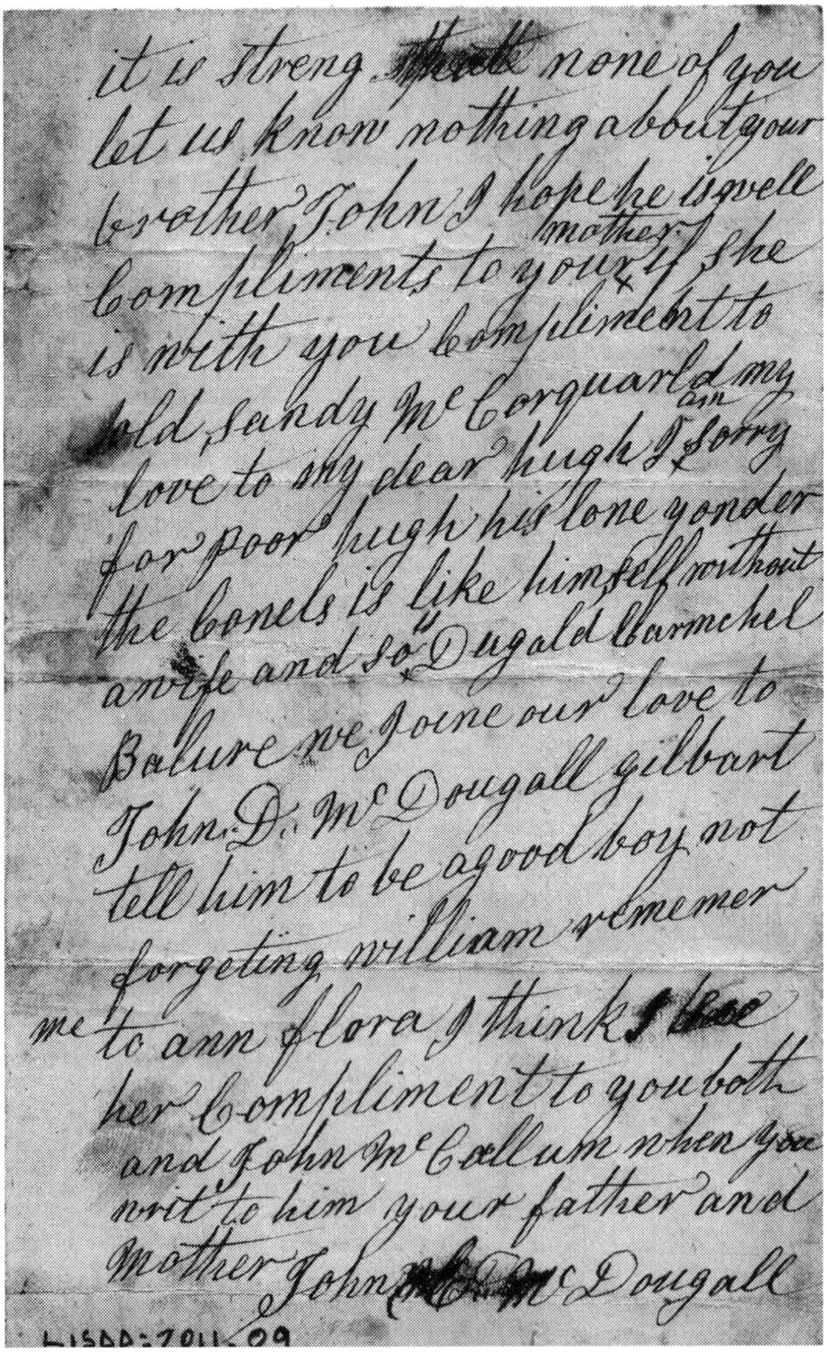

it is streng [illegible] none of you
let us know nothing abbut your
brother John I hope he is well
compliments to your mother if she
is with you compliment to
old Sandy McCorquarld my
love to my dear hugh I am sorry
for poor hugh his lone yonder
the bonels is like himself without
a wife and so Dugald Carmchel
Balure we joine our love to
John D. McDougall gilbart
tell him to be a good boy not
forgeting william rememer
me to ann flora I think [illegible]
her Compliment to you both
and John McCollum when you
writ to him your father and
Mother John [illegible] McDougall

Image db093

LETTER FROM JOHN MCDOUGALL (b. 1803 Lismore) AND CATHERINE MCCALLUM MCDOUGALL (b. 1809 Lismore) WHO LIVED AT BALLIMACKILLICHAN, ISLE OF LISMORE TO JOHN MCDOUGALL (b. 1837) DELHI, REDWOOD COUNTY, MINNESOTA USA

... it is streng [strange] that none of you let us know nothing about your brother John I hope he is well Compliments to your mother if she is with you Compliments to old Sandy McCorquarld my love to my dear hugh I am sorry for poor hugh his lone yonder the Conels is like himself without a wife and so is Dugald Carmchel Balure we joine our love to John D. McDougall gilbart tell him to be a good boy not forgeting william rememer me to ann flora I think I see her Compliment to you both and John McCallum when you write to him

Your father and Mother

John and C. McDougall

Plate 30.1. Three MacDougall Brothers and their Wives, about 1917
(back, left to right) John Dougald MacDougal (b. 1877),
William Moore MacDougall (b. 1883), Gilbert Hugh MacDougall (b. 1881)
(front, left to right) William's wife, Maude Ellen
Scribner; Gilbert's wife, Maude Welder

John Dougald, William Moore and Gilbert Hugh were the three oldest sons of John McDougall (b. 1837) and Isabel McCallum.

Notes:

1. This letter mentions four children of John McDougall and Isabel McCallum McDougall: John Dougal (born 1877), Anna Flora (born 1879), Gilbert (born 1881) and William (born 1883). It does not mention the youngest child, Donald (born 1885); therefore, the letter is likely to have been written before his birth.

2. The phrase, "your brother John", might refer to Isabel McCallum McDougall's brother, John McCallum, born 1847, who migrated to the United States. His status would have been of interest to John McDougall (weaver) and Catherine McCallum because, like Isabel, he was a child of Catherine's brother, Gilbert McCallum (born 1813, Lismore), and his wife, Ann McCallum (born 1814 Lismore).

3. Anne Aburn, New Zealand, a descendant of Ann McCallum McCallum's sister, Katherine McCallum (b. 1822 Killean, Lismore), provides the following additional information:

    Ann [McCallum] married Gilbert McCallum son of John McCallum and Ann Carmichael of Balure, Lismore. Gilbert McCallum died in 1849 leaving her with two small children John b.1847 and Isabella b. 1850. In 1851 she was living with her parents at Killean [Lismore]. According to family tradition Ann went to join her brothers Duncan (Jnr) and John in America. While at Caledonia Ann married a Mr Fraser and soon after was widowed a second time. ...

    By 1870 Ann, her son John and daughter Isabel, brother Duncan (Jnr) and family and possibly brother Archibald had moved to Minnesota.

    Ann McCallum's daughter, Isabel married John McDougall in 1877. He was born in 1837 the son of John McDougall and Catherine McCallum (sister of Gilbert McCallum Ann's first husband) of Ballimackillichan, Lismore and had followed some of the McCallums to USA in 1872.

    John and Isabel McDougall settled in Delhi, Redwood Falls, Minnesota. They farmed 160 acres. Descendants live in the region.

    Isabel's brother John McCallum and their mother Ann settled at Ortonville, Big Stone Co, Minnesota. Eventually he owned a large holding which he named "Lismore". John married and had nine children. He has descendants in the area. (Aburn, 2000)

    Census records for Minnesota show the following:

    <u>1870 Census</u>

    <u>Cottage Grove, Washington Co. Minnesota</u>

			Value	*Personal Value*	
Frazier, Anna	54	Keeping house	3,000	896	b. Scot
McCallum, John	23	Farming			
" Bell	20	at home			

    (Aburn, 2013a)

4. John and Isabel McDougall's farm in Delhi, Redwood County, Minnesota, "adjoined land owned by McCorquordales also from Lismore." (Aburn, 2013a)

5. The closing reference to "John McCallum when you writ to him" could be a reference to:

    - Isabel McCallum McDougall's brother, John (born 1847), mentioned in Note 2, above
    - Her cousin, John McCallum (born 1852 in Scotland, died 1919 in Minnesota). He was the son of Ann McCallum McCallum's brother, Duncan (Jnr), mentioned in Note 3, above, or
    - Ann McCallum McCallum's brother, John (born 1830 Lismore, died 1915 in Caledonia, New York.)

    (Aburn, 2013c)

Letter **#31**

July 30th 1884

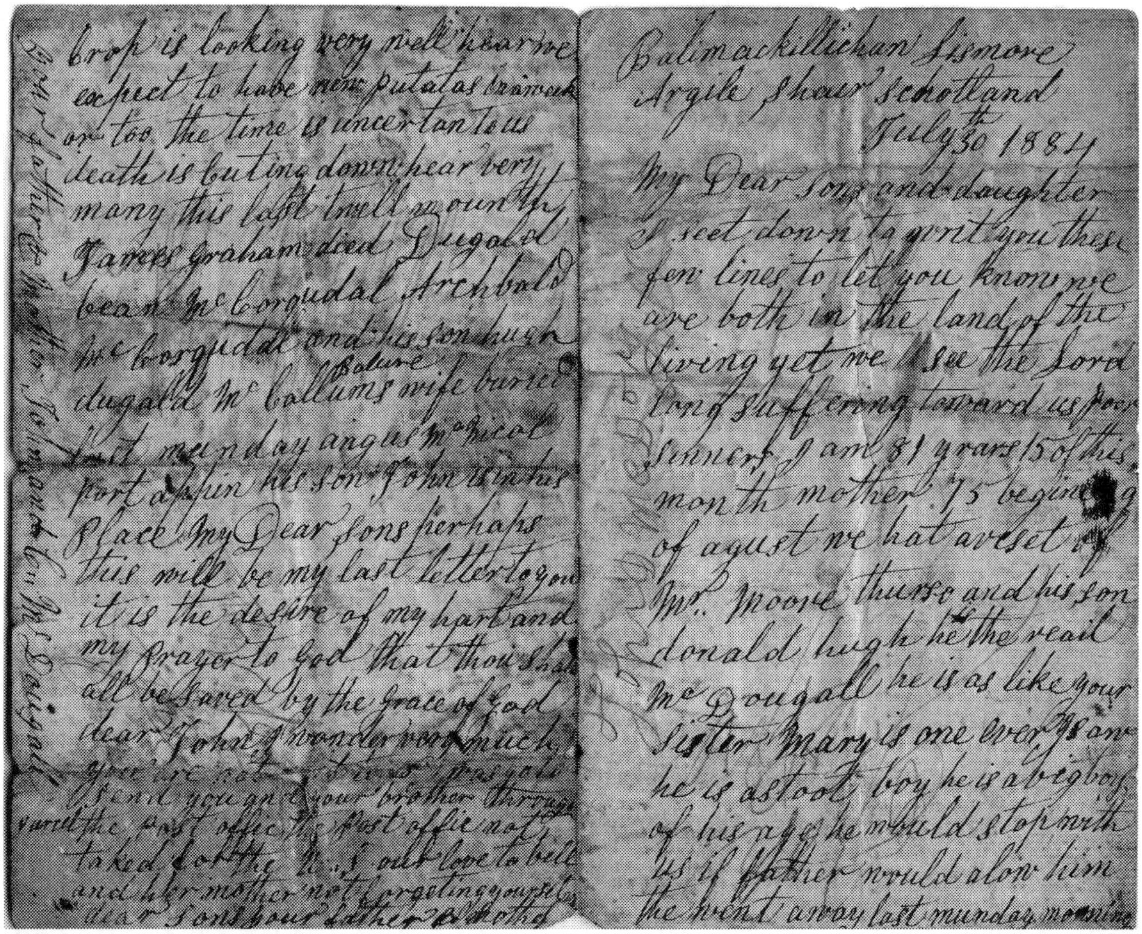
brop is looking very well hear we
expect to have new putatas [illegible]
or too the time is uncertan to us
death is buting down hear very
many this last twell mounthy
James graham died Dugald
bean Mc Corqudal Archbald
Mc Corqudal and his son hugh
dugald Mc Callums wife buried Balure
last munday angus Mc nicol
port a fuin his son John is in his
Place My Dear sons perhaps
this will be my last letter to you
it is the desire of my hart and
my prayer to God that thou shall
all be saved by the grace of God
dear John I wonder very much
[illegible]
I send you and your brother through
the post office the post office not
taked for the [illegible] our love to bell
and her mother not forgeting yourself
dear sons your father & mother

father & Mother To John and Colin McDougall

Balimackillichan Lismore
Argile Shaur Schottland
July 30th 1884
My Dear sons and daughter
I seet down to writ you these
few lines to let you know we
are both in the land of the
living yet we see the Lord
long suffering toward us poor
sinners I am 81 years 15 of this
month mother 75 begining
of agust we hat a vesel of
Mr. Moore thurso and his son
donald hugh he the real
Mc Dougall he is as like your
sister Mary is one ever I saw
he is a stool boy he is a big boy
of his age he would stop with
us if father would alow him
he went away last munday morning

Image db196

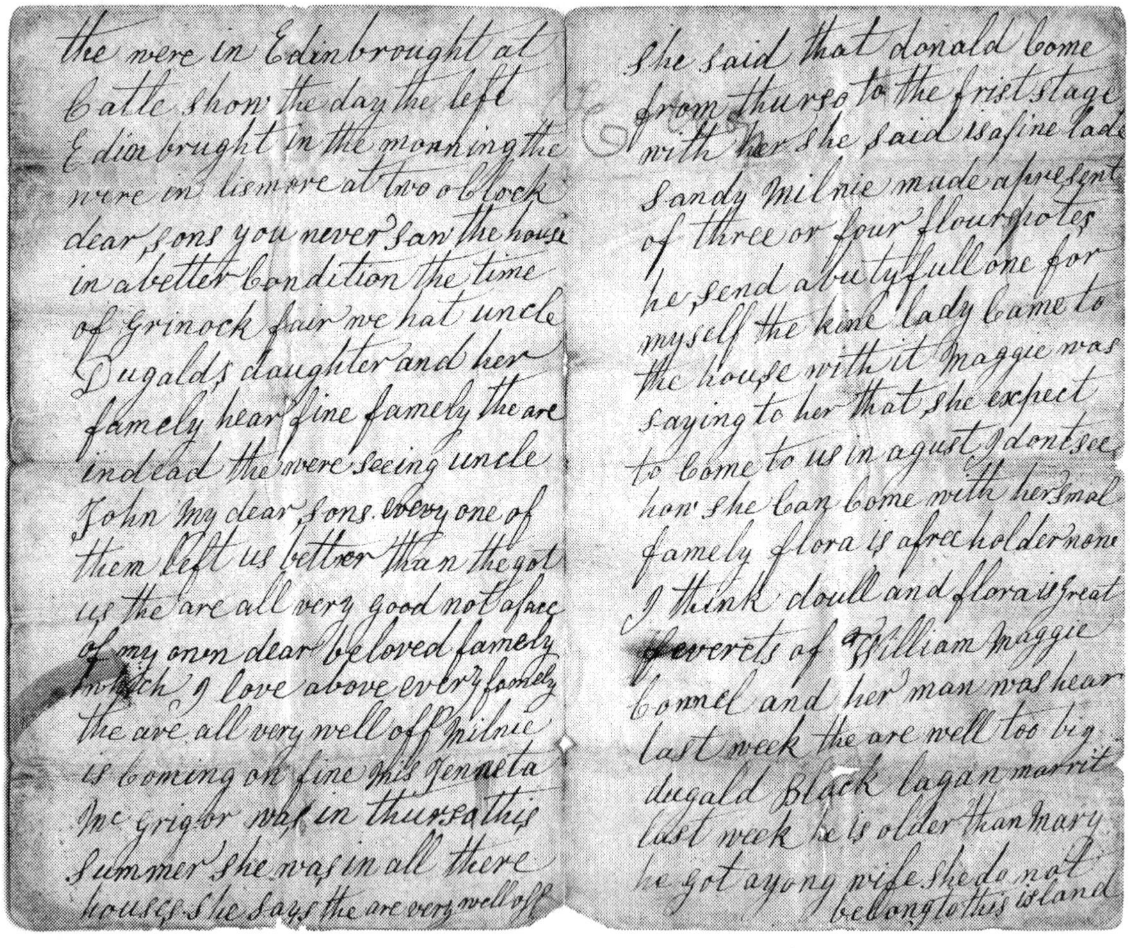

the were in Edinbrought at
Catle show the day the left
Edinbright in the morning the
were in lismore at two oclock
dear sons you never saw the house
in a better condition the time
of Grinock fair we hat uncle
Dugalds daughter and her
famely hear fine famely the are
indead the were seeing uncle
John my dear sons every one of
them left us better than the got
us the are all very good not a free
of my own dear beloved famely
which I love above every famely
the are all very well off Milnie
is coming on fine Miss Jenneta
Mc grigor was in thurso this
summer she was in all there
houses she says the are very well off

She said that donald come
from thurso to the frist stage
with her she said is a fine lade
Sandy Milnie made a present
of three or four flour potes
he send a buty full one for
myself the kine lady came to
the house with it Maggie was
saying to her that she expect
to come to us in agust I dont see
how she can come with her smal
famely flora is a free holder none
I think doull and flora is great
feverets of William Maggie
Connel and her man was hear
last week the are well too big
dugald Black lagan marrit
last week he is older than Mary
he got a yong wife she do not
belong to this island

Image db197

LETTER FROM JOHN MCDOUGALL (b. 1803 Lismore) AND CATHERINE MCCALLUM MCDOUGALL (b. 1809 Lismore) WHO LIVED AT BALLIMACKILLICHAN, ISLE OF LISMORE TO THEIR SONS JOHN MCDOUGALL (b. 1837 Lismore) AND HUGH MCDOUGALL (b. 1842 Lismore) MINNESOTA

Balimackillichan Lismore
Argile Shair
Schotland
July 30th 1884

My Dear Sons and daughter

I seet down to writ you these few lines to let you know we are both in the land of the living yet we see the Lord long suffering toward us poor sinners I am 81 yrars 15 of this month mother 75 beginning of agust we hat a veset of Mr. Moore thurso and his son donald hugh he is the reail McDougall he is as like your sister mary is one ever saw he is a stoot boy he is a big boy of his age he would stop with us if father would alow him the went away last munday morning the were in Edinbrought at Cattle show the day the left Edinbrught in the morning the were in lismore at two oClock dear sons you never saw the house in a better Condition the time of grinock [Greenock?] fair we hat uncle Dugalds daughter and her famely hear fine famely the are indead the were seeing uncle John my dear sons. every one of them left us better than the got us the are all very good not a face of my own dear beloved famely which I love above every famely the are all very well off Milnie is Coming on fine Mis Jenneta McGrigor [Revd. Gregor McGregor's daughter] was in thurso this Summer she was in all there houses she says the are very well off

She said that donald come from thurso to the frist stage with her she said is a fine lade

Sandy Milnie made a present of three or four flourpotes [flowerpots] he send a butyfull one for myself the kine lady Came to the house with it Maggie was saying to her that she expect to come to us in agust I dont see how she Can Come with her smal famely flora is a freeholder now I think doull and flora is great feverets of Willam [Moore] Maggie Connel and her man was hear last week the are well too big dugal Black lagan marrit last week he is older than Mary he got a yong wife she do not belong to this island

Crop is looking very well hear we expect to have new putatas in a week or too the time is uncertan to us

death is cuting down hear very many this last twell [twelve?] mounth James Graham died Dugald bean [wife] McCorqudal Archbald McCorqudal and his son hugh dugald McCallums Balure wife buried last munday angus McNicol port appin his son John is in his Place My Dear sons perhaps this will be my last letter to you it is the desire of my hart and my prayer to God that thou shall all be saved by the Grace of God dear John I wonder very much you are not___[?]to___[?]I was go to send you and your brother through purcel the post offic the post offic not taked for the U.S. our love to bell and her mother not forgeting yourselvs dear Sons your father & Mother your father & Mother John & C. McDougall

Plate 31.1. Duncan Street, Thurso
1965

Margaret McDougall and Alexander Milne lived on Duncan Street where three of their sons were born: William in 1883, Dougald in 1885 and Joseph in 1886.

Plate 31.2. View North from Lismore at Lagan

Letter #32

February 21, 1886

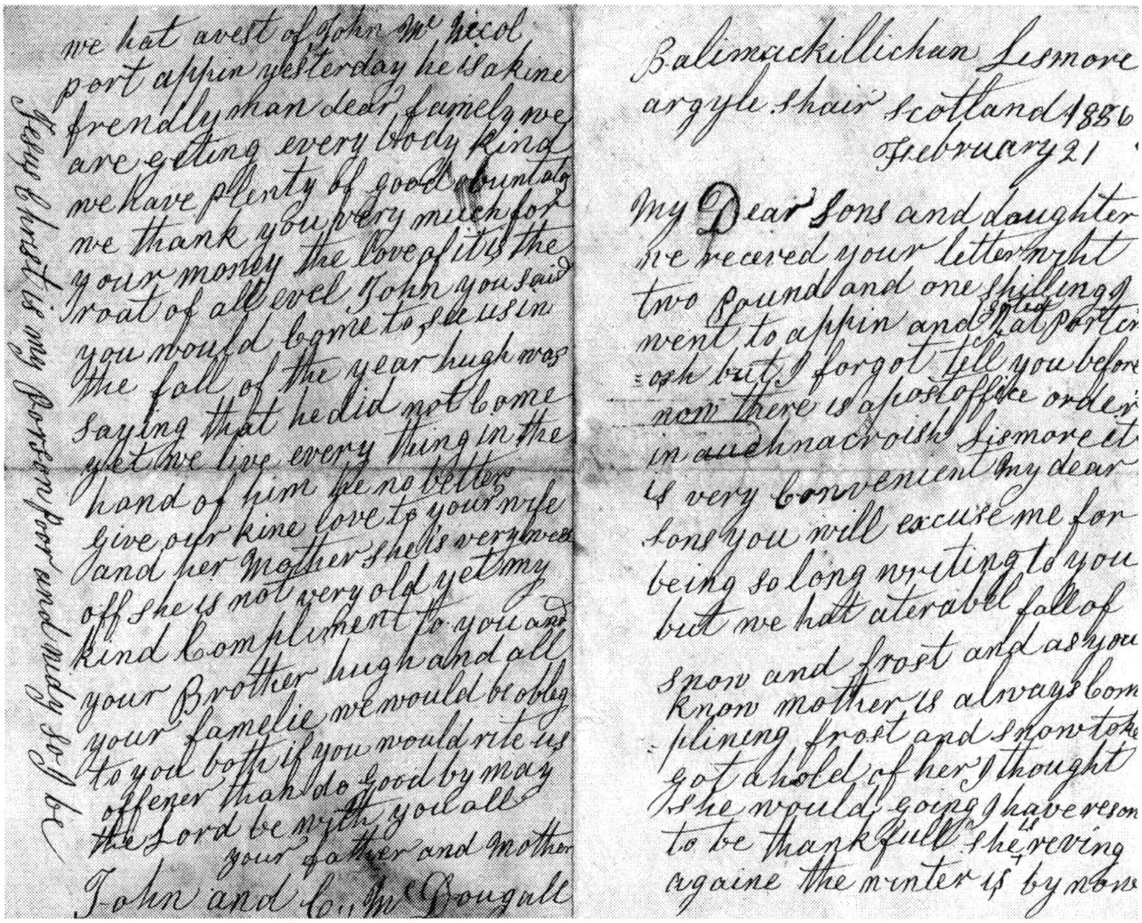
Balimackillichan Lismore
argyle shair Scotland 1886
February 21

My Dear Sons and daughter
we receved your letter night
two pound and one shillings
went to appin and [illegible] at port[illegible]
ash but I forgot tell you before
now there is a post office order
in auchnacroish Lismore it
is very convenient my dear
sons you will excuse me for
being so long writing to you
but we hat aterabel fall of
snow and frost and as you
know mother is always com
plining frost and snow toke
got a hold of her I thought
she would going I have reson
to be thankfull she is reving
againe the winter is by now

we hat a vest of John Mc Nicol
port appin yesterday he is a kine
frendly man dear famely we
are geting every body kind
we have plenty of good [illegible]
we thank you very much for
your money the love of it is the
roat of all evel John you said
you would come to see us in
the fall of the year hugh was
saying that he did not come
yet we live every thing in the
hand of him see no better
give our kine love to your wife
and her mother she is very [illegible]
off she is not very old yet my
kind compliment to you and
your Brother hugh and all
your famelie we would be obleg
to you both if you would rite us
offener than do Good by may
the Lord be with you all
your father and mother
John and C. Mc Dougall

Jesus Christ is my Portion for and [illegible]

Image db199

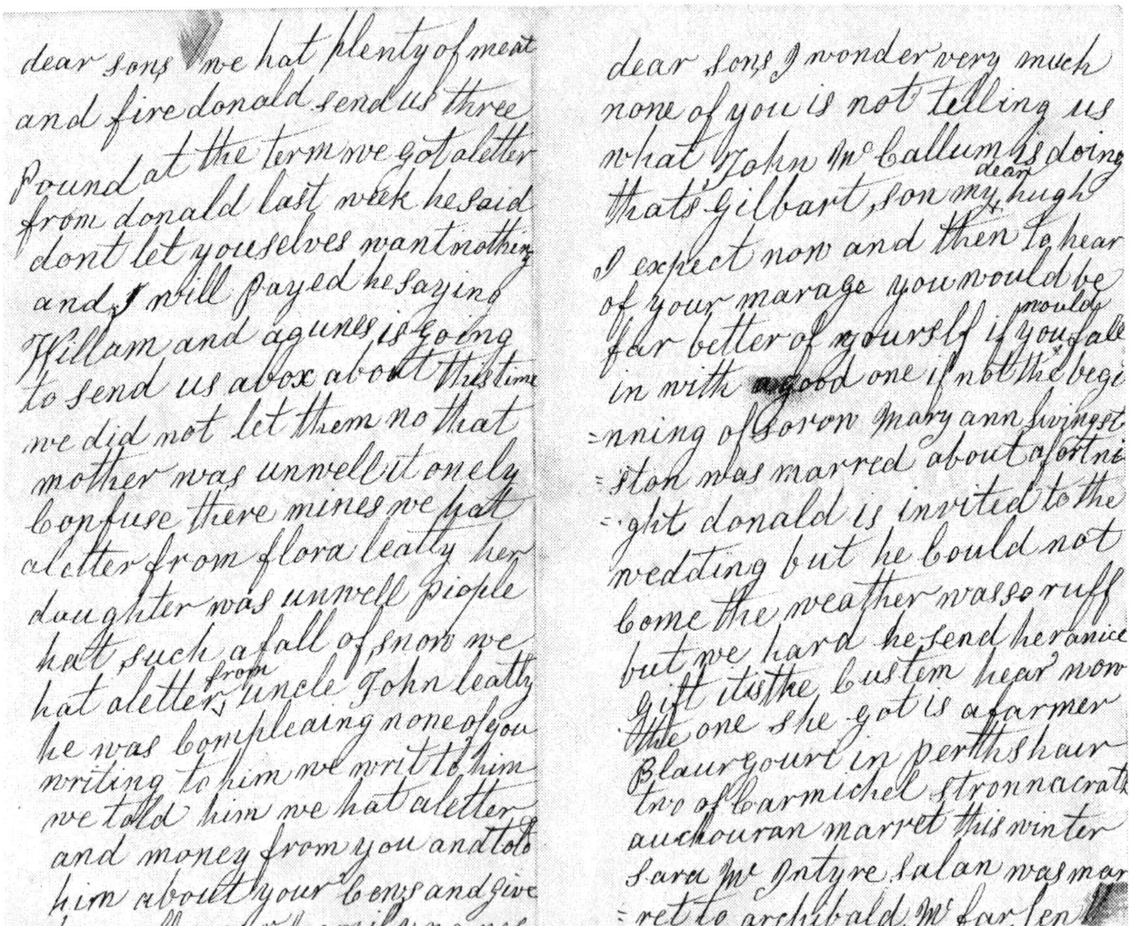

dear sons we hat plenty of meat
and fire donald send us three
Pound at the term we got aletter
from donald last week he said
dont let youselves want nothing
and I will payed he saying
Willam and agunes is going
to send us abox about this time
we did not let them no that
mother was unwell it onely
Confuse there mines we hat
aletter from flora leatty her
doughter was unwell piople
hat such a fall of snow we
hat aletter from uncle John leatty
he was compleaing none of you
writing to him we writ to him
we told him we hat aletter
and money from you and told
him about your Cenrs and give
him all your faemily names

dear sons I wonder very much
none of you is not telling us
what John Mc Callum is doing
thats Gilbart, son my dear hugh
I expect now and then to hear
of your marage you would be
far better of yourslf if you would fall
in with agood one if not the begi
=nning of soron mary ann livingst
=ston was marred about afortni
=ght donald is invited to the
wedding but he could not
come the weather was so ruff
but we hard he send her anice
gift it is the custem hear now
the one she got is a farmer
Blaurgourt in perthshair
two of carmichel stronnacrat
auchouran marret this winter
Sara Mc Intyre salan was mar
=ret to archibald Mc farlen
Gran son marten tirlagan

Image db200

LETTER FROM JOHN MCDOUGALL (b. 1803 Lismore) AND CATHERINE MCCALLUM MCDOUGALL (b. 1809 Lismore) WHO LIVED AT BALLIMACKILLICHAN, ISLE OF LISMORE TO THEIR SONS JOHN MCDOUGALL (b. 1837 Lismore) AND HUGH MCDOUGALL (b. 1842 Lismore) IN MINNESOTA

Balimackillichan Lismore
argyle Shair
Scotland
1886 February 21

My Dear Sons and daughter

We receved you letter wiht two pound and one shilling I went to appin and I goted at portenosh [Portnacroish (Appin)] but I forgot tell you before now there is a post office order in auchnacroish Lismore it is very Convenient my dear Sons you will excuse me for being so long writing to you but we hat a terabel fall of snow and frost and as you know mother is always Complining frost and snow toke got a hold of her I thought she would going I have reson to be thank full she is reving againe the winter is by now dear sons we hat plenty of meat and fire donald send us three Pound at the term we got a letter from donald last week he said dont let youselves want nothing and I will payed he saying Willam and agunes is going to send us a box about this time we did not let them no [know] that mother was unwell it onely Confuse there mines we hat a letter from flora leatly her daughter was unwell piople hat such a fall of snow we hat a letter from uncle John leatly he was compleaing [complaining] none of you writing to him we writ to him we told him we hat a letter and money from you and told him about your Cows and give him all your faemily names dear Sons I wonder very much none of you is not telling us what John McCallum is doing thats Gilbart son my dear hugh I expect now and then to hear of your marage you would be far better of yourself if you would fall in with a good one if not the beginning of sorow Mary ann Livingston was marred about a fortnight donald is invited to the wedding but he Could not Come the weather was so ruff but we hard he send her a nice Gift it is the Custem hear now the one she got is a farmer Blaurgouri [Blairgowrie] in perthshair two of Carmichel Stronnacrath auchouran marret this winter Sara McIntyre Salan was marret to archibald Mcfarlen Gran son marten tirlagan

we hat a vest [visit?] of John McNicol port appin yesterday he is a kine frendly man dear famely we are geting every body kind we have plenty of good obuntatas [potatoes?] we thank you very much for your money the love of it is the roat of all evel John you said you would Come to see us in the fall of the year hugh was saying that he did not Come yet we live every thing in the hand of him he no better

Give our kine love to your wife and her Mother she is very well off she is not very old yet my kind Compliment to you and your Brother hugh and all your famelie we would be obleg to you both if you would rite us offener than do Good by may the Lord be with you all

Your father and mother

John and C. McDougall

Jesus Christ is my porson [portion] poor and nidy [needy] so I be

Notes:

The following phrase, "you is not telling us what John McCallum is doing thats Gilbart son" probably refers to John McCallum (b. 1847), son of Gilbert McCallum (b. 1813 Balure) and Ann McCallum McCallum (b. 1814 Lismore). John McCallum (b. 1847) was the brother of John McDougall's (b. 1837) wife, Isabel. (See notes following letters 26 and 30, above.)

Gilbert died in 1849, a few weeks before the birth of John McDougall's (b. 1837) future wife, Isabel McCallum. Ann McCallum McCallum migrated to the US about 1855 with her son, John, and daughter, Isabel, eventually settling in Minnesota. Gilbert was a brother of Catherine McCallum McDougall, making him the maternal uncle of Isabel's husband, John McDougall (b. 1837). "John McCallum Gilbart's son" and Isabel would have been John McDougall's (b. 1837) cousins. For more information about the McCallum families of Balure and Killean, see Appendix 9.

Plate 32.1. Stronacroibh, Lismore 2013

Letter **#33**

March 22[d] 1886

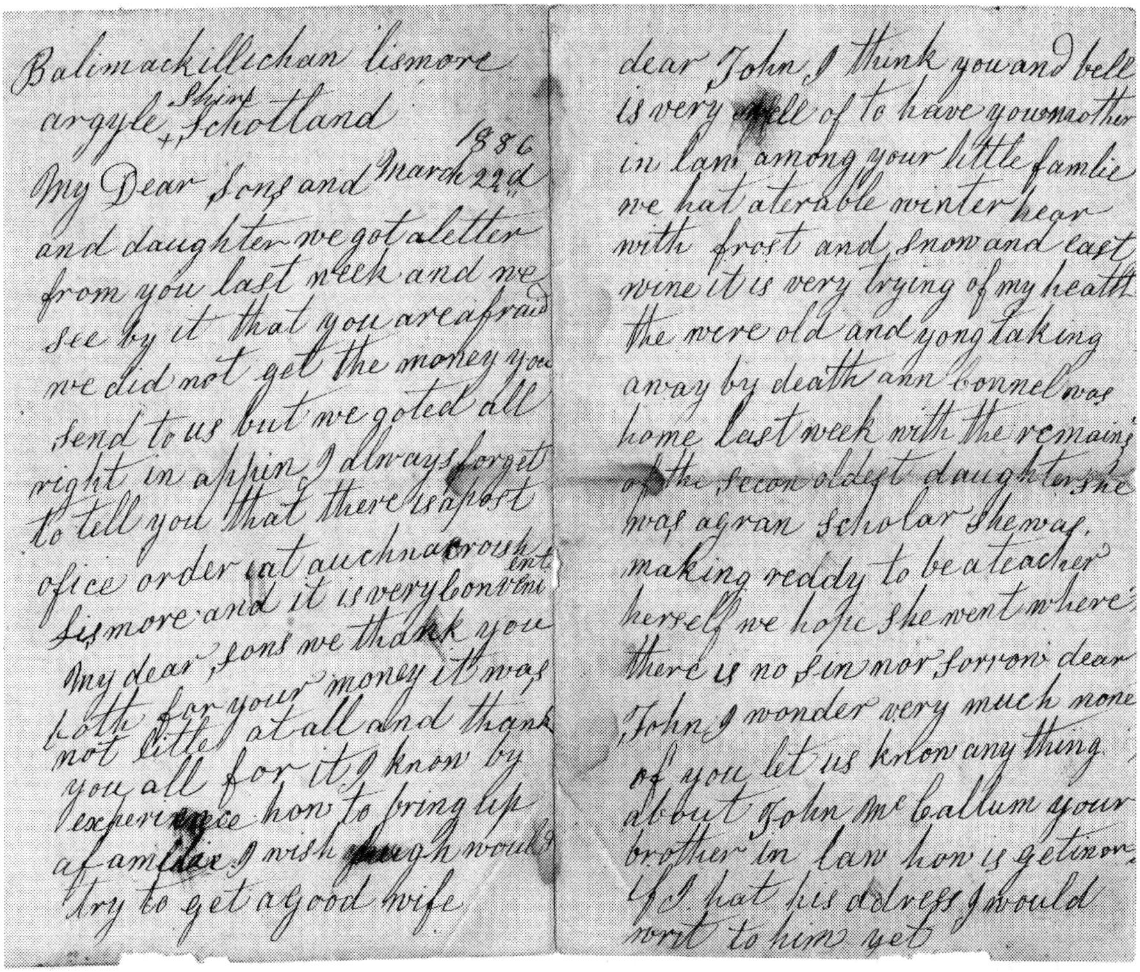
Balimackillichan lismore
argyle Shire Schottland
1886
My Dear Sons and March 22d
and daughter we got a letter
from you last week and we
see by it that you are afraid
we did not get the money you
send to us but we goted all
right in appin I always forget
to tell you that there is a post
ofice order at auchnacroish
lismore and it is very convenient
My dear sons we thank you
both for your money it was
not littel at all and thank
you all for it I know by
experience how to bring up
a famlie I wish hugh would
try to get a good wife

dear John I think you and bell
is very well of to have your mother
in law among your little famlie
we hat a terable winter hear
with frost and snow and east
wine it is very trying of my health
the were old and yong taking
away by death ann Connel was
home last week with the remains
of the secon oldest daughter she
was a gran scholar she was
making reddy to be a teacher
herself we hope she went where
there is no sin nor sorrow dear
John I wonder very much none
of you let us know any thing
about John Mc Callum your
brother in law how is getin on
if I hat his adress I would
writ to him yet

Image db203

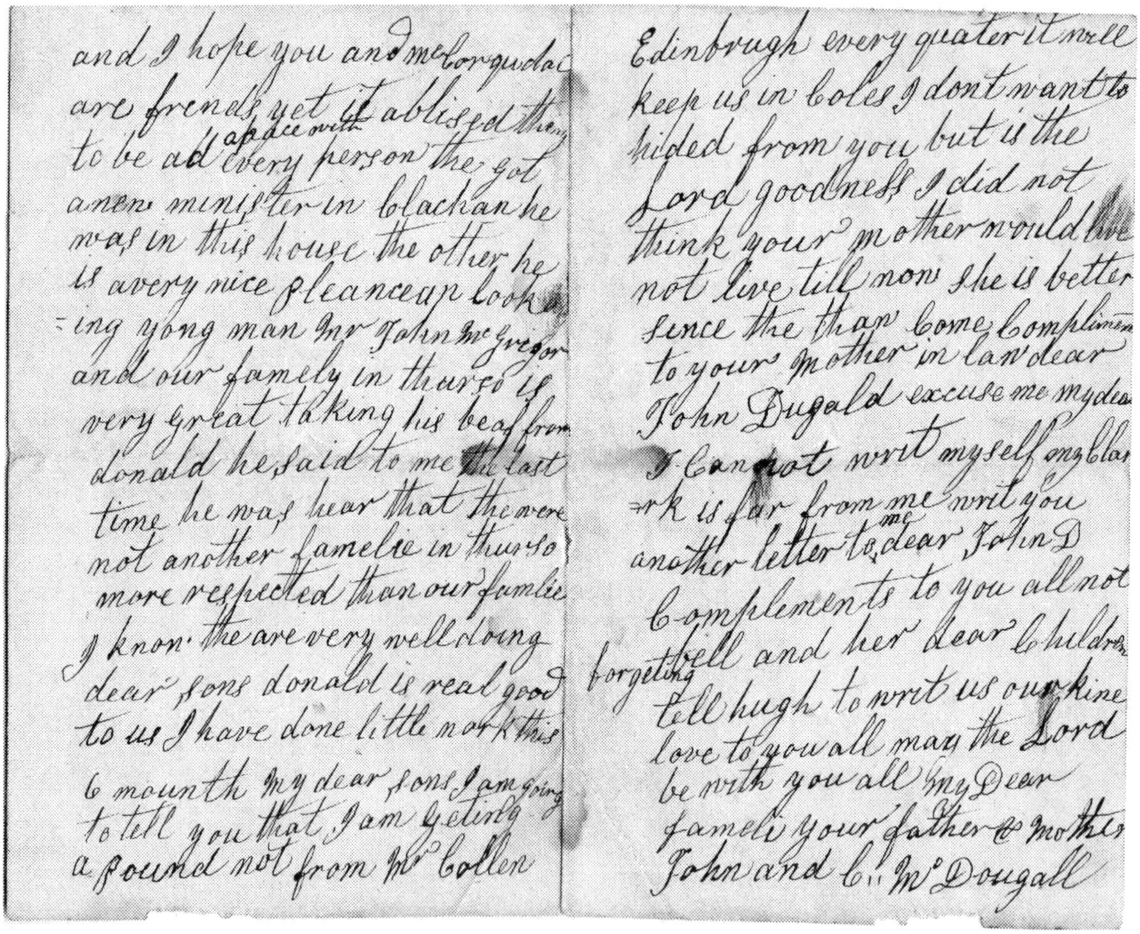
and I hope you and Mc Corquedal
are frends yet it ablissed them
to be at apace with every person the got
anew minister in blachan he
was in this house the other he
is avery nice pleanceup look
=ing yong man Mr John McGregor
and our famely in thurso is
very Great taking his beaf from
donald he said to me the last
time he was hear that thewere
not another famelie in thurso
more respected than our famlie
I know the are very welldoing
dear sons donald is real good
to us I have done little work this
6 mounth my dear sons I am going
to tell you that I am geting
a pound not from Mr Collen

Edinbrugh every quater it will
keep us in Coles I dont want to
hided from you but is the
Lord goodness I did not
think your mother would live
not live till now she is better
since the than Come Complimen
to your mother in law dear
John Dugald excuse me my dea
I Can not writ myself ony Clar
=rk is far from me writ you
another letter to me dear John D
Complements to you all not
forgeting bell and her dear Children
tell hugh to writ us our kine
love to you all may the Lord
be with you all my Dear
famelie your father & mother
John and C.. McDougall

Image db204

LETTER FROM JOHN MCDOUGALL (b. 1803 Lismore) AND CATHERINE MCCALLUM MCDOUGALL (b. 1809 Lismore) WHO LIVED AT BALLIMACKILLICHAN, ISLE OF LISMORE TO THEIR SON JOHN MCDOUGALL (b. 1837 Lismore) IN MINNESOTA

Balimackillichan lismore
argyle Shire Schotland
1886 March 22d

My Dear Sons and and daughter we got a letter from you last week and we see by it that you are afraid we did not get the money you send to us but we goted all right in appin I always forget to tell you that there is a post ofice order at auchnacroish Lismore and it is very convenient My dear sons we thank you both for your money it was not litle at all and thank you all for it I know by experience how to bring up a familie I wish hugh would try to get a good wife

dear John I think you and bell is very well of to have your mother in law among your little famlie we hat a terable winter hear with frost and snow and east wine [wind?] it is very trying of my health the were old and yong taking away by death ann Connel was home last week with the remains of the secon oldest daughter she was a gran scholar she was making reddy to be a teacher herself we hope she went where there is no sin nor sorrow dear John I wonder very much none of you let us know any thing about John McCallum your brother in law how is getin on if I hat his adress I would writ to him yet

and I hope you and McCorqudal are frends yet is a blised thing to be ad apace with every person the got a new minister in Clachan he was in this house the other he is a very nice pleancean looking yong man Mr John McGrigor and our famely in thurso is very great taking his beaf from donald he said to me the last time he was hear that the were not another famelie in thurso more respected than our famlie I know the are very well doing dear Sons donald is very good to us I have done little work this 6 mounth My dear Sons I am going to tell you that I am geting a pound not from Mr Collen Edinbrugh every quater it will keep us in Coles I dont want to hided from you but is the Lord goodness I did not think your mother would not live till now she is better since the thaw Come Compliments to your Mother in law dear John Dugald excuse me my dear I Cannot writ myself my Clark is far from me writ you another letter to me dear John D

Complements to you all not forgeting bell and her dear Children

tell hugh to writ us our kine love to you all may the Lord be with you all My Dear fameli

your father & Mother

John and C. McDougall

Notes:

1. "John McCallum your brother in law" would have been John McCallum (b. 1847), son of Ann McCallum McCallum (b. 1814) and Gilbert McCallum (b. 1813 Balure). He was the brother of Isabel McCallum McDougall and migrated to the US in 1855 with his mother and sister, eventually settling to farm in Minnesota. (See notes following Letters 2, 7, 26, 30 and Appendix 9.)
2. For information about Mr. John McGregor, see the note following Letter 23, December 6, 1881.

Plate 33.1. Achnacroish, Lismore from the Oban Ferry

Plate 33.2. Lismore Spring Lamb

Letter **#34**

Undated

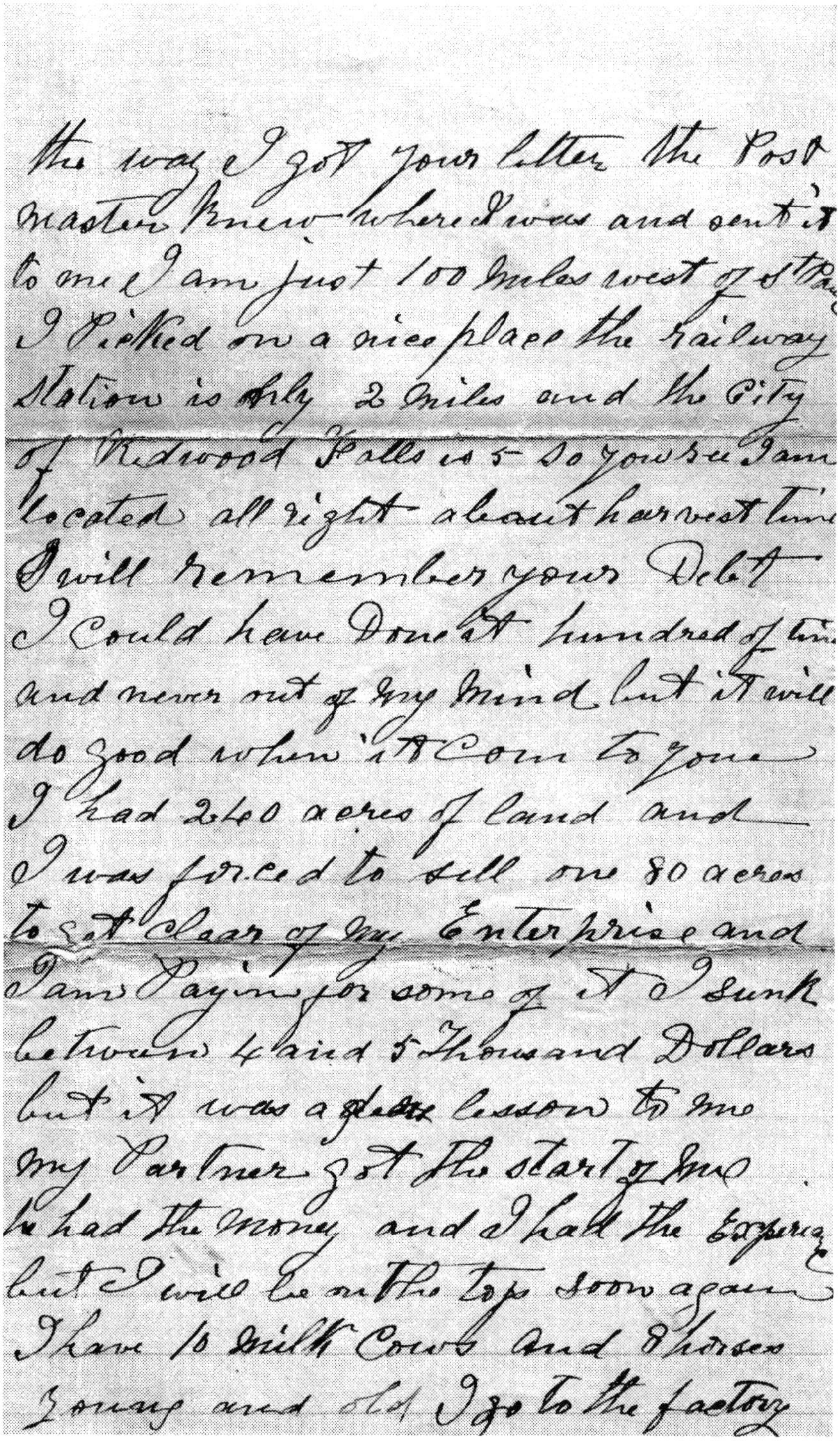
the way I got your letter the Post
Master knew where I was and sent it
to me I am just 100 Miles west of St Pau
I Picked on a nice place the Railway
Station is only 2 Miles and the City
of Redwood Falls is 5 So you see I am
located all right about harvest time
I will remember your Debt
I Could have Done it hundred of tim
and never out of my Mind but it will
do good when it Com to you
I had 240 acres of land and
I was forced to sell one 80 acres
to get Clear of my Enterprise and
I am Payin for some of it I sunk
between 4 and 5 Thousand Dollars
but it was a lesson to me
my Partner got the start of me
he had the money and I had the Experie
but I will be on the top soon again
I have 10 Milk Cows and 8 horses
young and old I go to the factory

Image db224

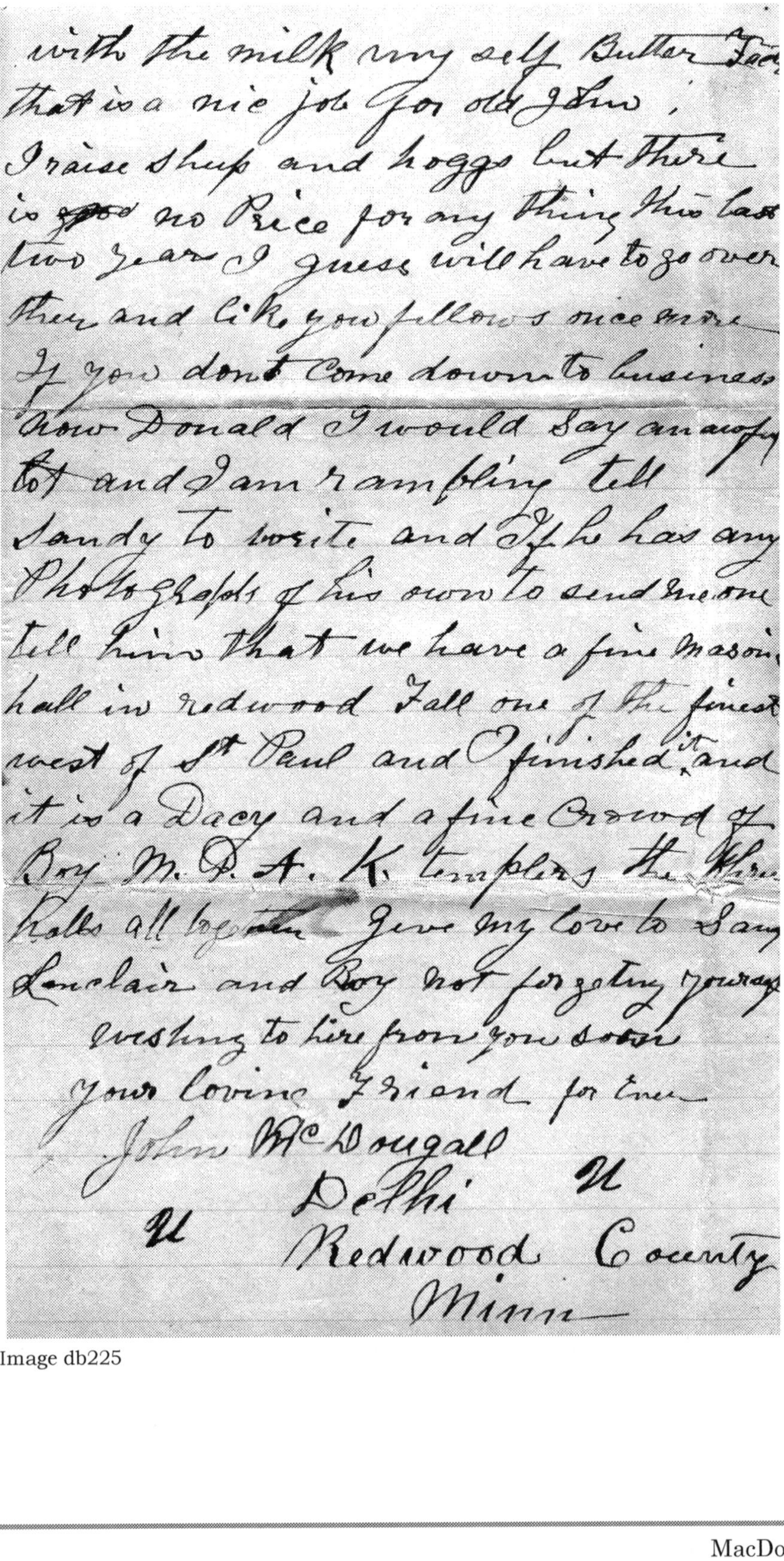
with the milk my self Butter Fac
that is a nie job for old John,
I raise sheep and hoggs but there
is ~~good~~ no Price for any thing this last
two year I guess will have to go over
ther and lik you fellows once more
If you dont Come down to business
Now Donald I would Say an awfu
lot and I am rambling tell
Sandy to write and If he has any
Photographs of his own to send me one
tell him that we have a fine Mason
hall in redwood Fall one of the finest
west of St Paul and I finished it and
it is a Dacy and a fine Crowd of
Boy M. D. A. K. templers the Whi
Kalbs all together Give my love to Sam
Sinclair and Boy not forgeting yourself
wishing to hire from you soon
your loving Friend for Ever
John McDougall
U Delhi U
Redwood County
Minn

Image db225

LETTER FROM JOHN MCDOUGALL (1837 - 1896) LIVING IN MINNESOTA TO DONALD MCCONOCHIE IN OBAN

[undated]

the way I got your letter the Post Master knew where I was and sent it to me I am just 100 miles west of St. Paul I Picked on a nice place the railway station is only 2 miles and the City of Redwood Falls is 5 so you see I am located all right about harvest time I will remember your Debt I could have Done it hundred of time and never out of my Mind but it will do good when it com to you

I had 240 acres of land and I was forced to sell one 80 acres to get clear of my Enterprise and I am Payin for some of it I sunk between 4 and 5 Thousand Dollars but it was a good[?] lesson to me my Partner got the start of me he had the Money and I had the Experience but I will be on the top soon again I have 10 milk cows and 8 horses young and old I go to the factory with the milk my self Butter Fac... That is a nic job for old John:

I raise sheep and hoggs but there is no Price for any thing this last two years I guess will have to go over ther and like you fellows once more

If you dont come down to business now Donald I would say an awful lot and I am rambling tell Sandy [Sinclair, friend, Oban] to write and If he has any Photographs of his own to send me one Tell him that we have a fine Masonic hall in redwood Fall one of the finest west of St Paul and I finished it and it is a Dacy and a fine Crowd of Boy M.P.A.K. templars the three halls all together Give my love to Sandy Sinclair and Boy not forgeting yourself

Wishing to hire from you soon

Your loving Friend for Ever

John McDougall

Delhi

Redwood County

Minn

Plate 34.1. Masonic Hall, Mill & 3rd Streets
Redwood Falls, Minnesota

Plate 34.2. Masonic Hall, Redwood Falls
The date above the windows suggests the letter was written in 1886 or later.

In addition to performing woodwork on the Masonic Lodge and other buildings in Redwood Falls, John McDougall (b. 1837) and his brother-in-law, Alexander Milne, performed woodwork on the interior of the Redwood Falls Presbyterian Church, pictured below.

Plate 34.3. First Presbyterian Church
Redwood Falls, Minnesota

Plate 34.4. First Presbyterian Church, Redwood Falls
2014
Woodwork by John McDougall (b. 1837 Lismore) and
his Brother-in-law, Alexander Milne

Letter **#35**

Undated (about 1887)

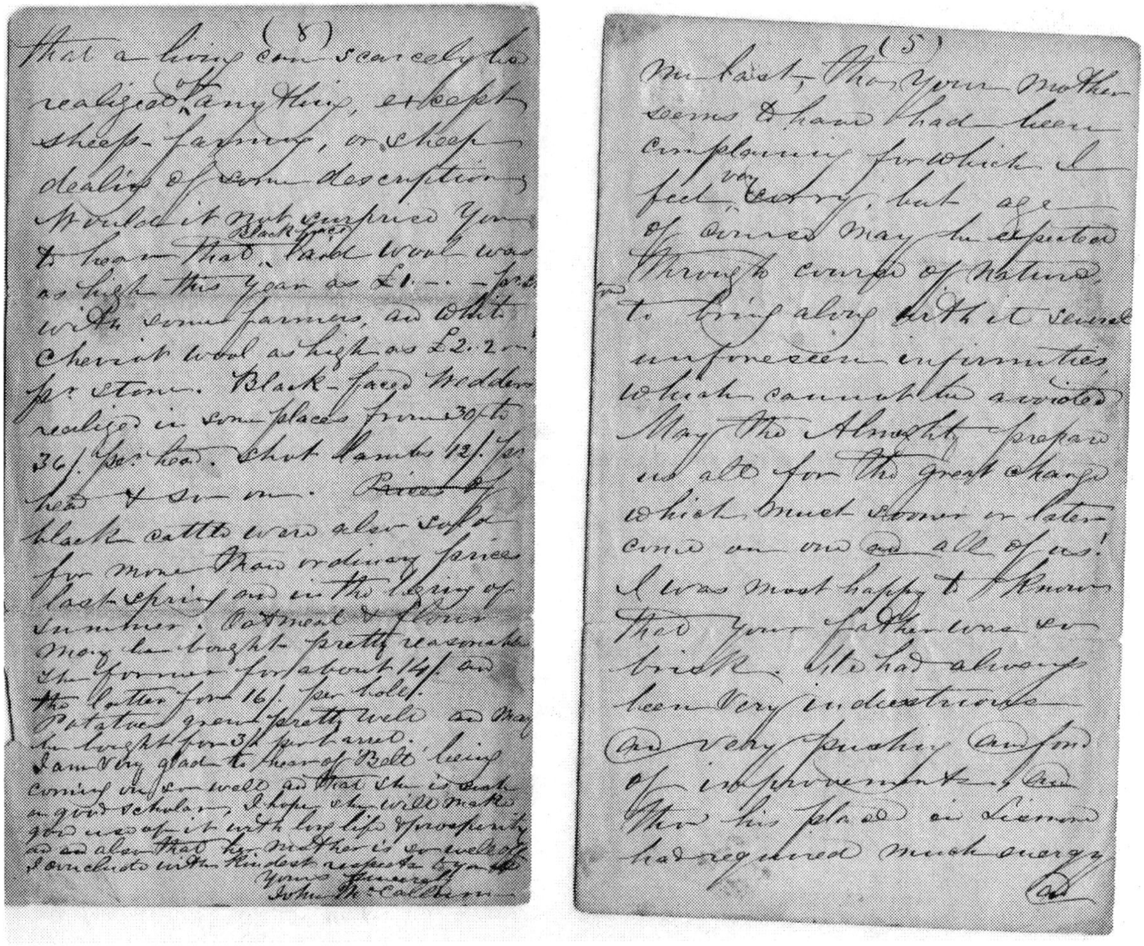
(8)

that a living can scarcely be
realized of anything, except
sheep-farming, or sheep
dealing of some description.
Would it not surprise you
to learn that Black-faced Laid Wool was
as high this year as £1.-.- per
with some farmers, and White
Cheviot wool as high as £2.2.-
per stone. Black-faced Wedders
realized in some places from 30/- to
36/- per head. Cheviot Lambs 12/- per
head & so on. ~~Prices of~~
black cattle were also sold
for more than ordinary prices
last spring and in the beginning of
summer. Oatmeal & flour
may be bought pretty reasonable
The former for about 14/- and
the latter for 16/- per boll.
Potatoes grew pretty well and may
be bought for 3/- per barrel.
I am very glad to hear of 'Bell' being
coming on so well and that she is such
a good scholar, I hope she will make
good use of it with long life & prosperity
and also that her mother is so well off.
I conclude with kindest respects to you all
Yours sincerely
John McCallum

(5)

me last, tho' your mother
seems to have had been
complaining for which I
feel very sorry, but age
of times may be expected
through course of nature,
to bring along with it several
unforeseen infirmities
which cannot be avoided.
May the Almighty prepare
us all for the great change
which must sooner or later
come on one and all of us!
I was most happy to know
that your father was so
brisk. He had always
been very industrious
and very pushing and fond
of improvements, and
then his place in Lismore
had required much energy
and

Image db206

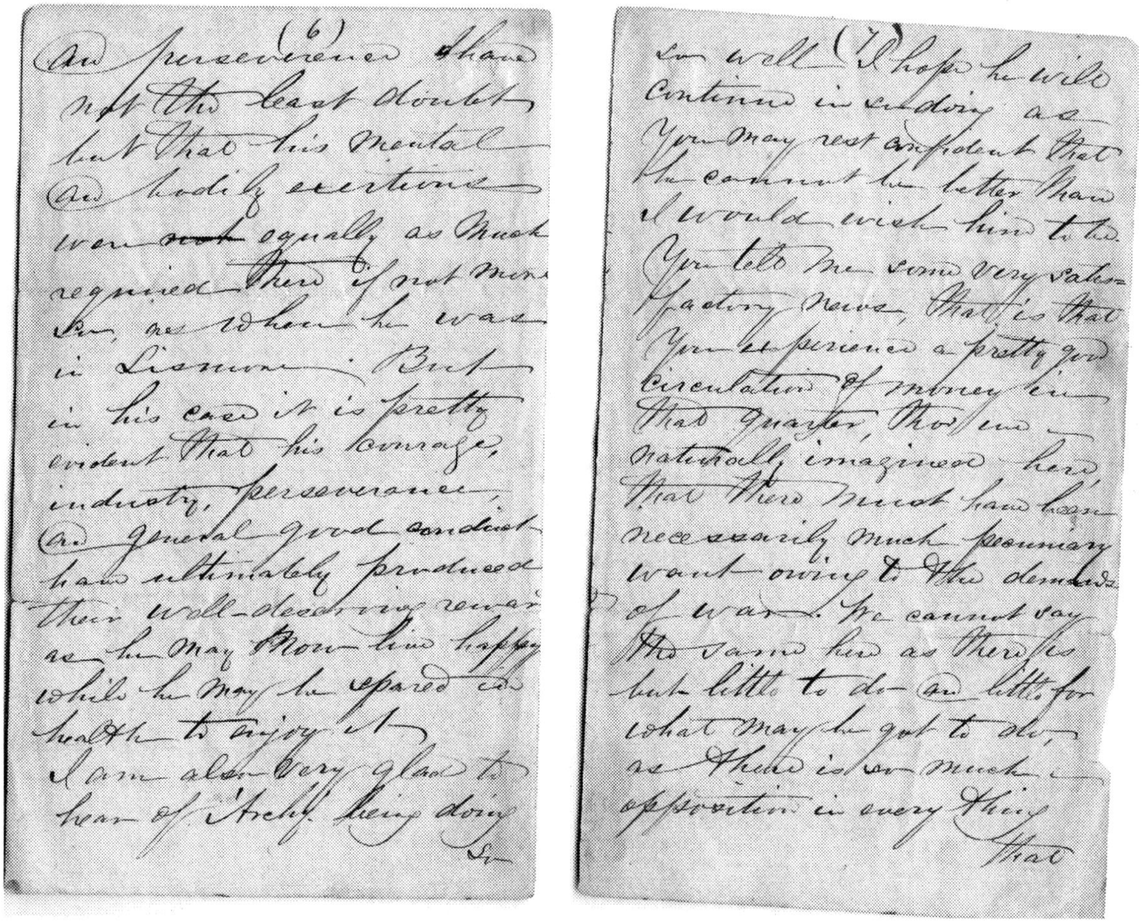

(6)
an perseverance I have
not the least doubt
but that his mental
and bodily exertions
were ~~not~~ equally as much
required there if not more
so, as when he was
in Lismore. But
in his case it is pretty
evident that his courage,
industry, perseverance,
and general good conduct
have ultimately produced
their well-deserving reward
as he may know live happy
while he may be spared in
health to enjoy it.
I am also very glad to
hear of Archy being doing
so

(7)
so well. I hope he will
continue in so doing as
you may rest confident that
he cannot be better than
I would wish him to be.
You tell me some very satisfactory news, that is that
you experience a pretty good
circulation of money in
that quarter, tho' we
naturally imagined here
that there must have been
necessarily much pecuniary
want owing to the demands
of war. We cannot say
the same here as there is
but little to do and little for
what may be got to do,
as there is so much
opposition in every thing
that

Image db207

TO JOHN MCDOUGALL (b. 1837 Lismore)
USA
FROM JOHN MCCALLUM BALURE
LISMORE

Written after Catherine McCallum McDougall died and her husband, John McDougall, moved to Thurso to stay with their children, about 1887

(partial letter)

[___?] last, tho your mother seems to have had been complaining for which I feel very sorry, but age of course may be expected through the course of nature, to bring along with it several unforeseen infirmities, which cannot be avoided

May the Almighty prepare us all for the great changes which must sooner or later come on one and all of us! I was most happy to know that your father was so brisk. He had always been very industrious and very pushing[?] and fond of improvements, and then his place in Lismore had required much energy and perseverance I have not the least doubt but that his mental and bodily exertions were equally as much required there if not more so as when he was in Lismore. But in his case it is pretty evident that his courage, industry, perseverance and general good conduct have ultimately produced their well-deserving reward as he may now live happy while he may be spared in health to enjoy it.

I am also very glad to hear of Archy [McCallum in New York, USA] being doing so well I hope he will continue in so doing as you may rest confident that he cannot be better than I would wish him to be.

You tell me some very satisfactory news, that is that you experience a pretty good circulation of money in that quarter, tho we naturally imagined here that there must have been necessarily much pecuniary want owing to the demand of war. We cannot say the same here as there is very little to do and little for what may be got to do, as there is so much opposition in every thing that a living can scarcely be realized of anything, except sheep-farming, or sheep dealing of some description. Would it not surprise you to hear that Black face laid wool was as high this year as £1._._ pr. stone with some farmers, and white Cheviot wool as high as £2.2_ pr. stone. Black faced Wedders realized in some places from 30/_ to 36/. per head. shot lambs 12/. pr head & so on. Black cattle were also sold for more than ordinary prices last spring and in the begining of summer. Oatmeal & flour may be bought pretty reasonable the former for about 14/. and the latter for 16/. per bole.

Potatoes grew pretty well and may be bought for 3/. per barrel.

I am very glad to hear of 'Bell' being coming on so well and that she is such a good scholar. I hope she will make good use of it with long life & prosperity and also that her mother [Ann McCallum] is so well off I conclude with the kindest respect to you all

Yours
sincerely

John
McCallum

Plate 35.1. Lismore Sheep

Plate 35.2. Balure

Plate 35.3. Memorial Stone for Joseph Milne, Son of Alexander Milne and Margaret McDougall Milne
Redwood Falls Cemetery, Redwood Falls, Minnesota
Joseph died in Scotland, March 14, 1887, age 9 months, 12 days.

Plate 35.4. Alexander Milne, Margaret McDougall Milne and their Children
The photo was taken in Scotland before the family left for the US in May 1887. The children are Dougald [b. 1885] on Margaret's lap, William (Billy) [b. 1883] on the floor. Behind him is Donald [b. 1882] and behind Donald, with a hand on his shoulder is James (Jim) [b. 1877]. Alexander [b. 1850] is behind Jim. On the other side, we think John [b. 1878] is standing with his hand on Alexander "Alec" and sometimes "Sandy" [b. 1880]. (Tiffany, S. October 16, 2012)
See Appendix 8, Family Tree #5 (the family tree of Margaret McDougall and Alexander Milne) for more information.

Letter **#36**

July 27th 1888

This letter is from Donald McDougall in Thurso
to his brother, John, in Minnesota.

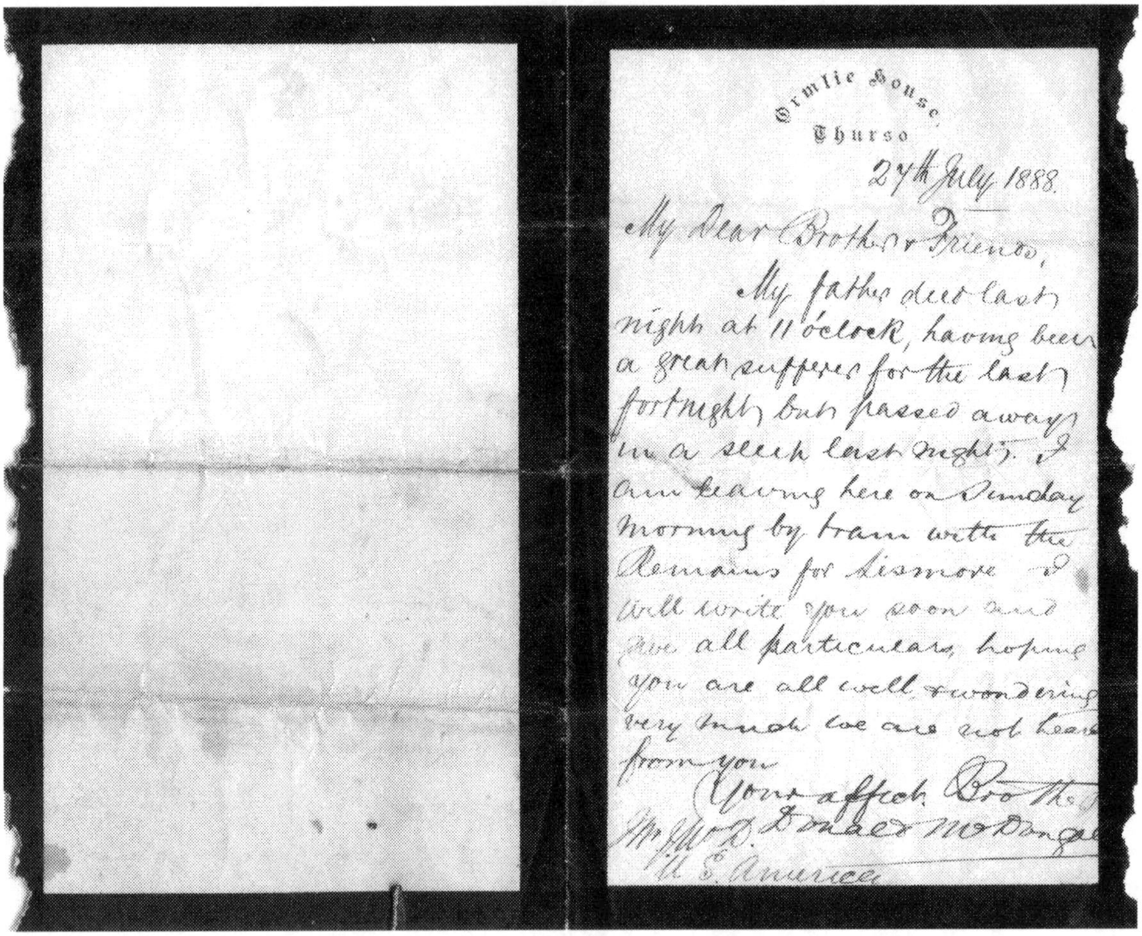
Ormlie House
Thurso

27th July 1888.

My Dear Brother & Friends,

My father died last night at 11 o'clock, having been a great sufferer for the last fortnight but passed away in a sleep last night. I am leaving here on Sunday morning by train with the Remains for Lismore. I will write you soon and give all particulars, hoping you are all well & wondering very much we are not hear from you

Your affect. Brother
Mr J McD. Donald McDougall
U S America

Image db209

LETTER TO JOHN MCDOUGALL (b. 1837 Lismore)
DELHI, REDWOOD COUNTY, MINNESOTA U.S.A.
FROM HIS BROTHER DONALD MCDOUGALL (b. about 1845 Lismore)
REGARDING
THEIR FATHER'S (John McDougall b. 1803 Lismore) DEATH

Ormlie House
Thurso
27th July 1888

My Dear Brother & Friends,

My father died last night at 11:00 o'clock, having been a great sufferer for the last fortnight, but passed away in a sleep last night. I am leaving here on Sunday morning by train with the Remains for Lismore I will write you soon and give all particulars, hoping you are all well, & wondering very much we are not heard from you

Your affect. Brother
Donald McDougall

Mr J.McD.
U.S. America

Plate 36.1. Memorial Stone for John McDougall (weaver), Catherine McCallum and their Children Lismore Parish Church, Old Graveyard, Gravestone #229

Inscription: "Erected by their son Donald in memory of John McDougall died July 28. [18]88. Catherine McCallum died May 26.[18]86 also their family Dougall died June [18]55, Mary died June 18 [18]74, Margaret died Oct 16. [18]88, John died Feb 5. [18]96, Flora died Apr 1929 aged 78 interred at Thurso 'Blessed are the dead which die in the Lord'" (White, A., 2009)

Plate 36.2. Lismore Parish Church, Old Graveyard
Facing Memorial to John McDougall, Catherine McCallum
and their Children
2011

Plate 36.3. View from Lismore Parish Church, Old Graveyard to the Main Road Easter Sunday, April 2011

Letter #37

January 20th 1896

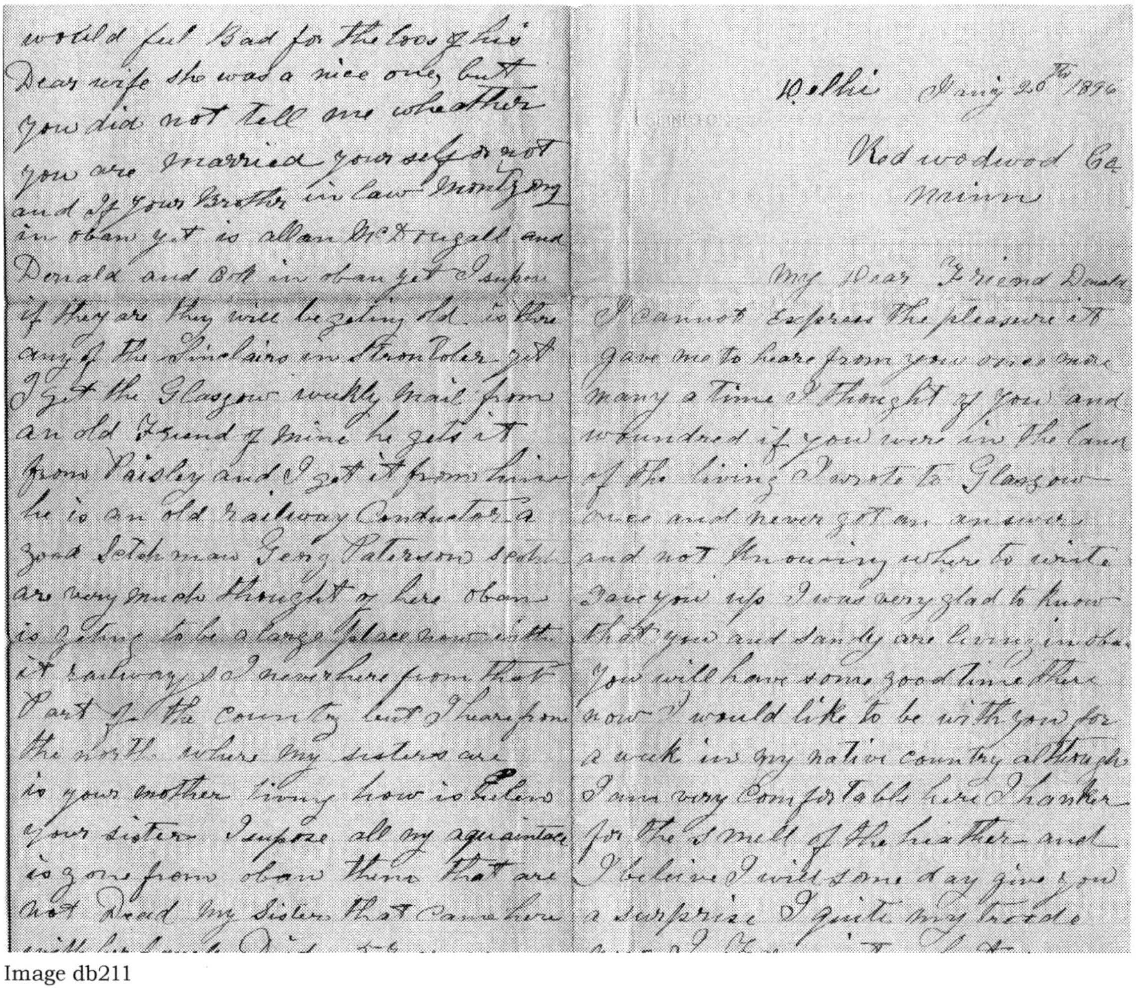

Delhi Jany 20th 1896

Redwodwod Co

Maine

My Dear Friend Dona

I cannot Express the pleasure it
gave me to heare from you once more
many a time I thought of you and
wondred if you were in the land
of the living I wrote to Glasgow
once and never got an answer
and not knowing where to write
gave you up I was very glad to know
that you and Sandy are living in oban
you will have some good time there
now I would like to be with you for
a week in my native country although
I am very Comfortable here I hanker
for the smell of the heather and
I believe I will some day give you
a surprise I quite my trade

would feel Bad for the loss of his
Dear wife she was a nice one, but
you did not tell me whether
you are married your self or not
and if your Brother in law montgomery
in oban yet is allan McDougall and
Donald and Bob in oban yet I supose
if they are they will be geting old is there
any of the Sinclairs in Strontolier yet
I get the Glasgow weekly mail from
an old friend of mine he gets it
from Paisley and I get it from him
he is an old railway Conductor a
good Scotchman Geng Paterson scotch
are very much thought of here oban
is geting to be a large place now with
it railway I never here from that
Part of the Country but I heare from
the north where my sisters are
is your mother living how is Helen
your sister I supose all my aquaintace
is gone from oban them that are
not Dead my Sister that Came here

Image db211

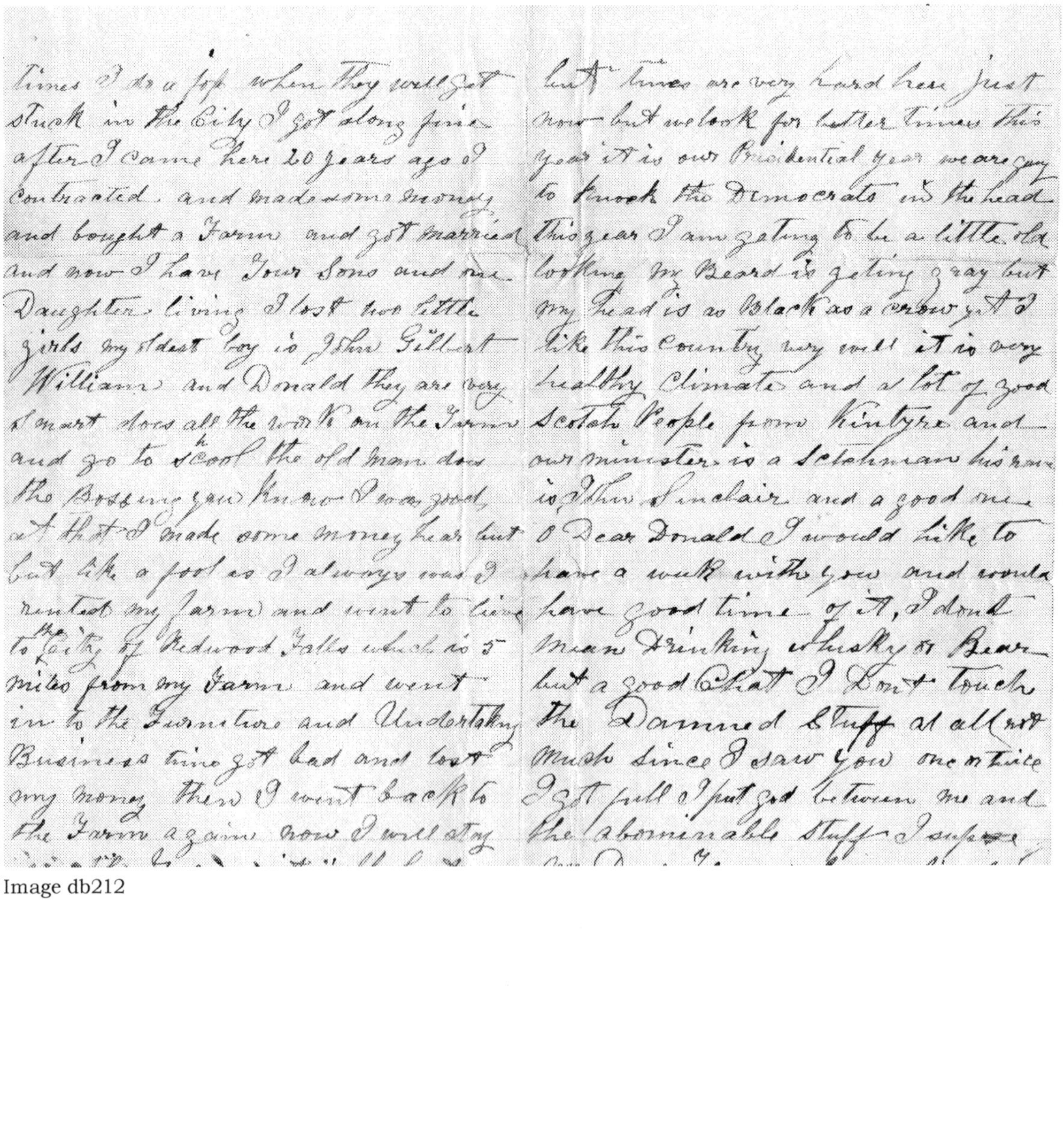
times I do a job when they will get
stuck in the City I got along fine
after I came here 20 years ago I
contracted and made some money
and bought a Farm and got married
and now I have Four Sons and one
Daughter living I lost two little
girls my oldest boy is John Gilbert
William and Donald they are very
smart does all the work on the Farm
and go to school the old man does
the Bossing you know I was good
at that I made some money hear but
but like a fool as I always was I
rented my Farm and went to live
to the City of Redwood Falls which is 5
miles from my Farm and went
in to the Furniture and Undertaking
Business times got bad and lost
my money then I went back to
the Farm again now I will stay

but times are very hard here just
now but we look for better times this
year it is our Presidential year we are going
to knock the Democrats in the head
this year I am geting to be a little old
looking my Beard is geting gray but
my head is as Black as a crow yet I
like this Country very well it is very
healthy Climate and a lot of good
Scotch People from Kintyre and
our minister is a Scotchman his name
is John Sinclair and a good one
O Dear Donald I would like to
have a walk with you and would
have good time of it, I dont
mean drinking whisky or Bear
but a good Chat I Don't touch
the Damned Stuff at all not
much since I saw you once or twice
I got full I put god between me and
the abominable stuff I suppose

Image db212

LETTER FROM JOHN MCDOUGALL (b. 1837 Lismore) WRITING FROM MINNESOTA, USA TO FRIEND DONALD MCCONOCHIE IN OBAN

Delhi Jan'y 20th 1896
Redwodwod Co.
Minn

My Dear Friend Donald

I cannot Express The pleasure it gave me to heare from you once More Many a time I thought of you and woundred if you were in the land of the living I wrote to Glasgow once and never got an answer and not knowing where to write gave you up I was very glad to know that you and Sandy are living in Oban You will have some good time there now I would like to be with you for a week in my native country although I am very comfortable here I hanker for the smell of the heather and I beleive I will some day give you a surprise I quite my trade now I farm it but some times I do a job when they will get stuck in the City I got along fine after I came here 20 years ago I contracted [construction/carpentry] and made some money and bought a Farm and got married and now I have Four Sons and one Daughter living I lost two little girls my oldest boy is John [b. 1877] Gilbert [b. 1881] William [b. 1883] and Donald [b. 1885] They are very smart does all the work on the Farm and go to school the old man does the Bossing you know I was good at that I made some money hear but but like a fool as I always was I rented my farm and went to live to the City of Redwood Falls which is 5 miles from my Farm and went in to the Furniture and Undertaking Business time got bad and lost my money then I went back to the Farm again now I will stay on the Farm it is the best but times are very hard here just now but we look for better times this year it is our Presidential year we are going to knock the Democrats in the head this year I am geting to be a little old looking my Beard is geting gray but my head is as Black as a crow yet I like this country very well it is very healthy climate and a lot of good Scotch People from Kintyre and our minister is a Sctchman his name is John Sinclair and a good one

O Dear Donald I would like to have a week with you and would have a good time of it, I dont mean Drinking whiskey or Bear but a good Chat I Dont touch the Damned Stuff at all not much since I saw you onc or twice I got full I put god between me and the abominable stuff I supose my Dear Friend Sandy Sinclair would feel Bad for the loss of his Dear wife she was a nice one, but you did not tell me wheather you are married yourself or not and If your Brother in law Montgomery in Oban yet is Allan Macdougall and Donald and Cole in Oban yet I supose if they are they will be geting old is there any of the Sinclairs in Strontoler[?] yet I get the Glasgow weekly mail from an old Friend of mine he gets it from Paisley and I get it from him he is an old railway Conductor a good Sctchman Georg Paterson Scotch are very much thought of here Oban is geting to be a large place now with it railways I never here from that Part of the Country but I heare from the north where my sisters are is your Mother living how is Eilen your sister I supose all my aquaintace is gone from oban them that are not Dead My Sister that came here with her family Died 5 years ago

(Rest of letter missing)

Note: John McDougall (b. 1837 Lismore), son of John McDougall (weaver) and Catherine McCallum McDougall, passed away on February 5, 1896, 16 days after writing this letter.

Plate 37.1.
Article about John McDougall's Death
***Redwood Reveille*, February 8, 1896**

REDWOOD REVEILLE

HISTORICAL SOCIETY.

VOL. XI. REDWOOD FALLS, MINNESOTA, SATURDAY, FEBRUARY 8, 1896. NO 16.

AN OLD SETTLER KILLED.

John McDougal Falls From His Wagon.

And Death Results Shortly Afterward.

We much regret the sad circumstances necessitating us to chronicle the death of John McDougal, an enterprising and respected farmer of Delhi township, which occurred near the hour of five o'clock on Wednesday afternoon, in this city, as a result of an accident. Mr. McDougal had arrived in town near noon, as was his custom in delivering milk to the creamery here. Near four o'clock, after attending to business matters, he, mounted his wagon, then standing in front of A. Miline's shop, on Mill Street, and started for home. Several citizens were upon the street and shortly after the team had passed the city watering fountain, Mr. McDougal was seen to pitch suddenly forward and fall between the team and wagon. He was hastily picked up and carried to Mr. Miline's shop and although Dr. Flinn, assisted by others, exerted every effort to save him death, came after some forty-five minutes.

In falling the unfortunate man had struck with his forehead and face upon the hard ground causing concussion of the brain, from which he died. Marks were to be seen upon his fore head and face, the worst being a cut upon the nose just below his left eye.

As to the cause of the accident no definite reason can be given, but it is thought that a stroke of heart disease or something similar was the cause of his falling forward so suddenly.

Deceased some fifty-five years of age and leaves a widow and seven children, the eldest a son 18 years of age, to mourn his death. He was a Scotchman by birth but settled in Redwood Falls at an early day when he engaged in the furniture business, but of late years has been an upright and industriour farme of Delhi. Upright and honest, had John McDougal lived, and his warm friends can be counted by the score; and to the widow and children is extended the deep sympathy of a sorrowing community.

The funeral took place yesterday, the service being held at the house by Rev. John Sinclair, in which Rev. H. Mc Henry also took part.

The Masons, of which Mr. McDougal was a member, met the cortege outside town and marched in front of the hearse to the cemetery. After prayer by Mr. Sinclair at the grave, the Masons conducted their service which is always pretty and impressive.

Provided by Redwood Falls Public Library

REDWOOD REVEILLE

Vol. XI REDWOOD FALLS, MINNESOTA, SATURDAY, FEBRUARY 8, 1896 No. 16

AN OLD SETTLER KILLED

John McDougal Falls From His Wagon.

And Death Results Shortly Afterward.

We much regret the sad circumstances necessitating us to chronicle the death of John McDougal, an enterprising and respected farmer of Delhi township, which occurred near the hour of five o'clock on Wednesday afternoon, in this city, as a result of an accident. Mr. McDougal had arrived in town near noon, as was his custom in delivering milk to the creamery here. Near four o'clock, after attending to business matters, he, mounted his wagon, then standing in front of A. Miline's shop, on Mill Street, and started for home. Several citizens were upon the street and shortly after the team had passed the city watering fountain, Mr. McDougal was seen to pitch suddenly forward and fall between the team and wagon. He was hastily picked up and carried to Mr. Miline's shop and although Dr. Flinn, assisted by others, exerted every effort to save him death, came after some fort-five minutes.

In falling the unfortunate man had struck with his forehead and face upon the hard ground causing concussion of the brain, from which he died. Marks were to be seen upon his fore head and face, the worst being a cut upon the nose just below his left eye.

As to the cause of the accident no definite reason can be given, but it is thought that a stroke of heart disease or something similar was the cause of his falling forward so suddenly.

Deceased some fifty-five years of age and leaves a widow and seven children, the eldest a son 18 years of age, to mourn his death. He was a Scotch man by birth but settled in Redwood Falls at an early day when he engaged in the furniture business, but of late years has been an upright and industriousr farme of Delhi. Upright and honest, had John McDougal lived, and his warm friends can be counted by the score; and to the widow and children is extended the deep sympathy of a sorrowing community.

The funeral took place yesterday, the service being held at the house by Rev. John Sinclair, in which Rev. H. McHenry also took part.

The Masons, of which Mr. McDougal was a member, met the cortege outside town and marched in front of the hearse to the cemetery. After prayer by Mr. Sinclair at the grave, the Masons conducted [....] service which is always pretty and impressive.

(Redwood Reveille, February 8, 1896)

Plate 37.2. Gravestone of John McDougall (b. 1837)
Redwood Falls Cemetery, Redwood Falls, Minnesota

"Born April ... 1837
Died Feb. 5 1896
At Rest
McDougall"

Plate 37.3

"Catherine, Daughter of John
& Isabell McDougall
Died June 11, 1889, Age ..."

Plate 37.4

"Mary, Daughter of J&I McDougall
Died March ..., 1893, Age ..."

Gravestones for Daughters of John and Isabel McCallum McDougall
Redwood Falls Cemetery, Redwood Falls, Minnesota

"My Sister [Margaret McDougall Milne] that came here with her family Died 5 years ago"

[Margaret Milne died October 16, 1888.]

Plate 37.5. Gravestone of Margaret McDougall Milne
Redwood Falls Cemetery, Redwood Falls, Minnesota

Plate 37.6. Alexander Milne (b. 1850) with his Children after the Death of their Mother, Margaret McDougall Milne

Front row (left to right): John Milne (b. 1878) or Alexander Milne (b. 1880),
Dougald McDougall Milne Tiffany (b. 1885),
Irma [Catherine] Milne Houghmaster (b. 1887) (on her father's lap),
Alexander Milne (b. 1850), William Milne Smith (b. 1883) and Donald Milne (b. 1882)
Standing behind (left to right): James Alexander Milne (b. 1877) and John or Alexander Milne
[Family notes are not clear which child is John and which is Alexander in the photo above.]

The Brothers Milne in 25-year reunion

By Mary Doms

Three brothers, each with a different surname, held a brief reunion in Redwood Falls Monday, the first time they were together in 25 years.

Dougald Tiffany, W.M. Smith, both of Redwood Falls, and Donald Milne of Rochester were joined by their first cousin, Gilbert MacDougall of Redwood Falls, at lunch in the Cardinal cafe and visited other relatives around town. Also at lunch with them were Tiffany's son, Gilbert, and Smith's daughters, Mrs. James Fitzpatrick and Mrs. S.P. Inglis.

All of the brothers and cousin are close to their ninetieth birthdays. Mac Dougall will be 90 November 12. Milne will celebrate his ninetieth birthday next March 1. Smith is 88 years old and Tiffany, 87.

The brothers were all Milnes in their early childhoods. Their mother died in 1888 at the age of 36, just a year after Alexander and Margaret MacDougall Milne brought the family to Redwood Falls from their native Thurso, Scotland.

The father was a master cabinet maker, one of his works being the hand-made spooled cherry breakfront in the west front office of the Stanhope clinic, 121 West Fourth street. He is also credited with creating a series of black walnut cabinets in the waiting room there.

He and his brother-in-law, John Mac Dougall, worked on the Presbyterian

(CONTINUED on Page Two)

HAPPY TOGETHER Meeting after a quarter-century were three brothers, from left, W.M. Smith, Donald Milne and Dougald Tiffany, and their first cousin, Gilbert MacDougall.

★ Milne brothers reunited

(CONTINUED from Page One)

church and some of Milne's cabinet work is still one of its beauties.

After the death of his wife, Milne was unable to keep the family together. It included five surviving of six sons and a daughter.

William was adopted by Isabella Smith, an unmarried woman, and the papers added Smith to his name, William Gunn Milne.

Jared J. Tiffany and his wife, Mary Miller Tiffany, took Dougald, 3 1/2 years old at the time of his mother's death, into their Redwood Falls township farm home. The adoption procedure was completed in 1889.

A sister, Catherine, born in Redwood Falls, had Mr. and Mrs. George Houghmaster as foster parents. Houghmaster was in real estate and had a store where Wilson's Clothing now stands. The couple changed Catherine's name to Irma.

Donald lived with the Houghmasters, graduating from high school here in 1904, but was not adopted.

He spent some of his youth with his father in Butte, Mont. A retired Rochester furniture dealer, in recent years he had been employed by the Masonic order as a greeter to visit patients in hospitals there. Like Smith, he is now afflicted with failing eyesight.

Smith is retired from the insurance and real estate business; Tiffany has retired from farming and is living in the city; MacDougall, formerly in the oil business, is a resident of Lakeside Manor.

Asked if MacDougall was also born in Scotland, Tiffany said: "No, He's a substitute."

Permission of *Redwood Falls Gazette*

Plate 37.7. From *Redwood Falls Gazette*, 1971 or 1972

The Brothers Milne in 25-year reunion

By Mary Doms

Three brothers, each with a different surname, held a brief reunion in Redwood Falls Monday, the first time they were together in 25 years.

Dougald Tiffany, W.M. Smith, both of Redwood Falls, and Donald Milne of Rochester were joined by their first cousin, Gilbert MacDougall of Redwood Falls, at lunch in the Cardinal café and visited other relatives around town. Also at lunch with them were Tiffany's son, Gilbert, and Smith's daughters, Mrs. James Fitzpatrick and Mrs. S.P. Inglis.

All of the brothers and cousin are close to their ninetieth birthdays. MacDougall will be 90 November 12. Milne will celebrate his ninetieth birthday next March 1. Smith is 88 years old and Tiffany, 87.

The brothers were all Milnes in their early childhoods. Their mother died in 1888 at the age of 36, just a year after Alexander and Margaret MacDougall Milne brought the family to Redwood Falls from their native Thurso, Scotland.

The father was a master cabinet maker, one of his works being the handmade spooled cherry breakfront in the west front office of the Stanhope clinic, 121 West Fourth street. He is also credited with creating a series of black walnut cabinets in the waiting room there.

He and his brother-in-law, John MacDougall, worked on the Presbyterian church and some of Milne's cabinet work is still one of its beauties.

After the death of his wife, Milne was unable to keep the family together. It included five surviving of six sons and a daughter.

William was adopted by Isabella Smith, an unmarried woman, and the papers added Smith to his name, William Gunn Milne.

Jared J. Tiffany and his wife, Mary Miller Tiffany, took Dougald, 3 ½ year old at the time of his mother's death, into their Redwood Falls township farm home. The adoption procedure was completed in 1889.

A sister, Catherine, born in Redwood Falls, had Mr. and Mrs. George Houghmaster as foster parents. Houghmaster was in real estate and had a store where Wilson's Clothing now stands. The couple changed Catherine's name to Irma.

Donald lived with the Houghmasters, graduating from high school here in 1904, but was not adopted.

He spent some of his youth with his father in Butte, Mont. A retired Rochester furniture dealer, in recent years he had been employed by the Masonic order as a greeter to visit patients in hospitals there. Like Smith, he is now afflicted with failing eyesight.

Smith is retired from the insurance and real estate business; Tiffany has retired from farming and is living in the city; MacDougall, formerly in the oil business, is a resident of Lakeside Manor.

Asked if MacDougall was also born in Scotland, Tiffany said: "No, He's a substitute."

(*Redwood Falls Gazette,* 1971 or 1972)

Plate 37.8. Margaret McDougall's Husband, Alexander Milne, with their Daughter Catherine (Irma Houghmaster) (b. 1887)

Photo date unknown

Plate 37.9. Margaret McDougall's Husband, Alexander Milne with their Son, Alexander (b. 1880)

Photo date unknown

Letter **#38**

March 31st 1913

This letter is from Donald McConochie, Oban, to John Dougald McDougall (b. 1877), son of John McDougall (b. 1837), grandson of John McDougall (weaver) and Catherine McCallum.

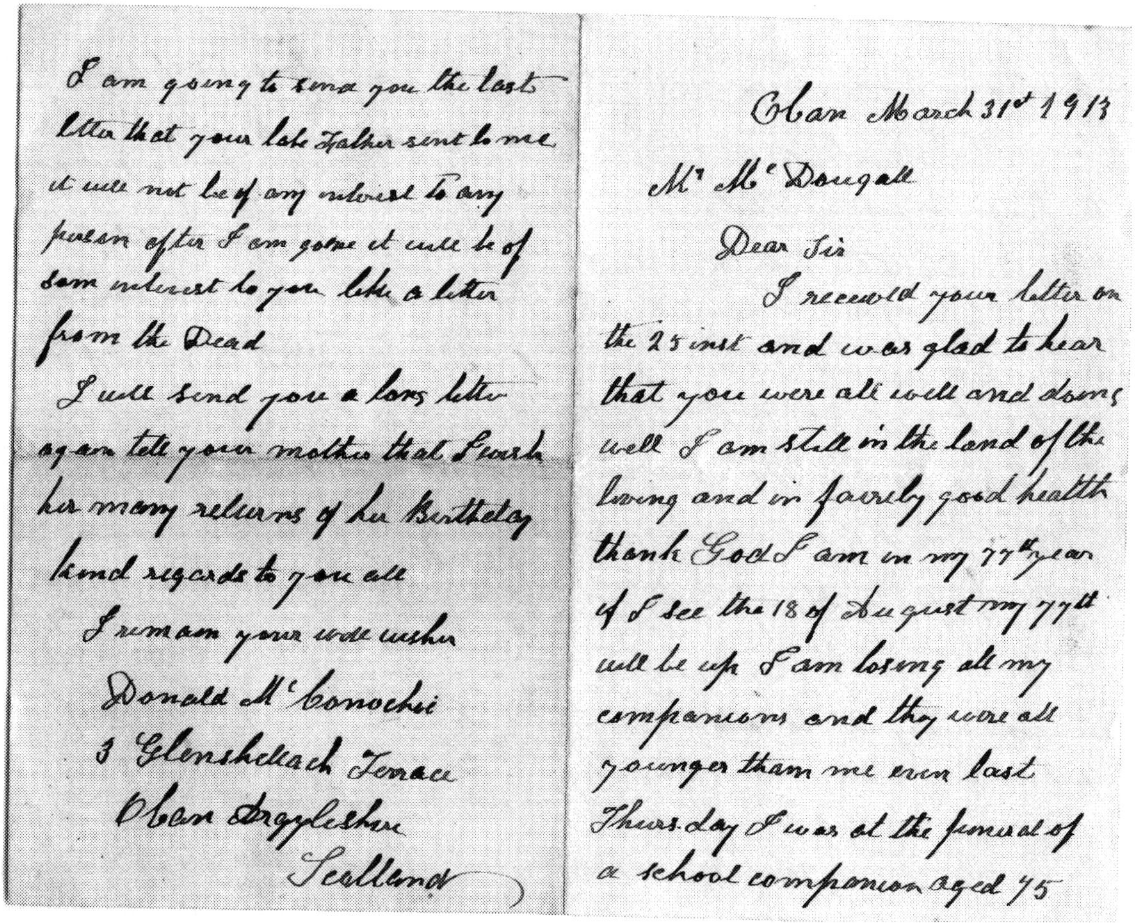

Oban March 31st 1913

Mr McDougall

Dear Sir

I received your letter on the 25 inst and was glad to hear that you were all well and doing well I am still in the land of the living and in fairly good health thank God I am in my 77th year if I see the 18 of August my 77th will be up I am losing all my companions and they were all younger than me even last Thursday I was at the funeral of a school companion aged 75

I am going to send you the last letter that your late Father sent to me it will not be of any interest to any person after I am gone it will be of som interest to you like a letter from the Dead

I will send you a long letter agan tell your mother that I wish her many returns of her Birthday kind regards to you all

I remain your well wisher

Donald McConochie

3 Glenshellach Terrace

Oban Argyleshire

Scotland

Image db230

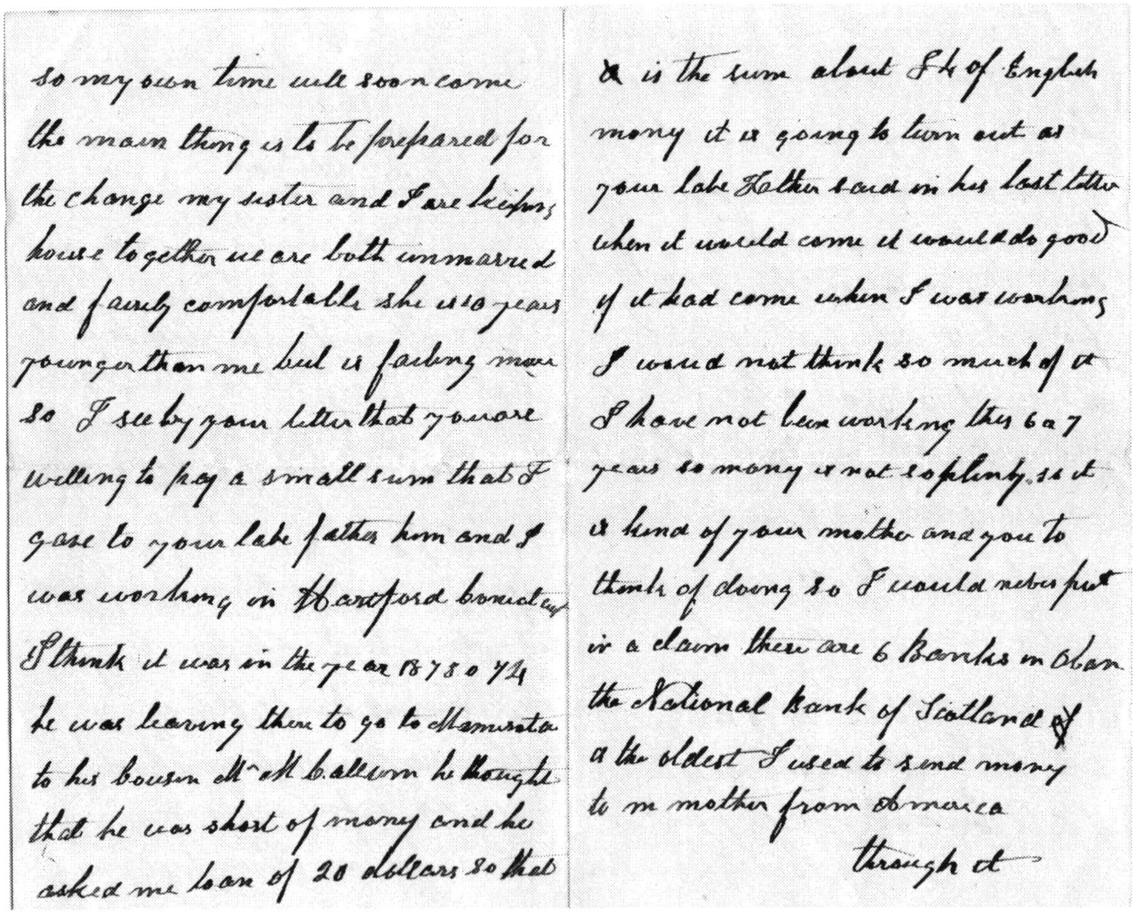

so my own time will soon come
the main thing is to be prepared for
the change my sister and I are keeping
house together we are both unmarried
and fairly comfortable she is 10 years
younger than me but is failing more
so I see by your letter that you are
willing to pay a small sum that I
gave to your late father him and I
was working in Hartford Connecticut
I think it was in the year 1873 or 74
he was leaving there to go to Minnesota
to his cousin Mr McCallum he thought
that he was short of mony and he
asked me loan of 20 dollars so that

& is the sum about £4 of English
mony it is going to turn out as
your late Father said in his last letter
when it would come it would do good
if it had come when I was working
I would not think so much of it
I have not been working this 6 or 7
years so mony is not so plenty so it
is kind of your mother and you to
think of doing so I would never put
in a claim there are 6 Banks in Oban
the National Bank of Scotland &
is the oldest I used to send mony
to my mother from America

through it

Image db231

LETTER TO JOHN DOUGALD MCDOUGALL (b. 1877 in Minnesota) SON OF JOHN MCDOUGALL (b. 1837 Lismore) AND ISABEL MCCALLUM MCDOUGALL (b. 1850 SCOTLAND), GRANDSON OF JOHN MCDOUGALL (b. 1803 Lismore) AND CATHERINE MCCALLUM MCDOUGALL (b. 1809 Lismore) FROM DONALD MCCONOCHIE, OBAN

Oban March 31st 1913

Mr McDougall
Dear Sir

I received your letter on the 25 inst [instant] and was glad to hear that you were all well and doing well I am still in the land of the living and in fairely good health thank God I am in my 77th if I see the 18 of August my 77th will be up I am losing my companions and they were all younger than me even last Thursday I was at the funeral of a school companion aged 75 so my own time will soon come the main thing is to be prepared for the change my sister and I are keeping house together we are both unmarred and fairely comfortable she is 10 years younger than me but is failing more so I see by your letter that you are willing to pay a small sum that I gave to your late father him and I was working in Hartford Conecticut I think it was in the year 1873 or 74 he was leaving there to go to Minnesota to his cousin Mr McCallum he thought that he was short of mony and he asked me loan of 20 dollars so that is the sum about £4 of English mony it is going to turn out as your late Father said in his last letter when it would come it would do good if it had come when I was working I woud not think so much of it I have not been working this 6 or 7 years so money is not so plenty, so it is kind of your mother and you to think of doing so I would never put in a claim there are 6 Banks in Oban the National Bank of Scotland a the oldest I used to send money to m mother from America through it

I am going to send you the last letter that your late Father sent to me it will not be of any interest to any person after I am gone it will be of som interest to you like a letter from the Dead

I will send you a long letter again tell your mother that I wish her many returns of her Birthday

Kind regards to you all

I remain your well wisher
Donald McConochie
3 Glenshellach Terrace
Oban Argylshire
Scotland

Plate 38.1. Children of John McDougall (b. 1837)
and Isabel McCallum McDougall
With their Mother

(Left to right)

Front: John Dougald MacDougal, Isabel McCallum McDougall, William (Bill) MacDougall

Back: Gilbert Hugh (Gib) MacDougall, Anna MacDougall Aufderheide, Donald Fraser MacDougall

Appendix 1

Table A1.1
The Letters – A List

No.	Date Written	From	Location	To	Location	Summary
1	December 13, 1870	John McDougall (weaver)	Ballimackil-lichan, Isle of Lismore	John McDougall (b. 1837) (his son)	Dunoon	He reports news of family members, reports that daughters Mary and Maggie are planning to be married and expresses fear that they are going astray. He thanks son John for a top coat and indicates John will receive a pair of drawers soon and a pair of hose when he goes to Glasgow.
2	January 16, 1871	John McDougall (weaver)	Ballimackil-lichan, Isle of Lismore	John McDougall (b. 1837) (his son)	Dunoon	He reports that his son John's mother, Catherine McCallum McDougall, has been unwell and expresses concern about daughter Mary's health. He reports on a letter from "uncle John". He reports on the death of Rev. Gregor MacGregor's wife. He praises his son for "keeping steadfast against strong drink."
3	April 4, 1871	John McDougall (weaver)	Ballimackil-lichan, Isle of Lismore	John McDougall (b. 1837) (his son)	Glasgow	He asks his son John if he received plaiden (blankets). He mentions lack of response from children to a letter. He reports on the brothers of Catherine McCallum ("uncle malcom" and "uncle John.") He reports that poor health prevents him and Catherine McCallum from planting potatoes and reports on a death in the community.
4	1871	John McDougall (weaver)	Ballimackil-lichan, Isle of Lismore	John McDougall (b. 1837) (his son)	Glasgow	He reports on his and Catherine McCallum's health and expresses a wish to have son John nearby. He reports that potatoes are expensive and that a member of the community is unwell. He extends greetings to his children Mary, Hugh and Maggie.
5	March 1, 1872	John McDougall (weaver)	Ballimackil-lichan, Isle of Lismore	John McDougall (b. 1837) (his son)	Glasgow	He writes about many deaths in the community and reports on a letter from "your uncle John [McCallum's] daughter" indicating her father had made many coffins. He comments that daughter Maggie (Margaret McDougall) had not written and expresses concern.
6	August 29, 1872	John McDougall (weaver) & Catherine McCallum McDougall	Ballimackil-lichan, Isle of Lismore	John McDougall (b. 1837) (his son)	East Coast, USA [New York?]	He provides the address of cousin John McCallum in Cottage Grove, Minnesota. He reports that daughter Ann (Agnes Moore) and her husband William had just visited. He writes that Mary is doing well in a shop and Maggie is with her. He reports that Hugh had been to visit. He reports on the death of "Aleser Carmichael Balure" and the marriage of cousin Ann McNicol He encourages son John to find a healthier place than New York.
7	June 6, 1873	John McDougall (weaver)	Ballimackil-lichan, Isle of Lismore	John McDougall (b. 1837) (his son)	Delhi, Redwood County, Minnesota	He reports on Catherine McCallum's visit to Glasgow where she saw daughter, Mary, and son, Hugh. He reports his pride on receiving money from son John. He reports on family friends in Glasgow, including the death of Sandy Carmichael. He reports on a letter from John McCallum in Minnesota (possibly Catherine McCallum's nephew, son of her brother, Gilbert McCallum). He sends the address for Catherine McCallum's brother, "your uncle"

No.	Date Written	From	Location	To	Location	Summary
						John McCallum, which is Strontian, Sunart. He reports on "Malcolm Ft. William", possibly Catherine McCallum's brother, Malcolm McCallum (b. 1811 Balure.)
8	Undated	John McDougall (weaver) & Catherine McCallum McDougall	Ballimackil-lichan, Isle of Lismore	John McDougall (b. 1837) (their son)	Delhi, Minnesota	Fragments. They report on deaths in the community, the death of daughter Agnes Moore's infant daughter, and the construction of a new house on Lismore. They report "Uncle John" and Malcolm were at a funeral and remind son to abstain from strong drink.
9	April 17, 1874	John (weaver) & Catherine McCallum McDougall	Ballimackil-lichan, Isle of Lismore	John McDougall (b. 1837) (their son)	Delhi, Redwood County, Minnesota	They thank son, John, for sending money and express appreciation for help he received from Ann McCallum and her daughter, Isabel. They indicate son, Hugh, is in England; said they received letter from (son?) Donald who went to daughter Mary's wedding in Glasgow. They write approvingly of Mary's husband. John (weaver) reports on the presentation of a new watch to him at a soiree. [Note: The watch was presented at the "annual soiree in connection with the Auchuaran Sabbath School", in the Independent Chapel, Lismore, to "Mr John Macdougall, superintendent of the Sabbath School" for his 30 years' service and "on account of his sterling worth and exemplary Christian character". (*The Oban Times*, 21 February 1874)] They report being lonesome without their children and would go to America if they were younger.
10	March 12, 1875	John McDougall (weaver) & Catherine McCallum McDougall	Ballimackil-lichan, Isle of Lismore	John McDougall (b. 1837) (their son)	Delhi, Minnesota	They report Catherine McCallum was "very unwell the whole winter" and that son Hugh is going where son John is. They report on letters from the Moore family in the north. They report Maggie is doing well in Glasgow and provide her address. They report death of Donald Carmicel (Auchouran) from strong drink and report on uncles John (b. 1818) and Malcolm (b. 1811) McCallum. They don't mention daughter Mary's death in 1874, but do report that their mother, Catherine McCallum, and their sister, Maggie, have her rings and earrings. They send love to Bella [Isabel] and her mother, Ann McCallum. [Note: John and Isabel eventually marry. Family notes suggest they married in or near Ortonville, Minnesota, January 1877.]
11	December 11, 1875	John McDougall (weaver) & Catherine	Ballimackil-lichan, Isle of Lismore	John McDougall (b. 1837) and Hugh		They report Dugald Carmichel Balure thatched their house without charge. They indicate they had been invited to spend the winter in the north but had declined. They report the winter is

No.	Date Written	From	Location	To	Location	Summary
		McCallum McDougall		McDougall (b. 1842) (their sons)		very cold and that tradesmen are idle. They report on the status of several people and provide spiritual guidance.
12	January 1876	Hugh McDougall (b. 1842)	Glasgow	John McDougall (b. 1837) (his brother)	Minnesota	Hugh congratulates John on becoming a contractor and a farmer. He reports on the departure of several friends for Africa, the return of several friends from the United States, and the health and well-being of others in Glasgow, Greenock and Dunoon.
13	January 30, 1877	John Moore (son of Agnes McDougall and William Moore, grandson of John McDougall (weaver) & Catherine McCallum)	Brown Hill Cottage, Thurso	John McDougall (b. 1837) and Hugh McDougall (b. 1842) (John Moore's uncles)	Ballmackillichan Estate, Redwood Falls, Redwood County, Minnesota	John Moore (age 18 or 19 at the time) provides an update on the weather and mentions shipwrecks on the Aberdeen coast and the status of his father's farming. He also reports that his aunt Margaret (Maggie) McDougall, married Alexander Milne in November 1876. He reports that his aunt, Flora McDougall, and a "Donald" (possibly Maggie's brother, Donald McDougall), attended the wedding in Glasgow. (Margaret's sister, Flora McDougall, witnessed the marriage.) See the marriage record. (NRS, 1855-2013c; GROS, number 644/10 0261). John and Hugh McDougall, to whom he wrote the letter, were Maggie's brothers. (See family trees, Appendix 8.) John Moore reports that his brother, Donald Hugh, misses his Uncle Hugh [in the US.] He reports on prices for sheep, wool, and crops and mentions his sister, Catherine Mary Anne, indicating she was 7 months old at the time. He writes that Flora is not yet married and provides news of Lismore and information about his father's civic affairs.
14	August 18, 1877	John McDougall (weaver) & Catherine McCallum McDougall, transcribed by their grandson, John Moore	Ballimackillichan, Isle of Lismore	John McDougall (b. 1837), Hugh McDougall (b. 1842) (their sons) and Isabel McCallum (b. 1850), their daughter-in-law		The parents express relief that their son, John McDougall (b. 1837), has married. They report on visits from friends and family. John Moore adds a note, indicating his aunt, Maggie (Margaret McDougall Milne), has had a baby boy and provides her address in Glasgow. [The baby would have been James Alexander Milne.] He indicates his grandparents are doing well on Lismore.
15	January 29, 1879	Author not identified. Written from home of Agnes (Ann)	Ormlie House, Thurso	America Friends		The author refers to a letter he or she had sent 3 or 4 months earlier, chides the recipients on not sending a reply, and refers to good crops but low prices. The author writes about the severe winter. Compares breakdown of the Caledonian Bank to the Glasgow Bank failure. Mentions

No.	Date Written	From	Location	To	Location	Summary
		McDougall and William Moore				forthcoming trial of the Glasgow Bank's shareholders and directors. Mentions new calves.
16	February 17, 1879	Margaret McDougall Milne (b. 1851 or 1852)	Bishop Mill, Elgin	John McDougall (b. 1837) (her brother)	Minnesota	Margaret reports on the severe winter (9th week since snow commenced), comments on her brother John McDougall's (b. 1837) marriage, indicates she has two sons. Refers to her husband Alexander Milne's difficulty working for himself; mentions low prices for his work. Refers to the "great Bank failure." Asks for advice on going to America, including the cost. Indicates her husband had considered migrating to New Zealand. Provides information about Alexander's skills (cabinetmaking). Reports that her sister, Flora, is married; provides information about Flora's husband (a plumber). Reports that her sister, Agnes (Ann) McDougall Moore, and family saw Maggie and her family in the summer. Reports she hasn't seen her parents since she got married. Sends greetings to her brother John's wife and his son, brother Hugh, and "cousin John" [possibly John McCallum (b. 1847), son of Gilbert McCallum and Ann McCallum McCallum. See Appendix 9.]

No.	Date Written	From	Location	To	Location	Summary
17	July 29, 1879	Margaret McDougall Milne (b. 1851 or 1852)	Thurso	John McDougall (b. 1837) (her brother)	Minnesota	Maggie writes that she and her husband had packed and sold their belongings to leave for the US. However, she reports William (Moore) invited them to visit before leaving. When they reached the Moore's home they found that the Moore's daughter, baby Katy (Catherine Mary Anne), was sick and that she died the next day. She reports that: - Brother Donald works for William Moore in his shop, is head of the shop and talks about going home to visit (Lismore); - William Moore asked them to stay in Thurso and provided a house for them; - Flora is married and that Flora's husband is doing well; - Her husband, Alexander Milne, is working at Ormlie (William Moore's home.) She indicates Thurso is cold and reports missing ("miny") her friends. She sends her brother, John, a photograph of herself with her family and requests a photo from him. She indicates her parents are glad she didn't go to the US. She refers to her health and appearance and suggests a wife for her brother, Hugh. She remarks on the news that her brother John McDougall's little boy, John (b. 1877, Minnesota), speaks some Gaelic.
18	August 22, 1879	John McDougall (weaver)	Ballimackil-lichan, Isle of Lismore	John McDougall (b. 1837) and Hugh McDougall (b. 1842) (their sons) and Isabel McCallum (b. 1850), their daughter-in-law		He refers to the death of Katy Mary Anne and provides information about Margaret and Alexander Milne's decision to remain in Scotland. He reports that William Moore has provided Maggie and Alexander a house and shop free of rent and that Alexander Milne is working in Thurso. He refers to Margaret's health, indicating she doesn't look well in her photograph. He reports on the status of shearings(?). He reports that Donald (his son) plans to come visit and that Flora (his daughter) has a baby boy. He reports on the visit of Aunt Cristy Black from Fort William and the deaths of people on Lismore. He reports the summer has been wet and cold.

No.	Date Written	From	Location	To	Location	Summary
19	August 23, 1879	John McDougall (weaver) (first part of letter) John McDougall (weaver) & Catherine McCallum McDougall (second part)	Ballimackil-lichan, Isle of Lismore	John McDougall (b. 1837) and Hugh McDougall b. 1842) (their sons)	Minnesota	First part: John McDougall (weaver) reports that his son, Donald McDougall (b. 1845), did arrive from Thurso the night before and shares Donald's information about the family in Thurso. Second part: They report on the difficulty of Lismore residents finding work, comment on conditions in Glasgow, provide information about aunties. They inquire about John McCallum and his mother (probably Isabel McCallum McDougall's brother, John McCallum, and mother, Ann McCallum McCallum, in Minnesota.)
20	Unknown (about 1879)	John McDougall (weaver) & Catherine McCallum McDougall	Ballimackil-lichan, Isle of Lismore	John McDougall (b. 1837) (their son)	Delhi, Redwood County, Minnesota	They comment on their desire for their son, Hugh, to marry, and ask that he write them. They ask Isabel McCallum McDougall to look for a wife for Hugh and suggest someone from Lismore. They note that "Uncle John" is waiting for a letter from John McDougall (b. 1837) and John McCallum. They refer to receiving Ann Flora's hair and wish she could be with them on Lismore. [Note: Ann Flora would be John and Isabel McCallum McDougall's daughter, Anna MacDougall Aufderheide, born November 9, 1879.]
21	December 27, Year Unknown	John McDougall (weaver) & Catherine McCallum McDougall	Ballimackil-lichan, Isle of Lismore	John McDougall (b. 1837) and Hugh McDougall (b. 1842) (their sons) and Isabel McCallum (b. 1850), their daughter-in-law	Minnesota	They send greetings to their sons, John and Hugh, John's wife, Bella, and her mother, as well as the children. They admonish Hugh to marry. A note added early the morning of December 27 refers to a heavy storm but that "not as much of a roof was steared on the house." [The letter refers to more than one child. Therefore, it would have been written after Anna MacDougall's birth in November 1879 and possibly after the birth of other grandchildren, as well.]
22	March 22, 1881	John McDougall (weaver) & Catherine McCallum McDougall	Ballimackil-lichan, Isle of Lismore	John McDougall (b. 1837) and Hugh McDougall (b. 1842) (their sons)	USA	They tell their son, Hugh, they just want to hear from him. They report the winter has been extremely cold in Scotland, that they had a freeze the night before, and that it is snowing. They report on the deaths of many people on Lismore and elsewhere. They ask about "little anny" [most likely Anna MacDougall, born 1879.] They report their daughter, Flora, has a son named

No.	Date Written	From	Location	To	Location	Summary
						William Moore. They report that Alexander Milne and William Moore (sons-in-law) and Donald (possibly their son, Donald, or son-in-law, Donald Doull) each sent money from Thurso and that Donald (possibly their son) says Maggie is well. They report that Maggie has three sons. They ask for photos of their two grandchildren in Minnesota and of John McCallum's son who, they understand, is named Gilbert. [Note: Family records indicate Isabel McDougall's brother, John McCallum (b. 1847), who lived in Minnesota, and his wife, Mary Secrest (b. 1850) had a son named Gilbert Sawyer McCallum, born October 1878. (Aburn, 2013c) See photograph, "Members of the MacDougall, Aufderheide and McCallum Families", following letter of March 22nd 1881.] They also mention a John McCallum in Ft. William, who might be John McCallum (also born 1847), the son of Catherine McCallum's brother, Malcolm (b. 1811 Balure).
23	December 6, 1881	John McDougall (weaver) & Catherine McCallum McDougall	Ballimackil-lichan, Isle of Lismore	Sons and daughter (John McDougall (b. 1837) and Hugh McDougall (b. 1842), their sons, and Isabel McCallum (b. 1850), their daughter-in-law)		They report on a severe storm that damaged the island, especially Port Ramsay and receiving money. They report that Mr. John McGregor, minister, visited the family in Thurso and that they are well off. They report Maggie is happy and that Agnes is doing well. John McDougall (weaver) reports that he is doing little but his health is good. He reports that "poor mother" (Catherine McCallum McDougall) is failing. They send news from their son Donald McDougall (b. 1845) in Thurso about grandson John Moore and others. They report on various deaths.

No.	Date Written	From	Location	To	Location	Summary
24	December 31, 1881	James Moore (b. 1868) (their grandson)	Ormlie House, Thurso	John McDougall (weaver) & Catherine McCallum McDougall	Ballimackil-lichan, Isle of Lismore	James Moore reports the death of his brother and their grandson, John Moore (b. 1858).
25	January 10, 1882	1st part: James Moore (b. 1868) 2nd part: John Moore (b. 1858) before his death	Ormlie House, Thurso	John McDougall (b. 1837) and Hugh McDougall (b. 1842) (their uncles) and Isabel McCallum (b. 1850), (their aunt)	Delhi, Redwood County, Minnesota	1st part: James Moore reports on the death of his brother, John Moore. 2nd part: In this letter, the last written before his death, John Moore reports on events in Scotland and asks about a "sad calamity" in Minnesota reported in the news a few months earlier.
26	January 24, 1882	John McDougall (weaver) & Catherine McCallum McDougall	Ballimackil-lichan, Isle of Lismore	Presumably John McDougall (b. 1837) (their son)	Minnesota	They rejoice at news of the birth of John and Isabel's second son, Gilbert Hugh (Gib MacDougall).They comment on his name, noting that "Gilbert" was a good man and that "Hugh" supported one of them in a spiritual experience. They describe the experience and provide advice. They refer to "my dear Mary's" rings and a broch, stating "it is my own brother's daughter I would like to have them.". They report on the death of their grandson, John Moore, indicating they received a letter from their son, Donald, as requested by John Moore before he died. They report on the deaths of a cousin, Ann McNicol, and others. See editor's notes following the letter for additional information.
27	Undated	John McDougall (weaver) & Catherine McCallum McDougall	Ballimackil-lichan, Isle of Lismore	John McDougall (b. 1837) (their son)	Delhi, Redwood County, Minnesota	They express thanks for a lock of Gilbert Hugh's hair and express hope their son, John, will be reading "Mr McCheynes book." They provide information about three bachelors "as ill to plase for wemen as our own hugh", and inquire about family and friends in Minnesota.

No.	Date Written	From	Location	To	Location	Summary
28	Undated	John McCallum (b. 1818 Balure) (Brother of Catherine McCallum McDougall)		John McDougall (b. 1837) (his nephew)	Delhi, Redwood County, Minnesota	He writes about making many coffins, reports many deaths have occurred. He extends greetings to nephew John's wife, family, mother-in-law, and John's brother, Hugh.
29	December 31, 1883	John McDougall (weaver) & Catherine McCallum McDougall	Ballimackil-lichan, Isle of Lismore	Presumably John McDougall (b. 1837) (their son)	Minnesota	They report receiving money and express appreciation for the generosity of their family. They report on the deaths of Uncle Malcolm [McCallum] and others and the health of others. Catherine reports she couldn't go to her brother's burial, but that another brother and John McNicol came to see her. They mention having spun and woven two blankets, that their father didn't do much this winter, and that the winter was very wet and stormy. They provide the price of potatoes and other items, indicating it's cheaper to buy tea and butter from Glasgow than locally. They report gifts from Alexander Milne and that Maggie has five sons. They express happiness that John and Isabel have another son. They ask Hugh to write. They refer to neighbors, the Carmichaels from Park, indicating that "they were badly used hear" and that their son, Duncan, wants to know if John and Hugh would recommend he go to America. They indicate they are still looking for a wife for Hugh and report on a letter from their grandson, James Moore.
30	About 1884	John McDougall (weaver) & Catherine McCallum McDougall	Probably from Ballimackil-lichan, Isle of Lismore	John McDougall (b. 1837) (their son) and Isabel McCallum (b. 1850)	Minnesota	They inquire about "your brother", express concern that Hugh has not married, extend their love to John and Isabel's four oldest children (John, Gilbert, Anna Flora and William), and extend greetings to Isabel's mother, "old Sandy McCorquarld", and "John McCallum."
31	July 30, 1884	John McDougall	Ballimackil-	Presumably	Minnesota	They report their ages.

No.	Date Written	From	Location	To	Location	Summary
		(weaver) & Catherine McCallum McDougall	lichan, Isle of Lismore	John McDougall (b. 1837) and Hugh McDougall (b. 1842) (their sons)		They report on a visit from their son-in-law, William Moore, and his son, Donald Hugh. They report that Ms. Janetta MacGregor (daughter of Rev. Gregor MacGregor) visited the homes of their children in Thurso and returned with gifts from them. They report on gifts from Alexander Milne and that Maggie expects to visit in August. They report that Flora and her husband are freeholders. They report on crops, a marriage, and various deaths on Lismore.
32	February 21, 1886	John McDougall (weaver) & Catherine McCallum McDougall	Ballimackil-lichan, Isle of Lismore	Presumably John McDougall (b. 1837) and Hugh McDougall (b. 1842) (their sons)	Minnesota	They express thanks for money sent by their sons and mention the post office at Achnacroish, Lismore. They report on the severe winter weather and the health of John and Hugh's mother. They mention a letter from Flora, indicating that her daughter was unwell. They mention the kindness of family and friends. They mention several weddings and deaths on Lismore. They ask about Isabel's brother, John McCallum ("that's Gilbart son".) They indicate they'd like to hear from Hugh that he is married. They request more frequent letters.
33	March 22, 1886	John McDougall (weaver) & Catherine McCallum McDougall	Ballimackil-lichan, Isle of Lismore	Presumably John McDougall (b. 1837) and Hugh McDougall (b. 1842) (their sons)	Minnesota	They express thanks for funds received and report on deaths. They ask about John McDougall's brother-in-law (Isabel's brother), John McCallum, and request his address. They mention they "have done little work this 6 mounth." They report compliments from Mr. John McGregor on their family

No.	Date Written	From	Location	To	Location	Summary
						in Thurso and mention the arrival of a new minister on Lismore. They report on news from Donald in Thurso. They inquire about Isabel's brother, John McCallum, and extend greetings to her mother. They mention receiving "a pound not" quarterly from Edinburgh.
34	Undated – 1886 or later	John McDougall (b. 1837)	Delhi, Minnesota	Donald McConochie (his friend)	Oban, Argyll	John McDougall (b. 1837) provides information about his farm in Minnesota and his experience with a business partner. He refers to a debt he owes Mr. McConochie, sends greetings to a mutual friend, and mentions his work on the Masonic Hall in Redwood Falls.
35 .	No date – possibly 1887	John McCallum (b. 1818 Balure), brother of Catherine McCallum McDougall	Not specified	Presumably John McDougall (b. 1837) (his nephew)	USA	John McCallum reports on death of his sister, Catherine McCallum McDougall. He comments on health of John McDougall (weaver) and his move to Thurso. He reports on prices of wool, sheep, lambs and cattle, oatmeal, flour and potatoes. He extends greetings to Isabel McDougall and her mother, Ann McCallum.
36	July 27, 1888	Donald McDougall (b. 1845)	Ormlie House, Thurso	John McDougall (b. 1837) (his brother)	Minnesota	Donald McDougall reports on the death of their father, John McDougall (weaver)
37	January 20, 1896	John McDougall (b. 1837)	Minnesota	Donald McConochie	Oban, Argyll	In this letter, his last to Donald McConochie, John McDougall (b. 1837) describes his farm work, his business ventures, and his family, and asks about mutual friends. He mentions the Redwood area's "good Scotch people" and his minister (a Scotchman). He also mentions the death of his sister a few years earlier (Margaret McDougall Milne).
38	March 31, 1913	Donald McConochie	Oban, Argyll	John McDougall (b. 1877), son of John McDougall and Isabel McCallum McDougall, Minnesota	Minnesota	Mr. McConochie forwards the last letter (January 20, 1896) he received from John McDougall (b. 1837 Lismore). He thanks the younger John McDougall (b. 1877 Minnesota) for offering to pay off the debt owed by his late father. Mr. McConochie provides instructions for sending the payment and extends birthday greetings to the young man's mother, Isabel McCallum McDougall.

Appendix 2

Figure A2.1
Timeline of Family Events

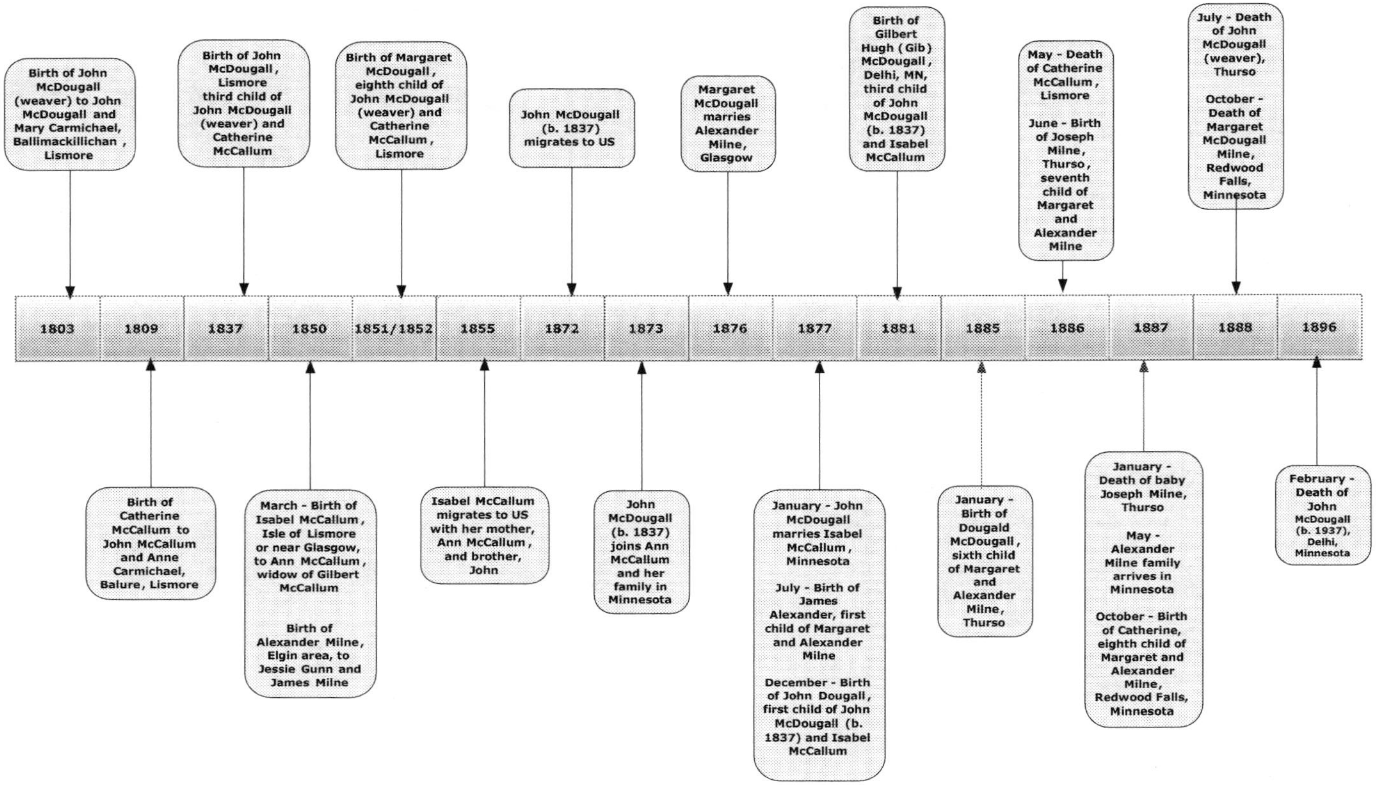

Table A2.1. Timeline of Family Events

Note: This timeline is based on several sources, listed below. They include an inscription on Memorial Stone #229, erected by Donald McDougall in memory of his parents, John McDougall (weaver) and Catherine McCallum, in the Old Graveyard, Lismore Parish Church Isle of Lismore. A photograph of the stone and a copy of the inscription appear immediately after the letter of July 27th 1888.

Date	Event	Place	Sources of the Information
July 15, 1803	John McDougall (weaver) born to John McDougall and Mary Carmichael	Ballimackillichan, Isle of Lismore	See Old Parish Registers (OPR) Births, which state, "1803. August 10th, John son to John M.Dugald and Mary Carmichael in Ballemacilichan" (NRS, Pre-1855a, General Register Office for Scotland, GROS, number 525/00 0010 0169). See, also, letter of July 30, 1884 from John McDougall (weaver).
August 1, 1809	Catherine McCallum born to John McCallum and Anne Carmichael who married about 1802	Balure, Isle of Lismore	See Old Parish Registers (OPR) Births, which state, "1809. August 1. Cathrine daughter to John McCallum & Anne Carmichael Balure" (NRS, Pre-1855a; GROS number 525/00 0010). See, also, letter of July 30, 1884 from John McDougall (weaver).
September 1, 1813	Gilbert McCallum born to John McCallum and Anne Carmichael	Balure, Isle of Lismore	See Old Parish Registers (OPR) Births which report, "1813 . Sept[r] 1. Gilbert son to John McCallum & Ann Carmichael Balure" (NRS, Pre-1855a; GROS number 525/00 0010).
October 6, 1814	Ann McCallum McCallum born to Duncan McCallum (b. 1789) and Isabella McColl (b. 1790, Lismore)	Achnacroish, Isle of Lismore	See Aburn (2013c). "Outline Descendant Report for Duncan McCallum." See, also, Old Parish Registers (OPR) Births, which report, "1814. October 6. Ann daughter to Duncan McCallum & Bell McColl Achnacroish" (NRS, Pre-1855a; GROS number 525/00 0010 0202).
February 23,1833	Agnes (Ann) McDougall born to John McDougall (weaver) and Catherine McCallum	Isle of Lismore	See Old Parish Registers (OPR) Births which report, "1833. Feby 23 Ann daughter to John McDugald & Cathrine McCallum Balemakilichan" (NRS, Pre-1855a; GROS number 525/00 0020 0050) See also Wilcox (1977), p. 149.
April 6, 1835	Mary McDougall born to John McDougall (weaver) and Catherine McCallum	Isle of Lismore	See Old Parish Registers (OPR) Births which report, "1835. Apr. 6 Mary daughter to John McDugald & Cathrine McCallum Balemakilichan" (NRS, Pre-1855a; GROS number 525/00 0020 0057).
April 1, 1837	John McDougall born to John McDougall (weaver) and Catherine McCallum	Isle of Lismore	See Old Parish Registers, Births, which report, "1837. April 1. John son to John McDugald & Cathrine McCallum Balemakilichan boy" (NRS, Pre-1855a; GROS number 525/00 0020 0065).
November 20, 1839	Dugald McDougall born to John McDougall (weaver) and Catherine McCallum	Isle of Lismore	See - Old Parish Registers (OPR), Births, which state, "1839. Nov. 20 Dugald son to John McDugald & Cathrine McCallum Balemakilichan" (NRS, Pre-1855a; GROS number 525/00 0020 0070). - Census, Parish of Lismore & Appin; McDugald, John (June 6, 1841) which includes Dugald, age 1 (NRS, 1841; GROS number 525/00 004/00 011) - Memorial Stone #229, Old Graveyard, Lismore Parish Church, Isle of Lismore.
1841	In addition to John McDougall and Catherine McCallum, census records show four children in	Isle of Lismore	See Census, Parish of Lismore & Appin; McDugald, John (June 6, 1841) (NRS, 1841; GROS number 525/00 004/00 011)

Date	Event	Place	Sources of the Information
	the John McDougall household in Ballimackillichan, Isle of Lismore: John, Dugald, Agnes and Mary.		
April 13, 1842	Hugh McDougall born to John McDougall (weaver) and Catherine McCallum	Isle of Lismore	See Old Parish Registers (OPR), Births, which state, "1842. Apr. 13 Hugh son to John McDugald & Cathrine McCallum Balemakilichan" (NRS, Pre-1855a; GROS number 525/00 0020 0074).
Uncertain - c.1845	Donald McDougall born to John McDougall (weaver) and Catherine McCallum	Isle of Lismore	Public and family records differ about his date of birth. The 1851 census (Census, Parish of Lismore & Appin, John McDougald, March 30, 1851) includes a son, Donald, age 3, suggesting a birth year of 1847 or 1848. (NRS, 1851; GROS number 525/00 001/00 014) The statutory record of his death reports his age as 69, suggesting a birth year of 1853. ("1922. Deaths in the Parish of Kiltearn in the County of Ross and Cromarty," NRS 1855-2013b; GROS number 070/00 0012) Inglis (undated) reports a birth year of about 1845.
1847	John McCallum born to Ann McCallum McCallum (b. 1814) and Gilbert McCallum (b. 1813 Balure)		Aburn (2013c) "Outline Descendant Report for Duncan McCallum"
October 31, 1849	Ann MacLennon born [Ann MacLennon became the wife of Hugh McDougall, son of John McDougall (weaver) and Catherine McCallum.]		Gravestone for Ann MacDougall and Hugh McDougall, Redwood Falls Cemetery, Redwood Falls, Minnesota
December 1849	Death of Gilbert McCallum (b. 1813, Balure) Cause of death: Appendicitis		Aburn (2013c) "Outline Descendant Report for Duncan McCallum" and Aburn (2014a)
1850	Alexander Milne is born to James Milne and Jessie Gunn Milne	Probably Elgin area, Scotland	Wilcox (1977), p. 151
March 1850	Isabel McCallum is born to Ann McCallum McCallum (b. 1814), widow of Gilbert McCallum (b. 1813, Balure)	Isle of Lismore or near Glasgow	See 1930 U.S. Census for Redwood County, Minnesota, which lists her age as 80, and Aburn (2013c)
1851	In addition to John McDougall and Catherine McCallum McDougall, census records show six children in the John McDougall household at Ballimakillichan, Isle of Lismore. They are John, Dugald, Hugh, Flory, Donald and Peggy (age 6 months). By this time, Agnes (Ann) and Mary, who appeared in the census of 1841, are not listed.	Isle of Lismore	See Census, Parish of Lismore & Appin, John McDougald (March 30, 1851). (NRS, 1851; GROS number 525/00 001/00 014)
1851	Flora McDougall is born to John McDougall (weaver) and Catherine McCallum		The following records are consistent with a birth year of 1851: - Memorial Stone #229, Old Graveyard, Lismore Parish

Date	Event	Place	Sources of the Information
			Church Isle of Lismore. It shows her age at death, which occurred in 1929, as 78. (Wilcox shows her age at death to be 77. Wilcox, 1977, p. 149). - Family notes of birth and death for Flora McDougall and her descendants, show a birth year of 1851. (Guthrie, December 10, 2013) However, the 1851 census shows a child named Flory, age 6, in the John McDougall household, suggesting a birth year of 1845. See Census, Parish of Lismore & Appin, John McDougald (March 30, 1851). (NRS, 1851; GROS number 525/00 001/00 014)
1851 or 1852	Margaret McDougall is born to John McDougall (weaver) and Catherine McCallum McDougall	Isle of Lismore	Her Gravestone, Redwood Falls Cemetery, Redwood Falls, Minnesota, shows her year of birth as 1852. However, census records for 1851 show a child named Peggy 6 months old in the John McDougall household, suggesting a birth year of 1850 or 1851. See Census, Parish of Lismore & Appin, John McDougald (March 30, 1851.) (NRS, 1851; GROS number 525/00 001/00 014)
1855	Ann McCallum migrates to New York with her children, John (b. 1847) and Isabel (b. 1850).	New York	Inglis (undated), Aburn (2013c)
June 1855	Death of Dougall, son of John McDougall (weaver) and Catherine McCallum		See inscription on Memorial Stone #229, Old Graveyard, Lismore Parish Church, Isle of Lismore.
November 6, 1858	John Moore, grandson of John McDougall and Catherine McCallum, is born to Agnes (Ann) McDougall and William Moore	Thurso	See "1858. Births in the Parish of Thurso in the County of Caithness" (Statutory Births). (NRS, 1855 – 2013a; GROS number 041/00 0130)
1860	Census records show Ann McCallum McCallum in Caledonia, New York, with her children.	Caledonia, New York	See 1860 U.S. Census, Livingston County, New York.
December 1868	James Moore, grandson of John McDougall and Catherine McCallum, is born to Agnes (Ann) McDougall and William Moore.	Thurso	See "1869. Births in the Parish of Thurso in the County of Caithness" (Statutory Births). (NRS, 1855 – 2013a; GROS number 041/00 0009)
By 1870	Ann McCallum McCallum had moved to Cottage Grove, Minnesota with her son, John McCallum (b. 1847) and daughter, Isabel McCallum (b. 1850).	Cottage Grove, Minnesota	US Census of 1870 summarized in Aburn (2013a)
Between March 22, 1872 and August 29, 1872	John McDougall (son of John McDougall, weaver, and Catherine McCallum) migrates to USA		See letter of August 19, 1872, from John McDougall (weaver) to his son which indicates John McDougall (son) has migrated.
September 26, 1873	Mary McDougall, daughter of John McDougall and Catherine McCallum, marries Jacob Swanson, a merchant seaman. Witnesses include Hugh McDougall.	Glasgow (Mary's address at the time: 79 Carrick Street, Glasgow)	See "1873. Marriages in the District of Blythewood in the Burgh of Glasgow," (Statutory Marriages) (NRS, 1855 – 2013c; GROS, number 644/06 0345). See, also, letter of April 17, 1874, from John McDougall (weaver) and Catherine McCallum to son, John, in

Date	Event	Place	Sources of the Information
			Minnesota.
Between June 1873 and April 1874	John McDougall (son of John McDougall, weaver, and Catherine McCallum) moves from the East Coast, United States, to Cottage Grove, Minnesota	Cottage Grove, Minnesota	See Inglis (undated), "John and Isabel McCallum MacDougall"
June 18, 1874	Death of Mary McDougall, wife of Jacob Swanson, daughter of John McDougall (weaver) and Catherine McCallum (Cause of death: Heart disease)	79 Carrick Street, Glasgow	See "1874. Deaths in the District of Clyde in the Burgh of Glasgow," (Statutory Deaths) (NRS, 1855 – 2013b; GROS number 644/05 0324) and inscription on Memorial Stone #229, Old Graveyard, Lismore Parish Church Isle of Lismore.
Between March 12, 1875 and December 11, 1875	Hugh McDougall may have gone to the US		See letter of March 12, 1875, from John McDougall (weaver) and Catherine McCallum to their son, John (b.1837) and letter of December 11, 1875, to their sons, John and Hugh.
July 12, 1876	Birth of Catherine Mary Ann, granddaughter of John McDougall (weaver) and Catherine McCallum, is born to Agnes (Ann) McDougall and William Moore	Brownhill Cottage, Thurso	See "1876. Births in the Parish of Thurso in the County of Caithness" (Statutory Births). (NRS, 1855 – 2013a; GROS number 041/00 0101)
November 17, 1876	Margaret McDougall marries Alexander Milne, a cabinetmaker. Witnesses: William Milne, Flora McDougall	371 Dumbarton Road, Glasgow (Partick Church)	See "1876. Marriages in the District of Anderston in the Burgh of Glasgow" (Statutory Marriages). (NRS, 1855 – 2013c; GROS number 644/10 0261)
Between January 1876 and letter of January 30,1877	Hugh McDougall migrates to the United States (Minnesota)		See letter of January 1876 from Hugh McDougall in Glasgow to John McDougall in Minnesota and letter of January 20, 1877, from John Moore to his uncles John and Hugh McDougall in Redwood Falls, Minnesota. The letters suggest Hugh McDougall migrated to the US between January 1876 and January 30, 1877.
January 1877	John McDougall (b. 1837) and Isabel McCallum marry		See the following item which appeared in *The Redwood Gazette:* "Mr. John McDougall returned last evening with a better half." (*The Redwood Gazette,* Thursday, Feb 1, 1877, Local News, last page) The item provides no additional information. Family notes indicate the couple married in or near Ortonville, Minnesota. (Inglis, undated)
July 10, 1877	James Alexander Milne, grandson of John McDougall and Catherine McCallum, is born to Margaret and Alexander Milne	Near Elgin	See Wilcox (1977), p. 151.
December 12, 1877	John Dougald McDougall, grandson of John McDougall (weaver) and Catherine McCallum, is born to John McDougall (Minnesota) and Isabel McCallum	Minnesota	See Minnesota Birth & Christening Index, 1840-1980, FamilySearch. Obtained through Archives.com, April 14, 2014.
July 12, 1878	Flora McDougall marries Donald Doull, master plumber.	Thurso	See "1878. Marriages in the Parish of Thurso in the County of Caithness" (Statutory Marriages). (NRS, 1855 – 2013c; GROS number 041/00 0021) See, also, letter of February 17, 1879, in

Date	Event	Place	Sources of the Information
			which Maggie (Margaret McDougall Milne) reports that Flora has married.
December 5, 1878	John Milne, grandson of John McDougall and Catherine McCallum, is born to Margaret and Alexander Milne		See "1878. Births in the District of Elgin in the County of Elgin" (Statutory Births). (NRS, 1855 – 2013a; GROS number 135/00 0255)
May 1879	John Doull, grandson of John McDougall and Catherine McCallum, is born to Flora McDougall and Donald Doull.	Thurso	See "1879. Births in the Parish of Thurso in the County of Caithness" (Statutory Births). (NRS, 1855 – 2013a; GROS number 041/00 0079) See, also, letter of August 22, 1879.
June 14, 1879	Death of Catherine Mary Ann, daughter of Agnes (Ann) McDougall and William Moore. Cause: diphtheria	Ormlie House, Thurso	See "1879. Deaths in the Parish of Thurso in the County of Caithness" (Statutory Deaths). (NRS, 1855 -2013b; GROS number 041/00 0055) See, also, letter of August 22, 1879.
November 9, 1879	Anna Flora, granddaughter of John McDougall (weaver) and Catherine McCallum, is born to John McDougall (Minnesota) and Isabel McCallum		See gravestone for Anna MacDougall Aufderheide, Redwood Falls Cemetery, Redwood Falls, Minnesota and Aburn (2013c).
July 1, 1880	Alexander Milne, grandson of John McDougall and Catherine McCallum, is born to Margaret and Alexander Milne	Banneck St., Thurso	See "1880. Births in the Parish of Thurso in the County of Caithness" (Statutory Births). (NRS, 1855 – 2013a; GROS number 041/00 0102)
October 23, 1880	William Moore Doull, grandson of John McDougall and Catherine McCallum, is born to Flora McDougall and Donald Doull	Thurso	See "1880. Births in the Parish of Thurso in the County of Caithness" (Statutory Births). (NRS, 1855 – 2013a; GROS number 041/00 0160) See, also, letter of March 22, 1881.
November 12, 1881	Gilbert Hugh (Gib) McDougall, grandson of John McDougall and Catherine McCallum, is born to John McDougall (Minnesota, b. 1837) and Isabel McCallum	Delhi, Minnesota	See gravestone, Redwood Falls Cemetery, Redwood Fall, Minnesota, family records (Christensen, 2014)
December 31, 1881	Death of John Moore, son of Agnes (Ann) McDougall and William Moore. Born 1858, died at age 23.	Thurso	See "1882. Deaths in the Parish of Thurso in the County of Caithness" (Statutory Deaths) (NRS, 1855 – 2013b; GROS number 041/00 0002) and letter of December 31, 1881 from James Moore.
February 26, 1882	Donald Dougald Milne, grandson of John McDougall and Catherine McCallum, is born to Margaret and Alexander Milne	Princes St., Thurso	See "1882. Births in the Parish of Thurso in the County of Caithness" (Statutory Births). (NRS, 1855 – 2013a; GROS number 041/00 0032)
August 3, 1883	William Gunn Milne [SMITH], grandson of John McDougall and Catherine McCallum, is born to Margaret and Alexander Milne	Duncan St., Thurso	See "1883. Births in the Parish of Thurso in the County of Caithness" (Statutory Births). (NRS, 1855 – 2013a; GROS number 041/00 0104)
23 Sep 1883	William Moore MacDougall, grandson of John McDougall (weaver) and Catherine McCallum, is born to John McDougall (Minnesota, b. 1837) and Isabel McCallum	Delhi, Minnesota	See Aburn (2013c).
September 18, 1884	Catherine ("Cousin Kate") Doull, granddaughter of John McDougall and Catherine McCallum, is born to Flora	Thurso	See "1884. Births in the Parish of Thurso in the County of Caithness" (Statutory Births). (NRS, 1855 – 2013a; GROS number 041/00 0111)

Date	Event	Place	Sources of the Information
	McDougall and Donald Doull		
January 22, 1885	Dougald McDougall Milne [TIFFANY], grandson of John McDougall and Catherine McCallum, is born to Margaret and Alexander Milne	Duncan St., Thurso	See "1885. Births in the Parish of Thurso in the County of Caithness" (Statutory Births). (NRS, 1855 – 2013a; GROS number 041/00 0028)
February 19, 1885	Donald Fraser MacDougall, grandson of John McDougall (weaver) and Catherine McCallum, is born to John McDougall (Minnesota, b. 1837) and Isabel McCallum	Delhi, Minnesota	See Aburn (2013c).
May 26, 1886	Death of Catherine McCallum, wife of John McDougall (weaver)	Ballimackillichan, Isle of Lismore	See "1886. Deaths in the District of Lismore in the County of Argyll." (Extract of an entry from the REGISTER OF DEATHS in Scotland) (NRS, 1855 – 2013b; GROS number 525/01 0009) See also Memorial Stone #229, Old Graveyard, Lismore Parish Church Isle of Lismore.
June 13, 1886	Joseph Milne, grandson of John McDougall and Catherine McCallum, is born to Margaret and Alexander Milne	Duncan St., Thurso	See "1886. Births in the Parish of Thurso in the County of Caithness" (Statutory Births). (NRS, 1855 – 2013a; GROS number 041/00 0071) See, also, Wilcox (1977), p. 151.
January 20, 1887	Death of Joseph Milne	Duncan St., Thurso	See "1887. Deaths in the Parish of Thurso in the County of Caithness." (Extract of an entry from the REGISTER OF DEATHS in Scotland) (NRS, 1855 – 2013b; GROS number 041/00 0005) [Note: Wilcox provides a different date. See Wilcox (1977), p. 151.]
May 1887	Alexander Milne family arrives in Redwood Falls, Minnesota	Redwood Falls, Minnesota	See Christmas Letter, 1966 from Dougald Milne and Jennie June Tiffany, reproduced in this book, Appendix 3.
October 16, 1887	Catherine Milne [Irma HOUGHMASTER], granddaughter of John McDougall and Catherine McCallum, is born to Margaret McDougall and Alexander Milne	Redwood Falls, Minnesota	See Wilcox (1977), p. 151 and Minnesota Birth and Christening Index, 1840-1980. [Note: The Minnesota Birth and Christening Index reports a birth date of November 16, 1887, for Catherine Milne. Accessed through http://www.Archives.com, May 14, 2014.]
July 26, 1888	Death of John McDougall (weaver)	Ormlie, Thurso	See "1888. Deaths in the Parish of Thurso in the County of Caithness" (Extract of an entry from the REGISTER OF DEATHS in Scotland) (NRS, 1855 – 2013b; GROS number 525/00 00100169)
October 16, 1888	Death of Margaret McDougall Milne	Redwood Falls, Minnesota	See Wilcox (1977), p. 151.
1888	Catherine Milne is adopted by Mr. & Mrs. George Houghmaster, renamed Irma, taking the surname Houghmaster.	Redwood Falls, Minnesota	See Inglis (undated) and Wilcox (1977), p. 151.
1889	Dougald MacDougall Milne is adopted by Mr. & Mrs. Jared Jerome Tiffany, taking the surname Tiffany.	Redwood Falls, Minnesota	See Inglis (undated) and Wilcox (1977), p. 151.
1892	William Gunn Milne is adopted by Miss Isabella Smith, taking the surname Smith.	Redwood Falls, Minnesota	See Inglis (undated) and Wilcox (1977), p. 151.

Date	Event	Place	Sources of the Information
February 5, 1896	Death of John McDougall, son of John McDougall (weaver) and Catherine McCallum	Delhi, Minnesota	See State of Minnesota, Certificate of Death, John McDougal. See also *Redwood Reveille*, February 8, 1896, which describes his fatal accident and Memorial Stone #229, Old Graveyard, Lismore Parish Church Isle of Lismore.
February 2, 1911	Death of Hugh McDougall, son of John McDougall (weaver) and Catherine McCallum	Delhi, Minnesota	See gravestone, Redwood Falls Cemetery, Redwood Falls, Minnesota. See also Wilcox (1977), p. 149, which mentions his place of death.
February 17, 1915	Death of Agnes (Ann) McDougall Moore	Thurso	"1915. Deaths in the Parish of Thurso in the County of Caithness", p. 6 (NRS, 1855 – 2013b; GROS number 041/00 0018)
August 13, 1922	Death of Donald McDougall, son of John McDougall (weaver) and Catherine McCallum	Drummond	"1922. Deaths in the Parish of Kiltearn in the County of Ross and Cromarty," p. 4. (NRS, 1855 – 2013b; GROS number 070/00 0012) The report gives his age as 69 years.
1925	Death of Alexander Milne	Redwood Falls, Minnesota	See Wilcox (1977), p. 147.
December 27, 1927	Death of Anna Flora MacDougall Aufderheide, daughter of John McDougall (b. 1837) and Isabel McCallum	Lamberton, Minnesota	See Aburn (2013c).
April 18, 1929	Death of Flora McDougall Doull, daughter of John McDougall (weaver) and Catherine McCallum	Thurso	See "1922. Deaths in the Parish of Kiltearn in the County of Ross and Cromarty," p. 4. (NRS, 1855 – 2013b; GROS number 041/00 0023) See also Memorial Stone #229, Old Graveyard, Lismore Parish Church Isle of Lismore.
November 27, 1937	Death of Ann MacLennon, wife of Hugh McDougall [son of John McDougall (weaver) and Catherine McCallum]		See gravestone of Ann MacDougall and Hugh MacDougall, Redwood Falls Cemetery, Redwood Falls, Minnesota.
July 3, 1961	Death of James Alexander Milne, son of Margaret McDougall and Alexander Milne		See Wilcox (1977), p. 151.
August 14, 1962	Death of Catherine Milne (Irma HOUGHMASTER), daughter of Margaret McDougall and Alexander Milne, adopted daughter of Mr. & Mrs. George Houghmaster		See Wilcox (1977), p. 151.
December 30, 1962	Death of John Dougald MacDougal, son of John McDougall (b. 1837) and Isabel McCallum	Agate Beach, Oregon	Standard Certificate of Death, State of Oregon
November 22, 1966	Death of Donald Fraser MacDougall, son of John McDougall (b. 1837) and Isabel McCallum	Redwood Falls, Minnesota	See Aburn (2013c).
January 11, 1972	Death of Catherine Doull Guthrie, daughter of Flora McDougall Doull and Donald Doull	Brechin	See "Extract of an entry from the Register of Deaths in Scotland", General Register Office for Scotland, issued December 3, 2012. See also NRS (1855 – 2013b; GROS number 367/00 0010).
August 10, 1973	Death of William Moore MacDougall, son of John McDougall (b. 1837) and Isabel McCallum	St. Paul, Minnesota	See Aburn (2013c).
July 5, 1975	Death of Gilbert Hugh (Gib) McDougall, son of John McDougall (b. 1837) and Isabel McCallum	Bloomington, Minnesota	Minnesota Historical Society, Minnesota Death Certificates Index, **CERTID# 1975-MN-017066.** See also gravestone, Redwood Falls

Date	Event	Place	Sources of the Information
			Cemetery, Redwood Falls, Minnesota.
May 24, 1977	Death of Dougald MacDougall Milne Tiffany, son of Margaret McDougall and Alexander Milne, adopted son of Mr. & Mrs. Jared Jerome Tiffany	Redwood Falls, Minnesota	Minnesota Historical Society, Minnesota Death Certificates Index, **CERTID# 1977-MN-011848.**

Appendix 3

Plate A3.1
Christmas Letter, 1966
Dougald Milne and Jennie June Tiffany

Season's Greetings Season's Greetings Season's Greetings

Dear Folks,

With Christmas so near, we are sending good will messages to friends and relatives. Important events (to us) have taken place this year.

In the spring, our daughter, Margaret, wrote us that the Ford Foundation had persuaded Bob (her husband) to go back to India and that she and Barbara would show us the way if we wanted to visit Scotland. We were delighted to go. Then we found out there was quite a bit to do to get ready, including smallpox vaccinations and passports. Since Dougald was born in Scotland and the family came to Redwood Falls in May, 1887, it was necessary for us to prove he was a citizen of the United States. John and Sue took us to St. Paul to the Immigration Office for a conference and a certificate of citizenship. The strike of machinists of airplanes caused us some difficulty. Margaret and Barbara were brought here by car instead of flying.

We left here at 4 a.m., Sunday, July 24. Bill and Catherine took us to the Minneapolis airport where we boarded a plane for Chicago, then to New York, where we left at 9 p.m. by plane for Scotland. About 9 a.m. Monday, Scotland time, we landed in Prestwick, went through customs, got a little lunch, and boarded a bus for Edinburgh. We were amazed at the beauty of the country as we saw it on the way. Arriving in Edinburgh we found we were dressed too thinly, so we soon changed to warmer clothing, which we wore all of the time we were in Scotland.

Next day we took a guided tour through a very old church, the Place where Queen Elizabeth lives when she is in the city on business, and the remarkable old Edinburgh castle which was started in 1076. That evening we saw a dance in front of an outdoor theater. There was a professional troupe who were dressed in typical Scottish costumes--the men wearing kilts and tartans, the women in white dresses, also wearing tartans. Our landlady at the hotel had given us a heavy blanket to put over our knees as we sat and watched the dancing, for which we were very grateful. Then we walked up out of the ravine onto Princes St., the main street of Edinburgh. We found a good restaurant and had a steak dinner after 9 p.m. It was very light at that time, as Edinburgh is quite far north. Wednesday was a fine day but cool. We took two tours around Edinburgh, then went to the open air theater again. There was a band concert featuring bagpipers, sword dancing, and the Highland Fling. Then the telephone chorus gave a very fine concert. They closed by singing several American songs which sounded good to us. Thursday noon we got a good Hertz car and drove to Brechin, arriving at the home of Dougald's cousin, Mrs. Kate Guthrie. She put on a fine tea and we stayed with her until about 9 p.m., when we went to a hotel. Friday it rained a little and was cool. Taking Cousin Kate with us, we drove around the country and saw Glamis Castle, from a distance, where the Queen's Mother was born. Next day we drove up to Peterhead to the home of Donald Guthrie, Cousin Kate's son. We spent the afternoon with them and the night in a hotel. Sunday we attended a church of Scotland, which is much like our Presbyterian Church. After church we drove to Banff, where we had a good dinner, then proceeded to Evanton to spend the night. Next day, Aug. 1, we drove to Thurso, stopping at Wick for dinner. Arrived at Thurso about 3:30 p.m. and stopped at a shop kept by Mr. Shearer. Since Thurso is the palce where Dougald was born, we found his birthplace, with the help of a man pushing a wheelbarrow. The lady who lives there very hospitably invited us to come in. We enjoyed seeing the house and the lovely back yard. We walked to the Royal Hotel to see James Munro, with whom Dougald had corresponded. We had a fine dinner in the hotel with Mr. and Mrs. Shearer as our guests. Tuesday was a rainy day, but the rain didn't stop us. We drove up to John O'Groat's house, the most northern house on the mainland. On the way we saw the castle where the Queen Mother stays in the summer. On Wednesday we drove down to Evanton to have a good visit with Allen Moore (the son of Donald Moore, a cousin of Dougald's), his wife, and their three lovely daughters. Allen took us all around his 770 acre farm. Thursday was rainy again and we started southward over highways that have good tar roadbeds but are very narrow. In some places, when meeting a vehicle, Margaret would stop to allow it to pass. In that country everyone drives on the left side of the road and the driver sits on the right. They don't drive nearly as fast there as we do in the U.S. On this day our route took us through the mountains, which are especially beautiful in the Glen Co. region. About the middle of the afternoon we drove into the little town of Tyndrum, and were graciously entertained at tea by Kathleen MacDonald Brodie and her two little children. We had met Kathleen about ten years ago and had entertained her in our home when she was spending a year in the U.S. We drove to Oban but stayed there only one night. Next day we drove to Ayr, stopping at an eating place on the bank of the celebrated and beautiful Loch Lomand, and the following day drove on to Brig O'Doon, which was mentioned in Burns' writing. It is a very old bridge but not now used for travel, although it looks as sturdy as when it was built centuries ago. We traveled on to Culzean Castle and were given a guided tour through the two lower stories. The third story had been given to Gen. Eisenhower. We drove on to Edinburgh that afternoon, completing nearly 1200 miles, and got rooms in the Thistle Hotel, where we had stayed before. Scotland is a beautiful country. Their crops, wheat, barley, oats, and potatoes, were luxuriant and the flowers are magnificent. It is said that the Scottish barley has the highest yield in the world. In all the pastures were cattle and sheep, fattened on the pasture, and we were told there was no need to salt the animals in the pasture. It was cool there and we wore warm clothing most of the time and enjoyed the hot water bottles the landladies put in the beds.

Sunday, Aug. 7, Margaret and I went to church services in St. Mary's Cathedral, an Episcopal church only a block from our hotel.

Monday we flew to London and stayed there until Friday. We went on several tours in London, through Westminster Abbey, St. Paul's Cathedral and the "Changing of the Guard" at Buckingham Palace, where the crowd was so great we caught only a glimpse of the ceremony. We enjoyed the waxworks and we liked London, with its many parks and statues. The air strike at that time caused us considerable trouble to come home, but with the help of quite a number of people, one of whom is the American Attache in the Embassy, we were able to board in Brussells, Belgium, for Montreal, missing our first plane from there to New York, and finally arriving in New York the evening of Aug. 12. Margaret and Barbara stayed in London, and flew to Stockholm, Sweden, where they met Bob and Dondee. After a short visit there they flew on to India.

In New York we were met by our son, Bob, Clarine, and Julie. We stayed with them until the following Wednesday, when we flew home. It was a wonderful trip and we enjoyed every minute of it.

Now we wish you all a very "Merry Christmas".

Sincerely and lovingly,

Dougald + Jennie

Season's Greetings

Dear Folks,

With Christmas so near, we are sending good will messages to friends and relatives. Important events (to us) have taken place this year.

In the spring, our daughter, Margaret, wrote us that the Ford Foundation had persuaded Bob (her husband) to go back to India and that she and Barbara would show us the way if we wanted to visit Scotland. We were delighted to go. Then we found out there was quite a bit to do to get ready, including smallpox vaccinations and passports. Since Dougald was born in Scotland and the family came to Redwood Falls in May, 1887, it was necessary for us to prove he was a citizen of the United States. John and Sue took us to St. Paul to the Immigration Office for a conference and a certificate of citizenship. The strike of machinists of airplanes caused us some difficulty. Margaret and Barbara were brought here by car instead of flying.

We left here at 4 a.m., Sunday, July 24. Bill and Catherine took us to the Minneapolis airport where we boarded a plane for Chicago, then to New York, where we left at 9 p.m. by plane for Scotland. About 9 a.m. Monday, Scotland time, we landed in Prestwick, went through customs, got a little lunch, and boarded a bus for Edinburgh. We were amazed at the beauty of the country as we saw it on the way. Arriving in Edinburgh we found we were dressed too thinly, so we soon changed to warmer clothing, which we wore all of the time we were in Scotland.

Next day we took a guided tour through a very old church, the Place where Queen Elizabeth lives when she is in the city on business, and the remarkable old Edinburgh castle which was started in 1076. That evening we saw a dance in front of an outdoor theater. There was a professional troupe who were dressed in typical Scottish costumes – the men wearing kilts and tartans, the women in white dresses, also wearing tartans. Our landlady at the hotel had given us a heavy blanket to put over our knees as we sat and watched the dancing, for which we were very grateful. Then we walked up out of the ravine onto Princes St., the main street of Edinburgh. We found a good restaurant and had a steak dinner after 9 p.m. It was very light at that time, as Edinburgh is quite far north. Wednesday was a fine day but cool. We took two tours around Edinburgh, then went to the open air theater again. There was a band concert featuring bagpipers, sword dancing, and the Highland Fling. Then the telephone chorus gave a very fine concert. They closed by singing several American songs which sounded good to us. Thursday noon we got a good Hertz car and drove to Brechin, arriving at the home of Dougald's cousin, Mrs. Kate Guthrie. She put on a fine tea and we stayed with her until about 9 p.m., when we went to a hotel. Friday it rained a little and was cool. Taking Cousin Kate with us, we drove around the country and saw Glamis Castle, from a distance, where the Queen's Mother was born. Next day we drove up to Peterhead to the home of Donald Guthrie, Cousin Kate's son. We spent the afternoon with them and the night in a hotel. Sunday we attended a church of Scotland, which is much like our Presbyterian Church. After church we drove to Banff, where we had a good dinner, then proceeded to Evanton to spend the night. Next day, Aug. 1, we drove to Thurso, stopping at Wick for dinner. Arrived at Thurso about 3:30 p.m. and stopped at a shop kept by Mr. Shearer. Since Thurso is the place where Dougald was born, we found his birthplace, with the help of a man pushing a wheelbarrow. The lady who lives there very hospitably invited us to come in. We enjoyed seeing the house and the lovely back yard. We walked to the Royal Hotel to see James Munro, with whom

Dougald had corresponded. We had a fine dinner in the hotel with Mr. and Mrs. Shearer as our guests. Tuesday was a rainy day, but the rain didn't stop us. We drove up to John O'Groat's house, the most northern house on the mainland. On the way we saw the castle where the Queen Mother stays in the summer. On Wednesday we drove down to Evanton to have a good visit with Allen Moore (the son of Donald Moore, a cousin of Dougald's), his wife, and their three lovely daughters. Allen took us all around his 770 acre farm. Thursday was rainy again and we started southward over highways that have good tar roadbeds but are very narrow. In some places, when meeting a vehicle, Margaret would stop to allow it to pass. In that country everyone drives on the left side of the road and the driver sits on the right. They don't drive nearly as fast there as we do in the U.S. On this day our route took us through the mountains, which are especially beautiful in the Glen Co region. About the middle of the afternoon we drove into the little town of Tyndrum, and were graciously entertained at tea by Kathleen MacDonald Brodie and her two little children. We had met Kathleen about ten years ago and had entertained her in our home when she was spending a year in the U.S. We drove to Oban but stayed there only one night. Next day we drove to Ayr, stopping at an eating place on the bank of the celebrated and beautiful Loch Lomand, and the following day drove on to Brig O'Doon, which was mentioned in Burns' writing. It is a very old bridge but not now used for travel, although it looks as sturdy as when it was built centuries ago. We traveled on to Culzean Castle and were given a guided tour through the two lower stories. The third story had been given to Gen. Eisenhower. We drove on to Edinburgh that afternoon, completing nearly 1200 miles, and got rooms in the Thistle Hotel, where we had stayed before. Scotland is a beautiful country. Their crops, wheat, barley, oats, and potatoes, were luxuriant and the flowers are magnificent. It is said that the Scottish barley has the highest yield in the world. In all the pastures were cattle and sheep, fattened in the pasture, and we were told there was no need to salt the animals in the pasture. It was cool there and we wore warm clothing most of the time and enjoyed the hot water bottles the landladies put in the beds.

Sunday, Aug. 7, Margaret and I went to church services in St. Mary's Cathedral, an Episcopal church only a block from our hotel.

Monday we flew to London and stayed there until Friday. We went on several tours in London, through Westminster Abbey, St. Paul's Cathedral and the "Changing of the Guard" at Buckingham Palace, where the crowd was so great we caught only a glimpse of the ceremony. We enjoyed the waxworks and we liked London, with its many parks and statues. The air strike at that time caused us considerable trouble to come home, but with the help of quite a number of people, one of whom is the American Attache in the Embassy, we were able to board in Brussells, Belgium, for Montreal, missing our first plane from there to New York, and finally arriving in New York the evening of Aug. 12. Margaret and Barbara stayed in London, and flew to Stockholm, Sweden, where they met Bob and Dondee. After a short visit there they flew on to India.

In New York we were met by our son, Bob, Clarine, and Julie. We stayed with them until the following Wednesday, when we flew home. It was a wonderful trip and we enjoyed every minute of it.

Now we wish you all a very "Merry Christmas".

Sincerely and lovingly,
Dougald and Jennie

Editor's Note: Sent from Redwood Falls, Minnesota, 1966

Appendix 4

Index of Names Mentioned in the Letters

Table A4.1
Letter Numbers and their Dates

No.	Date Written	No.	Date Written	No.	Date Written
1	December 13, 1870	14	August 18, 1877	27	Undated
2	January 16, 1871	15	January 29, 1879	28	Undated
3	April 4, 1871	16	February 17, 1879	29	December 31, 1883
4	1871	17	July 29, 1879	30	About 1884
5	March 1, 1872	18	August 22, 1879	31	July 30, 1884
6	August 29, 1872	19	August 23, 1879	32	February 21, 1886
7	June 6, 1873	20	Unknown (about 1879)	33	March 22, 1886
8	Undated	21	Undated – "December 27"	34	Undated – 1886 or later
9	April 17, 1874	22	March 22, 1881	35	No date – possibly 1887
10	March 12, 1875	23	December 6, 1881	36	July 27, 1888
11	December 11, 1875	24	December 31, 1881	37	January 20, 1896
12	January 1876	25	January 10, 1882	38	March 31, 1913
13	January 30, 1877	26	January 24, 1882		

Table A4.2
Names and Descriptive Information of People Mentioned in the Letters

Numbers in italics are plates in which photographs of the people appear.

Names and Descriptive Information	Letter Numbers; *Plate Numbers*
Anderson, Hugh	22
Bannerman, John	13
Black, Ann; "ann black baligarve"	3
Black, Christy; "Christy Black beside ... us"	11
Black, Dugal; "big dugal Black lagan"	31
Campbell, Duncan	12
Cannachanach, Pegge [Buchanan]	18
Carmicel, Donald; "Donald Carmicel auchouran"	10
Carmichael, Aleser; "Aleser Carmichael Balure"	6
Carmichel; "two of Carmichel Stronnacrath auchouran"	32
Carmichel; "Carmichels from park"	29
Carmichel, Donald	10
Carmichel, Ducan [Duncan?]	19
Carmichel, Duncan; youngest son of the Carmichaels from the Lismore township of Park	29
Carmichel, Dugald; "dugald Carmichel Balure"	11, 30
Carmichel, Dugald	27, 29
Carmichel, Hugh	19
Carmichel, Nell; "yong Nell Carmichel Park"	18
Carmichel, Nile; Niel	5
Carmichel, Sandy; "Sandy Carmichel balure"	1, 7
Chirsty; "anty Chirsty from fort william"	18, 22
"Cole"	37
Collen; "Mr Collen Edinbrugh"	33
Colquhoun	12
Connel, Ann	33
Connel; "the Connels"; "Conels"	11, 23, 29, 30
Connel, Donald	9
Connel, John	27
Connel, Maggie	31
Connel, Malcom	27
Crawford, Duncan	12
"Donald"	5, 18, 22, 23, 24, 26, 29, 31, 32, 33, 37

Names and Descriptive Information	**Letter Numbers;** ***Plate Numbers***
"Dougald"	7
Doull, Donald (b. 1850); husband of Flora McDougall	16, 17, 18, 31
Doull, John (b. 1879); first child of Flora McDougall and Donald Doull; "flora has a son", "flora frist son"	18, 22
Doull, William Moore (b. 1880); son of Flora McDougall and Donald Doull; "we got flora frist son but she has another son Called William Moore"	22
"dugald"; brother of "Mary McCallum"	29
"dugald post" [post runner]	18
"Dugald"; "uncle Dugalds daughter"	31
Duglas; "Mr duglas"	1
"duncans wife"	22
Ferguson, Malcolm	12
Fibelvie	12
Graham, James	31
Gregorson	8
"hugh"; "he has two men for by hugh working with him"	2
"hugh"; "he was your uncle hughs image"	5
"hugh"; "Gilbart was a good man and so hugh should be", "he was as tall is hugh"	26
"Hugh"	28
"Johnie"; "Johnie Hugh's son"	28
Livingston, Dugald; "dugald livingston bauchule"	26
Livingston, Duncan	7
Livingston, Kety	7
Livingston, Maggie	7
Livingston, Mary Ann	32
Livingston, Mrs.; "Mrs livingston bauchel"	9
Livingston, Mr	11
Livingston, Nele; "Nele Livingston Bauchle"	22
Livingstone, Coll	8
Livingstone, John	6
Livingstone, Sara; "sara livinstone balure"	23
Lose; "Brother Lose"	12
MacDougall, Allan	37
MacGregor, Rev. Gregor (b. 1797); Lismore Parish Minister 1836-1885 (See Scott, 1923, p. 100 for more details.)	
MacGregor, Janetta (b. 1851); daughter of Rev. Gregor MacGregor (Scott, 1923, p. 100)	31
MacGregor, John; "John McGrigor Stronacronaha"	3
MacGregor, John (b. 1847); "Mr john McGrigor minister", son of Rev. Gregor MacGregor (Scott, 1923, p. 100)	23, 33
MacGregor, Mrs.; "Mrs McG", wife of Rev. Gregor MacGregor, died 6th January 1871 (Scott, 1923, p. 100)	2
Mary	26, 31
Mary; "anty Mary"	23
Maxwell	12
McArthur, Mrs.; "Mrs McArthur inverrary"	9
McCallum	7
McCallum, Ann (b. 1863); daughter of John McCallum (b. 1818 Balure) and Flora Carmichael; "your uncle John daughter". Married Alexander McMaster.	5
McCallum, Ann McCallum (b. 1814 Achnacroish, Lismore); "your mother in law"; "your aunt"; "Mrs McCallum"; "my brother wife"; "your mother"; daughter of Duncan McCallum and Isabella McColl; married Gilbert McCallum (b. 1813 Balure); mother of John McCallum (b. 1847) and Isabel McCallum (b. 1850)	9, 10, 11, 14, 16, 19, 21, 27, 28, 29, 30, 31, 32, 33, 35
McCallum, Archibald; "Archy"; probably a reference to Archibald McCallum (b. 1833 Killean), son of Duncan McCallum and Isabella McColl, brother of Ann McCallum McCallum	35
McCallum, Catherine (b. 1809 Balure); Catherine McCallum McDougall; "your mother"; "her mother"; "Grand Mother"	1, 2, 4, 5, 6, 7, 10, 14, 17, 19, 20, 21, 22, 23, 24, 27, 29, 30, 31, 32, 33, 35; *1.1, 1.2*

Names and Descriptive Information	**Letter Numbers; *Plate Numbers***
McCallum, Donald (b. 1803 Balure); oldest brother of Catherine McCallum	29
McCallum, Donald (b. about 1852); son of Malcolm McCallum, lived in Fort William	28
McCallum, Dugald; "Dugald McCallums Balure wife"	31
McCallum, Duncan (b. 1820 Lismore); brother of Ann McCallum McCallum	10
McCallum, Duncan (b. about 1850); son of Malcolm McCallum	29
McCallum, Gilbert (b. 1813 Balure); "Gilbart"; brother of Catherine McCallum, father of Isabel McCallum (b. 1850) and John McCallum (b. 1847). Married Ann McCallum McCallum.	29, 32
McCallum, Gilbert Sawyer (b.1878 Minnesota); "gelbart"; son of John McCallum (b. 1847 Lismore) and Mary Secrest (b. 1850). He would have been a nephew of Isabel McCallum and John McDougall (b. 1837) and grandson of Ann McCallum McCallum. (Source: Aburn 2013c)	22, *22.5*
McCallum, Isabel (b. 1850); "Bell"; "Belle"; "dear bella"; "bela"; "your wife"; daughter of Gilbert McCallum & Ann McCallum McCallum; married John McDougall (b. 1837). Possibly "my own brothers daughter." (See Letter #26).	9, 11, 14, 16, 17, 18, 19, 20, 21, 22, 26, 27, 28, 29, 30, 31, 32, 33, 35, 38; *9.1, 9.3, 22.1, 38.1*
McCallum, John (b. 1818 Balure); "uncle John", "your uncle John", brother of Catherine McCallum	1, 2, 3, 7, 8, 9, 10, 14, 18, 20, 28, 29, 31, 32, 35
McCallum, John (b. 1847); "your brother in law", "Gilbart son", "your cousin", "cousin John"; son of Gilbert McCallum & Ann McCallum McCallum; lived in Cottage Grove and Ortonville, Minnesota. Possibly also "John McCallum Minisota." (See John McCallum, b. 1852, below.)	6, 7, 14, 16, 19, 20, 21, 22, 27, 30, 32, 33, 38
McCallum, John (b. 1847); "your cousin John McCallum", son of Malcolm McCallum, lived in Fort William	14, 22, 28
McCallum, John (b. 1852); son of Duncan McCallum (b. 1820), lived in Cottage Grove, Minnesota. Possibly also "John McCallum Minisota." (See John McCallum, b. 1847, above.)	7
McCallum, Malcolm (b. 1811 Balure); "your uncle malcom", brother of Catherine McCallum	3, 6, 7, 9, 10, 21, 29
McCallum, Mary; possibly Mary McPhee, wife of Duncan McCallum. Duncan was born about 1850 and was the son of Catherine McCallum's brother, Malcolm.	29
McCheyne, Robert Murray (1813-1843); Scottish theologian	27
McColl	7
McColl, Dougall	14
McColl, John	2, 4
McConchar	22
McConochie, Donald	34, 37, 38
McConochie, Eilen; "Eilen your sister"	37
McCormmick, Duncan	18
McCorquodale; "McCorqudal", "the McCorqudal", "Mr McCorqudal and famely"	18, 19, 27, 33
McCorqudal, Archibald	31
McCorqudal, Dugald; "Dugald bean [wife] McCorqudal"	31
McCorqudal, Hugh; "Archbald McCorqudal and his son Hugh"	31
McCorqudal, John	23
McCorqudal, Sandy; "compliments to old Sandy McCorquarld"	30
McDonald, Angus	20
McDonald, Ducan	23
McDougall, Agnes (Ann) (b. 1833); "agunes", "Agness", "Angnes", daughter of John McDougall (weaver) and Catherine McCallum; married William Moore	6, 8, 13, 16, 19, 23, 25, 32, 35; *6.1*
McDougall, Ann (b. 1879); "ann flora", "little anny", daughter of John McDougall and Isabel McCallum	20, 22, 30, 37; *22.1, 22.3, 26.2, 26.3, 38.1*

Names and Descriptive Information	Letter Numbers; *Plate Numbers*
McDougall, Donald (b. about 1845, Lismore); son of John McDougall (weaver) and Catherine McCallum	9, 13, 17, 19, 36 (See also "donald" above.)
McDougall, Donald (b. 1885, Minnesota); son of John McDougall and Isabel McCallum	37, *26.2, 26.3, 38.1*
McDougall, Flora (b. 1851); "Flory", daughter of John McDougall (weaver) and Catherine McCallum	7, 13, 16, 17, 18, 22, 23, 29, 31, 32
McDougall, Gilbert Hugh (Gib) (b. 1881 Delhi, Minnesota); son of John McDougall and Isabel McCallum	26, 27, 30, 37; *22.5, 26.2, 26.3, 26.4, 30.1, 37.7, 38.1, A8.1*
McDougall, Hugh (b. 1842, Lismore); son of John McDougall (weaver) and Catherine McCallum	1, 2, 3, 4, 5, 6, 7, 9, 10, 11, 12, 13, 14, 16, 17, 18, 19, 20, 21, 22, 28, 29, 30, 31, 32, 33
McDougall, John (weaver) (b. 1803); "your father", "my father"	1, 2, 3, 4, 5, 6, 7, 8, 9, 10, 11, 14, 16, 17, 19, 20, 21, 22, 23, 24, 27, 29, 30, 31, 32, 33, 35, 36; *1.1*
McDougall, John (b. 1837, Lismore); son of John McDougall (weaver) and Catherine McCallum	1, 2, 3, 4, 5, 6, 7, 8, 9, 10, 11, 12, 13, 14, 16, 17, 18, 19, 20, 21, 22, 23, 26, 27, 29, 30, 31, 32, 33, 34, 36, 37, 38; *1.3, 9.3*
McDougall, John D. (b. 1877, Minnesota); "little John McDougall"; "John Dugald"; "John Dugald McDougall"; "J.. D.. McDougall"; "yong John dugald McDougall"; "dear John D"; "John Dugald MacDougal"; railroad engineer; son of John McDougall (b. 1837) and Isabel McCallum	16, 17, 18, 20, 22, 26, 29, 30, 33, 37, 38; *20.1, 26.2, 26.3, 30.1, 38.1*
McDougall, Margaret (b. 1851 or 1852); "Maggie", "My Sister that came here with her family", Mrs. Alexander Milne, daughter of John McDougall (weaver) and Catherine McCallum	1, 3, 4, 5, 6, 7, 9, 10, 11, 13, 14, 16, 17, 18, 22, 23, 26, 29, 31, 37; *1.8, 16.1, 35.4*
McDougall, Mary (b. 1835); "your sister mary", daughter of John McDougall (weaver) and Catherine McCallum	1, 2, 3, 4, 6, 7, 9, 10, 31
McDougall, William Moore (b. 1883); son of John McDougall (b. 1837) and Isabel McCallum; "we was happy to hear that the Lord give you another Son"	29, 30, 37; *26.2, 26.3, 30.1, 38.1*
McDouglas	12
McFarlane, Archibald	32
McFarlane, Bill	12
McFarlane, Marten; "archibald Mcfarlen Gran son marten tirlagan"	32
McIntyre, Mrs.; "Mrs McIntyre Salan"	4
McIntyre, Sara; "Sara McIntyre Salan"	32
McKinnon, Bob	12
McLaren, Dan	12
McNicol, Angus; "angus McNicol port appin"	31
McNicol, Ann; "Your cousin Ann McNicol"; "your Cusen ann McNicol Mrs McPerson"	6, 9, 25
McNicol, Donald	8
McNicol, John; "John McNicol port appin"; "Angus McNicol port appin his son John is in his place"	29, 31, 32
McPhail, Adam; "Adam Mcphell"	20
McPherson, John; "Pt Appin Police Man John McPherson"	6
McQueens; "McQuenz"	9
McRae, Jamie	12
McRindle, Beatrice	17

Names and Descriptive Information	Letter Numbers; *Plate Numbers*
Milne, Alexander (b. 1850); "Alesar"; "Alastair"; "Sandy Miline"; "Milnie"; husband of Margaret McDougall; son-in-law of John McDougall (weaver) and Catherine McCallum	13, 14, 16, 17, 18, 19, 22, 23, 29, 31; *35.4, 37.6, 37.9*
Milne, James Alexander (b. 1877); oldest child of Margaret McDougall & Alexander Milne	14, 16; *14.1, 14.2, 14.3, 35.4, 37.6*
Milne, John (b. 1878); "Jonnie", second child of Margaret McDougall & Alexander Milne	16, 17, 22; *16.1, 35.4, 37.6*
Montgomery; brother-in-law of Donald McConochie	37
Moody	11
Moore, Donald Hugh (b. 1870); son of Agnes (Ann) McDougall and William Moore	13, 23, 31
Moore, Catherine Mary Ann (b. 1876); "Katy", "kety mary ann", daughter of Agnes (Ann) McDougall and William Moore	13, 17, 18
Moore, James (b. 1868); son of Agnes (Ann) McDougall and William Moore	13, 24, 25, 26, 29; *6.3*
Moore, John (b. 1858); son of Agnes (Ann) McDougall and William Moore	10, 13, 14, 17, 22, 23, 24, 25, 26
Moore, William (b. 1834); "william"; "Mr. Moore thurso"; husband of Agnes (Ann) McDougall; son-in-law of John McDougall (weaver) and Catherine McCallum	1, 3, 6, 9, 10, 13, 16, 17, 18, 23, 25, 29, 31, 32; *6.2*
Niven, Archy	12
Otter, Admiral; "admoral otter oban"	9
Paterson, Georg	37
Robinson	12
Ross	12
Sallan; "the Sallan girls"	11
Sara; "poor anty Sara"	22
Sinclair, Rev.; minister, Redwood Falls, Minnesota	37
Sinclair	12, 37
Sinclair, Sandy; Oban (possibly "Sandy Singelar" in Letter #22)	22, 33, 37
Smith, Dan	12
Stuart, James; "James Stwuart port Ramsa"	18
Stuart, Sandy [Stewart?]; "Sandy Stwuard"	23
Turner	12
White; "Mr White"	1
"William"	22
Young, Susan; "Miss Young a Merchant's daughter"; married Catherine McCallum's nephew, John McCallum (b. 1847), of Fort William	14

Appendix 5

Table A5

Places Mentioned in the Letters

Place Name (Variations)	Letter Number
Aberdeen, Scotland	13
Achnacroish, Lismore (Auchnacroish)	32, 33
Africa	12
America	2, 4, 6, 9, 11, 15, 16, 17, 26, 38
Appin	2, 3, 7, 23, 32, 33
Argyllshire	38
Auchouran, Lismore (Achuaran)	9, 10, 32
Bachuil, Lismore (Bauchel, Bauchle, bauchule)	9, 22, 26
Baligarve, Lismore	3
Ballimackillichan, Lismore	1, 2, 3, 4, 5, 6, 7, 8, 9, 10, 11, 14, 18, 22, 26, 27, 29, 31, 32, 33
Balure, Lismore	1, 6, 11, 23, 31
Blairgowrie ("Blaurgouri")	32
Caithness	13, 17
California	12
Clachan, Lismore	33
Corran	2
Cottage Grove, Minnesota	6
Delhi, Minnesota	34, 37
Dunoon	1, 12
Edinburgh ("Edinbrought", "Edinbrught", "Edinbruch")	14, 15, 31, 33
Eilean nan Caorach (Eellan na Caorach) (Sheep Island)	19
Elgin; "Elgen"	13, 16, 18, 22
England	9
Fort William	7, 14, 18, 22, 28
Glasgow	1, 4, 6, 7, 9, 10, 11, 12, 13, 14, 15, 29, 37
Govan	12
Greenock ("grinock")	12, 31
Hartford	12
Hartford, Connecticut	38
Hill Head	12
Invereray (Inverray, inverera)	9, 10
Ireland	25
Killean, Lismore	Undated letter – Mentioned in transcriber's note about birthplace of Ann McCallum McCallum
Kintyre	37
Lagan, Lismore (Laggan)	31
Lismore	7, 9, 11, 13, 14, 18, 20, 21, 22, 23, 26, 27, 29, 31, 32, 33, 35, 36
Minnesota	6, 7, 25, 34, 37, 38
New York	6
New Zealand	16
Oban	9, 22, 37, 38
Paisley	37
Park, Lismore	18, 29
Perthshire ("perthshair")	32
Point, Lismore	14

Place Name (Variations)	Letter Number
Port Appin	6, 29, 31, 32
Port Maluag, Lismore	9
Port Ramsay, Lismore ("port Ramsa", "Portramsa")	18, 23
Portnacroish ("portenosh")	32
Redwood County, Minnesota	34, 37
Redwood Falls, Minnesota	13, 34, 37
Salan, Lismore (Sailean, Sallan)	4, 11, 32
Scotland ("Schotland", "Scothland")	6, 18, 22, 25, 26, 27, 31, 32, 33, 38
Sheep Island	See Eilean nan Caorach, above.
St. Paul, Minnesota	34
Stronacroibh, Lismore ("Stronacrie", "Stronacronaha", "Stronnacrath")	3, 19, 32
Stronation, Sunart	7
Strontoler	37
Thurso	13, 14, 15, 17, 18, 19, 22, 23, 24, 25, 31, 33, 36
Tirlaggan, Lismore (Tirlagan)	2, 32
Virginia	12
Washington County, Minnesota	6

Appendix 6

Certificates of Births and Deaths

Entries from the Registers of Births and Deaths in Scotland and Minnesota

The following records include the following, from the and from Redwood County, Minnesota.

- Record of birth for Dougald McDougall Milne [Tiffany] (b. 1885, Thurso).

- Records of death for:
  - Catherine McCallum McDougall (b. 1809, Lismore)
  - Joseph Milne (b. 1886, Thurso)
  - John McDougall (weaver, b. 1803, Lismore)
  - John McDougall (b. 1837, Lismore, son of John McDougall, weaver and Catherine McCallum McDougall)

The record of Catherine McCallum's death appears to have been signed by her husband, John McDougall, with an "X". The record of death for John McDougall (weaver, b. 1803, Lismore), which occurred in Thurso, appears to have been signed by his son, Donald (D. McDougall.) The record of infant Joseph Milne's death, which also occurred in Thurso, was signed by his father, Alexander, cause of death: hydrocephalus.

Plate A6.1

Record of Birth for Dougald McDougall Milne [Tiffany] (b. 1885, Thurso)

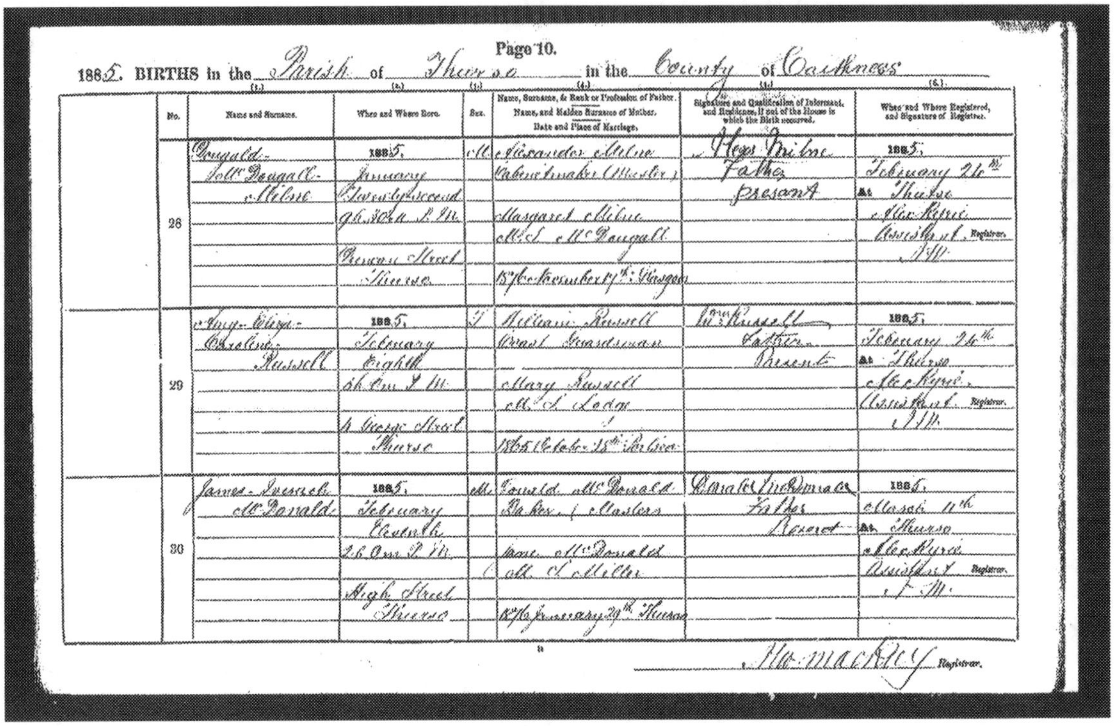

Page 10.

1885. BIRTHS in the Parish of Thurso in the County of Caithness

No.	Name and Surname.	When and Where Born.	Sex.	Name, Surname, & Rank or Profession of Father. Name, and Maiden Surname of Mother. Date and Place of Marriage.	Signature and Qualification of Informant, and Residence, if out of the House in which the Birth occurred.	When and Where Registered, and Signature of Registrar.
28	Dougald McDougall Milne	1885. January Twenty second 9h. 30m P.M. Duncan Street Thurso	M	Alexander Milne Cabinetmaker (Master) Margaret Milne M.S. McDougall 1876 November 17th Glasgow	Alex Milne Father Present	1885. February 2[illegible]th At Thurso Alex [illegible] Assistant Registrar. [illegible]
29	Amy Eliza Caroline Russell	1885. February Eighth 5h 0m P.M. 4 George Street Thurso	F	William Russell Coast Guardsman Mary Russell M.S. Lodge 1865 October 18th [illegible]	Wm Russell Father Present	1885. February 26th At Thurso Alex [illegible] Assistant Registrar. [illegible]
30	James Russell McDonald	1885. February Eleventh 2h 0m P.M. High Street Thurso	M	Donald McDonald Baker (Master) Jane McDonald M.S. Miller 1876 January 29th Thurso	Donald McDonald Father Present	1885. March 11th At Thurso Alex [illegible] Assistant Registrar. [illegible]

[illegible] Mackay Registrar.

Reproduced with the kind permission of the Registrar General for Scotland.

Plate A6.2

Dougald McDougall Milne Tiffany at his birthplace, Duncan Street, Thurso, 1966
with his daughter, Margaret Tiffany Wilcox, and his wife, Jennie June Peabody Tiffany

Plate A6.3
Record of Death for Catherine McCallum McDougall (b. 1809, Lismore)

Extract of an entry from the REGISTER OF DEATHS in Scotland

188*6*. DEATHS in the *District* of *Lismore* in the *County* of *Argyll*

No.	(1.) Name and Surname. Rank or Profession, and whether Single, Married, or Widowed.	(2.) When and Where Died.	(3.) Sex.	(4.) Age.	(5.) Name, Surname, & Rank or Profession of Father. Name, and Maiden Surname of Mother.	(6.) Cause of Death, Duration of Disease, and Medical Attendant by whom certified.	(7.) Signature & Qualification of Informant, and Residence, if out of the House in which the Death occurred.	(8.) When and where Registered, and Signature of Registrar.
9	Catherine McDougall Married to John McDougall	1886. May twenty-sixth 5h. 0 m. [sic] Ballimackillichan Lismore	F	77 yrs	John Maccallum Farmer (deceased) Anne Maccallum M.S. Carmichael (deceased)	Chronic Bronchitis As certified by Archd. Mackay M.D.	John X McDougall his mark husband, Present James Wilson Regr. Witness	1886. May 28th At Lismore James Wilson Registrar.

This official document is issued by the General Register Office for Scotland, New Register House, 3 West Register Street, Edinburgh EH1 3YT under the Seal of that Office on 9 February 2013

The above particulars incorporate any subsequent corrections or amendments to the original entry made with the authority of the Registrar General.

Warning

It is an offence for any person to pass as genuine any copy or reproduction of an extract issued from the General Register Office for Scotland if it has not been authenticated by the Seal of that Office.

Any person who falsifies or forges any of the particulars on this extract or knowingly uses, gives or sends as genuine any false or forged extract is liable to prosecution.

5977127 CE

Plate A6.4
Record of Death for Joseph Milne (b. 1886, Thurso)

Extract of an entry from the REGISTER OF DEATHS in Scotland

1887. DEATHS in the Parish of Thurso in the County of Caithness

No.	(1.) Name and Surname. Rank or Profession, and whether Single, Married, or Widowed.	(2.) When and Where Died.	(3.) Sex.	(4.) Age.	(5.) Name, Surname, & Rank or Profession of Father. Name, and Maiden Surname of Mother.	(6.) Cause of Death, Duration of Disease, and Medical Attendant by whom certified.	(7.) Signature & Qualification of Informant, and Residence, if out of the House in which the Death occurred.	(8.) When and where Registered, and Signature of Registrar.
5	Joseph Milne Single	1887. January Twelfth 4h 30m A.M. Duncan Street Thurso	M	7 Months	Alexander Milne Cabinetmaker, Master Margaret Milne M. S. McDougall	Hydrocephalus 2 Months As cert by Dr J. B. Arnott Thurso	Alex Milne Father Present	1887. January 21st At Thurso Alex Rhine Assistant Registrar. A.M.

This official document is issued by the General Register Office for Scotland, New Register House, 3 West Register Street, Edinburgh EH1 3YT under the Seal of that Office on 12 February 2013

The above particulars incorporate any subsequent corrections or amendments to the original entry made with the authority of the Registrar General.

Warning
It is an offence for any person to pass as genuine any copy or reproduction of an extract issued from the General Register Office for Scotland if it has not been authenticated by the Seal of that Office.
Any person who falsifies or forges any of the particulars on this extract or knowingly uses, gives or sends as genuine any false or forged extract is liable to prosecution.

5980507 CE

Reproduced with the kind permission of the Registrar General for Scotland.

Plate A6.5
Record of Death for John McDougall (b. 1803, Lismore)

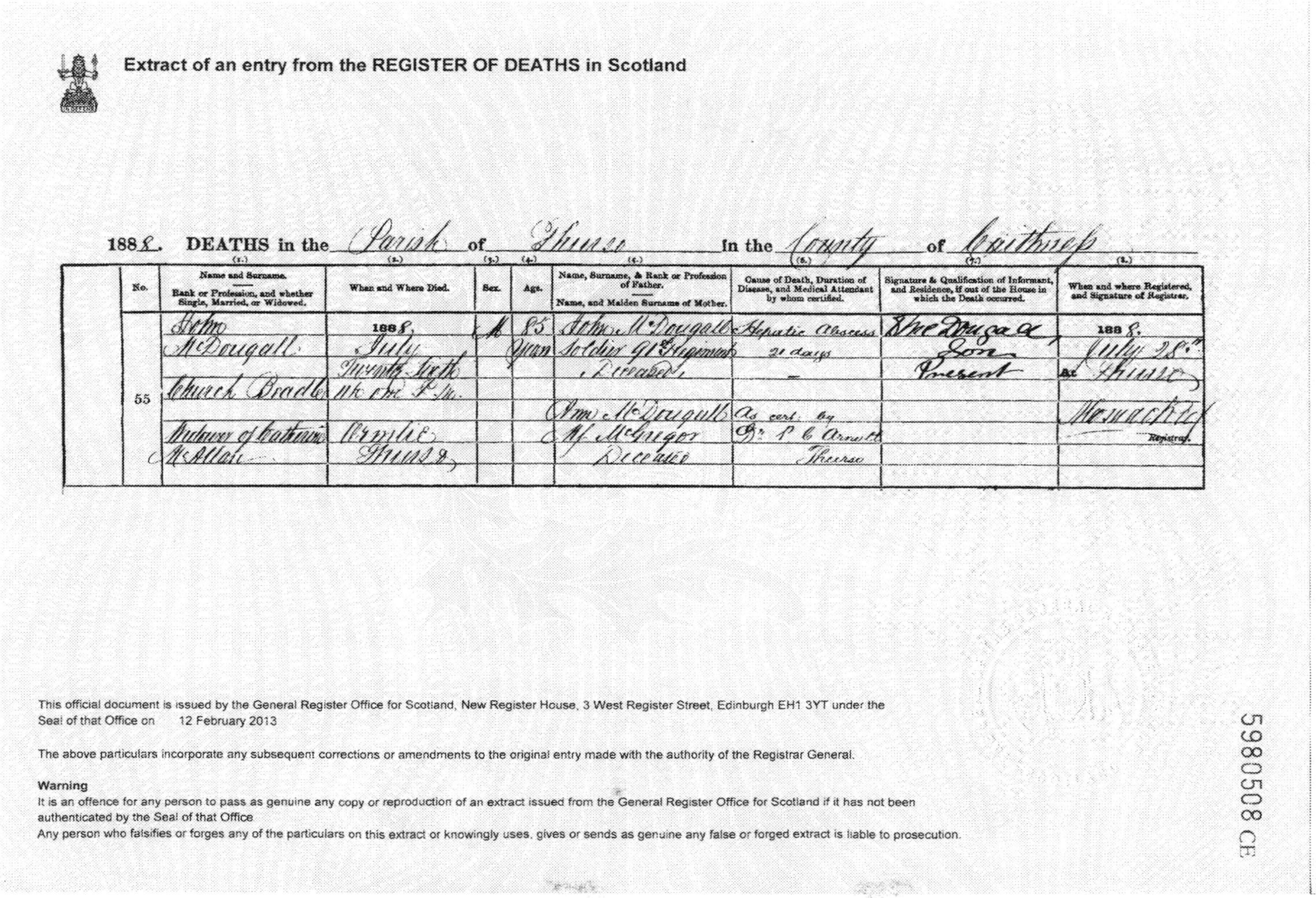

Extract of an entry from the REGISTER OF DEATHS in Scotland

1888. DEATHS in the Parish of Thurso in the County of Caithness

No.	Name and Surname. Rank or Profession, and whether Single, Married, or Widowed. (1.)	When and Where Died. (2.)	Sex. (3.)	Age. (4.)	Name, Surname, & Rank or Profession of Father. Name, and Maiden Surname of Mother. (5.)	Cause of Death, Duration of Disease, and Medical Attendant by whom certified. (6.)	Signature & Qualification of Informant, and Residence, if out of the House in which the Death occurred. (7.)	When and where Registered, and Signature of Registrar. (8.)
55	John McDougall Church Beadle Widower of Catherine McAllan	1888 July Twenty Sixth 11h 0m P.M. Ormlie Thurso	M	85 Years	John McDougall Soldier 91st Regiment (Deceased) Ann McDougall MS McGregor Deceased	Hepatic Abscess 21 days — As cert. by Dr P C Arnott Thurso	[illegible] McDougall Son Present	1888 July 28th At Thurso [illegible] Registrar.

This official document is issued by the General Register Office for Scotland, New Register House, 3 West Register Street, Edinburgh EH1 3YT under the Seal of that Office on 12 February 2013

The above particulars incorporate any subsequent corrections or amendments to the original entry made with the authority of the Registrar General.

Warning

It is an offence for any person to pass as genuine any copy or reproduction of an extract issued from the General Register Office for Scotland if it has not been authenticated by the Seal of that Office.

Any person who falsifies or forges any of the particulars on this extract or knowingly uses, gives or sends as genuine any false or forged extract is liable to prosecution.

5980508 CE

Reproduced with the kind permission of the Registrar General for Scotland.

Plate A6.6

Certificate of Death for John McDougall (b. 1837, Lismore)

Redwood County Recorder
Joyce Anderson, Recorder
PO Box 130
403 S Mill Street
Redwood Falls MN 56283
Phone (507) 637-4032 Fax (507) 637-4064

Certificate of Death

State of Minnesota

Deceased First Name	Middle Name	Last Name	Suffix
John		Mc Dougal	

Deceased Maiden Surname; Deceased Alias First Middle Last Name Suffix

Sex	Social Security No.	Date of Death	County of Death
Male	------	02/05/1896	Redwood

City or Township of Death	Age: Year	Month	Days
Delhi	58	11	24

City and State of Foreign County of Birth

Scotland

Father's First	Middle	Last Name	Place of Birth
John		Mc Dougal	England

Mother's First	Middle	Last Name	Place of Birth
Catherine		Mc Dougal	Scotland

Marital Status	Spouse's First	Middle	Last or Maiden Surname
Married			

Name of Funeral Est.

Date of Documentation of death was filed

02/24/1896

Cause of Death – Concussion of Brain

Immediate Cause of Death-

Underlying Cause of Death-

Conditions contributing to the death-

Manner of Death;

Names and address of Physician who provided cause of death information-

Amendments to death records; notation.

This is a Non-Certified Copy
Not to be used for legal purposes

Courtesy of Margaret Carasik

Appendix 7

Maps

Plate A7.1
North Atlantic - Scotland to Minnesota

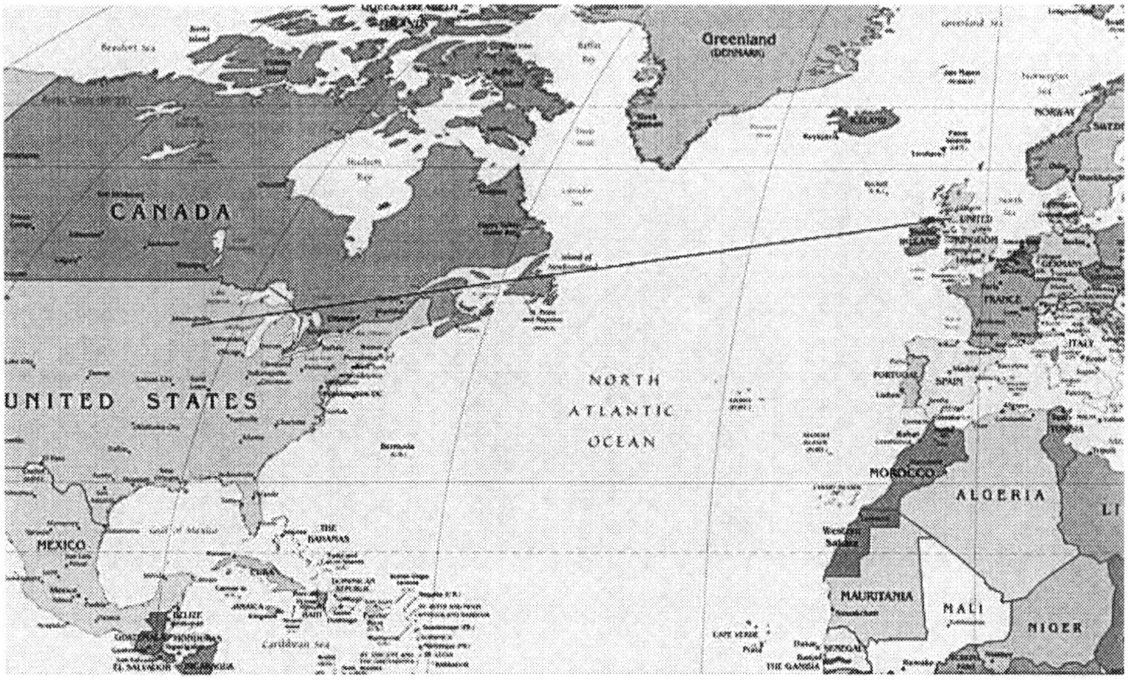

Source (Base Map): Perry-Castañeda Library Map Collection, University of Texas, Austin

Plate A7.2
Scotland - Places Mentioned in the Letters
(Repeated from Introduction)

Lynn D. Miller

Plate A7.3
Lismore - Places Mentioned in the Letters

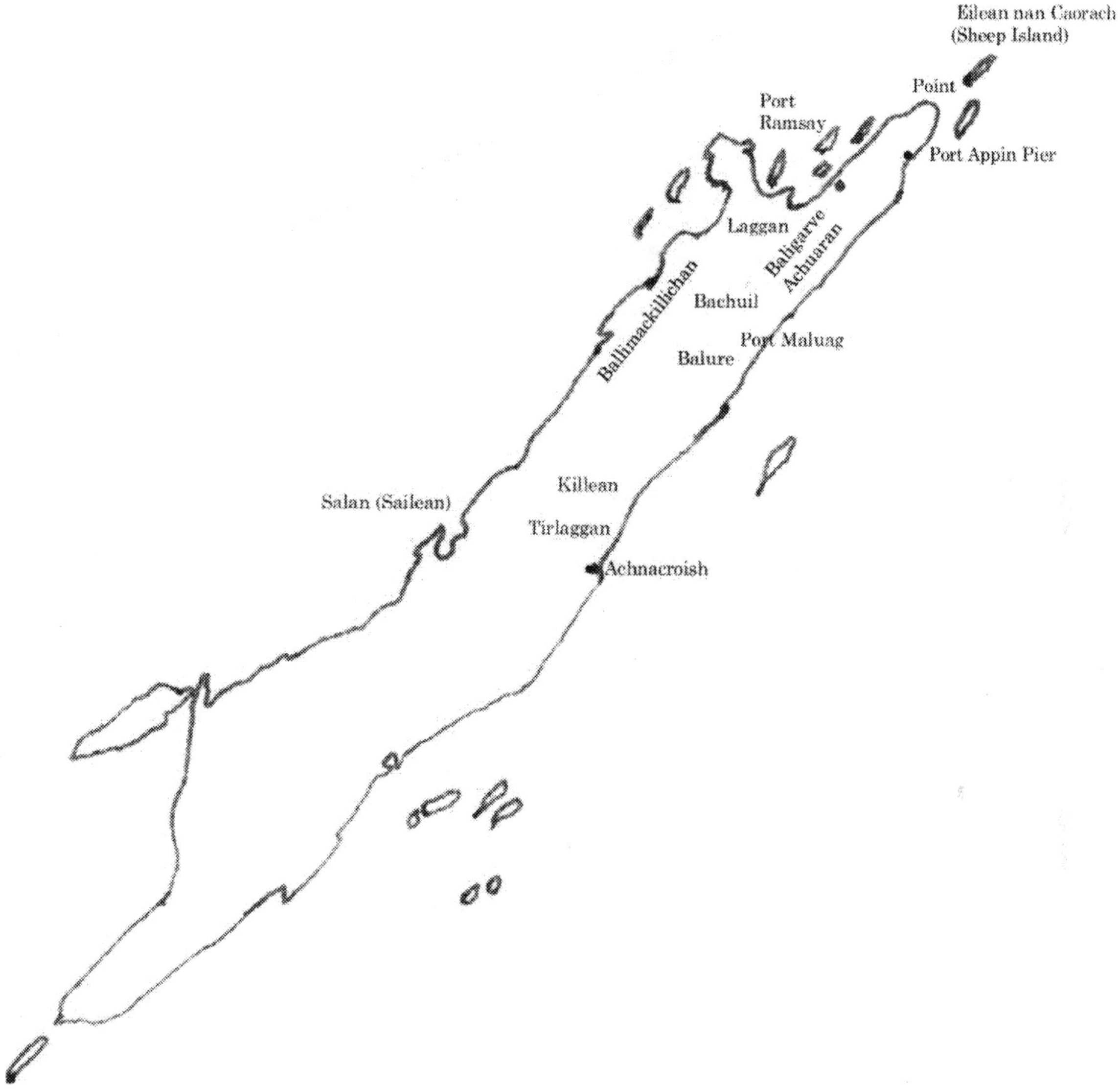

Lynn D. Miller

Lismore Detailed Maps

Plate A7.4.1
Castle Coeffin, Ballimackillichan, Cathedral of St. Maluag, Bauchuil, Baptist Chapel, Independent Chapel
Survey Date: 1871-1872

Scale for this map: ⟵ **1 mile** ⟶

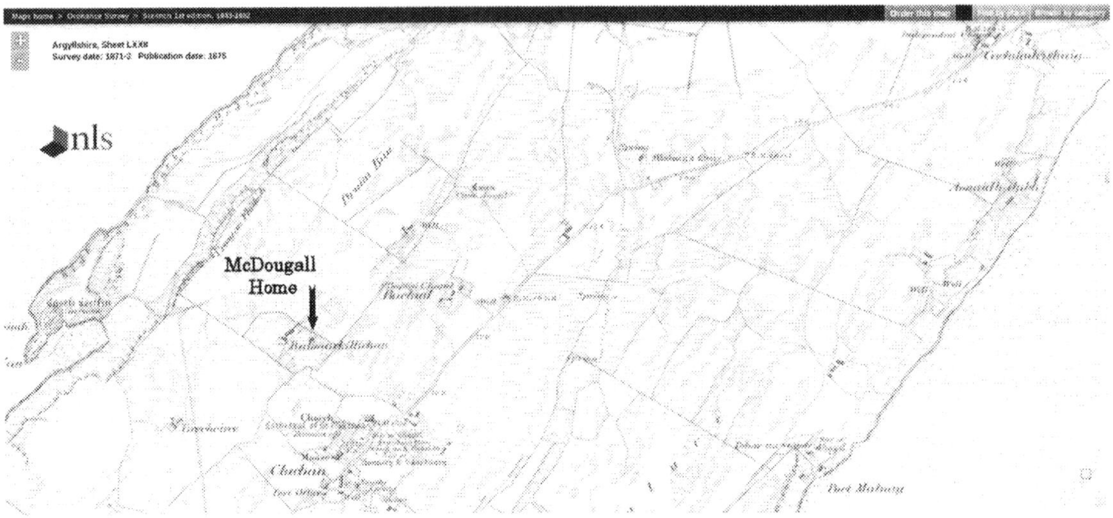

Reproduced by Permission of the National Library of Scotland

Plate A7.4.2
Castle Coeffin, Ballimackillichan, Cathedral of St. Maluag, Bachuil, and Baptist Chapel
Survey Date: 1871

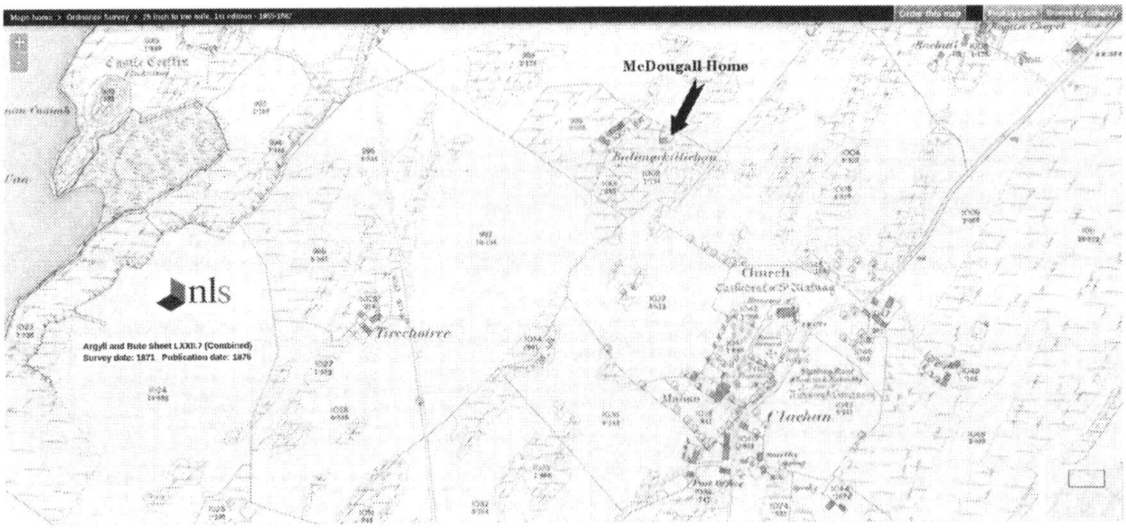

Reproduced by Permission of the National Library of Scotland

Plate A7.4.3
Ballimackillichan, Bachuil and Baptist Chapel
Survey Date: 1871

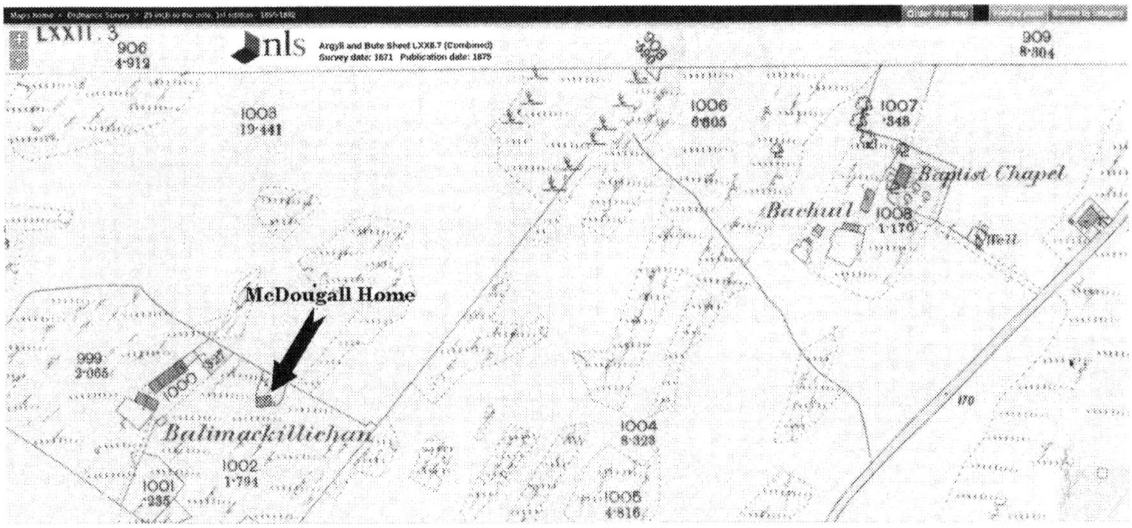

Reproduced by Permission of the National Library of Scotland

Plate A7.4.4
Ballimackillichan and Cathedral of St. Maluag
Survey Date: 1871

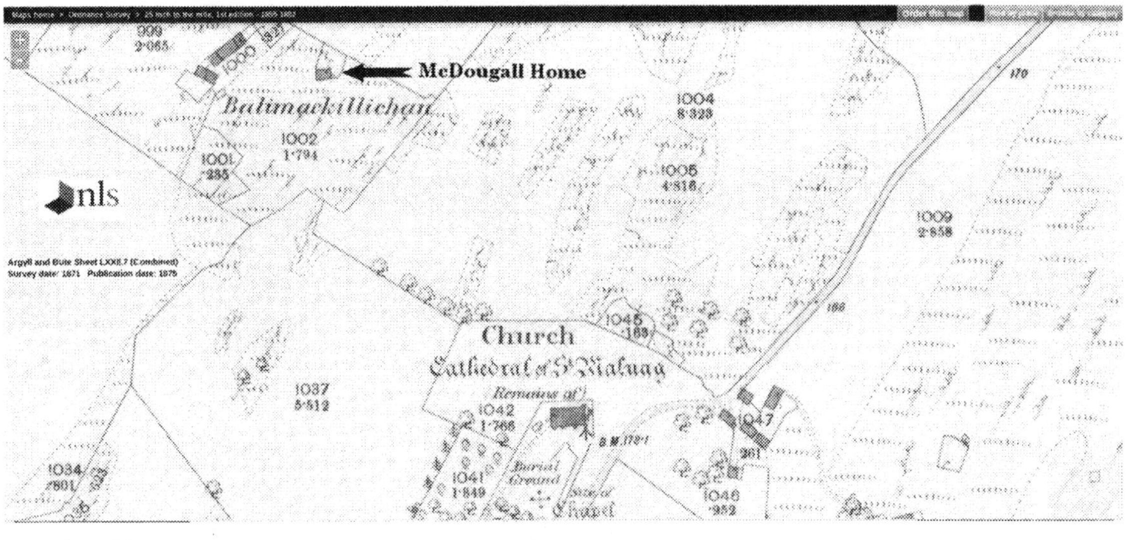

Reproduced by Permission of the National Library of Scotland

Plate A7.4.5
Lismore Showing Locations of
Independent Chapel and Achuaran School

Argyllshire, Sheet LXXII
Survey date: 1871-2 Publication date: 1875

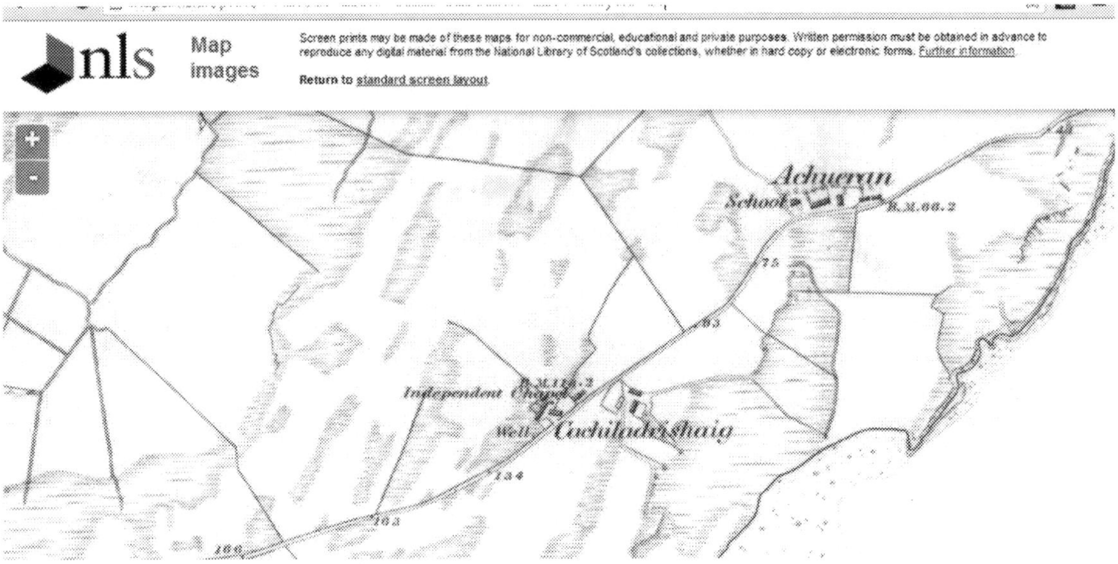

Reproduced by Permission of the National Library of Scotland

Plate A7.5
United States Showing Minnesota and New York Communities Mentioned in the Letters

University of Texas Libraries

Minnesota

University of Texas Libraries

United States

Lynn D. Miller, editor

Appendix 8

Family Trees for John McDougall (weaver) (b. 1803 Lismore), Catherine McCallum (b. 1809 Lismore) and their Children

The following high-level family trees identify the children and grandchildren of John McDougall (weaver) and Catherine McCallum. They are complete for Catherine Doull Guthrie (daughter of Flora McDougall and Donald Doull), Gilbert Hugh MacDougall (son of John McDougall and Isabel McCallum) and Margaret Tiffany Wilcox (granddaughter of Margaret McDougall and Alexander Milne). They are a starting point for other, more detailed family trees.

Family Tree #1
John McDougall (weaver) and Catherine McCallum
(Repeated from Introduction)

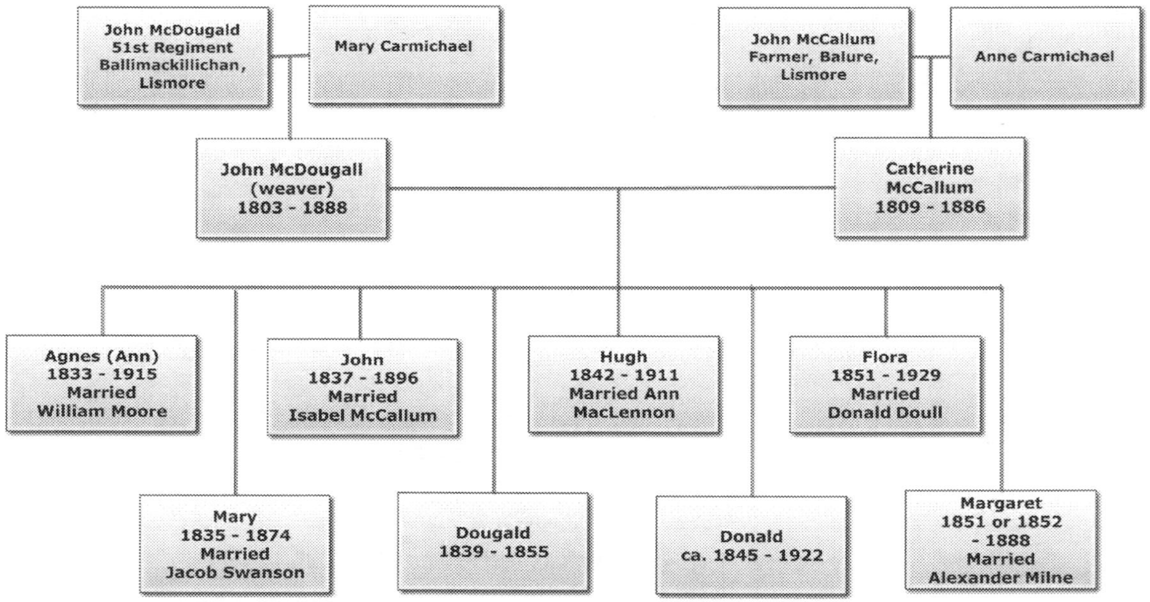

Family Tree #2
Ann (Agnes) McDougall (1833 - 1915) and William Moore
Agnes' Parents: John McDougall (weaver) (b. 1803, Lismore) and Catherine McCallum (b. 1809, Lismore)

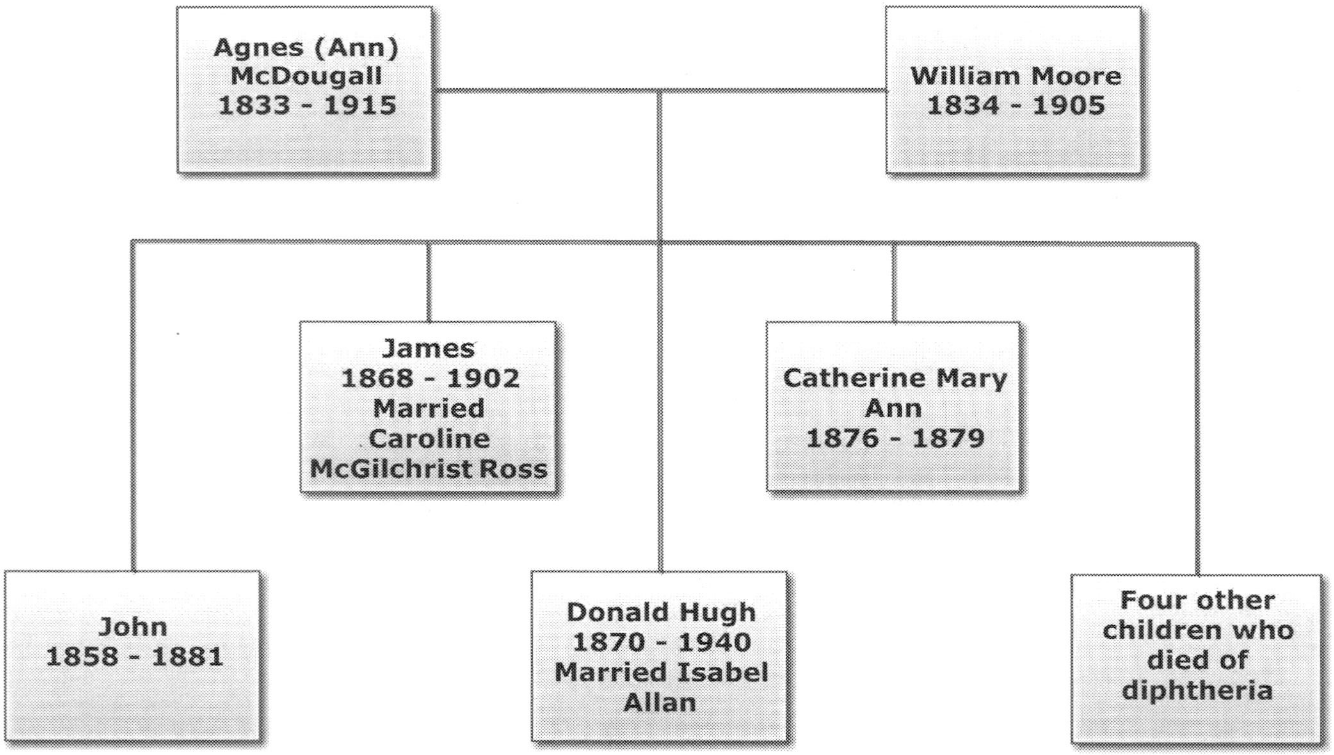

Family Tree #3
John McDougall (1837-1896) and
Isabel McCallum (1850 - 1935)

John's Parents: John McDougall (weaver) (b. 1803, Lismore) and Catherine McCallum (b. 1809, Lismore)

Isabel's Parents: Gilbert McCallum (b. 1813, Balure, Lismore), brother of Catherine McCallum, and Ann McCallum McCallum (b. 1814, Lismore)

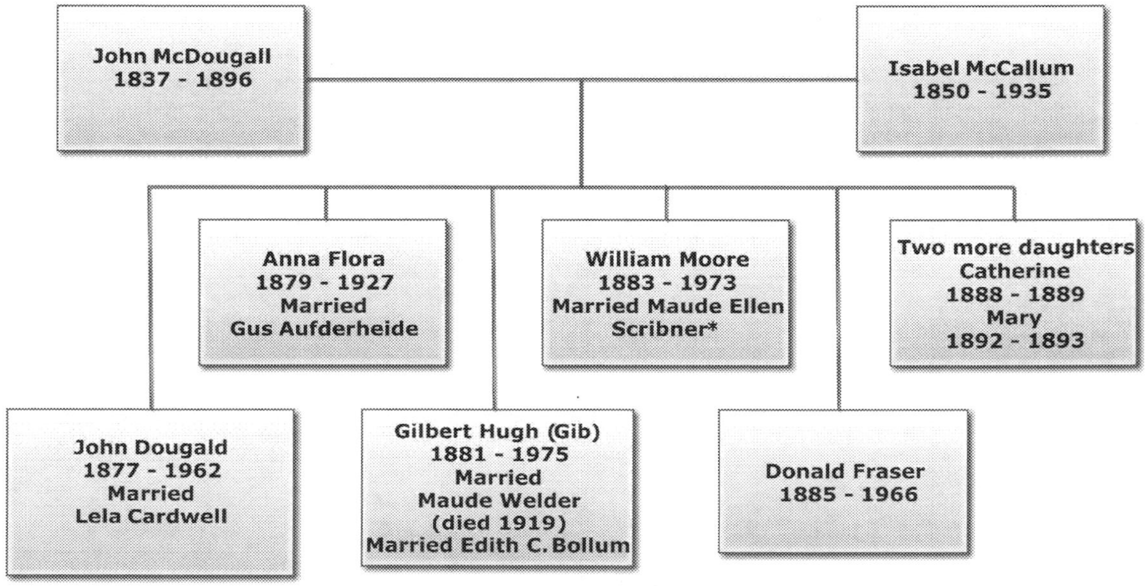

*The name of William Moore MacDougall's wife may have been Maude Ellen Osborne. (Stark, 2014e)
Catherine's and Mary's years of death are from photos of their gravestones in the Redwood Falls Cemetery.

Additional descendants: The following tree provides a complete list of Gilbert Hugh MacDougall's descendants. His sister, Anna MacDougall Aufderheide, and his brother, William Moore MacDougall, also had children.

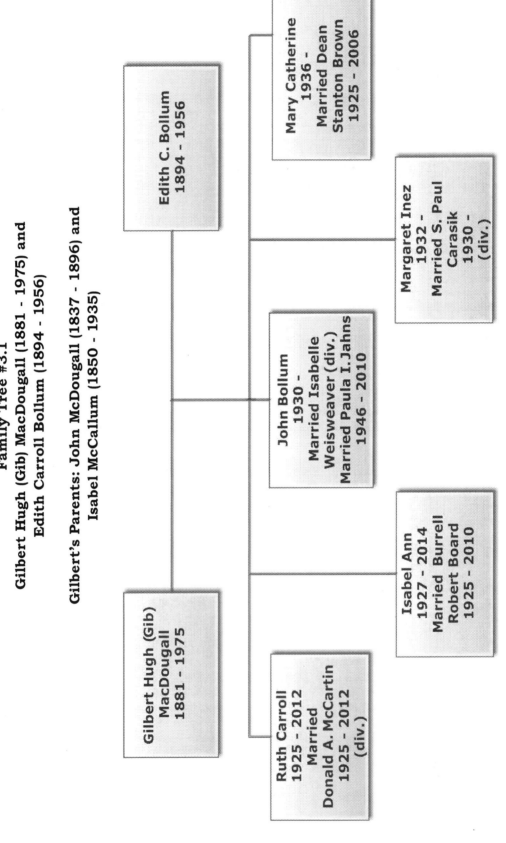

Family Tree #3.1
Gilbert Hugh (Gib) MacDougall (1881 - 1975) and
Edith Carroll Bollum (1894 - 1956)

Gilbert's Parents: John McDougall (1837 - 1896) and
Isabel McCallum (1850 - 1935)

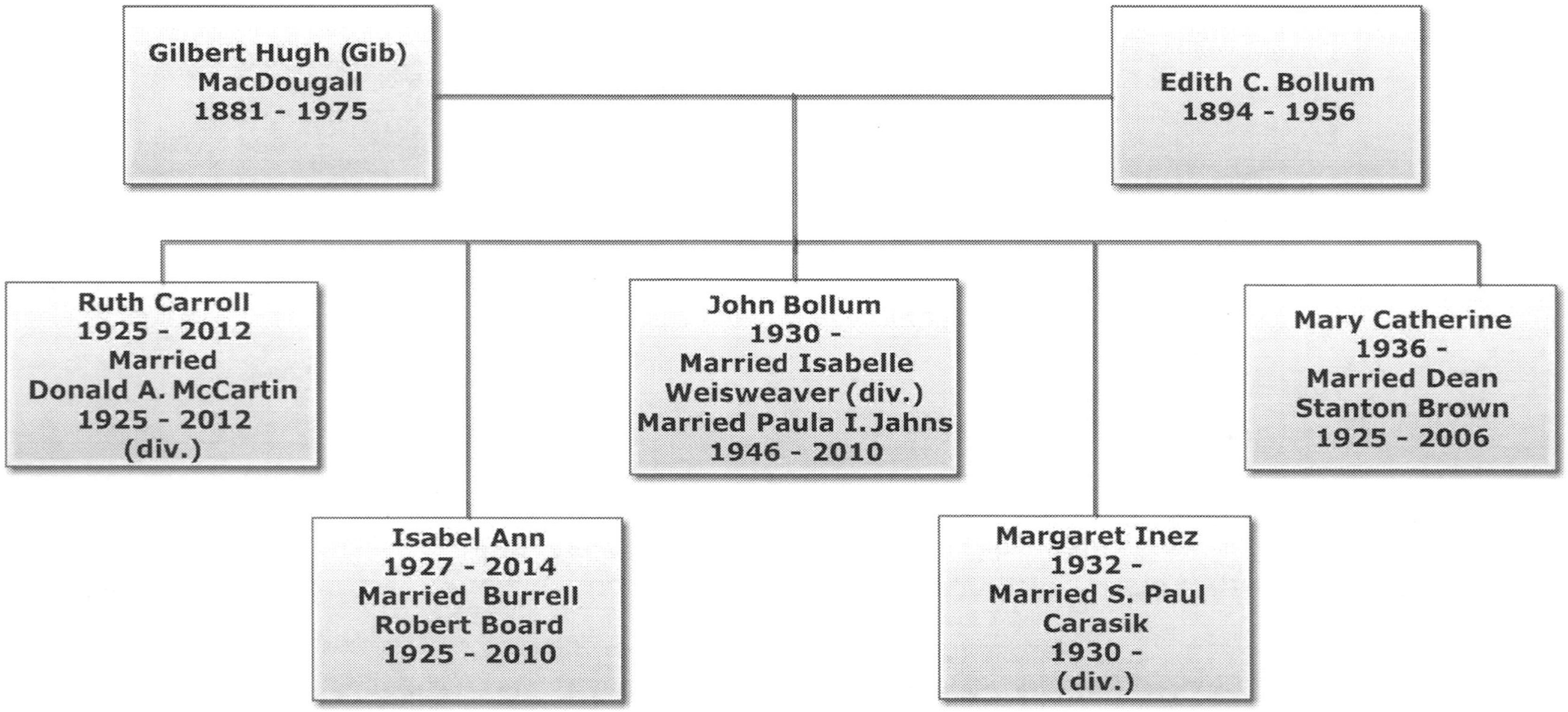

Key: (div.) – divorced

Plate A8.1
Gilbert Hugh (Gib) MacDougall with his Children, 1971
(Left to Right) Isabel MacDougall Board, Ruth MacDougall McCartin, Margaret MacDougall Carasik, Gilbert Hugh (Gib) MacDougall, John MacDougall, Mary MacDougall Brown

Family Tree #3.1.1
Children and Grandchildren of
Gilbert Hugh (Gib) MacDougall and Edith C. Bollum

Children	Grandchildren			
Ruth Carroll 1925 - 2012 Married Donald A. McCartin 1925 - 2012 (div.)	Michael Sterling 1949 - Married June McKee (div.) Married Catherine G. Lacuesta	Mark John 1954 - Married Cheryl Cooke	Casey Hugh 1957 - 2014 Married Geraldine A. Serdenia	Duff Patrick 1959 -
Isabel Ann 1927 - 2014 Married Burrell Robert Board 1925 - 2010	Connie Lynne 1947 - Married James Thomas Horton (div.) Married John Edward Meyer (div.)	Stephen Robert 1948 - Married Cathleen Ann Salemme	Sandra Lee 1951 - Married Eric Henry Christensen	Beryl Ann 1959 - Married Susan Reed
John Bollum 1930 - Married Isabelle Weisweaver (div.)	Alec John (Jock) 1961 - Married Theresa Sepulveda	Edith Ann (Dee) 1962 - Married Jeffrey Scott Anderson	Eric James (Jim) 1965 - Married Morgynne Clarrissa Ann Northe	
Married Paula I. Jahns 1946 - 2010				
Margaret Inez 1932 - Married S. Paul Carasik 1930 - (div.)	John Samuel Carasik 1969 - 2002			
Mary Catherine 1936 - Married Dean Stanton Brown 1925 - 2006				

Key: (div.) – divorced

Family Tree #3.1.1.1
Children and Grandchildren of
Ruth Carroll MacDougall and Donald A. McCartin

Children	Grandchildren					
Michael Sterling McCartin 1949 - Married June McKee (div.)	Laurie Erin 1974 -	Megan Anne 1979 -	Jennifer Sue 1979 - Married Andrew Arnold Hock Children: Paige Cameron 2010 - Samuel Aaron 2013 -			
Married Catherine G. Lacuesta	Cameron Michael 1996 -					
Mark John McCartin 1954 - Married Cheryl Cooke	Jennifer Lorraine 1976 -	Shaun Mark 1987 -	Casey James 1988 - Married Kelly Craft Nolan James 2014 -	Taryn Carol 1990 -	Cheyenna Dawn 1991 -	
Casey Hugh McCartin 1957 - 2014 Married Geraldine A. Serdenia						
Duff Patrick McCartin 1959						

Family Tree #3.1.1.2
Children and Grandchildren of Isabel Ann MacDougall and Burrell Robert Board

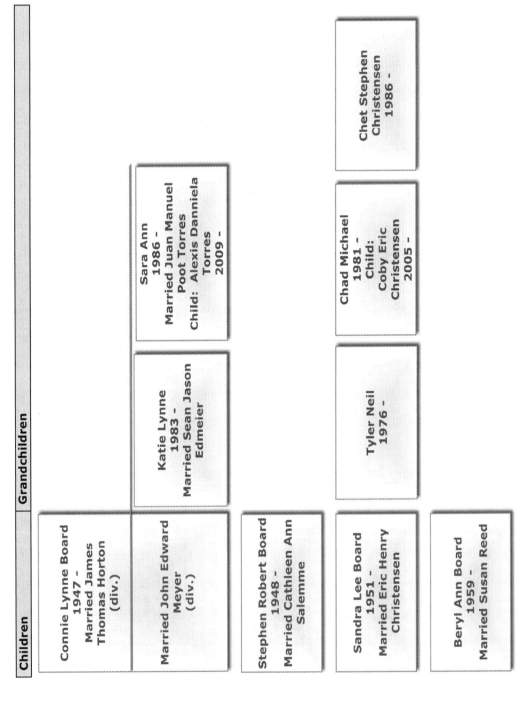

Children	Grandchildren		
Connie Lynne Board 1947 - Married James Thomas Horton (div.)			
Married John Edward Meyer (div.)	Katie Lynne 1983 - Married Sean Jason Edmeier	Sara Ann 1986 - Married Juan Manuel Poot Torres Child: Alexis Danniela Torres 2009 -	
Stephen Robert Board 1948 - Married Cathleen Ann Salemme			
Sandra Lee Board 1951 - Married Eric Henry Christensen	Tyler Neil 1976 -	Chad Michael 1981 - Child: Coby Eric Christensen 2005 -	Chet Stephen Christensen 1986 -
Beryl Ann Board 1959 - Married Susan Reed			

Family Tree #3.1.1.3
Children and Grandchildren of John MacDougall and Isabelle Weisweaver MacDougall

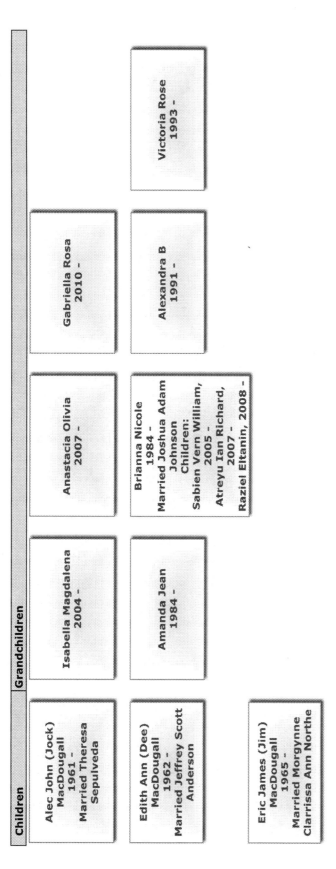

Children	Grandchildren			
Alec John (Jock) MacDougall 1961 - Married Theresa Sepulveda	Isabella Magdalena 2004 -	Anastacia Olivia 2007 -	Gabriella Rosa 2010 -	
Edith Ann (Dee) MacDougall 1962 - Married Jeffrey Scott Anderson	Amanda Jean 1984 -	Brianna Nicole 1984 - Married Joshua Adam Johnson Children: Sabien Vern William, 2005 - Atreyu Ian Richard, 2007 - Raziel Eltanin, 2008 -	Alexandra B 1991 -	Victoria Rose 1993 -
Eric James (Jim) MacDougall 1965 - Married Morgynne Clarrissa Ann Northe				

Family Tree #3.1.1.4
Children of Margaret Inez MacDougall
and S. Paul Carasik

Children	Grandchildren
John Samuel Carasik 1969 - 2002	

Family Tree #3.1.1.5
Children of Mary Catherine MacDougall
and Dean Stanton Brown

Children	Grandchildren

Family Tree #4
Flora McDougall (1851-1929) and Donald Doull
Their Children and Grandchildren
Flora's Parents: John McDougall (weaver) (b. 1803, Lismore) and Catherine McCallum (b. 1809, Lismore)

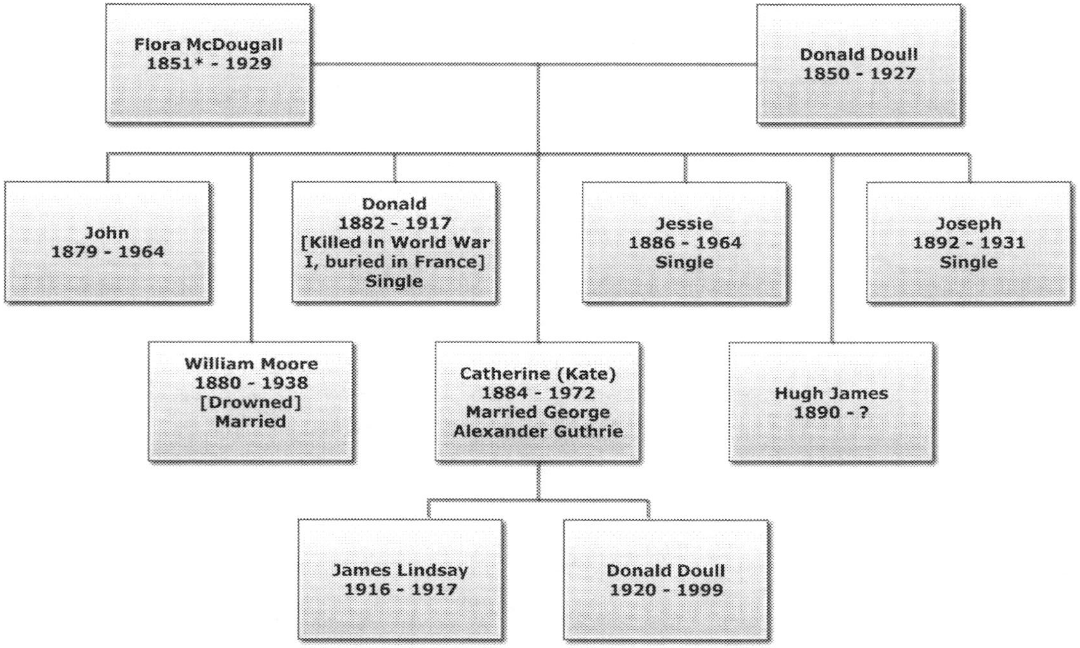

Sources: Guthrie (2014); National Records of Scotland, Old Parish Registers and Statutory Registers of Births, Marriages and Deaths
*Note: Scottish Census of 1851 includes a daughter " Flory", age 6, in John McDougall household, Ballimackillichan, Lismore. Nonetheless, family records show that she was born in 1851 (Guthrie 2013). The record of her marriage (1878) shows her age as 28.

Family Tree #4.1
Descendants of Flora McDougall and Donald Doull's Daughter, Catherine (Kate), and her Husband, George Alexander Guthrie

Family notes suggest that Flora McDougall and Donald Doull may have had just two grandchildren through their daughter, Catherine (Kate). (See Family Tree #4, above.) Therefore, the following chart of Catherine's descendants may be a complete list of Flora McDougall's descendants, as well.

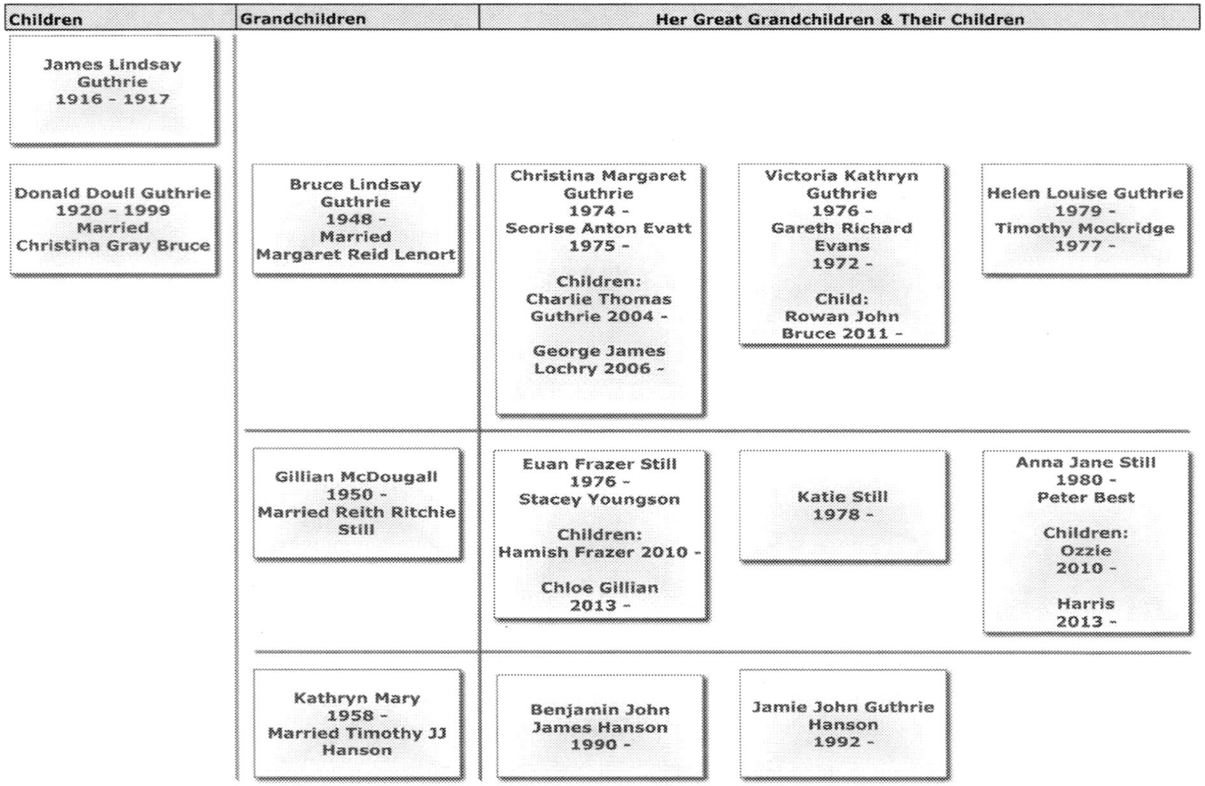
Children
Grandchildren
Her Great Grandchildren & Their Children
James Lindsay Guthrie 1916 - 1917
Donald Doull Guthrie 1920 - 1999 Married Christina Gray Bruce
Bruce Lindsay Guthrie 1948 - Married Margaret Reid Lenort
Christina Margaret Guthrie 1974 - Seorise Anton Evatt 1975 -
Children: Charlie Thomas Guthrie 2004 -
George James Lochry 2006 -
Victoria Kathryn Guthrie 1976 - Gareth Richard Evans 1972 -
Child: Rowan John Bruce 2011 -
Helen Louise Guthrie 1979 - Timothy Mockridge 1977 -
Gillian McDougall 1950 - Married Reith Ritchie Still
Euan Frazer Still 1976 - Stacey Youngson
Children: Hamish Frazer 2010 -
Chloe Gillian 2013 -
Katie Still 1978 -
Anna Jane Still 1980 - Peter Best
Children: Ozzie 2010 -
Harris 2013 -
Kathryn Mary 1958 - Married Timothy JJ Hanson
Benjamin John James Hanson 1990 -
Jamie John Guthrie Hanson 1992 -

Plate A8.2
Donald Doull Guthrie (center) with his Son, Bruce Lindsay Guthrie, and Daughter, Gillian McDougall Guthrie, 1966

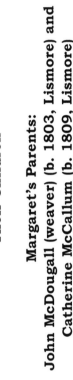

Family Tree #5
Margaret McDougall (1851 or 1852 - 1888) and Alexander Milne (1850 - 1925)
Their Children

Margaret's Parents:
John McDougall (weaver) (b. 1803, Lismore) and
Catherine McCallum (b. 1809, Lismore)

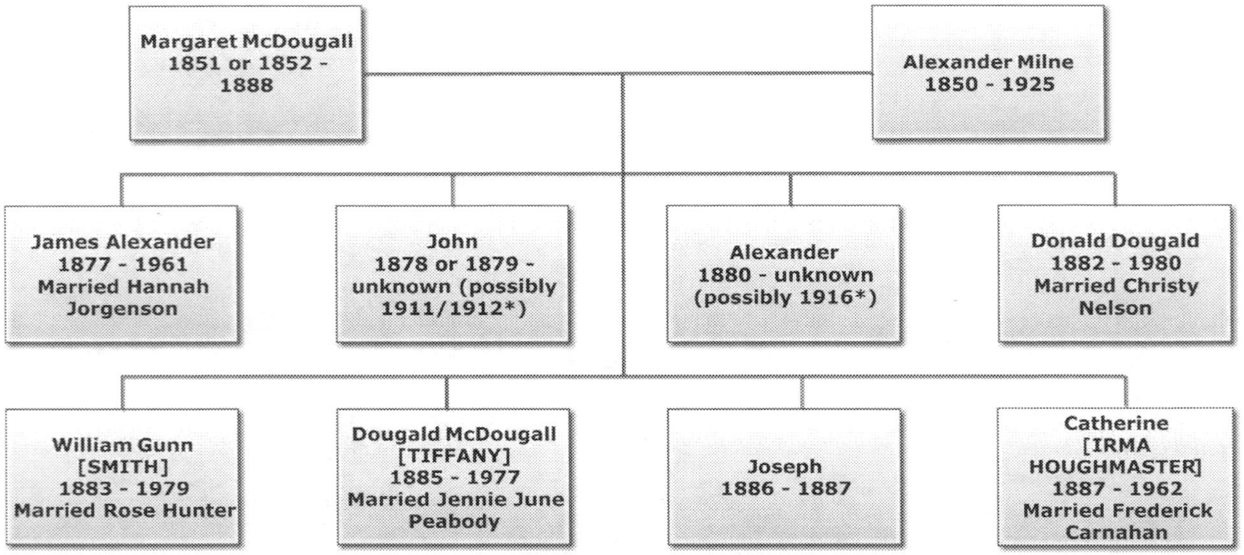

*Inglis (undated)

Notes:

The adoptive names of William Gunn, Dougald McDougall, and Catherine appear in capital letters above. They were the youngest surviving children of Margaret McDougall and Alexander Milne and were adopted by other families in the Redwood Falls community after Margaret's death.

Additional descendants: Although Margaret McDougall died in her 30s, she had given birth to eight children. All except Joseph survived her. Family records for two of the surviving children, John (b. 1878) and Alexander (b. 1880), are not clear after their childhoods. (Wilcox 1977) The other five children (James, Donald, William, Dougald and Catherine) lived into adulthood and married. The six children and twenty-seven grandchildren of Dougald and his wife, Jennie June Tiffany, are identified in the following chart. The family continues to grow; therefore, the following tree is a reference point for additional family trees. (However, Family Tree #5.1.1 for Dougald and Jennie's daughter, Margaret Elizabeth, is a list of her descendants.)

Family Tree #5.1
Dougald McDougall Milne Tiffany (1885 - 1977) and Jennie June Peabody: Their Children and Grandchildren

Dougald's Parents: Margaret McDougall and Alexander Milne
Adopted by: Jared Jerome Tiffany and Mary Calista Miller, taking the surname Tiffany

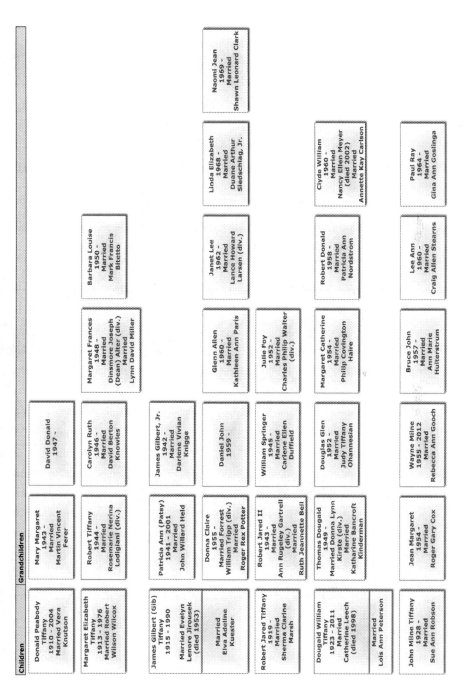

Children	Grandchildren						
Donald Peabody Tiffany 1910 - 2004 Married Vera Knutson	Mary Margaret 1943 - Married Martin Vincent Ferer	David Donald 1947 -					
Margaret Elizabeth Tiffany 1913 - 1976 Married Robert Wilson Wilcox	Robert Tiffany 1944 - Married Rosemarie Nerina Lodigiani (div.)	Carolyn Ruth 1946 - Married David Berton Knowles	Margaret Frances 1948 - Married Dinsmore Joseph (Dean) Alter (div.) Married Lynn David Miller	Barbara Louise 1950 - Married Mark Francis Bitetto			
James Gilbert (Gib) Tiffany 1915 - 1990 Married Evelyn Lenore Jirousek (died 1953)	Patricia Ann (Patsy) 1941 - 2001 Married John Willard Held	James Gilbert, Jr. 1942 - Married Darlene Vivian Knigge					
Married Elva Adeline Kuester	Donna Claire 1955 - Married Forrest William Tripp (div.) Married Roger Rex Potter	Daniel John 1959 -	Glenn Allen 1960 - Married Kathleen Ann Paris	Janet Lee 1962 - Married Lance Howard Larsen (div.)	Linda Elizabeth 1968 - Married Duane Arthur Siedschlag, Jr.	Naomi Jean 1969 - Married Shawn Leonard Clark	
Robert Jared Tiffany 1919 - Married Sherma Clarine Marsh	Robert Jared II 1943 - Married Ann Rugeley Gartrell (div.) Married Ruth Jeannette Bell	William Springer 1945 - Married Carlene Ellen Duffield	Julie Foy 1952 - Married Charles Philip Walter (div.)				
Dougald William Tiffany 1923 - 2011 Married Catherine Leech (died 1998)	Thomas Dougald 1949 - Married Donna Lynn Kirste (div.) Married Katharine Bancroft Kinderman	Douglas Glen 1952 - Married Judy Tiffany Ohannesian	Margaret Catherine 1954 - Married Philip Covington Haire	Robert Donald 1958 - Married Patricia Ann Nordstrom	Clyde William 1960 - Married Nancy Ellen Meyer (died 2002) Married Annette Kay Carlson		
Married Lois Ann Peterson							
John Milne Tiffany 1928 - Married Sue Ann Robson	Jean Margaret 1954 - Married Roger Gary Cox	Wayne Milne 1955 - 2012 Married Rebecca Ann Gooch	Bruce John 1957 - Married Ann Marie Hulterstrum	Lee Ann 1960 - Married Craig Allen Stearns	Paul Ray 1964 - Married Gina Ann Goslinga		

Plate A8.3
Dougald Milne Tiffany, Jennie June Tiffany and their Children (1963)
Redwood Falls, Minnesota

Seated (left to right): Dougald William (Bill), Jennie June Peabody Tiffany, Dougald Milne Tiffany, John Milne
Standing (left to right): Robert Jared (Bob), Margaret Elizabeth, James Gilbert (Gib), Donald Peabody (Don)

Plate A8.4
Grandchildren of Dougald Milne and Jennie June Tiffany
Twenty-six of the Tiffany's twenty-seven grandchildren appear in this photo, in birth order.
June 2000, Redwood Falls Presbyterian Church
Redwood Falls, Minnesota

The grandchildren are
(back row, left to right) James Gilbert Tiffany, Jr., Mary Margaret Tiffany Ferer, Robert Jared Tiffany II, Robert Tiffany Wilcox, William Springer Tiffany, Carolyn Wilcox Knowles, David Donald Tiffany, Margaret A. Miller, Thomas Dougald Tiffany, Barbara Wilcox Bitetto, Julie Tiffany Walter, Douglas Glen Tiffany, Jean Margaret Tiffany Cox, Margaret Tiffany Hare, Wayne Milne Tiffany

(front row, left to right) Donna Tiffany Potter, Bruce John Tiffany, Robert Donald Tiffany, Daniel John Tiffany, Lee Tiffany Stearns, Clyde William Tiffany, Glenn Allen Tiffany, Janet Lee Tiffany, Paul Ray Tiffany, Linda Tiffany Seidschlag, Naomi Tiffany Clark
Not pictured: Patricia Tiffany Held

Family Tree #5.1.1
Descendants of Margaret Elizabeth Tiffany (1913 - 1976) and Robert Wilson Wilcox

Margaret's Parents: Dougald McDougall Milne Tiffany (b. 1885, Thurso) and Jennie June Peabody

Children	Grandchildren	
Robert Tiffany 1944 - Married Rosemarie Nerina Lodigiani (div.)	James Dougald Wilcox 1972 - Married Chiaki Nakatani Children: Misaki Julie, 2007 - Kento Ryan, 2010 -	David Michael Wilcox 1976 -
Carolyn Ruth 1946 - Married David Berton Knowles	Margaret Ann Knowles 1974 - Married David Brent Pease	Kathryn Elizabeth Knowles 1976 -
Margaret Frances 1948 - Married Dinsmore Joseph (Dean) Alter (div.) Married Lynn David Miller	Martha Catherine Alter 1977 - Married Taylor Spight Hines (div.) Children: Alexander Thomas, 2007 - Abigail Elizabeth, 2012 -	Elizabeth Ann Alter Married 1979 - Married Luis Sahit Santiago Children: Kaden Sahit, 2005 - Isabella Kaya Marie, 2009 -
Barbara Louise 1950 - Married Mark Francis Bitetto	Krista Louise Bitetto 1982 -	Joseph David Bitetto 1986 - Married Paule Lynn Brown

Plate A8.5
Grandchildren of Margaret E. Tiffany and Robert W. Wilcox

Plate A8.5.1
Margaret Tiffany Wilcox with her Grandson, James Dougald Wilcox, 1974

Plate A8.5.2
(clockwise from left)
Kathryn Knowles, Margaret Knowles [Pease],
Martha Alter [Hines],
Elizabeth Alter [Santiago] (in front), 1981

Plate A8.5.3
(left to right)
Martha Alter Hines, Holding her Son, Alexander;
Krista Bitetto, David Wilcox
and Joseph Bitetto, 2010

Plate A8.6
Great Grandchildren of Margaret E. Tiffany and Robert W. Wilcox, 2014

Plate A8.6.1
Alexander and Abigail Hines

Plate A8.6.2
Kento and Misaki Wilcox

Plate A8.6.3
Kaden and Kaya Santiago

Appendix 9

McCallum Families, Lismore
John McCallum (Balure), Duncan McCallum (Killean)
Early 19th Century

John McDougall (b. 1837 Lismore) and his wife, Isabel (b. 1850), appear to have been first cousins through John's mother, Catherine McCallum, and Isabel's father, Gilbert McCallum, who were sister and brother. The family trees and tables below provide additional detail.

Family Tree #9.1
John McCallum (Farmer) (b. ?, d. ?) Married about 1802
Wife: Anne Carmichael (b. 1771/1772 Appin, d. 1860 Balure, Lismore)

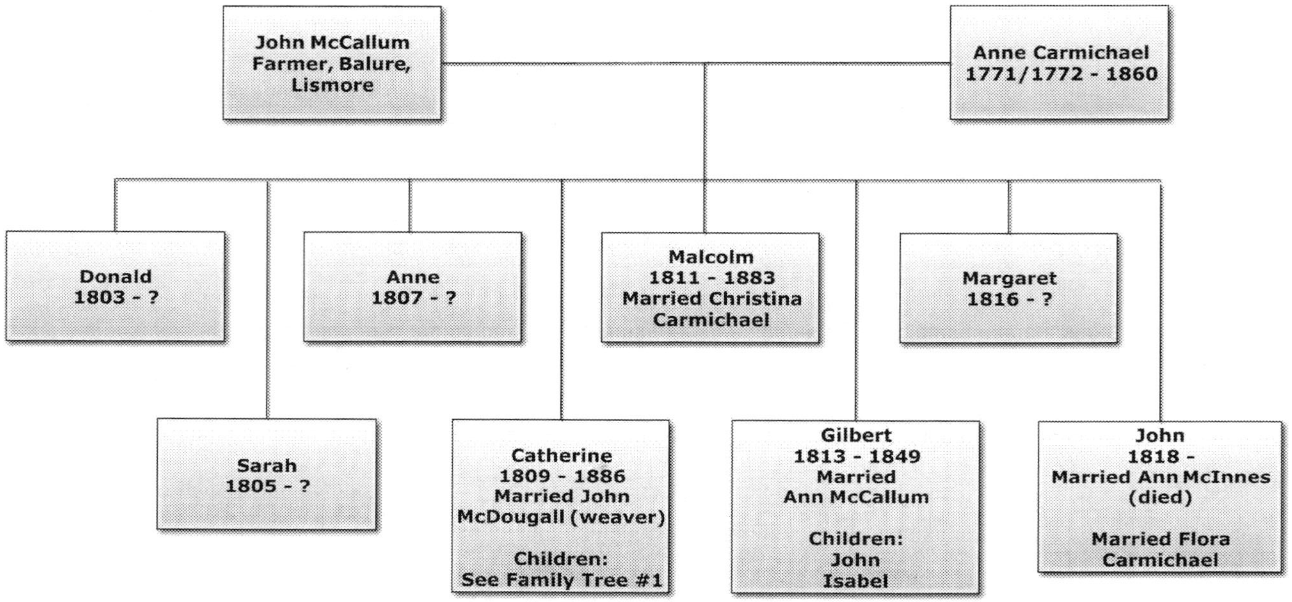

Sources: NRS, pre-1855a; Gloag, 2014b; Aburn, 2013a

Family Tree #9.1.1
Children of John McCallum and Anne Carmichael

The following table lists the children of John McCallum and Anne Carmichael. The children, who were born in the Lismore hamlet of Balure, include Catherine McCallum McDougall (b. 1809), mother of John McDougall (b. 1837). They also include Catherine's brother, Gilbert McCallum (b. 1813), father of Isabel McCallum (b. 1850.)

Children	Birth & Death	Spouse	Grandchildren		
			Names	Birth & Death	Children's Spouses
Donald	1803 - ?				
Sarah	1805 - ?				
Anne	1807 - ?				
Catherine	**1809 - 1886**	**John McDougall (weaver) (1803 - 1888)**	See Family Tree #1. Their children include John (b. 1837), who married Isabel McCallum (b. 1850).		
Malcolm	1811 - 1883	Christina Carmichael (Ballimackillichan)	Catherine	1844 - ?	
			John	1847 - ?	Susan Young (m. 1877)
			Duncan	c1850 - 1883	Mary McPhee
			Donald	c1852 - 1890	Never married
Gilbert	**1813 – 1849**	**Ann McCallum (1814 - 1903)**	John	1847 – 1927	Mary Secrest (b. 1850)
			Isabel	**1850 – 1935**	**John McDougall (b. 1837)**
Margaret	1816 - ?				
John	1818 -1894	Ann McInnes (1st wife) (m. 1854)			
		Flora Carmichael (2nd wife) (m. 1860)	Hugh Carmichael (stepson)	1849 – 1935	Julia McIntyre
			Ann	1863 - ?	Alexander McMaster

Sources: Gloag (2014a and 2014b), Inglis (undated), Aburn (2000, 2002, 2013a, 2013c, 2014a), NRS (pre-1855a and pre-1855b) and the letters of this book.

Key: Catherine McCallum, Gilbert McCallum and their spouses appear in bold. A blank or question mark means the editor does not have the information.

Family Tree #9.2
Children and Grandchildren of Gilbert McCallum and Ann McCallum

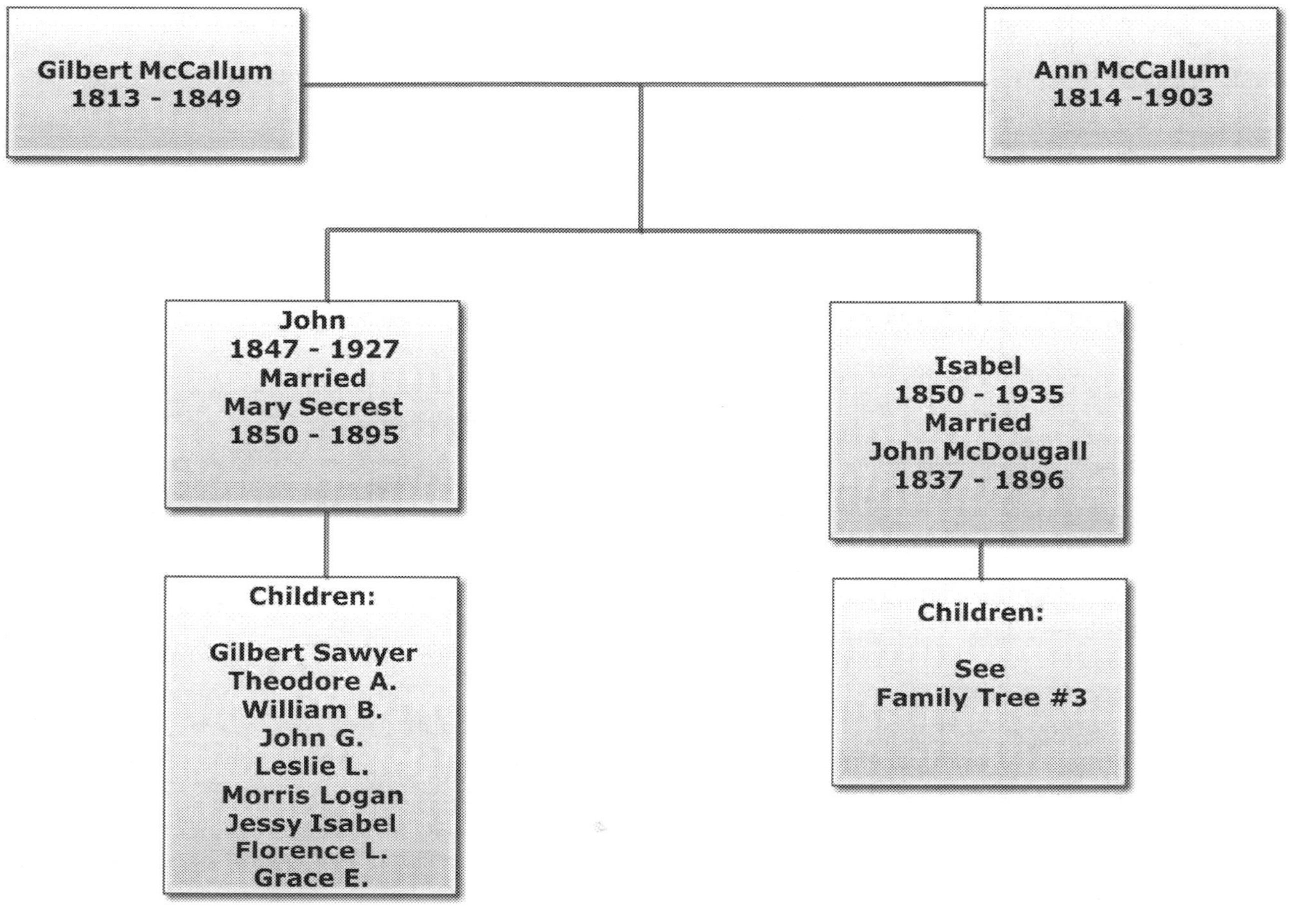

Source: Aburn, 2013c

Family Tree #9.3
Duncan McCallum (1789 - 1883) Married about 1813
Wife: Isabella McColl (1788 - 1880)

The following table identifies the children of Duncan McCallum (b. 1879) and his wife, Isabella McColl (b. 1788). The children, born on Lismore and raised in the hamlet of Killean, include Ann McCallum, identified in Family Trees 9.1 and 9.2, above. Her husband, Gilbert, died in December 1849, a few weeks before the birth of their daughter, Isabel. Duncan and Isabella McCallum migrated to the US between 1851 and 1855, joining members of their family in Caledonia, New York, where they died years later. Ann migrated to New York with her young children in 1855 where she joined her family. Ann's sister, Katherine, married in Scotland and migrated with young children to New Zealand in 1855. (Aburn, 2013c)

Child	Birth & Death	Spouse	Migrated to (Destination & Timeframe)	Children		
				Children's Names	Birth & Death	Children's Spouses
Ann	**1814 - 1903**	**Gilbert McCallum (1813 - 1849)**	LeRoy, New York; Cottage Grove, Minnesota (by 1870); Bigstone County, Minnesota; Delhi, Minnesota	John	1847 - 1927	Mary Secrest (b. 1850)
				Isabel	**1850 - 1935**	**John McDougall (b. 1837)**
Neil	1818 - ?		Canada			
Duncan ["Duncan jnr"]	1820 - ?	Catherine McCormick	Caledonia, New York (before 1850); Cottage Grove, Minnesota (by 1870)	Archibald	1851 - ?	
				John	1852 - 1919	Catherine McDonald
Katherine	1822 - 1912	Donald Sinclair	New Zealand (1855)	John	1850 - 1914	Katherine Ward
				Isabella	1852 - 1897	George White
				Angus	1855 - 1930	
				Rachael	1857 - 1929	John McKenzie
				Sarah	1860 - 1943	James Sutherland
				Ann	1862 - 1958	
				Mary Ann	1864 - 1948	Donald Sutherland
Dugald	1825 - ?					
John	1830 - 1915		Caledonia, New York (before 1850)			
Archibald	1833 - 1892	Mary Taggart	Caledonia, New York (between 1851 & 1855 with his parents); Minnesota (possibly) (by 1870)	Archibald	1863 - 1914	Never married

Source: Aburn (2013c, 2014b)

Appendix 10

Plates, Figures, Tables and Family Trees that Appear in the Book

Numbering of Images

Images of the handwritten letters and family trees are numbered sequentially as they appear in the book. See Appendix 1 for a list of the handwritten letters and the numbers assigned to them.

The plates, tables and figures are numbered sequentially in relation to the handwritten letters after which they appear or the index in which they appear. For example, the photograph of Margaret McDougall, which appears after Letter #1, is labeled Plate 1.8. The list of places mentioned in the letters, which appears in Appendix 5, is labeled Table A5.

Plate	Caption
5.2, 5.3	Inside the Building
6.1	Ann (Agnes) McDougall, Daughter of John McDougall (weaver) and Catherine McCallum
6.2	William Moore, Husband of Ann (Agnes)
6.3	James Moore (b. 1868), Son of Ann (Agnes) McDougall and William Moore
6.4	Drummond, Home of William Moore Family, Evanton
6.5	Looking toward Eileen Dubh (Black Island) near Balure
6.6	The Broch, near Balure
6.7	Port Appin
6.8	Port Appin Pier
6.9	Port Appin Beach and Pier, June 2010, with Lismore in the Distance
7.1	Sign on the Village Shop, Strontian, Sunart, September 2014
9.1	Isabel McCallum
9.2	Photo Back
9.3	John McDougall (b. 1837) and Isabel McCallum McDougall (b. 1850)
9.4	*The Oban Times,* February 21, 1874, Article about the Achuaran Soiree
9.5	Bachuil (Bauchel)
9.6	Achuaran, Isle of Lismore
9.7	The Independent Chapel Building, Achuaran
11.1	Remains of John McDougall's (weaver) House, Ballimackillichan
11.2	Thatched Crofter's Cottage, Lismore Historical Society, Isle of Lismore
12.1	Gravestone of Hugh MacDougall and his Wife, Ann MacDougall, Redwood Falls Cemetery, Redwood Falls, Minnesota
12.2	Jared Jerome Tiffany, with his Granddaughter, Margaret Elizabeth Tiffany, Redwood Falls, 1917
12.3	Dougald Milne Tiffany Farm, Redwood Falls, Minnesota, 1917
12.4	Dougald Milne Tiffany Farm, Redwood Falls, Minnesota, 1940s
12.5	Moving Cattle, Dougald Milne Tiffany Farm, Redwood Falls, 1948
12.6	Robert Tiffany Wilcox, Grandson of Dougald Milne Tiffany, on his Grandfather's Allis Chalmers Tractor, Redwood Falls, 1949
12.7	Cattle on the Dougald Milne Tiffany Farm, Redwood Falls, January 1950
13.1	Alexander Milne with his Parents and Siblings, 1875
13.2	Partick South Parish Church (Scale Model), Glasgow, 2010
13.3, 13.4	The Partick South Parish Church, 259 Dumbarton Road, Glasgow, 1983, Before It Was Replaced
13.5	Catherine (Kate) Doull Guthrie with Dougald Milne Tiffany at her Home in Montrose, Scotland
14.1	James Alexander Milne with Grand Nephew, Robert Tiffany Wilcox and Grand Niece, Carolyn Ruth Wilcox
14.2	James Alexander Milne with Niece Margaret Tiffany Wilcox and her Children at her Home, Boise, Idaho
14.3	James Alexander Milne with Carolyn Ruth Wilcox, Robert Tiffany Wilcox, Robert Wilson Wilcox, Margaret Frances (Dondee) Wilcox and George A. Wilcox
14.4	Margaret Milne Marquardt and her Cousin, John Milne Tiffany
14.5	Point, Isle of Lismore, Looking toward Sheep Island
16.1	Margaret McDougall Milne ("Maggie") Holding Baby John Milne, Alexander Milne Holding James Alexander Milne, 1878
16.2	Cabinet Made by Margaret McDougall's Husband, Alexander Milne At Clinic of Dr. S. Francis Ceplecha, Redwood Falls, Minnesota

Plate	Caption
16.3	Dougald Milne Tiffany (1885 – 1977), Son of Margaret McDougall and Alexander Milne, Feeding Cattle on his Farm, Redwood Falls, Minnesota, January 1950, Temperature: - 25° F (- 31.7° C)
16.4	Margaret Tiffany Wilcox, Granddaughter of Margaret McDougall and Alexander Milne, Viewing a Backdoor Garden, Elgin, August 1966
18.1	Fort William Railway Station, Train to Mallaig
18.2	Catherine (Kate) Doull Guthrie with Margaret Tiffany Wilcox
18.3	Port Ramsay, Lismore 2013
19.1	Eilean na Caorach (Sheep Island)
19.2	Eilean na Caorach with Lime Kiln and Cottage Faintly Visible near the Shore
19.3	Southern End of Eilean na Caorach (Sheep Island)
19.4	Eilean na Caorach, Inn Island, Port Appin and Lismore Communities of Park and Port Ramsay
20.1	John Dougald MacDougal (b. 1877, Delhi, Minnesota), First Child of John McDougall (b. 1837), with his Wife, Lela Cardwell MacDougal
22.1	Anna MacDougall (b. 1879) and her Mother, Isabel (Bella) McCallum McDougall
22.2	Photo Back
22.3	Gustave (Gus) and Anna MacDougall Aufderheide: Their Wedding Photo, 1916
22.4	Gravestone of Anna MacDougall Aufderheide (b. 1879), Redwood Falls Cemetery, Redwood Falls, Minnesota
22.5	Members of the MacDougall, Aufderheide and McCallum Families, Redwood Falls, Minnesota, July 1953
26.1	Marriage Banns for Gilbert McCallum (b. 1813) and Ann McCallum (b. 1814), Lismore, 13th July 1842
26.2	Children of John McDougall and Isabel (Bell) McCallum McDougall, about 1886
26.3	Children of John McDougall (b. 1837) and Isabel (Belle) McCallum McDougall
26.4	Gilbert Hugh (Gib) MacDougall (b. 1881) with his Cousin, Dougald Milne Tiffany (b. 1885), Redwood Falls, Minnesota, 1971
26.5	Children of Gilbert (Gib) MacDougall and Dougald Milne Tiffany, June 2008
26.6	Gravestone of Gilbert Hugh (Gib) MacDougall, Redwood Falls Cemetery, Redwood Falls, Minnesota
26.7	Gravestone of Gilbert (Gib) MacDougall's Wife, Edith Bollum, Redwood Falls Cemetery, Redwood Falls, Minnesota
27.1	Along the Main Road, Lismore in Killean
27.2	Killean
28.1	Graveyard, Lismore Parish Church
29.1	Gravestones of William Moore MacDougall and his Wife, Maude Ellen Scribner, Redwood Falls Cemetery, Redwood Falls, Minnesota
30.1	Three MacDougall Brothers and their Wives, about 1917
31.1	Duncan Street, Thurso, 1965
31.2	View North from Lismore at Lagan
32.1	Stronacroibh, Lismore, 2013
33.1	Achnacroish, Lismore from the Oban Ferry
33.2	Lismore Spring Lamb
34.1	Masonic Hall, Mill & 3rd Streets, Redwood Falls, Minnesota
34.2	Masonic Hall, Redwood Falls
34.3	First Presbyterian Church, Redwood Falls, Minnesota
34.4	First Presbyterian Church, Redwood Falls, 2014 Woodwork by John McDougall (b. 1837 Lismore) and his Brother-in-law, Alexander Milne
35.1	Lismore Sheep

Plate	Caption
35.2	Balure
35.3	Memorial Stone for Joseph Milne, Son of Alexander Milne and Margaret McDougall Milne, Redwood Falls Cemetery, Redwood Falls, Minnesota
35.4	Alexander Milne, Margaret McDougall Milne and their Children
36.1	Memorial Stone for John McDougall (weaver), Catherine McCallum and their Children, Lismore Parish Church, Old Graveyard, Gravestone #229
36.2	Lismore Parish Church, Old Graveyard, Facing Memorial to John McDougall, Catherine McCallum and their Children
36.3	View from Lismore Parish Church, Old Graveyard to the Main Road Easter Sunday, April 2011
37.1	Article about John McDougall's Death, *Redwood Reveille*, February 8, 1896
37.2	Gravestone of John McDougall (b. 1837), Redwood Falls Cemetery, Redwood Falls, Minnesota
37.3, 37.4	Gravestones for Daughters of John and Isabel McCallum McDougall, Redwood Falls Cemetery, Redwood Falls, Minnesota
37.5	Gravestone of Margaret McDougall Milne, Redwood Falls Cemetery, Redwood Falls, Minnesota
37.6	Alexander Milne (b. 1850) with his Children after the Death of their Mother, Margaret McDougall Milne
37.7	From *Redwood Falls Gazette*, 1971 or 1972
37.8	Margaret McDougall's Husband, Alexander Milne, with their Daughter, Catherine (Irma Houghmaster) (b. 1887)
37.9	Margaret McDougall's Husband, Alexander Milne with their Son, Alexander (b. 1880)
38.1	Children of John McDougall (b. 1837) and Isabel McCallum McDougall with their Mother
A3.1	Christmas Letter, 1966, Dougald Milne and Jennie June Tiffany
A6.1	Record of Birth for Dougald McDougall Milne [Tiffany] (b. 1885, Thurso)
A6.2	Dougald McDougall Milne Tiffany at his birthplace, Duncan Street, Thurso, 1966
A6.3	Record of Death for Catherine McCallum McDougall (b. 1809, Lismore)
A6.4	Record of Death for Joseph Milne (b. 1886, Thurso)
A6.5	Record of Death for John McDougall (b. 1803, Lismore)
A6.6	Certificate of Death for John McDougall (b. 1837, Lismore)
A7.1	North Atlantic - Scotland to Minnesota
A7.2	Scotland – Places Mentioned in the Letters
A7.3	Lismore - Places Mentioned in the Letters
A7.4.1	Castle Coeffin, Ballimackillichan, Cathedral of St. Maluag, Bauchuil, Baptist Chapel, Independent Chapel, Survey Date: 1871-1872
A7.4.2	Castle Coeffin, Ballimackillichan, Cathedral of St. Maluag, Bachuil, and Baptist Chapel, Survey Date: 1871
A7.4.3	Ballimackillichan, Bachuil and Baptist Chapel, Survey Date: 1871
A7.4.4	Ballimackillichan and Cathedral of St. Maluag, Survey Date: 1871
A7.4.5	Lismore Showing Locations of Independent Chapel and Achuaran School
A7.5	United States Showing Minnesota and New York Communities Mentioned in the Letters
A8.1	Gilbert Hugh (Gib) MacDougall with his Children, 1971
A8.2	Donald Doull Guthrie with his Son, Bruce Lindsay Guthrie, and Daughter, Gillian McDougall Guthrie, 1966
A8.3	Dougald Milne Tiffany, Jennie June Tiffany and their Children (1963)
A8.4	Grandchildren of Dougald Milne and Jennie June Tiffany
A8.5	Grandchildren of Margaret E. Tiffany and Robert W. Wilcox

Plate	Caption
A8.5.1	Margaret Tiffany Wilcox with her Grandson, James Dougald Wilcox, 1974
A8.5.2	Kathryn Knowles, Margaret Knowles [Pease], Martha Alter [Hines], Elizabeth Alter [Santiago], 1981
A8.5.3	Martha Alter Hines, Holding Her Son, Alexander; Krista Bitetto, David Wilcox and Joseph Bitetto, 2010
A8.6	Great Grandchildren of Margaret E. Tiffany and Robert W. Wilcox, 2014
A8.6.1	Alexander and Abigail Hines
A8.6.2	Kento and Misaki Wilcox
A8.6.3	Kaden and Kaya Santiago

Figure	Title
A2.1	Timeline of Family Events

Table	Title
A1.1	The Letters – A List
A2.1	Timeline of Family Events
A4.1	Letter Numbers and their Dates
A4.2	Names and Descriptive Information of People Mentioned in the Letters
A5	Places Mentioned in the Letters

Family Tree No.	Title
1	John McDougall (weaver) and Catherine McCallum
2	Ann (Agnes) McDougall (1833 - 1915) and William Moore
3	John McDougall (1837-1896) and Isabel McCallum (1850 – 1935)
3.1	Gilbert Hugh (Gib) MacDougall (1881 - 1975) and Edith Carroll Bollum (1894 – 1956)
3.1.1	Children and Grandchildren of Gilbert Hugh (Gib) MacDougall and Edith C. Bollum
3.1.1.1	Children and Grandchildren of Ruth Carroll MacDougall and Donald A. McCartin
3.1.1.2	Children and Grandchildren of Isabel Ann MacDougall and Burrell Robert Board
3.1.1.3	Children and Grandchildren of John MacDougall and Isabelle Weisweaver MacDougall
3.1.1.4	Children of Margaret Inez MacDougall and S. Paul Carasik
3.1.1.5	Children of Mary Catherine MacDougall and Dean Stanton Brown
4	Flora McDougall (1851-1929) and Donald Doull: Their Children and Grandchildren
4.1	Descendants of Flora McDougall and Donald Doull's Daughter, Catherine (Kate), and her Husband, George Alexander Guthrie
5	Margaret McDougall (1851 or 1852 - 1888) and Alexander Milne (1850 - 1925) and Their Children
5.1	Dougald McDougall Milne Tiffany (1885 - 1977) and Jennie June Peabody: Their Children and Grandchildren
5.1.1	Descendants of Margaret Elizabeth Tiffany (1913 - 1976) and Robert Wilson Wilcox
9.1	John McCallum (Farmer) (b. ?, d. ?) Married about 1802, Wife: Anne Carmichael (b. 1771/1772 Appin, d. 1860 Balure, Lismore)
9.1.1	Children of John McCallum and Anne Carmichael
9.2	Children and Grandchildren of Gilbert McCallum and Ann McCallum
9.3	Duncan McCallum (1789 - 1883) Married about 1813, Wife: Isabella McColl (1788 - 1880)

Photo Credits

Photographers

The following took photographs included in the book:

- Barbara Wilcox Bitetto, plates 13.5, 16.4, 26.5, A6.2, A8.2
- Mark F. Bitetto, plates 14.4, 22.4, 26.6, 35.3, 37.4, 37.5
- Jim Cassatt, author photo
- Martha C. Hines, plate A8.6.1
- Carolyn Wilcox Knowles, plates A8.5.1, A8.5.2
- Eric James MacDougall, plate 29.1
- Lynn D. Miller, plates 12.1, 37.2, 37.3
- Margaret A. Miller, cover photo, plates 1.5, 1.6, 1.9, 1.10, 1.11, 1.12, 1.13, 1.14, 1.15, 2.1, 2.2, 2.3, 2.4, 2.5, 3.1, 3.2, 3.3, 4.1, 4.2, 4.3, 4.4, 5.1, 5.2, 5.3, 6.5, 6.6, 6.7, 6.8, 6.9, 7.1, 9.5, 9.6, 9.7, 11.1, 11.2, 13.2, 14.5, 18.1, 18.3, 26.7, 27.1, 27.2, 28.1, 31.2, 32.1, 33.1, 33.2, 34.3, 35.1, 35.2, 36.1, 36.2, 36.3, A8.5.3, A8.6.3
- Lee Tiffany Stearns, plates 13.3, 13.4
- Jennie June Tiffany, plate 12.4
- Sue Robson Tiffany, plates 34.1, 34.2, 34.4, A8.4
- David H. White, plates 19.1, 19.2
- Chiaki Wilcox, plate A8.6.2
- Margaret T. Wilcox, plate 14.3
- Robert W. Wilcox, plates 1.1, 6.4, 12.5, 12.6, 12.7, 14.1, 14.2, 16.2, 16.3, 18.2, 22.5, 26.4, 31.1, A8.1, A8.3

Collections

The following provided images from their collections:

- Krista L. Bitetto, plates 1.8, 12.2, 12.3, 35.4, 37.8, 37.9
- Margaret MacDougall Carasik, plates 9.1, 9.2, 20.1, 22.1, 22.2, 26.1, 26.2, 30.1, 38.1, A6.6
- Alec John (Jock) MacDougall, plates 1.3, 1.4, 22.3
- Mark McCartin, plates 26.2, 26.3
- Jean Aufderheide Stark, plate 9.3
- Lee Tiffany Stearns, plates 1.2, 6.1, 6.2, 6.3, 13.1, 16.1
- Sue Robson Tiffany, plate 37.6

References

1860 U.S. Census, Livingston County, New York, "Schedule 1. – Free inhabitants in the Town of Caledonia in the County of Livingston, State of New York, enumerated on the fifteenth day of June 1860," p. 7 (penned), 527 (stamped), dwelling 51, family 49, Duncan McCallum household, digital image, *Archives.com*, URL: http://www.archives.com. [Accessed June 6, 2014]

1930 U.S. Census, Redwood County, Minnesota, "Fifteenth Census of the United States: 1930, Population Schedule", Enumerated April 30th 1930, Enumeration District Number 64-22, Supervisor's District No. 11, Sheet No. 22B (penned); dwelling number 509, family number 533, Isabel McDougall household, digital image *Archives.com* URL: http://www.archives.com. [Accessed June 6, 2014]

Aburn, Anne (2000) "Duncan McCallum and Isabella McColl," personal correspondence, received April 7, 2013.

Aburn, Anne (2002) "Katherine McCallum," personal correspondence, received April 7, 2013.

Aburn, Anne (2013a) "McCallum – Census, etc." personal correspondence, received April 7, 2013.

Aburn, Anne (2013b) "Outline Descendant Report for Catherine McCallum," personal correspondence, received April 13, 2013.

Aburn, Anne (2013c) "Outline Descendant Report for Duncan McCallum," personal correspondence, received April 7, 2013.

Aburn, Anne (2014a) "More bits – Anne Aburn", personal correspondence, received February16, 2014.

Aburn, Anne (2014b) "Update", personal correspondence, received June 25, 2014.

Am Faclair Beag (undated), URL: http://www.faclair.com. [Accessed April 2, 2014]

Bitetto, Krista L. (ed.) (undated a) "Tiffany Family Photos", a collection of photographs about the extended family of Dougald Milne Tiffany, provided by family members for the Tiffany Family Reunion, June 2012. URL: http://redwoodtiffanys.shutterfly.com/1645. [Accessed December 4, 2012]

Bitetto, Krista L. (ed.) (undated b) "Slides of Yore", URL: http://slidesofyore.shutterfly.com/. [Accessed December 4, 2012]

Bonar, A. (1843) *The Biography of Robert Murray M'Cheyne*. Tredition Classics. Charleston, SC: BiblioBazaar.

Carasik, Margaret MacDougall (April 2014) "The Family of Gilbert Hugh MacDougall", a chart showing descendants of Gilbert Hugh MacDougall and Edith Carroll Bollum MacDougall, prepared by Sandra Lee Board Christensen, personal correspondence.

Carmichael, Ian (1948) *Lismore in Alba*. Published privately.

Concise Scots Dictionary (2005) Scottish National Dictionary Association, Edinburgh: Edinburgh University Press Ltd.

Dictionary of the Scots Language (DSL) (2004) Scottish Language Dictionaries Ltd., URL: http://www.dsl.ac.uk. [Accessed August 25, 2013]

Doms, Mary (undated) "The Brothers Milne in 25-year Reunion", Redwood Falls: *Redwood Gazette*.

Dwelly-d (undated) *Dwelly's Classic Scottish Gaelic Dictionary*, URL: http://www.cairnwater.co.uk/gaelicdictionary/. [Accessed April 2, 2014]

Feiler, F. (March 15, 2013) "The Family Ties that Bind Us", *The New York Times*, URL: http://www.nytimes.com/2013/03/17/fashion/the-family-stories-that-bind-us-this-life.html?smid=pl-share&_r=0. [Accessed March 22, 2013]

Gloag, Laura (2014a) Email dated January 21, 2014, transmitting notes about John and Malcolm McCallum, brothers of Catherine McCallum McDougall. Subject: "John and Malcolm McCallum." Personal correspondence.

Gloag, Laura (2014b) Email dated January 22, 2014, containing notes about the mother of John McDougall (weaver), naming patterns and undated letter fragment from John McCallum, and information about Mary McDougall (b. 1835). Subject: "Lismore." Personal correspondence.

Guthrie, Bruce L. (December 10, 2013) Email to Margaret A. Miller about Flora McDougall descendants. Personal correspondence.

Hay, Robert (2009) *Lismore, the Great Garden*, Edinburgh: Birlinn Limited.

Hay, Robert (2010) "Improvement not Clearance: A Factor's instructions to his Ground Officers on the Isle of Lismore, 1831-46", *Review of Scottish Culture,* Vol 22, pp. 99-119.

Hay, Robert (2013) *How an Island Lost its People: Improvement, clearance and resettlement on Lismore, 1830 – 1914,* Kershader, South Lochs, Isle of Lewis: The Islands Book Trust.

Inglis, Gertrude Smith (undated) "McDougall/MacDougall Genealogy." (Research performed by Gertrude Smith Inglis in the 1980s and 1990s, provided to the editor by Mary MacDougall Brown, 2013). Unpublished.

Kidd, S. (2000) Social Control and Social Criticism: the nineteenth century

còmhradh. *Scottish Gaelic Studies* 20:pp. 67-87. URL: http://eprints.gla.ac.uk/4585/1/4585.pdf. [Accessed October 23, 2013]

Kurylo, E. (undated) "Family Storytelling may be Key to Resilience in Children", MARIAL Profile: Marshall Duke, MARIAL: the Emory Center for Myth and Ritual in American Life, URL: http://www.marial.emory.edu/faculty/profiles/duke.html. [Accessed March 22, 2013]

MacIntosh, A. (2010) "Alexander Carmichael's Testimonies to the Napier Commission on Crofting, 1883." URL: http://www.alastairmcintosh.com/general/resources/2010-Carmichael.pdf. [Accessed November 14, 2013]

MacLean, C. and Veitch, K. (eds) (2006) *Scottish Life and Society Volume 12: Religion, Compendium of Scottish Ethnology,* Edinburgh: Birlinn Limited.

McDougall, John (weaver), et al (1870 – 1913) "We are Still in the Land of the Living", Letters from John McDougall (weaver) and Catherine McCallum to their son, John McDougall (b. 1837). Lismore: Lismore Historical Society (Comann Eachdraidh Lios Mòr).

The Napier Commission (1883) *Evidence Taken by Her Majesty's Commissioners of Inquiry into the Conditions of the Crofters and Cottars in the Highlands and Islands of Scotland* as digitized in 2007 by Lochaber College, Maillaig. URL: http://www.whc.uhi.ac.uk/research/napier-commission. [Accessed November 14, 2013]

National Library of Scotland (1875a), Ordnance Survey map, 25-inch, 1st edition, Argyll & Bute, Sheets LXII.7 (published 1875).

National Library of Scotland (1875b), Ordnance Survey map, 6-inch, 1st edition, Argyllshire, sheet LXXII (published 1875).

National Library of Scotland (1885 - 1900), Ordnance Survey map, 1-inch to the Mile Maps of Scotland, 2nd edition, 1885 – 1900, Outline. URL: http://maps.nls.uk/geo/explore/#zoom=14&lat=56.56326&lon=-5.41347&layers=B000000000TFFF.[Accessed April 25, 2014]

National Library of Scotland (1885 - 1900), Ordnance Survey map, 1-inch to the Mile Maps of Scotland, 2nd edition (Hills), 1885 – 1900. URL: http://maps.nls.uk/geo/explore/#zoom=14&lat=56.55997&lon=-5.39978&layers=B000000000FTFF. [Accessed April 25, 2014]

National Records of Scotland (NRS) (1841) Census Records, URL: http://www.scotlandspeople.gov.uk/search/census/index.aspx?1841. [Accessed June 1, 2014]

National Records of Scotland (NRS) (1851) Census Records, URL: http://www.scotlandspeople.gov.uk/search/census/index.aspx?1851. [Accessed June 1, 2014]

National Records of Scotland (NRS) (Pre-1855a) Old Parish Registers, Pre 1855 Births & Baptisms, URL: http://www.scotlandspeople.gov.uk/search/oprbirth/index.aspx. [Accessed April 23, 2014]

National Records of Scotland (NRS) (Pre-1855b) Old Parish Registers, Pre 1855 Deaths and Burials, URL: http://www.scotlandspeople.gov.uk/search/oprdeath/index.aspx. [Accessed June 1, 2014]

National Records of Scotland (NRS) (1855 – 2013a) Statutory Births 1855 - 2013, URL: http://www.scotlandspeople.gov.uk/search/birth/index.aspx. [Accessed June 1, 2014]

National Records of Scotland (NRS) (1855 - 2013b), Statutory Deaths 1855 - 2013, URL: http://www.scotlandspeople.gov.uk/search/death/index.aspx. [Accessed April 23, 2014]

National Records of Scotland (NRS) (1855 – 2013c) Statutory Marriages 1855 – 2013, URL: http://www.scotlandspeople.gov.uk/search/marriage/index.aspx. [Accessed April 23, 2014]

National Records of Scotland (NRS) (undated) County Sutherland, Parish of Farr, *ScotlandsPlaces*, URL: http://www.scotlandsplaces.gov.uk/search/partner/Sutherland?class=county&id=31. [Accessed February 23, 2014]

Ordnance Survey (2009) *Lismore Placenames – Ainmean Liosmòr*, Ordnance Survey License number 100049636.

Oxford Dictionaries, URL: http://oxforddictionaries.com. [Accessed March 13, 2013]

Partick South Parish Church (2012) URL: http://www.particksouth.org.uk/. [Accessed December 7, 2012]

Redwood Falls Gazette, Redwood Falls, Minnesota. URL: http://www.redwoodfallsgazette.com/. [Accessed April 12, 2014]

Rosenblum, L. (December 1933) "The Failure of the City of Glasgow Bank", *The Accounting Review,* Vol. 8, No. 4 (Dec. 1933), pp. 285-291.

Scott, H. (1923) *Fasti Ecclesiae Scoticanae: The Succession of Ministers in the Church of Scotland from the Reformation, vol. 4, Synods of Argyll, and of Perth and Stirling.* Edinburgh: Oliver and Boyd. URL: https://ia600702.us.archive.org/35/items/fastiecclesiaesc04scot/fastiecclesiaesc04scot.pdf. [Accessed February 23, 2014]

Stark, Jean Aufderheide (2013) Letter to Margaret Carasik.

Stark, Jean Aufderheide (2014a) Letter to Margaret A. Miller, undated, written January 14, 2014, transmitting articles about and photographs of John McCallum (b. 1847) family, Ortonville, Minnesota.

Stark, Jean Aufderheide (2014b) Letter to Margaret A. Miller, written January 17, 2014, providing information about family names.

Stark, Jean Aufderheide (2014c) Letter to Margaret A. Miller, written April 11, 2014.

Stark, Jean Aufderheide (2014d) Letter to Margaret A. Miller, written April 30, 2014, personal correspondence.

Stark, Jean Aufderheide (2014e) Letter to Margaret A. Miller, written May 14, 2014, personal correspondence.

Stark, Jean Aufderheide (2014f) Letter to Margaret A. Miller, written September 21, 2014, personal correspondence.

The Gaelic-English Dictionary: Am Faclair Gaidhlig – Buerla, Mark, C. (2005), New York: Routledge.

The Oban Times, Oban, Argyll, URL: http://www.obantimes.co.uk/. [Accessed October 4, 2013.]

The Redwood Gazette (February 1, 1877) Local News. Redwood Falls, Minnesota.

The Scotsman (December 13, 1879) "Fatal Boat Accident At Appin- 13th December 1879", Scotsman Archives, URL: http://www.oldappin.com/article.asp?aid=220. [Accessed April 21, 2014]

The Spokesman-Review, Spokane, Washington, URL: http://www.spokesman.com/. [Accessed April 1, 2014]

Tiffany, Sue Robson (October 15, 2012) Personal correspondence.

Tiffany, Sue Robson (October 16, 2012) Personal correspondence.

University of Texas at Austin, Perry-Castañeda Library Map Collection. URL: http://www.lib.utexas.edu/maps/faq.html#2.html. [Accessed August 25, 2013]

University of the Highlands and Islands (undated) "Napier Commission", URL: http://www.whc.uhi.ac.uk/research-old/napier-commission%20. [Accessed November 27, 2013]

Unknown (March 4, 1871) "Lismore", Oban, Argyll: *The Oban Times.*

Unknown (February 8, 1874) "Presentation", Oban, Argyll: *The Oban Times.*

Unknown (January 9, 1875) "Lismore", Oban, Argyll: *The Oban Times.*

Unknown (March 18, 1876) "Lismore – Soiree", Oban, Argyll: *The Oban Times.*

Unknown (March 25, 1876) "Lismore – Revival", Oban, Argyll: *The Oban Times.*

Unknown (June 17, 1876) "Lismore – Sacrament", Oban, Argyll: *The Oban Times.*

White, A. M. (2009) *St. Moluag's Church, Isle of Lismore: Transcription of the gravestones in the old graveyard.* Published privately.

Wilcox, Margaret T. (1977) *Seasons and Songs*, Seattle: Impression Northwest.